Palgrave Macmillan Memory Studies

Series Editors
Andrew Hoskins
University of Glasgow
Glasgow, UK

John Sutton
Department of Cognitive Science
Macquarie University
Macquarie, Australia

The nascent field of Memory Studies emerges from contemporary trends that include a shift from concern with historical knowledge of events to that of memory, from 'what we know' to 'how we remember it'; changes in generational memory; the rapid advance of technologies of memory; panics over declining powers of memory, which mirror our fascination with the possibilities of memory enhancement; and the development of trauma narratives in reshaping the past. These factors have contributed to an intensification of public discourses on our past over the last thirty years. Technological, political, interpersonal, social and cultural shifts affect what, how and why people and societies remember and forget. This groundbreaking new series tackles questions such as: What is 'memory' under these conditions? What are its prospects, and also the prospects for its interdisciplinary and systematic study? What are the conceptual, theoretical and methodological tools for its investigation and illumination?

More information about this series at
http://www.palgrave.com/gp/series/14682

Sabine Marschall
Editor

Public Memory in the Context of Transnational Migration and Displacement

Migrants and Monuments

palgrave
macmillan

Editor
Sabine Marschall
School of Social Sciences
University of KwaZulu-Natal
Durban, KwaZulu-Natal, South Africa

Palgrave Macmillan Memory Studies
ISBN 978-3-030-41328-6   ISBN 978-3-030-41329-3 (eBook)
https://doi.org/10.1007/978-3-030-41329-3

© The Editor(s) (if applicable) and The Author(s), under exclusive licence to Springer Nature Switzerland AG 2020
This work is subject to copyright. All rights are solely and exclusively licensed by the Publisher, whether the whole or part of the material is concerned, specifically the rights of translation, reprinting, reuse of illustrations, recitation, broadcasting, reproduction on microfilms or in any other physical way, and transmission or information storage and retrieval, electronic adaptation, computer software, or by similar or dissimilar methodology now known or hereafter developed.
The use of general descriptive names, registered names, trademarks, service marks, etc. in this publication does not imply, even in the absence of a specific statement, that such names are exempt from the relevant protective laws and regulations and therefore free for general use.
The publisher, the authors and the editors are safe to assume that the advice and information in this book are believed to be true and accurate at the date of publication. Neither the publisher nor the authors or the editors give a warranty, expressed or implied, with respect to the material contained herein or for any errors or omissions that may have been made. The publisher remains neutral with regard to jurisdictional claims in published maps and institutional affiliations.

Cover illustration: Felix Lipov / Alamy Stock Photo
Cover design: eStudioCalamar

This Palgrave Macmillan imprint is published by the registered company Springer Nature Switzerland AG.
The registered company address is: Gewerbestrasse 11, 6330 Cham, Switzerland

Acknowledgements

This book project began with a vision to bring together two separate strands of my own research activity over the past years that had appeared disparate and resulted in distinct parallel publication streams, namely the field of heritage/public monuments and the field of migrants and their memories. First and foremost, I want to thank the editors of Palgrave Macmillan's Memory Studies series, Andrew Hoskins and John Sutton, for 'buying into' my vision by accepting my initial proposal and giving me the opportunity to develop this exciting project. Their scholarly expertise and leadership in the critical scrutiny and 'quality control' of the final manuscript is also highly appreciated.

Any edited volume relies most crucially on the scholarly expertise and professional commitment of individual chapter authors. My sincere gratitude goes out to all contributors, some of whom struggled with personal and professional challenges, yet excelled in working with me to develop, revise and finalize their chapters within a tight timeline. I'm moreover indebted to all colleagues and scholarly experts who kindly availed themselves to conduct the double blind peer review of all individual chapters; their familiarity with specific geo-social contexts and their scholarly expertise in specialized areas have enabled them to offer useful observations, critical thoughts, and constructive suggestions that have shaped the authors' revisions.

Several contributors presented their papers at the 2019 annual Memory Studies Association conference in Madrid, either as part of my panel on Migrants and Monuments or independently in other sessions. Valuable feedback and constructive suggestions were received from various members of the audience, which may have influenced the thinking of some authors and elements of which may have found their way into the final narrative. On behalf of all authors concerned, I express my appreciation.

While no specific funding is to be acknowledged for this project, institutional support came from the University of KwaZulu-Natal, notably the School of Social Sciences. Lastly, many thanks to the production team at Palgrave Macmillan for their professionalism and multifaceted support.

Contents

1 Monuments in the Context of Migration: An Introduction   1
Sabine Marschall

Part I   The Production and Contestation of Public Memory
Around Migration   29

2 Memorializing Migration: Immigrant Patronage, Public
Memory and the Syrian Centennial Monument to
Argentina (1910)   31
Caroline 'Olivia' M. Wolf

3 'Columbus Might Be Dwarfed to Obscurity': Italian
Americans' Engagement with Columbus Monuments in a
Time of Decolonization   61
Laura E. Ruberto and Joseph Sciorra

4 Long-Distance Nationalism: Ukrainian Monuments and
Historical Memory in Multicultural Canada   95
Per A. Rudling

5 Political and Social Contestation in the Memorialization
of 'Comfort Women'   127
Mary M. McCarthy

6 Contested Memory in an Eponymous City: The Robert
  Towns Statue in Townsville, Australia   157
  Rodney Sullivan and Robin Sullivan

Part II Refugees, Informal Memorials and the Dissolution of
         the Monument   187

7 Tracing Paths of Transcultural Memory: The Usage of
  Monuments in Guided Tours by Refugees   189
  Michal Huss

8 From Here because from Abroad? Migrants and
  Grassroots Memorials in Paris in the Aftermath of 13
  November 2015   219
  Sarah Gensburger and Gérôme Truc

9 Walter Benjamin in Fortress Europe: Refugees and the
  Ethics of Memory in an (Ex)Border Town   243
  Garikoitz Gómez Alfaro

10 Augmented Reality: Memorializing Deaths of Migrants
   Along the US-Mexico Border   267
   Jessica Auchter

11 Synthesis and Conclusions   293
   Sabine Marschall

Index   317

Notes on Contributors

Jessica Auchter is Guerry Professor and Associate Professor of Political Science at the University of Tennessee at Chattanooga. Her research focuses on visual politics and culture. Her book, *The Politics of Haunting and Memory in International Relations* (2014), examines memorialization and the politics and ethics of being haunted by the dead. Her work appears in *Critical Studies on Security, Journal of Global Security Studies, International Affairs, Millennium, Journal for Cultural Research, Global Discourse, Human Remains and Violence, Review of International Studies,* and *International Feminist Journal of Politics*, among others, and in several edited volumes. She is working on a book manuscript on the global politics of dead bodies.

Sarah Gensburger is a sociologist and a senior researcher in memory studies at the French National Centre for Scientific Research (CNRS). In her still ongoing work, she has been studying the governmentality of memory and the way it has become a category of public intervention in Western democracies. In 2019, in this perspective, she co-edited a special issue of the *International Journal of Politics, Culture and Society* entitled *Administrations of Memory*. Her last books are *Beyond Memory. Can We Really Learn from the Past?* (with Sandrine Lefranc, Palgrave Memory Studies Series, forthcoming); *Memory on My Doorstep. Chronicles of the Bataclan Neighbourhood (Paris, 2015–2016)* (2019); *National Policy, Global Memory. The Commemoration of the Righteous Among the Nations from Jerusalem to Paris (1942–2007)* (2016); and *Witnessing the Robbing of the Jews. A Photographic Album (Paris, 1943–1944)* (2015).

Garikoitz Gómez Alfaro lectures at the School of Environment and Technology, University of Brighton (UK). His main research focus is on commemorative geographies, cultural memory, affect theory and the politics of time. He is an affiliated researcher at the Centre for Research in Memory, Narrative and Histories, University of Brighton.

Michal Huss is an Economic and Social Sciences Research Council-sponsored doctoral student in the Department of Architecture at the University of Cambridge. The working title of her thesis is 'Walking in Landscapes of Displacement and Exile', and she is supervised by Dr Maximilian Sternberg. A recent article, 'Mapping the Occupation: Performativity and the Precarious Israeli Identity', was published in the journal *Geopolitics*. Prior to this, she studied Fine Art and Art History at Goldsmiths, University of London, before completing an MA in Art and Politics at the same institution. In 2016, Huss initiated the Order of Things Collective, which creates an ongoing mapping of Deptford, and hosts workshop events on radical cartography and map-making in and around the Deptford area. Between 2014 and 2016, Huss developed an educational counter-mapping project with the Hotel Elephant Gallery and several local schools.

Sabine Marschall is Professor of Cultural and Heritage Tourism (School of Social Sciences) at the University of KwaZulu-Natal, Durban (South Africa). She holds a PhD from the Eberhardt-Karls-University in Tübingen (Germany) and has published widely in the fields of South African art and architecture; commemoration and cultural heritage; and tourism and migration with a particular emphasis on issues of memory. Major publications include *Landscape of Memory: Commemorative Monuments, Memorials and Public Statuary in Post-apartheid South Africa* (2010); *Tourism and Memories of Home* (2017); and *Memory, Migration and Travel* (2018).

Mary M. McCarthy is Associate Professor of Politics and International Relations at Drake University in Des Moines, Iowa, USA. She specializes in Japan's domestic and foreign policies, and is editor of the *Routledge Handbook of Japanese Foreign Policy*. Her current research and most recent publications examine the historical legacies of the Asia-Pacific War on Japan's foreign relations, with a particular focus on the 'comfort women' issue. McCarthy is a Mansfield Foundation US-Japan Network for the Future Scholar and was a 2014 Japan Studies

Resident Fellow at the East-West Center in Washington, DC. She received her BA in East Asian studies and her PhD in political science from Columbia University.

Laura E. Ruberto is a Humanities professor at Berkeley City College, where she teaches courses in film and cultural studies. A past Fulbright Faculty Research Scholar to Italy, her research focuses on Italian and Italian American transnational and diasporic experiences and cultures, mainly vis-à-vis film and material culture. She is the author of *Gramsci, Migration, and the Representation of Women's Work in Italy and the U.S.* (2007). Her co-edited collections include *Italian Neorealism and Global Cinema* (2007), *Italian Americans and Television* (*Italian American Review*, 2016), and the two volumes *New Italian Migrations to the United States. Vol. 1: Politics and History since 1945* and *Vol. 2: Art and Culture since 1945* (2017). Her translations include *Such Is Life, Ma la vita e' fatta cosi: A Memoir* (2010). She is co-editor of the book series *Critical Studies in Italian America* for Fordham University Press and serves on the Editorial Board of the *Italian American Review*.

Per A. Rudling Associate Professor of History at Lund University, Per A. Rudling is a Wallenberg Academy Fellow (2019–2024), funded by the Knut and Alice Wallenberg Foundation. He is the author of *The Rise and Fall of Belarusian Nationalism, 1906–1931* (2015) and *The OUN, the UPA, and the Holocaust: A Study in the Manufacturing of Historical Myths* (2011).

Joseph Sciorra is Director of Academic and Cultural Programs at Queens College's John D. Calandra Italian American Institute, a City University of New York research institute. As a folklorist he has conducted ethnographic research on vernacular expressivity and published on material culture, religious practices and popular music. He was the editor (2011–2016) of the journal *Italian American Review* and of *Italian Folk: Vernacular Culture in Italian-American Lives* (2010), and co-editor of *Embroidered Stories: Interpreting Women's Domestic Needlework from the Italian Diaspora* (2014); *Neapolitan Postcards: The Canzone Napoletana as Transnational Subject* (2016); and *New Italian Migrations to the United States. Vol. 1: Politics and History since 1945* and *Vol. 2: Art and Culture since 1945* (2017). Sciorra is the author of *R.I.P: Memorial Wall Art* (1994; 2002), with photographer Martha Cooper, and *Built with Faith: Italian American Imagination and Catholic Material Culture in New York City* (2015).

Robin Sullivan is an honorary research associate professor in the School of Historical and Philosophical Inquiry at The University of Queensland. She was formerly Queensland Commissioner for Children and Young People and Director-General in the Queensland public service. Her publications include articles on labour history, education and family issues. She has co-authored recent articles on Irish memorials and symbols in Queensland. She holds honorary doctorates from the Queensland University of Technology and the Central Queensland University.

Rodney Sullivan is an honorary research associate professor in the School of Historical and Philosophical Inquiry at The University of Queensland and formerly an associate professor in the Department of History & Politics at James Cook University, Townsville. He has published in the fields of Australian and Philippine-American history. His recent research on the Irish in Queensland has focused on memory practices and sectarianism. He has contributed to the *Australian Dictionary of Biography* and the *Biographical Dictionary of the Australian Senate*. Rodney and Robin Sullivan are Honorary Historians of the Queensland Irish Association. They are writing a history of the Association to be published for its 125th anniversary in 2023.

Gérôme Truc is a sociologist, tenured research fellow at the French National Centre for Scientific Research (CNRS). His work focuses primarily on social reactions to terrorist attacks and their memorialization, and more generally on moral and political sociology. He leads the REAT research cluster, funded by the 'Attentats-Recherche' committee of the CNRS, and he is involved in the interdisciplinary 'November 13' research programme, directed by the CNRS and the INSERM. He is the author of *Shell Shocked: The Social Response to Terrorist Attacks* (2018) and has also contributed among others to *The Archivo del Duelo: Análisis de la respuesta ciudadana ante los atentados del 11 de marzo en Madrid*, directed by Cristina Sánchez-Carretero (CSIC, 2011).

Caroline 'Olivia' M. Wolf is Assistant Professor in Art History at the University of Tennessee at Chattanooga, USA. Her research explores migration and identity in the visual culture and built environment of Latin America, the Middle East and their global intersections. Her recent work focuses on the art and architectural patronage of Arabic-speaking diaspora (*mahjar*) communities in modern Argentina as a response to transnational migration. She also examines contemporary art in the context of migration debates in Latin America today. Wolf was recently selected as a 2018–2019 Calouste Gulbenkian Visiting Scholar, and her research has been supported by fellowships from the Fulbright-Hays DDRA, *Forum Transregionale Studien*, Max Weber Foundation, Society of Architectural Historians (SAH), and the National Endowment for the Humanities (NEH), among others.

LIST OF FIGURES

Fig. 2.1 *Monument of the Syrian Residents to the Argentine Nation, 1810–1910.* [Monumento de los Residentes Sirios a la Nación Argentina.] (Photograph by the author, Caroline Olivia M. Wolf, 2016)   32

Fig. 2.2 Detail of bas-relief, *Monumento de los Sirios a la Nación Argentina.* (Photograph by the author, Caroline Olivia Wolf, 2017)   49

Fig. 3.1 Columbus Monument, Columbus Circle, New York City, November 2019. (Courtesy of Joseph Sciorra)   65

Fig. 3.2 Columbus Statue, San Jose City Hall, February 2018. (Courtesy of Laura E. Ruberto)   82

Fig. 4.1 Tweet by Russian Embassy in Ottawa (15 October 2017). Thanks to Vasily Kultyshev of the Russian Embassy in Ottawa for the permission to reproduce. For copyright issues, the images of the Edmonton Shukhevych memorial along with the Oakville monuments to the UPA and veterans of the Waffen-SS *Galizien* have been removed. The tweet, with its images, is available online at ('Russia in Canada' 2017)   96

Fig. 4.2 Bust to Roman Shukhevych (pseud. Chuprynka), Ukrainian Youth Complex, Edmonton. (Photo courtesy of John-Paul Himka)   102

Fig. 4.3 Monument 'To the Fighters for Ukrainian Freedom', Edmonton, Alberta. (Photo by Erik Visser. Thanks to Marc Turgeon, Director of Cemeteries at the Ukrainian Catholic Eparchy of Edmonton for generously allowing author to use this illustration. Image from http://www.stmichaels-rosehill-cemetery.com/st-michaels-description.html. Accessed 31 July 2018.)   104

Fig. 4.4	'Monument to the Glory of the UPA', North Oakville, Ontario. Wikipedia commons, photo by Wikipedia user 'Lvivske'	107
Fig. 4.5	Monument 'To the Fighters for the Freedom of Ukraine', North Oakville, Ontario. Wikipedia commons, photo by Wikipedia user 'Lvivske'	108
Fig. 5.1	Column of Strength in San Francisco, California, erected 2017. (Source: Author, February 28, 2019)	140
Fig. 5.2	Comfort women memorial in Palisades Park, New Jersey, erected in 2010. (Source: Author, March 19, 2015)	143
Fig. 5.3	The Peace Monument in Glendale, California, erected in 2013. (Source: Author, June 10, 2015)	146
Fig. 6.1	South Sea Islanders outside overseer's hut, John Melton Black's plantation, Townsville, ca. 1870. State Library of Queensland.	162
Fig. 6.2	Robert Towns statue, Pioneers Walk, Townsville, unveiled 2005 (Authors' photograph)	176
Fig. 6.3	Eddie Mabo Memorial, Pioneers Walk, Townsville, unveiled 2007. (Authors' photograph)	179
Fig. 7.1	Map of Yasmin's tour, Berlin, and images of memorials along route, drawn or photographed by author	190
Fig. 7.2	Map of Wael's tour and sights along route, drawn or photographed by the author	203
Fig. 8.1	'Kabylia is Paris'. (© Paris Archives, document 3907W1-109)	226
Fig. 8.2	Messages left by the 'Free Syrians of France' in front of the Bataclan, 11 January 2016. (© Gérôme Truc)	227
Fig. 8.3	'I am Ouagadougou! with all my heart'. Bataclan, Paris, 18 January 2016. (© Gérôme Truc)	229
Fig. 8.4	The recurring banner. (© Sarah Gensburger)	237
Fig. 9.1	Glass panel in Karavan's Passages (1994). (Photograph by Caterina Nicolau Oliver 2012)	250
Fig. 9.2	Portbou's Cemetery. Stone laid in 1992 to commemorate the 100th Anniversary of Benjamin's birth. (Photograph by Caterina Nicolau Oliver, 2012)	252
Fig. 10.1	*Border Memorial: Frontera de los Muertos*, John Craig Freeman, augmented reality public art, Three Points, Arizona, 2015, courtesy of John Craig Freeman	280
Fig. 10.2	*Drift Alignment*, January 2017 grid, 2019, 15 digital pigment prints, 20″ x 20″ each. Image courtesy of Andrew O'Brien	284

CHAPTER 1

Monuments in the Context of Migration: An Introduction

Sabine Marschall

INTRODUCTION

Monuments and memorials as tangible commemorative markers in public places are always about remembering and appropriating the past for the needs of those in the present, but the context of migration, displacement and diaspora adds a peculiar dimension to such beacons of public memory. On the one hand, immigrants and refugees now constitute new, previously neglected and originally unintended audiences who bring transnational and transcultural perspectives to old monuments in host country settings. On the other hand, established migrant communities can become 'agents of memory' in their own right, who wish to contribute their own monuments and memorials to the memory landscape of their adoptive home. However, the public memory markers of diasporic minorities, migrants, refugees and even the internally displaced are always subject to negotiation with the host nation or local society, which usually holds hegemonic power over the production of public memory (Motte and Ohliger 2006). In addition, the visual, textual and contextual characteristics of migrant

S. Marschall (✉)
School of Social Sciences, University of KwaZulu-Natal,
Durban, KwaZulu-Natal, South Africa
e-mail: marschalls@ukzn.ac.za

monuments, whether merely tolerated by, erected with support of or temporarily set up in defiance of host country authorities, reveal much about inter- and intragroup relations and illustrate how memory is strategically deployed to stake claims and defend positions about identity and belonging. This setting gives rise to many nuances, permutations and complexities, some of which will be sketched in this introductory overview and others discussed in detail in the chapters of this book. It is first necessary to clarify who is considered a migrant and what is a monument for the purposes of this collection.

Who Is a Migrant?

For the sake of convenience, 'migrant' and 'immigrant' are used as umbrella terms in this volume, but in specific cases, this can refer to many different categories of mobile persons. These include temporary migrants, legal or undocumented; economic or elite migrants; sojourners or expatriates with first-hand memories and often strong transnational ties, many of whom are planning to return to their country of origin one day, many of whom are returning. It moreover includes those who are more settled with citizenship or permanent residence, who have established roots and families, and those of later generations who were born in the host country, forming ethnic minorities, belonging perhaps to a larger diaspora. Retaining a sense of difference, cultural identity and diasporic entanglement, they are to some extent perceived as Other by the host society.

Refugees, irregular or undocumented migrants, asylum seekers and forcibly displaced people are also subjects of investigation in this volume. Scholars and policy makers tend to distinguish quite clearly between forced and voluntary forms of mobility and resettlement, but neat divisions can in reality be blurred where a complex combination of push and pull factors, compulsion and choice influence migrants in their decision to move (see Van Hear (2010) on 'mixed migration'). Some scholars contest and others defend the status quo of migration and refugee studies as separate fields of academic enquiry, but scholarly work on the overlap of the two categories is increasing (Fiddian-Qasmiyeh et al. 2014). We frequently note disjuncture between self-identification and official classification, emic and etic perspectives. Later generations' understanding of their community's history and intergenerational family memory can add further distortions: refugees can morph into migrants (Raj 2000) and ancestors migrating for opportunistic reasons may become mythologized as victims of forcible displacement (Basu 2005).

Baldassar (2006, p. 44) identifies four competing and coexisting sets of identity discourses associated with migration: those (often muted) of the migrants themselves; those (often more powerful) of the 'mainstream host society'; those of the diaspora and those (largely unexamined) of the non-migrants, the stay-behinds. In this volume, one important addition is made to this typology, namely the identity discourses of competing migrant groups and ethnic minorities within the host country. As will be shown, most of these identity projects are based on cultural memories and shared understandings of the past, which may be subject to contestation from outside and even inside the group, as generational, gender, religious and other divisions manifest themselves. The production and reception of public memory markers are focal points and catalysts of negotiation over identity, belonging and power.

Migration and displacement are both about movements of people and mobility of memories. This includes the personal recollections literally carried across borders by individuals on the move and their potential transformation through transfer into new geographical and socio-political contexts. It moreover includes the nostalgic family memories of distant homes and pre-migration pasts; the transnational exchange of memory within diasporic families and communities; the 'performance' of collective remembrance embedded in cultural identity practices; the personal and cultural memories attached to objects sent from place to place; and—not least—the public identity statements made through commemorative monuments. If Memory Studies scholars have been advocating a shift of attention from static objects of memory and national *lieux de mémoires* to dynamics of memory or 'knots of memory', the circulation and 'travel' of memory and the constitution of memory through the movement of people, objects and media within the nation and across borders (Erll 2011a, b; Rigney 2005; Rothberg 2009), monuments in the context of migration certainly represent a fertile arena of empirical investigation.

What Is a Public Monument?

Much has been written about migration heritage and the multifarious tangible and intangible ways in which migrants and refugees preserve memories of their place of origin, their home culture and pre-migration past (e.g. Glynn 2012; Gouriévidis 2014; Innocenti 2016). Language, food, dress, architecture, religion, ritual, objects, performance culture and a host of other vehicles of memory have been investigated in the scholarly literature, but surprisingly little has been published on commemorative monuments in this context.

Unless specified otherwise, the terms monument and memorial in this volume denote a wide range of material artefacts set up in public places. This may include small plaques attached to buildings or simple support structures; plain steles and inscribed hewn rocks; busts and statues, from minute to gigantic; abstract or figurative sculptures; and architectural structures built as public monuments. What these objects have in common is that the intention of their creation and purpose of their existence is purely commemorative. It hence distinguishes them from so-called 'living monuments', that is functional buildings erected or named in memory of a person or event; museums, archives and heritage centres; memorials in private spaces as well as buildings and sites that have over time become recognized as symbolic of a migration-linked past or officially declared as monuments. While performative and intangible types of memorials are generally excluded from consideration in this volume, certain types of informal ephemeral monuments as well as online memorials are considered, especially where they aspire to emulate the aesthetic language of conventional monuments or are created to protest the impossibility of making a permanent statement in the physical landscape of public memory.

Monuments are representational battlegrounds that rely on visual and textual modes of expression to condense complex historical narratives, endorse selected value systems and transmit partisan 'messages'. Yet, as Kirk Savage's (1997) influential book *Standing Soldier, Kneeling Slave* illustrates, the design of a monument is never simply a question of aesthetics, but rather the outcome of a complex process of negotiation that is essentially determined by how different stakeholders understand the past and interpret its meaning. A close reading of the visual appearance of a monument, its location, scale, shape and materials; its design, symbols and imagery; the precise wording of its inscription; the choice of artist; references to well-known local and national landmarks that strategically seek connections and associations; the relationships established through sightlines with statues and symbols in the vicinity; and especially the genesis and reception of the final product reveals much about the complexities of inter- and intragroup relations.

By crystallizing in its visual and textual signifiers the history and experience of migration, a monument hence creates myths and implicitly suppresses or denies alternative motivations, experiences and perspectives, for instance the fact that many immigrants intended to return home and many indeed did return (Bodnar 1986). If all commemorative markers are installed to remember and socially transfer selected narratives of the past, the context of migration adds an important dimension: monuments and memorials are symbolic sites where transnational and transcultural memories manifest themselves.

MEMORY AND THE TRANSCULTURAL TURN

The 'transcultural turn' in memory studies has gained strong momentum during the course of the last decade, lending currency to such concepts as transcultural, transnational, global travelling and multidirectional memory (Crownshaw 2011; Erll 2011b; Assmann and Conrad 2010; Phillips and Reyes 2011; Rothberg 2009). In the 1990s, much scholarship in memory studies, influenced by Pierre Nora's (1989) seminal work on *lieux de mémoire*, analytically centred on site-bound memory within the nation, as well as within ethnic, religious and other groups envisaged as relatively homogenous and culturally bounded. Aleida and Jan Assmann's (1992, 2003) notion of cultural memory, broadly understood as the preservation, sharing and intergenerational transfer through artefacts (texts, objects and symbols) within the nation and cultural groups has enjoyed tremendous influence, especially in German-speaking scholarly circles. The concept has also drawn critique, as bounded conceptualizations of culture ('container-culture') receded behind the recognition of hybridity, permeability of cultural boundaries, fluidity and border-transcending dynamics. The micro and macro level effects of transnationalism, migration and other facets of global mobility, as well as advances in information and communications technology and mass media have rendered the nation state less self-evident as the logical site of investigation and analysis (Carrier and Kabalek 2014; De Cesari and Rigney 2014; Assmann and Conrad 2010; Bond and Rapson 2014).

Nation states in the age of globalization and neoliberalism are increasingly integrated into transnational networks, affecting decision-making at multifarious levels and influencing mnemonic dynamics within the collective political arena. Social media and other vehicles of global communication create new spaces of memory and circulate icons, images and narratives of the past, some of which become shared internationally on account of their strong cross-cultural resonance. Such circulation of memories and practices of commemoration forge global social movements into transnational memory communities and create a 'global memoryscape' (Phillips and Reyes 2011; Hoskins 2018; Assmann and Conrad 2010; Santino 2006). As Phillips and Reyes (2011, p. 15) put it, global frames of reference and the encounters and interactions of people of diverse origins create memories and memory practices that are by definition transnational—and, one might add, transcultural.

The consideration of border-transcending trajectories, transnational and transcultural forces, has not resulted in the abandonment of national memory as a primary site of investigation and framework for analysing the formation of collective memory and identity, but perhaps in its contextualization, decentring, destabilizing or reconfiguration (Phillips and Reyes 2011; Bond and Rapson 2014; De Cesari and Rigney 2014). Paradoxically, the globalization of memory practices can even reinforce the nation as identity framework and transnational institutions can 'inadvertently end up promoting ethno-nationalist memories' (De Cesari and Rigney 2014, p. 20), as will become evident in this collection. Transnational memory is not necessarily transcultural and vice versa, illustrate Moses and Rothberg (2014, p. 32) with respect to Europe, a transnational, yet ideologically relatively mono-cultural formation engaged in constructing a shared, exclusive memory around the notion of a common 'Judeo-Christian' culture.

Ironically, this occurs while immigration, the presence of refugees and other dynamics of globalization have rendered most places at the local level religiously diverse and deeply transcultural. This is epitomized by the multicultural classroom, where varied and potentially competing memories are crowded into small spaces (Assmann and Conrad 2010, p. 2). It can also be witnessed around commemorative sites and ceremonies, once intended to coalesce culturally similar people's ideas about the past, now exposed to culturally dissimilar audiences with different memorial references, which may confrontationally be mobilized in response to exclusive memory practices. Alternatively, memory once 'owned' by specific cultural groups can also be shared cross-culturally, strategically used or adopted 'prosthetically' (Landsberg 2004) by individuals and collectives in different cultural settings (Crownshaw 2011, p. 2; Rothberg and Yildiz 2011). Migrants and other marginalized groups interacting with and adopting memories of the dominant group leads to transculturation, the nuancing and transformation of the majority's memories (Carrier and Kabalek 2014, p. 55).

Whilst the terms transnational and transcultural memory focus on the transcendence of borders—political, geographical, social, cultural—it is hence equally important to investigate how such practices of remembrance can likewise reinforce borders or create new ones. Not all memories that transcended the confines of their specific places of origin attain global reach; transcultural memory can manifest itself at many different scales and very localized places. 'Transcultural memory ... offers a vision that cuts across the different scales evoked by the frameworks of transnational or global memory' (Moses and Rothberg 2014, p. 32).

As scholarship around transcultural (and transnational) memory grows, empirical investigation and analysis of memory formation between, across and beyond the boundaries of closed groups depends on what meanings are ascribed to the prefix 'trans' (Carrier and Kabalek 2014). Aleida Assmann (2014, p. 547) posits that trans stands both for 'transit', the movement across national borders, and 'translation', 'the cultural work of reconfiguring established national themes, references, representations, images and concepts'. One example of what this might mean in the context of this book is the development of a specific memory culture by those who transit (migrants and refugees), which involves the translation of collective memories of home, familiar tropes or national icons into a host nation context, whilst absorbing new impulses from the host society itself.

The context of migration represents a particularly fruitful arena of inquiry in this regard, not only because migration, diaspora and displacement invariably foster a wealth of transcultural memory. Migration encourages attention to memory at the micro level, the experiences of individuals and small groups, placing emphasis on subjectivity and transformation, in a context where the study of memory has often been bound up with the political and the macro level (Carrier and Kabalek 2014). Transcultural memory is not merely about the border-transcending dimensions of remembering and forgetting or about the global dissemination of cultural memory. Rather, it is about the potential emergence of a new type of collective memory that is produced at the interface of two or more memorial cultures. Transcultural memory entails new modes of remembrance and novel outlooks on the past resulting from the process of transcultural recollection among individuals and collectives within the nation and across borders. The chapters in this book empirically investigate commemorative monuments and memorials as one of the interfaces at which transcultural and transnational memories are forged.

Structure of This Book

The following will present an overview of pertinent conceptual issues and relevant empirical case studies featured in the extant scholarship, whilst simultaneously contextualizing the nine chapters in this volume, which are loosely arranged in two parts. The first section, comprising five chapters, considers the production and contestation of formal public memory markers by migrants, established diasporic groups and ethnic minorities in host country settings or settler nations (Argentina, United States, Canada, Australia). The four chapters in the second section concentrate on first-generation 'irregular' or undocumented migrants, refugees, asylum seekers and displaced people, notably in Europe and the United States. The case studies illuminate how these particularly vulnerable migrants are represented through public memory discourses and commemorative initiatives within the host society, but also how they represent themselves—through informal memory markers and strategic appropriation of host-country monuments for their own agendas and memory-based identity projects. Lastly, the collection ends with a conclusion that synthesizes insights from all chapters, structured around Kansteiner's (2002) hermeneutic triangle of media, makers and consumers of memory and drawing on relevant concepts from the field of memory studies.

Authored by scholars from different countries, the case studies explored in the chapters of this book cover a diversity of geographical, socio-political and historical contexts. The enquiries are conducted through a variety of epistemological approaches and disciplinary perspective, including art history, history, political science, international relations, sociology and cultural studies, each contributing unique facets to knowledge production in the broad fields of memory and commemoration; migration and refugee studies as well as identity and national belonging.

Commemorating Migration

In 1910, Argentina celebrated its 100-year anniversary of independence from Spain, an event that involved many inaugurations of monumental sculptures sponsored by immigrant groups, mostly of European origin. Olivia Wolf's Chap. 2 in this volume focuses more interestingly on the Monument of the Syrian Residents to the Argentine Nation, the first public memorial built by the diaspora community of former Ottoman subjects. Her careful art historical examination of the patronage, visual programme and inscriptions of this bronze memorial in the heart of Buenos Aires elucidates some core issues that have characterized migrant monuments ever since.

As a form of self-representation, public memorial sculptures visually enshrine preferred memories and ways of seeing, hence affording the immigrants an opportunity to address common stereotypes and counter anti-immigrant discourses (see also Wolf 2017). Landsberg (2004, p. 10) importantly reminds us that memories and traditions can 'flourish in the diaspora in ways they never did in the homeland'. Later waves of immigrants or later generations on touristic journeys may discover with interest or amusement how their ancestors preserved memories and inscribed their presence and values in public places upon settling in a foreign country (Marschall 2018). Wolf shows how the Syrians use the public memory marker to project a new collective, transnational identity and craft transnational allegiances. The transcultural dimension of this commemorative initiative hence manifests itself both locally in the negotiation of memories between different population groups, and more globally, as the monument symbolically connects the immigrants with the homeland, the wider Syrian diaspora and the international community.

As exemplified by the Argentinian case, anniversaries and centenaries are important triggers of personal recall and more importantly organized collective forms of remembrance that aim to consolidate and unify narratives of the past. Anniversaries can provide a significant push to the development of an historical consciousness within the migrant community or the host society in relation to the immigrants. Being a symbolic focal point of cultural identity and community memory, monument initiatives can generate much excitement and consolidation within groups, but also bring forgotten memories to the fore, become catalysts for debate and cause division (Raj 2000). Preparations for a centenary may offer competitive advantages in the *realpolitik* of dealings with local authorities, for instance by forcing their hand in providing a site for a monument, especially if it is donated to the city (Baldassar 2006). Once the monument is erected, it finds itself at the centre of future anniversary ceremonies and commemorative practices, where public remembrance is periodically stimulated. It is through the performativity involved in commemorative behaviour—ritual, habit and even bodily automatisms—that memory is activated and intergenerationally transferred within the community and beyond (Connerton 1989, pp. 4/5).

Of course, anniversaries and centenaries are also occasions for critical re-evaluation of memories, reflection on accustomed symbolic meanings and the reassessment of their relevance in relation to more recent understandings of the past and topical contemporary debates. This occurred during the 1992 Christopher Columbus quincentenary, when the simmering dispute over the navigator's legacy intensified in the United States and elsewhere, accompanied by calls to remove public statues and monuments in his honour. Many of these monuments had been commissioned and funded by Italian immigrants and their descendants during the course of the twentieth century, explain Laura Ruberto and Joseph Sciorra in Chap. 3. Italian immigrants historically used the figure of Columbus to symbolize a unified face—'the Italian'—while assimilating under the cover of whiteness. The authors focus on two cities, New York City and San Jose (California), both with Italian American mayors, which have seen varying efforts to remove or preserve these migrant-created monuments in light of shifting cultural politics. They examine how contemporary Italian Americans' attachment to Columbus *vis-à-vis* monuments and festivities creates a master narrative regarding earlier Italian migration, while also reaffirming a racialized ideology of privilege and exclusion.

Similar to the Syrian immigrants in Wolf's chapter, the American-Italian monuments implicitly engage with racial politics, cultural stereotypes, identity and belonging, but in this chapter, the intergenerational dimension is salient. Immigrants and ethnic diasporic communities are not homogenous groups, and the transcultural memory that emerged at the interface of first generation migrants and host society impulses does not necessarily resonate with descendants whose own memories are deeply rooted in the host country. Their reluctance, if not resistance, to embrace the narratives, symbols and iconographic references cherished by their forefathers is evident in Baldassar's (2006) study on Italian Australians. Yet, by the same token, immigrant community monuments can equally conceal intergenerational tensions about cultural identity and suitable ways of publicly representing Italianness (ibid, p. 43).

Migrant Memories and the Nation State

The experience of migration ruptures and reconfigures memory not only for migrants, their families and the society they leave behind, but—perhaps equally dramatically—the host country population and the nation state, often in ways that cut to the very core of how national identity and belonging are imagined. This is especially true in the European context, where the nation has historically been defined and politically and scientifically legitimated as a *Kulturnation* (cultural nation) based on shared culture, language and collective memory. Monuments and other sites of memory evidence the traditionally strong connection between public remembrance and the nation state, as national memory is visualized, materialized and disseminated in—and national identity forged through—symbolic practice and rituals of collective remembrance (Phillips and Reyes 2011). This explains the difficulties in integrating transnational and transcultural migrant memories into the collective master narrative and cultural memory of the nation and the reluctance in accommodating their public representation in monuments, especially in places conventionally reserved for the commemoration of national memory.

Paralleling the sovereign state's legal authority to determine its immigration policy, who is accepted as a migrant or refugee, the state's delegated authorities have the power to make decisions over the organization of public space, including who can erect a public monument, where and under what conditions (Kleist 2013). In the past decades, state authorities in many constitutional democracies have taken the initiative to sponsor institutionalized places dedicated to the memory of major immigration waves, notably museums, archives, interpretation centres, temporary exhibitions and to a lesser extent public monuments and memorials. The state as producer of public memory about migration, speaking on behalf of migrants and refugees, hence takes control over transcultural memory, pre-empts migrant self-representation and decides how migration-related events should be remembered for the sake of the nation.

State sponsorship can (but does not always) ensure the installation of mnemonic markers with carefully crafted non-confrontational messages; it allows for addressing a sense of guilt in measured ways or disseminating compromise statements, for instance in cases where minorities are keen to draw attention to public amnesia around unpalatable aspects of the host society's past (Siblon 2009; Hamilton and Ashton 2001; Kleist 2013). Just as the nation may be divided over their government's immigration policy, local communities and activists at the grassroots level dispute decisions affecting the representation of public memory. Because political leaders are ultimately concerned about electoral support, lack of public consensus about the historical meaning of the migration and the role of migrants in the social fabric of the local population can easily stall official monument initiatives, as illustrated by the case of 'guest worker' monuments in Germany (Motte and Ohliger 2006).

In such host country environments, commemorative markers initiated, designed and erected by migrants and diasporic communities themselves face even greater hurdles, because of the need for official support; unequal access to resources and not being part of networks and decision-making processes. Motte and Ohliger (2006, pp. 159/160) link monuments with citizenship rights for migrants and diasporic communities, arguing that a lack of participation in the production of public memory or denial of cultural representation in the memory landscape amounts to privation of full citizen rights and emotionally grounded membership in society. Hamilton and Ashton (2001, p. 28) similarly observe for the Australian context that 'The very act of trying to fit in belies the reality of not belonging or at best being on the margin'.

Where they do exist, migrant monuments—their visual and textual signifiers, their intended meaning and especially their location—can hence be read as an indicator of the acceptance and integration of immigrants. They reveal to what extent the native-born population and the immigration-based minorities form part of shared narratives of the nation rather than living in separate worlds of commemoration (Motte and Ohliger 2006). Vying for a share in the cultural capital of the nation in the face of social marginalization and spatial exclusion, migrant monuments tend to communicate in distinctly unthreatening ways: expressing gratitude; stressing the community's contribution to the host society and implying their worthiness (e.g. Frotscher 2015). While statements are overtly about the past—preserving the memory of migration-related events; acknowledging the contribution of the first generation; paying tribute to the dead—they are essentially about the present generation's own need for acknowledgement and the mobilization of memories for their own identity projects and political aims (Baldassar 2006; McMahon 2007).

As mentioned earlier, to what extent attempts at institutionalizing transcultural and transnational memories challenge, re-define or threaten the memory of the nation depends on how the nation is defined. Even in pluralist 'settler nations' composed of different waves of immigration and refugee arrivals, the national imaginary is circumscribed by foundation myths and societal discourses of exclusions based on race, religious affiliation or other characteristics. In Australia, where multiculturalism has been enshrined as the basis of national identity, monuments and memorials by indigenous and migrant groups have proliferated, but their capacity and power to embed transcultural perspectives into public memory are compromised where the emphasis is on 'political correctness' and distinctly uncontroversial representations (Hamilton and Ashton 2001).

Canada, another settler nation that has embraced multiculturalism, officially promotes and even lends state support to public commemorative initiatives by immigrant communities as an expression of multicultural national identity. However, as Per Anders Rudling shows with respect to monuments established by the Ukrainian diaspora (Chap. 4), this policy allows immigrants to foster a type of homeland politics and long-distance nationalism that ultimately defeats the object of Canadian national identity formation. His analysis of several monuments in honour of ultranationalist groups with a controversial Nazi-linked history illustrates how the host country context creates spaces for a memory culture around extremist ethno-nationalist values increasingly at odds with mainstream society in Canada (see also Rudling 2011). Paralleling McCarthy's case study introduced below, the memory agendas and commemorative initiatives of immigrant groups can cause friction, create challenges for the central government and result in diplomatic incidents that reverberate in far-away places.

Transcultural Memories of Victimization

As mentioned earlier, a memory culture and places of public remembrance can be developed in the diaspora to an extent that may not be possible or desirable in the homeland. This includes the nurturing of controversial victim narratives that fall on unsympathetic ears in the home country or are not sustained by mainstream socio-historical discourses (Frotscher 2015). Even where the historical facts of tragic past events are largely uncontested, the interpretation of their meaning and perceptions of their significance in the present are marked by divergence and dissonance between homeland and diaspora, as Crowley (2007) shows in his comparison of Irish famine monuments in Ireland and those erected by the Irish diaspora, especially in the United States. Controversial historical memories of suffering and death as a cornerstone of national identity constructs, political ideology and international relations management in the homeland reverberate in the diaspora and influence the transnational implanting of memories where they find fertile ground. Host country solidarity with diasporic communities' homeland politics and support for advocacy-oriented memory projects depend not only on how memories of traumatic loss and victimization resonate and find empathy among the host society, but also on its government's political will, ideological orientation and international relations.

Rudling mentions how the Ukrainian community in Canada pushed for the recognition of the so-called *Holodomor*, the long-suppressed memory of the 1930s great Ukrainian famine as a genocide committed by the Soviet Union against the Ukrainian people. While the causes of this tragic event are politically contested and lack consensus among historians, various countries with large Ukrainian immigrant groups began to bolster their position and create international awareness by initiating genocide memorials. This effort impressively culminated in the erection of a *Holodomor* memorial in Washington, DC, in 2015 (Pabst 2017).

The diaspora-coined term *Holodomor*, which according to Pabst (2017) references Ukrainian words for 'hunger' and 'murder', echoes the word Holocaust and represents one of many contemporary examples of an appropriation of Holocaust memory and more generally, the mobilization of a globally established memory culture around victimization. Emulating moreover the Armenian genocide memorials in France (Al-Rustom 2013; see below) and similar commemorative initiatives driven by diasporas around the world, it indicates the emergence of 'memory templates' that travel across boundaries (Erll 2014), both facilitated by and further stimulating the prevailing international discourse around genocide, victimization, historical justice and the transnational dimension of 'victimhood nationalism' (Lim 2010). If the power of a monument is determined by its capacity to influence public memory (Baldassar 2006, p. 44), the *Holodomor* memorial in Washington, DC, might indeed be very successful, as Pabst (2017) suggests that its efficacy in promoting popular knowledge about 'genocide' at an international level exceeds the evidence-based efforts of historians and scholarly experts.

An interesting dimension is added to the literature on diaspora mobilization of traumatic memories and the use of public monuments as instruments of advocacy by Mary M. McCarthy in Chap. 5. She examines memory-based identity politics in the context of nine public memorials established by the Korean community in the United States in commemoration of the tragic lives of Korean 'comfort women' used in servitude by the Japanese armed forces during the 1930s and 1940s. The Korean diaspora has solidified its identity through collective memories of its relationship *vis-à-vis* its former colonial power, Japan, and the perpetuation of a related moral narrative. Some members of the Japanese diaspora, however, are opposed to these memorials and perceive them as an attack on their group identity. McCarthy's chapter investigates the process of contestation between these two migrant groups in the United States and the arbiter role played by mainstream American society as the two groups negotiate claims to the historical narrative through political contests. Highlighting a different dimension of transcultural memory, this chapter hence extends dichotomous host-guest perspectives on the negotiation of public memory to interdiasporic group relations.

MIGRANTS AS CRITICAL AUDIENCE

As alluded to in the context of Columbus statues, monuments can be silent bystanders for decades, only to find themselves thrust into the limelight, subject to critical public scrutiny or outrage by detracting social identity groupings. This may occur suddenly in response to a topical debate or controversial incident with high media visibility, but alternative readings of accustomed mnemonic markers may also gradually emerge as a result of shifting socio-political value systems or changing demographics, including migration-related. Migrants, refugees and diasporic communities change the accustomed demographic structure and social order of the host society and form new audiences for existing and newly erected monuments, injecting previously unconsidered or largely ignored memories into the interpretive mix of the local landscape of memory. Established migrant groups and ethnic minorities emerge as stakeholders and may raise dissenting voices when newly erected monuments aspire to define national identity or local values, challenging authorities and heritage elites who have long been accustomed to decide what is historically significant in the city (McMahon 2007, p. 54).

Rodney and Robin Sullivan's Chap. 6 in this volume demonstrates the plurality and contradictions of urban memory in their analysis of the statue of Robert Towns, unveiled in 2005, in Townsville, Australia. Once again, the monument was the culmination of a centenary project to present Towns as a founding father congruent with the civic elite's vision of the city's past and future. This provoked bitter criticism from South Sea Islander descendants and other local groups who regarded Towns as a 'slave trader', ultimately prompting the expansion of Townsville's innercity memorial landscape to include monuments to Indigenous Australians, who, in the main, shared South Sea Islanders' counter-memory of the past and repudiation of Towns as a pioneer worthy of memorialization.

This chapter connects the collection's focus on migrants with earlier debates about the representation of indigenous people, ethnic minorities and the subaltern, part of the wider postmodern/late modern 'crisis of representation', advocacy of multicultural pluralism and emphasis on 'popular memory' (Lambek and Antze 1996). While migrants as marginalized residents share much with indigenous minorities in the politics and poetics of representation in museums, monuments and other public arenas of cultural and historical display (e.g. Karp and Lavine 1991), the chapter also illustrates what distinguishes the South Sea Islander descendants from Australian aborigines in relation to the reception and production of public memory, most notably their transnational link to the Melanesian ancestral homeland.

By the same token, we must consider what distinguishes migrants (especially those of the first and second generations) as viewers from international tourists and similar external audiences: it is their liminal status as simultaneously internal and external, outsiders and insiders, with memories shaped by transcendental links to distant homelands. Their relationship towards the local mnemoscape is influenced by their history, circumstances of migration and rapport with their chosen or forcibly allocated 'home'. How do migrants and refugees feel about statues of political 'heroes' who once subjugated their people, or memorials to soldiers who died in warfare against their country of origin? Very little may be known about this, especially where affront does not manifest itself in defacement or public protest. Recent arrivals and migrants with tenuous residency status often prefer to maintain a low profile or are simply overwhelmed with more pressing concerns of daily survival in an alienating environment. Within the family, community and among friends, migrants certainly develop their own codes and interpretive narratives about prominent statues in their midst (Peralta-Catipon 2009).

Carrier and Kabalek (2014, p. 50) remind us that the study of memory in transcultural contexts such as migration-related settings casts doubt on the commonly assumed link between memory and power and that the 'trans' in transcultural memory must be understood to be potentially subversive. The presence of migrants and refugees in public squares and prominent places adorned with statues redefines how such spaces are used and perceived, transforming them, for instance, into places of refuge and shared experiences amongst migrants, but potentially causing a sense of alienation and displacement for local residents. Such modifications of the contextual environment and accustomed location of statues and monuments impact their reception and meaning (Peralta-Catipon 2009). Entire bodies of commemorative monuments in cities and spatial precincts can be interpreted in different and contradictory ways, argues John Siblon (2009). Himself a London-born son of immigrants from the former colony of British Guiana, Siblon declares his sense of connectedness with London through familiarly, nationality and identity, while simultaneously feeling alienated and excluded by the city's public symbols and icons of national identity, the lack of monuments to non-white people.

Appropriation of Monuments

More interestingly, Siblon (2009) reflects on his childhood memories and examines photographs of weekend outings to the heart of London, where the family would pose in front of prominent buildings and monuments. He now understands that these pictures also told relatives and friends back home that his parents had 'made it' in Britain—in more than material terms; the backdrop of key icons of British heritage signified the parents' affirmation of British citizenship and implied a sense of connection and rootedness. Performative symbolic behaviour in the form of touring, photographing, posing, placing flowers, attaching notes and conducting rituals at monuments defines subject positions, signifying perhaps integration and assimilation; asserting political agency or manifesting the desire to maintain a culturally distinct identity.

Some immigrant communities strongly identify with selected commemorative markers, especially war memorials in host cities, and strategically appropriate them for their own identity politics. For the Armenian community in Paris, for instance, the tomb of the Unknown Soldier at the Arc de Triomphe, where the French victims of the two world wars are commemorated, has become an important symbolic centre and focal point for the commemoration of the Armenian genocide committed by Ottoman empirical forces in 1915 (Al-Rustom 2013). By tying the memory of the many Armenians who fought and died for France during both world wars—as a mark of their loyalty for the nation—with the memory of the Armenian genocide and loss of homeland, the descendants of exiled Armenians foster a unique kind of transcultural memory. Their commemorative practice justifies the descendants' position *vis-à-vis* the French state and its society, while simultaneously establishing their difference from and worthiness over other immigrant groups in France.

Similarly, at London's Memorial Gates Military memorial in Hyde Park (unveiled in 2002), which commends the Asian continent for its service in both world wars, members of Asian immigrant communities periodically attach handwritten notes, pictures and other small items that connect them to the memory of their forefathers. Such intimate, personal forms of interaction and engagement suggest that the memorial not only serves socio-political agendas or affirms group identity, but it seems to carry deeply felt, private subjective meanings for individuals. This helps us understand why in an alienating, sometimes hostile environment far away from home or origin, some immigrant groups desire to have a monument of their own, a meaningful symbolic site where their personal and collective memories can be not only publicly represented but also privately activated, shared and transmitted.

REFUGEES: THE SPACES AND TEXTURES OF PUBLIC MEMORIALIZATION

We now proceed from the consideration of established groups of migrants and official public monuments in the urban fabric to more precariously positioned migrants and less formal types of commemorative markers. From a memory perspective, the refugees examined in the second part of the book are distinguished by the fact that they belong to the first generation, who have personal and autobiographical memories of their place of origin and often traumatic, episodic memories of pre-migration experiences and the journey itself. They hence literally carry their memories, traumas and heritage into new societal and political contexts. As Assmann and Conrad (2010, p. 2) observe, while the media are widely recognized in the globalization of memory, the role of migrants and refugees as transnational and transcultural carriers of memory deserves more attention.

Refugees may not be in the position to establish their own monuments, but they are still resourceful memory agents who resort to a variety of strategies to make their mark on the local memory landscape. Michal Huss (Chap. 7) opens this section by discussing another type of appropriation, namely walking tours in Berlin guided by refugees. Focused on two specific memorials dedicated to traumatic events in German history, Huss examines how the refugee-guide maps his own traumatic memories of war and displacement onto these German memory markers in the heart of Berlin. He hence forges an alternative narrative and brings new meanings to old monuments, shared with the host society and external visitors. Huss argues that the tour can be understood as a form of transcultural memory activism (Gutman 2017), which undermines the fixed specialization of a singular cultural memory through transforming national sites of memory into transnational sites.

One might think that refugees and irregular migrants, constrained as they often are, by poverty, lack of legal status and documentation, homelessness, unemployment, ill health, communication barriers and a variety of other problems, have more pressing concerns than contributing to the local landscape of memory in their new place of residence. However, memory is an inescapable part of human existence, and the desire to remember and memorialize is both socio-culturally rooted and often perceived as a psychological need, no matter how precarious one's situation. Shifting from bronze statues and officially endorsed monumental commemorative markers, we now consider informal and alternative types of memory markers in the context of migration and displacement.

The practice of establishing temporary, so-called grassroots memorials (Margry and Sánchez-Carretero 2011) or 'spontaneous shrines' (Santino 2006) has become a widespread phenomenon in many, mostly western societies around the world, not least through the influence of conventional and especially social media. Accruements of flowers, candles, photos, cards, toys and religious symbols tend to 'pop up' quickly and sometimes expand massively at places of violent or traumatic death, from road side accident scenes to sites of terrorist attacks. In the latter case and wherever collective memories are at stake, spontaneous shrines frequently precede the later installation of formal markers or monumental memorial structures, epitomized by the commemoration of the 11 September World Trade Centre attack in New York.

All types of memorials commemorating victims of trauma are associated with public grief, outrage and coming to terms with horrific loss of life, but official public memorials are frequently criticized for selective remembering. They tend to produce hegemonic perspectives on the past that result in a hierarchical ordering of victims, valorizing some deaths over others. Even the much celebrated Vietnam Veterans Memorial in Washington, DC, which supposedly captures all names of American combatants of the Vietnam war, is underpinned by definitional criteria that render some deaths valiant and deserving of national honour, whilst justifying omission of others. In the case of the National September 11 Memorial & Museum and its ritualized annual public reading of the roll of names, victims who were undocumented migrants remain invisible. Even the best intentions of complete and non-judgemental inclusiveness are constrained by the larger societal reality of non-registered migrants and refugees, who are forced to spend their lives 'under the radar' and vanish without a trace in the public record.

Although very localized, spontaneous shrines, on the contrary, are inclusive and democratic by enabling anyone to actively participate, including the poor, the homeless, the powerless and marginalized, the refugees and undocumented migrants. Anyone can leave an object or a personal 'message'; engage in individual or communal ritualistic behaviour to articulate grief and take part in the public outpouring of sorrow and expression of empathy and solidarity. Given the proliferating scholarly literature on informal memorials, little is known about the specific ways in which migrants relate to and engage with such memory sites and practices in their host societies. Such research may be of particular interest where migrants emanating from societies with a different memory culture are relatively unfamiliar with the phenomenon of grassroots memorials. Sarah Gensburger and Gérôme Truc (Chap. 8) hence make an important contribution by exploring the voices and practices of migrants at grassroots memorials in Paris that emerged in the wake of terrorist attacks between 2015 and 2017. They note the transnational dimension of these improvised memorials: the commemorated victims were not necessarily French nationals; tourists and migrants from many countries deposited items at the expanding shrine. But interestingly, the messages left by migrants are distinguishable from those of tourists, because they show direct identification with the victims at the local level of the city, hence building an inclusive relation to the events and affirming a sense of belonging to an imagined community—not on the basis of French citizenship, but as residents of Paris.

HOST SOCIETY REPRESENTATIONS OF REFUGEES

Another dimension of transcultural memory is explored by Garikoitz Gómez Alfaro in Chap. 9, as he links the memory of the Holocaust and the mass movement of refugees caused by the Second World War with the contemporary refugee crisis in the Mediterranean. To this effect, the chapter analyses the changing narratives around a memorial to Walter Benjamin (1892–1940), designed by Dani Karavan and erected in Portbou (Spain) in 1994. Being a stateless refugee, the German author and philosopher had died trying to cross the French-Spanish border in escaping the horrors of Fascism.

Gómez examines the commemorative language around Benjamin and the changing public discourses around the memorial and the annual re-enactment of Benjamin's crossing. He argues that the commissioning of the memorial was seen as an 'atonement ritual', discursively tied to the institutionalization of Holocaust memory and implicitly celebrating the dissolution of the European Union's internal borders. Ironically, the emphasis on global human rights did not initially translate into contemporary migrant politics. It is only recently that attention has been drawn to the European external borders' enactment of a very similar kind of violence, this time upon the bodies of 'irregularized' migrants and refugees. His choice of terminology here reminds us of the ideological bias and constructedness of the term 'irregular migrants' commonly found in the public discourse about migration.

As migration and refugee movements increase around the world, many individuals lose their lives or 'disappear' along the exhausting and perilous journey. The Missing Migrants Project (2019), an initiative of the International Organization for Migration (IOM), 'tracks incidents involving migrants, including refugees and asylum-seekers, who have died or gone missing in the process of migration towards an international destination'. Constantly updated, detailed statistical information is presented along chronological and geographical categories in graphs and diagrams. At the time of writing (26 July 2019), the total number of migrant fatalities recorded worldwide for the year 2019 is 1442, of whom 686 died in the Mediterranean Sea. According to the Missing Migrants website, from 2014 to 2018, a combined total of 17,918 persons lost their lives in the Central, Eastern and Western Mediterranean.

In most cases, the bodies of these refugees vanish forever, some eventually wash up along the coastlines, where they are buried in mass graves or local cemeteries with simple head stones or other types of memorial markers (if any) (e.g. D'Ignoti 2018). 'Spontaneous shrines' are created at particularly emotional scenes of migrant deaths, for instance when the small body of three-year-old Kurdish Syrian refugee, Alan Kurdi, washed up on a Turkish beach on 2 September 2015 (Defend International 2015). Permanent and sometimes monumental public memorials have been erected in Lampedusa (Amani 2015) and various other places even outside the immediate border zone (e.g. Ajuntament de Barcelona n.d.). Such memorials are frequently initiated by humanitarian or faith-based organizations and sometimes activists and artists, but easily appropriated by the political leadership, potentially generating conflict between the local, national and international levels.

The memorialization of refugees and irregular migrants raises many other issues of contention that warrant investigation. While academic research in this field is still in its infancy, scholarly interest is definitely emerging (e.g. WUN 2019). Horsti (2017), for instance, examines the 'grievability' (Butler 2009) of migrant fatalities and official efforts of memorialization in the European border zone, particularly in Sicily, while Horsti and Neumann (2019) conduct a transnational comparison of memorials dedicated to two disastrous ship wrecks, involving the drowning of hundreds of irregular migrants bound for Italy and Australia, respectively. Despite many commonalities between the two disasters, the outcomes of their memorialization differ markedly due to dissimilar political and mediated contexts (2019, p. 143). This alerts us to the importance of paying close attention to local and national political dynamics; the specificity of migration-related discourses and socio-cultural responses within the prospective host society; the geographical location and aesthetic design of the memorials; and the local memory culture generated around them.

The commemoration of drowned migrants and missing persons is complicated by the fact that many remain unidentified and were not citizens or residents of the place they tried to reach. However, they were aspiring or potential citizens, especially since most of them had close ties to people already settled in Europe and Australia. Horsti (2017) examines how the memorials in Italy served the political, ideological and psychological needs of those instrumental in erecting them, whilst family members and diasporic connections were side-lined in official commemorative initiatives driven by political leaders. Countering the predominant treatment of irregular migrants as helpless victims and non-agents, Horsti (2017) explores how the Eritrean diaspora has harnessed social and mobile media technology to create innovative methods of commemoration that blur the boundaries between the living and the dead and assist in the formation of new diasporic communities of mourning.

This leads us to Jessica Auchter's Chap. 10, which is placed at the end of the collection, as it begins to transcend the parameters that define this book's investigative focus on space-bound, tangible markers of public commemoration. With special attention to the case study of migrants at the US-Mexican border and conceptually drawing on James Young's (1992, 1994) theorization of the counter-monument, Auchter considers how new technologies reshape our interactions with sites of death and remembrance. She discusses two projects by American artists who utilize virtual and augmented reality to memorialize migrants who died in the Mexican desert in their attempt at crossing the border. In the absence of physical commemorative markers and the absence of actual migrant bodies, technology renders the dead visible and inscribes their memory onto the desert landscape, across borders, but only for those who are prepared to actively engage and—in Auchter's words—'step up to accept that burden of memory'.

Memorialization and indeed memory itself is always dependent on media and mediation. The utilization of digital communication technology for the purpose of mourning; the creation of online memorials and other types of virtual memorialization in cyberspace and the use of artificial intelligence and augmented reality in rendering visible the invisible lives and deaths of migrant victims, all these new media open up innovative possibilities with distinctly transnational and transcultural dimensions for memorialization and commemoration of migrants or by migrants. Discussion of these opportunities and their respective limitations remains beyond the scope of this book, but would certainly warrant future research.

Conclusion

This chapter has defined key terms and conceptual boundaries that circumscribe the topic of the current collection, whilst explaining what makes the study of monuments in the context of migration interesting and significant, both within the broad fields of public memory and migration, diaspora and refugee studies. While this Introduction has attempted to contextualize the topic more broadly and the nine chapters specifically within the extant scholarship, the literature review is far from exhaustive and can only provide a cursory overview of historical developments and current debates. The careful, detailed probing of selected case studies presented in the following chapters, on the contrary, allows the reader to gain a much deeper understanding of the complexity and diversity of migration-linked memory issues in specific social and geo-political settings.

In addition to the variety of discipline-specific methodologies and theoretical perspectives that are brought to bear on the empirical data collected by each contributor, a consideration of pertinent issues and concepts drawn from the field of memory studies ties the chapters of this volume together. Some authors are experienced memory scholars, others relatively new to this rapidly expanding scholarly field; yet all have made a remarkable effort at examining their archival, ethnographic or other types of empirical material through a 'memory lens' or conceptual angles aligned to the objectives of this book. Despite the variety represented here, this collection still leaves many gaps. Several interesting proposals submitted for this collection could not be included or were later withdrawn for various reasons. It is hoped that this book will draw more attention to public commemorative markers in the context of migration and displacement as a neglected aspect of migration—within academia and beyond.

References

Al-Rustom, H. (2013). Diaspora Activism and the Politics of Locality. The Armenians of France. In A. Quayson & G. Daswani (Eds.), *A Companion to Diaspora and Transnationalism* (pp. 473–493). Hoboken: Wiley.
Ajuntament de Barcelona. (n.d.). Memorial for victims. Barcelona Ciutat Refugi. http://ciutatrefugi.barcelona/en/memorial
Amani. (2015). Porta di Lampedusa, porta d'Europa. http://www.amaniforafrica.it/cosa-facciamo/la-porta-di-lampedusa. Downloaded 26/7/19
Assmann, A. (2003). *Erinnerungsräume. Formen und Wandlungen des kulturellen Gedächtnisses*. München: C.H. Beck.
Assmann, J. (2002 [1992]). *Das kulturelle Gedächtnis. Schrift, Erinnerung und politische Identität in frühen Hochkulturen* (4th ed). München: C.H Beck.
Assmann, A. (2014). Transnational Memories. *European Review, 22*(4), 546–556.
Assmann, A., & Conrad, S. (Eds.). (2010). *Memory in a Global Age. Discourses, Practices and Trajectories*. New York: Palgrave Macmillan.
Baldassar, L. (2006). Migration Monuments in Italy and Australia: Contesting Histories and Transforming Identities. *Modern Italy, 11*(1), 43–62.
Basu, P. (2005). Roots-Tourism as Return Movement: Semantics and the Scottish Diaspora. In M. Harper (Ed.), *Emigrant Homecomings: The Return Movement of Emigrants, 1600–2000* (pp. 131–150). Manchester: Manchester University Press.
Bodnar, J. (1986). Symbols and Servants: Immigrant America and the Limits of Public History. *The Journal of American History, 73*(1), 137–151.
Bond, L., & Rapson, J. (2014). Introduction. In L. Bond & J. Rapson (Eds.), *The Transcultural Turn. Interrogating Memory Between and Beyond Borders* (pp. 1–26). Berlin: De Gruyter.
Butler, J. (2009). *Frames of War: When Is Life Grievable?* London: Verso.
Carrier, P., & Kabalek, K. (2014). Cultural Memory and Transcultural Memory – A Conceptual Analysis. In L. Bond & J. Rapson (Eds.), *The Transcultural*

Turn. Interrogating Memory Between and Beyond Borders (pp. 39–60). Berlin: De Gruyter.
Connerton, P. (1989). *How Societies Remember*. Cambridge: Cambridge University Press.
Crowley, J. (2007). Constructing Famine Memory: The Role of Monuments. In N. Moore & Y. Whelan (Eds.), *Heritage, Memory and the Politics of Identity: New Perspectives on Cultural Landscape* (pp. 55–67). Hamshire/Burlington: Ashgate.
Crownshaw, R. (2011). Introduction (Special Issue on Transcultural Memory). *Parallax, 17*(4), 1–3.
De Cesari, C., & Rigney, A. (2014). Introduction. In C. De Cesari & A. Rigney (Eds.), *Transnational Memory. Circulation, Articulation, Scales* (pp. 1–25). Berlin/Boston: De Gruyter.
Defend International. (2015). *Refugee Crisis: Minutes of Mourn for Alan Kurdi and Others*. https://defendinternational.org/minute-of-mourn-for-aylan-kurdi-and-others/
D'Ignoti, S. (2018, November 26). What Happens to the Bodies of Those Who Die in the Mediterranean? *Aljazeera News*. https://www.aljazeera.com/indepth/features/bodies-die-mediterranean-181125235524960.html
Erll, A. (2011a). *Memory in Culture*. London/New York: Palgrave.
Erll, A. (2011b). Travelling Memory. *Parallax, 17*(4), 4–18.
Erll, A. (2014). From 'District Six' to District 9 and Back: The Plurimedial Production of Travelling Schemata. In C. De Cesari & A. Rigney (Eds.), *Transnational Memory. Circulation, Articulation, Scales* (pp. 29–50). Berlin/Boston: De Gruyter.
Fiddian-Qasmiyeh, E., Loescher, G., Long, K., & Sigona, N. (Eds.). (2014). *The Oxford Handbook of Refugee and Forced Migration Studies*. Oxford: Oxford University Press.
Frotscher, M. (2015). A Lost Homeland, a Reinvented Homeland: Diaspora and the 'Culture of Memory' in the Colony of Danube Swabians of Entre Rios. *German History, 33*(3), 439–461.
Glynn, I. (2012). *History, Memory and Migration: Perceptions of the Past and the Politics of Incorporation*. London: Palgrave Macmillan.
Gouriévidis, L. (Ed.). (2014). *Museums and Migration: History, Memory and Politics*. London/New York: Routledge.
Gutman, Y. (2017). *Memory Activism: Reimagining the Past for the Future in Israel-Palestine*. Nashville: Vanderbilt University Press.
Hamilton, P. I., & Ashton, P. (2001). On Not Belonging: Memorials and Memory in Sydney. *Public History Review, 1*, 23–36.
Horsti, K. (2017). The Mediated Commemoration of Migrant Deaths at European Borders. In Cammaerts, B., Anstead N., & Stupart, R. (Eds.). Media@LSE

Working Paper Series. London: Media@LSE, London School of Economics and Political Science.
Horsti, K., & Neumann, K. (2019). Memorializing Mass Deaths at the Border: Two Cases from Canberra (Australia) and Lampedusa (Italy). *Ethnic and Racial Studies, 42*(2), 141–158.
Hoskins, A. (Ed.). (2018). *Digital Memory Studies: Media Pasts in Transition*. London/New York: Routledge.
Innocenti, P. (2016). *Migrating Heritage: Experiences of Cultural Networks and Cultural Dialogue in Europe*. London/New York: Routledge.
Kansteiner, W. (2002). Finding Meaning in Memory: A Methodological Critique of Collective Memory Studies. *History and theory, 41*(2), 179–197.
Karp, I., & Lavine, S. (Eds.). (1991). *Exhibiting Cultures. The Poetics and Politics of Museum Display*. Washington, DC/London: Smithsonian Institution Press.
Kleist, O. J. (2013). Remembering for Refugees in Australia: Political Memories and Concepts of Democracy in Refugee Advocacy Post-Tampa. *Journal of Intercultural Studies, 34*(6), 665–683.
Lambek, M., & Antze, P. (1996). Introduction. Forecasting Memory. In M. Lambek & P. Antze (Eds.), *Tense Past. Cultural Essays in Trauma and Memory* (pp. xi–xxxviii). New York/London: Routledge.
Landsberg, A. (2004). *Prosthetic Memory. The Transformation of American Remembrance in the Age of Mass Culture*. New York: Columbia University Press.
Lim, J. H. (2010). Victimhood Nationalism in Contested Memories: National Mourning and Global Accountability. In A. Assmann & S. Conrad (Eds.), *Memory in a Global Age. Discourses, Practices and Trajectories* (pp. 138–162). New York: Palgrave Macmillan.
Margry, P., & Sánchez-Carretero, C. (Eds.). (2011). *Grassroots Memorials: The Politics of Memorializing Traumatic Death*. Oxford: Berghahn.
Marschall, S. (2018). *Memory, Migration and Travel*. London/New York: Routledge.
McMahon, C. (2007). Montreal's Ship Fever Monument: An Irish Famine Memorial in the Making. *The Canadian Journal of Irish Studies, 33*(1), 48–60.
Missing Migrants Project. (2019). *International Organization for Migration (IOM)*. https://missingmigrants.iom.int/
Moses, A. D., & Rothberg, M. (2014). A Dialogue on the Ethics and Politics of Transcultural Memory. In L. Bond & J. Rapson (Eds.), *The Transcultural Turn. Interrogating Memory Between and Beyond Borders* (pp. 29–38). Berlin: De Gruyter.
Motte, J., & Ohliger, R. (2006). Men and Women with(out) History? Looking for 'lieux de mémoire' in Germany's Immigration Society. In M. König & R. Ohliger (Eds.), *Enlarging European Memory. Migration Movements in Historical Perspective* (pp. 147–160). Ostfildern: Thorbecke.
Nora, P. (1989). Between Memory and History: Les Lieux de Mémoire. *Representations, 26*(Spring), 7–25.

Pabst, S. (2017). *The Holodomor and the Ukrainian Diaspora: Historical Narratives in a Changing World*. Unpublished Thesis Presented in Partial Fulfillment of the Requirements for The Degree Bachelor of Arts with Honours Research Distinction in History. Columbus: Ohio State University.

Peralta Catipon, T. (2009). Statue Square as a Liminal Sphere: Transforming Space and Place in Migrant Adaptation. *Journal of Occupational Science, 16*(1), 32–37.

Phillips, K. R., & Reyes, G. M. (Eds.). (2011). *Global Memoryscapes. Contesting Remembrance in a Transnational Age*. Tuscaloosa: University of Alabama Press.

Raj, D. S. (2000). Ignorance, Forgetting, and Family Nostalgia: Partition, the Nation State, and Refugees in Delhi. *Social Analysis: The International Journal of Social and Cultural Practice, 44*(2), 30–55.

Rigney, A. (2005). Plenitude, Scarcity and the Circulation of Cultural Memory. *Journal of European Studies, 35*(1), 11–28.

Rothberg, M. (2009). *Multidirectional Memory: Remembering the Holocaust in the Age of Decolonization*. Stanford: Stanford University Press.

Rothberg, M., & Yildiz, Y. (2011). Memory Citizenship: Migrant Archives of Holocaust Remembrance in Contemporary Germany. *Parallax, 17*(4), 32–48.

Rudling, P. A. (2011). Multiculturalism, Memory, and Ritualization: Ukrainian Nationalist Monuments in Edmonton, Alberta. *Nationalities Papers, 39*(5), 733–768.

Santino, J. (2006). *Spontaneous Shrines and the Public Memorialization of Death*. New York/Houndmills: Palgrave Macmillan.

Savage, K. (1997). *Standing Soldiers, Kneeling Slaves: Race, War and Monument in 19th Century America*. Princeton: Princeton University Press.

Siblon, J. (2009). 'Monument Mania'? Public Space and the Black and Asian Presence in the London Landscape. In P. Ashton & H. Kean (Eds.), *People and Their Pasts. Public History Today* (pp. 146–162). London: Palgrave Macmillan.

Van Hear, N. (2010). Migration. In K. Knott & S. McLoughlin (Eds.), *Diasporas: Concepts, Intersections, Identities* (pp. 34–38). New York: Zed Books.

Wolf, O. (2017). Migrant Monuments, Monumental Migrants: São Paulo's Sculptural Homage to Syrian-Lebanese Friendship and the Crafting of Transnational Identity in Centennial Brazil. *TAREA, 4*(4), 120–152.

World Universities Network (WUN). (2019). Memorials to People Who Have Died and to Those Missing During Migration: A Global Project. https://wun.ac.uk/wun/research/view/memorials

Young, J. E. (1992). The Counter-Monument: Memory Against Itself in Germany Today. *Critical Inquiry, 18*(2), 267–296.

Young, J. E. (1994). *The Texture of Memory: Holocaust Memorials and Meaning*. New Haven: Yale University Press.

PART I

The Production and Contestation of Public Memory Around Migration

CHAPTER 2

Memorializing Migration: Immigrant Patronage, Public Memory and the Syrian Centennial Monument to Argentina (1910)

Caroline 'Olivia' M. Wolf

INTRODUCTION

Complex issues of identity and memory surrounding immigrants from the Eastern Mediterranean to Argentina at the turn of the twentieth century are embodied by the first public sculpture sponsored by this community in the nation's capital—the *Monument of the Syrian Residents to the Argentine Nation, 1810–1910*. The construction of this Centennial-era sculpture (Fig. 2.1) served as a centrepiece for nationalist debates on migration and art at an intensely Euro-centric moment in Argentina, which coincided with territorial loss and political turmoil in the final years of the Ottoman Empire, circa 1910–1922. Commissioned by the immigrant community in Buenos Aires that identified as Syrians, the statue was erected in 1913. It was part of the large-scale monument-building spree that swept Argentina in honour of the 100-year anniversary of independence from Spain, initiated in 1910, and sponsored by national and municipal

---

C. M. Wolf (✉)
The University of Tennessee at Chattanooga, Chattanooga, TN, USA
e-mail: Caroline-Wolf@utc.edu

© The Author(s) 2020
S. Marschall (ed.), *Public Memory in the Context of Transnational Migration and Displacement*, Palgrave Macmillan Memory Studies,
https://doi.org/10.1007/978-3-030-41329-3_2

Fig. 2.1 *Monument of the Syrian Residents to the Argentine Nation, 1810–1910.* [Monumento de los Residentes Sirios a la Nación Argentina.] (Photograph by the author, Caroline Olivia M. Wolf, 2016)

authorities, as well as international allies and its immigrant patrons. By exploring the negotiations and speeches tied to the Syrian Centennial monument, the community's awareness of nationalist discourses and the role of public art to construct a new transnational vision of the memory of migration are revealed.

HISTORICAL CONTEXT

On 16 January 1913, a jubilant crowd gathered to witness the public unveiling of the *Monumento de los Residentes Sirios a la Nación Argentina* in the heart of Buenos Aires at a small plaza located along the *Paseo de Julio* between Santa Fe avenue and Arenales street.[1] The enthusiastic reception of the monument by the general public and immigrant community both during the laying of its foundation stone on 16 June 1911 and its later inauguration upon completion on 16 January 1913 reverberated in the press, from the popular weekly *Caras y Caretas* to national newspapers, such as *La Nación*. The printed media reproduced images of the monument and key portions of the speeches delivered by community and political leaders present.

The immigrant-sponsored monument features two modelled bronzes— one male and one female—elaborated in an idealized Beaux Arts academic style at 1.5 scale to life. Arranged around an imported polished granite base, the inscription, '*Los Residentes Sirios a la Nación Argentina en el Centenario, 1810–1910*' [From the Syrian Residents to the Argentine Nation on the Centennial], was boldly inscribed in Spanish on the front of the pedestal and in Arabic on the back. Poised beside the red granite base, a bronze sculpture depicts a moustachioed, fez-capped man in European-style suit gesturing upwards towards the bronze female allegorical figure of the Argentine Republic. The Republic, in turn, stands grandly beside the national shield with laurel frond in hand, atop a pedestal adorned with bronze panels on its flanking sides. These pendant bas-relief panels bear idealized scenes of migration, with one side alluding to the patrons' Levantine port of embarkation and the opposite to their arrival in their new Argentine home.

The monument was originally located on the *Plazoleta Alem*—one of a string of small garden plazas that once ran along the bustling *Paseo de Julio* avenue. In 1910, these *plazoletas* flanked the grand Plaza San Martín and British clock tower erected for the Centennial in the capital. They were situated across from the bustling Retiro railway station and north of the *Hotel de Inmigrantes* in the flanking port. In the decades surrounding the Centennial, neighbouring *plazoletas* became the site of the *Monument of*

---

[1] Translations from original Spanish are my own. This avenue today is known as Leandro Alem Avenue. Location and inaugural date are cited in the *Archivo de Monumentos y Obras de Arte* (hereafter cited as MOA) in Buenos Aires.

the *Catalans* by Joseph Llimona Brughero, a Catalan sculptor hired by the same community in Argentina, and blocks away stood the *Monument to Columbus*, donated by prosperous Italian immigrant Antonio Devoto (Gutiérrez Viñuales 2004). Other donations by European communities for the Centennial include the colossal *Monument of the Carta Magna and the Four Argentine Regions*, given by the Spanish community, as well as Germany's *Monument to Argentina's Agro-Pescarian Wealth* and the *Homage by the French Colony to Argentina*—to name a few (Spinetto 2010). The ceremonial inaugurations of these monuments, sponsored by patrons who typically commissioned artists of the same nationality, involved public speeches and musical tributes that celebrated these sculptures as gifts to Argentina by its immigrant communities, activating them as avatars of identity and diplomacy. The *Monument of the Syrian Residents* contributed to this concert of immigrant-sponsored works honouring the 100-year anniversary of Argentina's May Revolution, whose diverse patronage signalled a layered system of public identities while highlighting their civic presence in the urban fabric.

The location, visual elements and Centennial theme of the Syrian monument also functioned in dynamic dialogue with a broader network of public sculptures sponsored by national and local authorities. These included smaller municipal monuments honouring Argentina's founding figures associated with national historical events such as the *Primera Junta*, Assembly of the Year XIII, and Tucuman Congress. Urban historian Adrian Gorelik (2001, p. 184) has demonstrated that the public space of the Centennial capital was powerfully reshaped by urban reform debates, mass occupation of the streets and the raising of commemorative monuments.

Collective Commission

Against this backdrop, the *Monument of the Syrian Residents* was sponsored by prominent members of the religiously diverse *Syrian Pro-Centennial Commission*, under the leadership of Manuel Manouk.[2] The group collectively identified as Syrian residents, although their homeland was still a province under Ottoman control at the time. The surnames of the committee reflect religious diversity, including Manouk, which signals

---

[2] In the original Spanish, the group was known as *Comisión Siria Pro-Centenario*. See *Los Sirios a La Argentina*, Inv: no 36, circumscription 14a, MOA.

Armenian heritage as a common abbreviation for Manoukian.[3] Other surnames were associated with Maronite, Orthodox Christian and Syrian Jewish traditions. Syrian Sephardic Jews on the committee played a key role in the monument's funding and logistics, visible in the *Club Israelita* offering of 50,000 pesos and negotiating land for the statue.[4] Prominent immigrant businessmen and leaders served as spokesmen for the commission, including Aiub Bestani, Gabriel Kairuz, José Bechelli, Juan Murat, Pedro J. Chaher and Salomón David—associated with Middle Eastern immigrant-owned textile, real estate and medical industries in the capital. That these diverse Arab-speaking immigrants to collectively commissioned the statue together as 'Syrian residents' suggests the stirrings of the Syrianist movement in Argentina, which advocated for regional, ethno-religious unity for the advance of political independence (Hyland 2014; Fahrenthold 2014). The title of the monument and its committee underscores the powerful circulation of these emergent political ideas in the diaspora.

Italian immigrant and sculptor, Garibaldi Affani, received the commission for the *Monument of the Syrians*.[5] Born in Parma in 1861, Affani became an Argentine resident in 1888, where he remained until his death in 1917. The *National Centennial Commission's* records show the sculptor worked prolifically in Argentina and offered his services for over ten commissions in 1909, including statues in Junin and Monuments to Humberto I and Tornquist in Mar del Plata. Affani also created the *Monument to Ramon L. Falcón (Pro National Culture)* in 1914. According to a press release from the monument's inauguration in January 1913, the artist also authored the 24 statues adorning the interior of the Congress' cupola—an impressive record.[6] Prior to his arrival in Argentina, Affani sculpted models of children for drawing studios in Rome, and forged the

---

[3] The press referred to Manouk as the president of the *Comision popular siria* (Syrian Popular Commission) and published a list of leading members. Nélida Boulgourdjian-Toufeksian has confirmed the surname Manouk is associated with Armenian heritage. Boulgourdjian-Toufeksian and Juan Carlos Toufeksian (2012, p. 61) recorded the entry of Manuel Manouk, as a businessman, travelling 3rd class with origins from the Levant via Marseilles in July of 1908.
[4] *Los Sirios a La Argentina,* Inv: no 36, circumscription 14a, MOA.
[5] Affani's authorship is documented at the AGN, MOAs and *Biblioteca Nacional.*
[6] 'El monumento a la Argentina ofrecido por la colectividad Siria', in *La Nación,* Jueves 16 de Enero 1913.

tomb of Anita Coresini in Parma's *camposanto* cemetery.[7] At a time in which Argentina was seeking to rapidly Europeanize the nation, the commission of an Italian or Italian-trained sculptor was regarded as prestigious (Berresford 2009). Thus, the community's selection of Affani as sculptor for the monument demonstrates a keen awareness of the dominant Eurocentric discourse on artistic taste in the era.

The Centennial monument in Buenos Aires represents the largest collective effort to sponsor a public sculpture by the Syrian immigrant community there to date. However, other Centennial homages were sponsored by the diaspora community of former Ottoman subjects in the interior provinces of Argentina. In Cordoba, the historic anniversary was honoured by Arabic-speaking artist Jorge Batica's donation of a richly handcrafted plaque on behalf of the community to the city, featuring the coat of arms of the province of Cordoba and Turkey amidst an array of artistic details.[8] Such commemorations were sponsored by communities of former Ottoman subjects across the Americas for their respective independence celebrations, allowing us to see unique continental and transnational configurations, as also seen in Brazil (Wolf 2017). These works responded to local taste and national contexts, and engaged with Ottoman commemorative traditions abroad to varying degrees. Thus, the *Monument of the Syrian Residents* was not an isolated case, but rather a unique component in a much larger wave of *mahjar*—or diasporic—*monuments* sponsored by diverse communities of former Ottoman subjects across the Americas to proclaim their civic presence while creatively crafting new collective identities.

MONUMENTAL INAUGURATION

At the inaugural unveiling of the Centennial statue in the nation's capital, schoolchildren from the nearby Syrian Argentine school (*Colegio Sirio Argentino*) ceremoniously sang the Argentine national anthem. This

[7] Inv: no 36, circumscription 14a, MOA. Art historian Laura Malosetti discussed the demand for Italian sculptors in Argentina at the turn of the century in her seminar, 'Arte Latinoamericano del Siglo XIX', at the Universidad Nacional San Martín-IDAES, Buenos Aires, Argentina, May–June 2014. On Italian sculptors in the global art market, see Sandra Berresford (2009).

[8] *Diario Sirio Libanés*, 'Una ofrenda de nuestra colectividad: En 1910 un nucleo de siriolibaneses donó una placa al gobierno de Cordoba en occasion del centenario de la independencia argentina', 23 April 1929.

school still operates today as the *Colegio San Marón*, highlighting its Maronite religious affiliation. The plaza was decorated with the Argentine flag and Syrian banners as the municipal police band performed. The national press noted the presence of the immigrant-produced local Arabic language newspaper, *Assalam*, crediting the periodical and its directors—including the aforementioned Schamún—as largely responsible for the success of the monumental initiative.[9] Schamún and Manuel Manouk spoke on behalf of the immigrant community. The newly appointed Ottoman consul to Argentina, Emir Emín Arslán, also gave a speech. Arslán had recently arrived in Buenos Aires at the request of the diaspora community to diplomatically represent the Ottoman provinces to Argentina, which included Greater Syria, still under the control of the empire at this time. Prominent figures from the nation's political ministries and conservative-leaning elite were also in attendance, including the Argentine Minister of External Relations; the Ministers of War and the Interior, Mayor Joaquín Samuel de Anchorena; and renowned lawyer, educator and senator Joaquín V. Gonzalez. Many of these individuals prominently ascribed to the Centennial era's 'spiritual re-awakening', which embraced conservative religious values while balking at rising cosmopolitanism and materialism in the country, and urging civic morality and nationalism (Gorelik 2001, pp. 181–185). The presence of these elites together with the immigrant community and its leaders highlights collective patronage of the monument as a strategic political tool to foment national allegiances among these social sectors.

The unveiling of the completed statue was followed by the public speeches of Manouk, Argentine dignitaries and Ottoman consuls, Arslán and Schamún. Manouk opened the discourse, lauding the monument as a testament to the manner in which the immigrant community 'could not remain indifferent to the momentous occasion of the Argentine Centennial' and symbolized the 'gratitude and love of my compatriots for the Republic'.[10] The monument was then accepted on behalf of the nation's president by Minister of External Relations, Dr. Bosch, stating,

> This act is greatly significant for us, as in addition to obliging our gratitude to its generous donors, it provides the intimate satisfaction of a gentle

[9] 'El Monumento de los Sirios: El acto inaugural de ayer', *La Prensa*, viernes 17 de enero, 1913.
[10] Ibid.

testament of appreciation by this foreign community for our hospitality, and externalized in this friendly manner, demonstrates their intent to continue taking root in our country.[11]

Voiced before the Argentine public, the immigrant community and its current ambassador, this national acknowledgement of the monument highlights its pivotal role in transnational diplomacy.

Yet the discourse of Ottoman consul Emín Arslán took a noticeably different turn. Acknowledging the relatively small size of the Syrian monument, he declared,

> As you can see, this work is modest compared to those offered by other nationalities. It is ... the violet in an immense bouquet of flowers ... On my part, I only feel – not to diminish the artistic valour or critique the commission...that our commemorative branch does not carry the perfume of the Orient that to this day does not cease to scent the world. I would have liked the monument to have been sculpted in a purer arabesque style, a style that today receives universal admiration, that art lovers seek in the beautiful architecture of Granada, Cordoba and Seville.[12]

Arslán's comments targeted what he interpreted as the prominence of Western academic traditions of the monument, revealing tensions surrounding the representation of the community as something overtly 'Oriental' versus 'European'. Despite the politeness and poetics of Arslán's statement, his words likely spurred a reaction among the immigrant leaders present who had laboured to fund, commission and ceremoniously unveil the Centennial monument.

Arslán's speech continued, outlining an artistic critique while making a marked effort to clarify the cultural value and historical contributions of the Ottoman Empire and its immigrant community. He first openly denounced prejudices surrounding Ottoman immigrants in Argentina, declaring,

> I would have liked this, in order to show before the sight of all a small trace of the civilization of our race, because today there shamefully still exists some mistaken ideas about the true value of the Ottoman community. It belongs to the race which gave the world its prophets and apostles: Moses,

[11] Ibid.
[12] Ibid.

Jesus Christ and Mohammed, that conquered the ancient world from the great walls of China to the Atlantic ... and these Asians founded an empire more vast and grand than that of the Roman or Greek empires ... I lament the general belief that all Ottomans are street hawkers, when only 10% of these residents exercise this commerce, while instead there are 50,000 with vigorous arms, with the energy that characterizes them, working Argentine soil, for the greater progress and development of the Argentine Republic. These modest workers, dispersed throughout the immense territory of the Republic are not recognized – only the ambulant workers are brought to the indulgent attention of the public.[13]

The ambassador's speech highlights bias against the monument's patrons in modern Argentina, and the key role of public sculpture in a climate of chronic discrimination. His critique of the lack of *arabesque* elements in the statue also sheds light on important disparate notions of identity between the Ottoman consul and his subjects during the Centennial moment. A close analysis of the statue's historical context during the era of mass migration, as well as its visual iconography, reveals complex issues of identity and reconstruction of collective memory at play.

SYRIAN IMMIGRATION TO ARGENTINA

Immigration from the Ottoman Empire to the Americas, and particularly to Brazil and Argentina in Latin America, was spurred by powerful 'push and pull' factors at the turn of the century. Argentina's lax immigration policies were a major attraction for those seeking economic and political refuge. The desire to populate and cultivate the nation agriculturally in the name of 'progress' was an ideological cornerstone of 'the Generation of 1880', the group of intellectuals associated with President Sarmiento, in power from 1868 to 1874. Open-door immigration was famously advocated by statesman Juan Bautista Alberdi in his 1852 epithet, 'To govern is to populate'.

Yet the nation's initial open-door policies were fuelled by government designs to colonize the country with northern Anglo-Saxon Europeans while filling labour shortages in the agricultural pampas. Early immigration law was designed to facilitate Eurocentric aims, with Article 25 of the Argentine Constitution of 1853 stating, 'The Federal Government will

[13] Ibid.

promote *European* immigration; it will not restrict, limit, or burden with tax the entry of foreigners into the Argentine territory who intend to work the land...'. However, the majority of immigrants coming to Argentina did not fulfil this northern Eurocentric and Anglo-centric vision. Instead, the vast majority of immigrant arrivals were of 'Latin' or Mediterranean origin with 30% hailing from Italy, and 35% from Spain (Devoto 2003; Bailey and Miguez 2003; Moya 1998). The arrival of Arabic-speaking and Armenian communities from the Eastern Mediterranean provinces of the Ottoman Empire in Argentina began as early as the 1850s (Klitch and Lesser 1996; Hyland 2017). Immigration statistics for the diverse Ottoman subjects that arrived in Argentina present difficult challenges, as official records of the entry into Argentina by sea only began in 1882 (Jozami 1993).

Between 1888 and 1914, an estimated 2.5 million immigrants settled in Argentina, with approximately 104,000 recorded to have come from the Levant and North Africa (Klitch 1993). Actual numbers are likely to have been much higher as border control statistics during this era are extremely unreliable. Immigrants who did not arrive by second or third class fare or entered through neighbouring countries, such as Brazil or Uruguay, often went undocumented by officials. Furthermore, many Armenian and Arabic-speaking immigrants carried French or European travel documents. In 1914—the year after the *Monument of the Syrian Residents* was inaugurated—immigrants represented 30% of the total population of the country, and 70% of the male population of Buenos Aires (Klitch 1993). Gladys Jozami (1993) has shown that Arabic-speaking immigrants appear for the first time in census records in 1895. The second national census reported 876 immigrants hailing from the Ottoman Empire, placing these immigrants under the official label 'turco', which reflected their legal status as Ottoman subjects (1993, p. 337). Yet in 1899, the national *Memoria de Inmigración* (Memory of Immigration) records book contained a chapter titled 'Inmigración Siria', which described a new group of Syrian immigrants, stating,

> among the exotic populations which arrive from abroad, the Christian contingent from Turkic Asia distinguishes itself. These Turks are from the province of Syria, belonging to the Catholic Maronite rite and for some years now have arrived in relatively considerable quantities. (Jozami 1993, p. 337)

Between 1883 and 1924, the *Dirección Nacional de Migraciones* register of the high seas immigration placed migrants from the Ottoman

Empire in the following categories: 'Arab, Asian, Babylonian, Caldean, Constantinopolitana, Egyptian, Levantine, Morrocan, Muslim, Ottoman, Palestinian, Syrian, Syrian-Lebanese, Turco, Turco-Arab, Turco-Asian, Turco-Syrian'. In contrast, the consular files of Emin Arslán from 1910 to 1915 simply refer to its emigrés as 'Ottoman subjects'. While this term circulated in the press, Jozami (1993) argues that whenever these immigrants wished to proclaim authority, they referred to themselves in distinct modes, such as 'Non-Muslim Syrians', 'of Arabia' or, even sometimes, as the *'colonia árabe'*—that is, the 'Arab colony'. This is supported by the title of the Syrian Centennial monument as the *Monument of the Syrian Residents*, chosen by its patron community.

The majority of early Eastern Mediterranean immigrants to Argentina sought economic prosperity, while later arrivals tended to flee war and religious conflicts in their homelands. Initial waves of immigrants from Ottoman provinces like Greater Syria arrived seeking commercial opportunities that had dwindled in their homelands, and often came from financially secure, prominent families associated with modern international (and often missionary) schools that facilitated mobility by stressing Western-influenced education, language and important global networks (Khater 2001; Hyland 2014). Economic factors were further provoked by Ottoman debt to Europe due to territorial losses as a result of the Crimean War in 1856 and the Russo-Turkish war in 1878. These losses, along with new trade routes fostered by the building of the Suez Canal in 1869, initiated devastating economic conditions aggravated by the 1890 collapse of the Lebanese silk industry, resulting in a greater impulse for Ottoman subjects to seek economic betterment by migrating abroad.

Political instability and religious conflicts also played an important role. The Young Turk revolution of 1908 resulted in the overthrowing of Sultan Abdülhamid II and the establishment of the Committee of Union and Progress. This party soon splintered, becoming radically nationalist in 1913, and placing restrictions on intellectual and religious freedoms that instigated further migration, particularly as a result of obligatory Ottoman military conscription for non-Muslims (Klitch 1993). In terms of sheer numbers, the largest wave of emigration from the Ottoman Empire occurred between 1910 and 1920—a period marked by the 1911 war in Tripolitania, economic and territorial loss in the Balkans in 1912, and the Ottoman Empire's entry into World War I in August 1914 via the Ottoman–German alliance (Fawaz 2014).

Christian minorities—particularly Armenians, but also Pontian Greeks and Arameans (known also as Assyrians or Syriacs)—were accused of conspiring against the empire by Ottoman authorities in the nineteenth century, as they received special protection from Europe and Russia, each with vested politico-economic interests in the area (Koutoudjian 2015). This resulted in the forced relocation of many minority Christians in the region, and the targeting of Armenians and Arameans in government-sponsored ethnic eradication campaigns in the region. Massacres of Christian minorities took place as early as 1822 under Sultan Abdul Hamid II, with the killing of 50,000 Greeks, followed by massacres of Armenians in 1865, and of Armenians, Pontian Greeks and Arameans again in 1895–1896, known as the Hamidian Massacres (Astourian 2012). Various countries in the United Nations now officially recognize the ethnic eradication campaigns against Christian minorities by the Ottoman government at the turn of the twentieth century as genocide. The Ottoman government's violent persecution and massacres of ethnic and religious minorities during this era led historian Reşat Kasaba (2009, p. 125) to observe that the Ottoman 'migrations of the late 19th and early 20th century were almost exclusively based on some aspect of identity of the people involved'. In 1860, religious conflicts between Muslim Druze and religious groups like the Maronites erupted in Mount Lebanon and Damascus, spurring another exodus of mainly Christians and Sephardic Jews from the Levant, with many fleeing to the Americas (Fawaz 1994; Grün 1996; Moore and Mathewson 2013).

Despite the statistical immigration record challenges of the Arabic-speaking community, historians have demonstrated that many Ottoman subjects powerfully shaped their adopted nation, while becoming highly visible in the city streets, as peddlers. By 1910, a Syrian-Lebanese and Armenian socio-economic network had taken root along Reconquista Street between Charcas and Córdoba Avenues. The small district was blocks away from the port and *Hotel de Inmigrantes,* a state-sponsored immigration shelter (Scobie 1974, p. 30).

Response to Anti-Immigration and Nationalist Discourses

With the arrival of immigrants from beyond Western Europe, political debates on immigration circulating since the nineteenth century became radicalized and proliferated around the Centennial celebrations, with an emergent strain of Argentine nationalism of increasingly xenophobic dimensions (Devoto 2002). Discourses calling for 'a new Argentine race' born of European miscegenation emerged (Ruggiero 2004, pp. 115, 122) and voiced in José Ingenieros' *Sociologia Argentina*:

> In the Argentine territory, liberated after a century by the wisdom and action of a thousand or ten-thousand 'euro-argentinos', there will be a race composed of twenty or ten million whites familiar with good hygiene and reading, symbols of civilization. In their hours of recreation, they will read legends of the extinguished races of indigenous peoples, and the stories of colonial racial *mestizaje*. (1913, p. 263)

During the same period, German immigration to Argentina and new nationalisms in Europe—particularly in the late nineteenth century and the 1930s—were on the rise. The increasingly xenophobic modes of nationalism surfacing in Germany, Italy and France had a powerful impact on transatlantic North-South cultural exchanges, inciting further scrutiny against Jewish and Muslim immigrants to Argentina (Goebel 2011; Foote and Goebel 2014).

José Ingenieros claimed that Europeanization of the nation was necessary to eradicate modern social ills. 'There is no remedy, then, but one against our calamities: to Europeanize...We will never be able to change our bloodlines nor history nor climate, but we can Europeanize our ideas, sentiments, passions' (Ingenieros cited in Gonzalez 2015, p. 48). These discourses on Argentine immigration during the Centennial moment reflect a racialized vision of cultural production fomented by industry, economy, education and the arts, lingering since the nineteenth century, and at the forefront of twentieth-century public debates. Such rhetoric evoked the ideology steeped within the 1902 *ley de residencia* (Residency law), which permitted the government to expel immigrants without a trial, agitating narratives of 'non-desirable' immigration.

Increasing nationalism also found its way into the educational and artistic curriculum of Argentina, particularly promoted by Ricardo Rojas— Argentine journalist, author and later Dean of the University of Buenos Aires—who penned his landmark text, *La restauracion nacionalista* (The Nationalist Restoration) in 1909. Here, Rojas urged for the establishment of a nationalist education, as well as a nationalist art programme as a direct response to compound fears regarding immigrants and 'exotic' influences. Rojas' text reflected the escalating social tensions and prejudices by which recent immigrants were claimed to be associated with anarchism and as potential threats to the nation. He championed an Argentinian nationalism, stressing its insertion within pedagogy as the foundation of a strong nation. He argued that public sculpture in particular could play a key role in the construction of the nation and its history.

> History is not only taught in classroom lectures: the feeling of history, without which it is sterile, is formed within the spectacle of daily life, in the traditional naming of places and sites associated with historic memories, in the vaults of museums and commemorative monuments whose influence over the imagination I have dubbed the *pedagogy of statues*. (Rojas 1971 [1909], p. 139)

Gorelik (2001, p. 214) has keenly described Rojas' awareness of the role of monuments 'as one of the fundamental instruments of the nationalizing task, learned from Europe, where public art is abundant'. Rojas believed in the need to clearly define the relationship between new monuments and patrimony in order to re-appropriate the city, which he believed was at the mercy of 'foreign nations ... symbolically occupying our territory'. While Gorelik (2001, p. 214) argues that Rojas' reference to 'foreign nations' here likely refers to the cosmopolitan capitalist powers, rather than immigrants, the statement is ambiguous and appears to have been designed to appeal to anti-cosmopolitan and anti-immigrant nationalists alike.

Considering the climate of nationalism, the role of the *Monument of the Syrian Residents* in representing its immigrant patrons in a positive light was all the more salient. Noufouri (1999, p. 150) has demonstrated the circulation of anti-'turco' discourses during the Centennial, arguing that the monument's patrons adopted a European style to suppress 'fears of Turkification'. At this time, reactionary anti-immigration politicians and conservative elites attempted to pass a law banning the entry of Arab immigrants to Argentina, claiming they belonged 'to a race unable to adapt', on 12 September 1910 during the 36th Ordinary Session of the Honourable Senate of the National Congress. During this session, Joaquín V. González—the same senator later present at the Syrian monument's inauguration in 1913—argued that distinctions needed to be made between 'turco' and Syrian immigration, stating the Syrian shows conditions much more acceptable to our civilization than others... this immigration perfectly assimilates to our customs and ways of working, and also adopts with admirable facility our political customs to such a degree that it is almost difficult to distinguish them, in the interior of the Republic, from the population that we commonly call our gauchos or farmers of the country.[14]

Interestingly, González avoided comment on the hotly disputed presence of these immigrants in the city as street merchants, while he subtly merged the image of the Syrian immigrant with the Argentine nationalistic figure of the gaucho, in the only defence of the migrant community against virulent anti-'turco' voices at the session. The xenophobic racism of the opposition circulating at the hearing is embodied in the words of Dr. Lainez, who proclaimed,

how can we reject the Mohammedan or Jewish Berbers and all that overflowing Moroccan and Levantine (human) foam from one side of the Mediterranean from the civilization which lies on its other side, as if they were divided by a wall, if we accept these Syrians? Such immigration... represents part of a movement which obliges us to backwardness and burdens the country with dead weight, illiteracy and primitive customs, still uncontrollable.[15]

González responded to such arguments by stating,

I would like to remind the Senate that the Syrians, in a certain sense, are the Europeans of Asia, with its ancient civilization, morals, and Christian culture, who have come under the protection of European powers, whose education, language and progress they have assimilated and now practice like Europeans.[16]

González' defence of Syrian immigrants is cautious but also problematic in its association with European neo-colonial thinking, Christian emphasis and lack of defence for Levantine culture or the Syrian Jewish or Muslim immigrants that also arrived in Argentina. Yet his Eurocentric

---

[14] 36th *Sesión Ordinaria de la Honorable Cámara de Senadores*. September 12, 1910, (ed.) Congreso de la Nación Argentina, (1911), p. 555.
[15] Ibid.
[16] Ibid, p. 558. Also cited in Noufouri et al., *Tinieblas del Crisol de Razas*, p. 155.

rhetoric strategically manipulated assimilationist discourses to connote Eastern Mediterranean migrants as 'Western' and ultimately stopped the ban on Arab migration to the nation.

A Transnational Visual Programme

In light of these debates circulating during the Centennial, the monument's nationalist and Eurocentric visual elements, artistic production, materials and patronage can all be seen as a reaction to ethnocentric discourses spurred by tensions surrounding migration and modernization. The monument also reflects the desire to craft a new transnational identity and non-sectarian allegiances in the region. Rather than dismiss the *Monument of the Syrian Residents* as a simple exercise in European academic aesthetics that rejected associations with the 'Orient', the statue reveals a keen negotiation of nationalist discourses. This was visually accomplished by heavily borrowing from both local and global visual referents such as the Argentine *Monuments of the May Founding Fathers* series, as well as modern monumental practices in the Syrian provinces.[17]

Sponsored by patrons who self-identified as Syrian residents of Argentina and designed by an Italian-Argentine immigrant sculptor on Argentine soil in honour of the Centennial, the monument inherently embraces pluralistic notions of nationality. The diverse forces fuelling its creative production allow the monument to be seen as cosmopolitan and transcultural in nature. Transcultural visual references embedded within the statue blend to innovatively portray the immigrant community as loyal, upstanding Ottoman-Argentine citizens and 'desirable' immigrants during an increasingly xenophobic era. A transnational analysis of the monument—which carefully reads its production and visual elements as the combined result of distinct traditions transformed by mass migration—allows us to understand it as a reflection of intersecting notions of modernity and shifting global identities.

The statue's imagery signals its transnational dimensions. The *Monument of the Syrian Residents*' strong use of allegory resonates with Western and Argentine iconography in public sculpture. The Syrian monument's polished pedestal is topped with a bronze female as symbol of the Argentine republic crowned with a Phrygian cap and laurel wreath, employing Western symbols of liberty and peace. In her right hand, the

[17] The Spanish title is *Monumentos de los próceres de Mayo*.

Republic holds a laurel frond, and under her left, the Argentine shield. An interesting parallel exists between this figure and that of the May pyramid in the *Plaza de Mayo*, originally constructed in 1811 and altered with the additional topping of the female allegory of Liberty in 1856 (Payro 1970). Both figures wear classical robes with cap and bare right shoulder, traditional allusions to the goddess Athena (Burucúa and Campagne 1994, pp. 349–81). Thus, the monument visually quotes a landmark national icon to show allegiance with Argentine values and identity. While the allegorical figure in the May monument holds a spear, the *Monument of the Syrian Residents* exchanges the weapon for the laurel—replacing a symbol of war for one of peace. The May pyramid allegory stands in defensive *contrapposto*, while the Republic figure is fuller and in flowing robes, suggesting national bounty and serenity. The polished aesthetic and symbolism of the Syrian monument implies a dual interest in crafting an image readily identifiable with classical and national iconography while publically embracing liberty.

Yet the complex visual programme of the monument reaches well beyond national associations. At the base of the pedestal stands a second bronze depicting a moustached gentleman in an elegant suit and fez simultaneously, sporting a combination of west-east attire then described as *ala franga*, associated with Europe and elite class status in the empire. The fez was also linked to Ottomanism—a concept circulating in the empire between 1876 and the first Balkan wars in 1912, which promoted equality of all Ottoman subjects before the law, influenced by the French Revolution (Deringil 1993). The fez carried a political charge, as it was introduced by Ottoman decree under Sultan Mahmud II in 1829 with the goal of replacing the turban, associated with Muslim elites, with a form of universal, secular headgear to be worn by elites regardless of religion throughout the Empire (Quataert 1997). The fez consequently bears layers of meaning, melding modernizing processes (such as social homogenization and secularization) with Ottoman allegiance. During the Argentine Centennial, various medallions circulated among immigrant communities of Ottoman subjects in Buenos Aires that incorporated both the image of the fez and the *Monument of the Syrian Residents* itself, forging a layered image of transnational Syrian-Argentine identity that conveyed palimpsest notions of modernity. Rather than portray a specific individual, the bronze re-casts its collective patrons from Greater Syria as model, modern migrants.

Gesturing towards the pedestal's inscription and placed below the figure of the Republic in a position of submission, the emblematic modern Ottoman Argentine figure looks out towards the viewer, who stands as witness to the monumental dedication of the immigrant community to its new homeland. Noufouri (1999, p. 151) interprets the sculpture of the ambiguously unidentified Ottoman immigrant as precariously perched, linking this visual instability to the shifting immigration politics of the era. Yet the fez-bearing Syrian figure of the monument can alternatively be understood a symbolic visual surrogate, serving as a universal representative for the modern Syrian-Argentine collective community. By adopting the modern fez and avoiding specific references to religion via headgear, this idealized Syrian immigrant figure physically embodied a positive image of its multi-faith, transnational patrons within the public sphere.

Positioned on each side of the inscription on the northern and southern faces of the pedestal, two bronze friezes in sculptural bas-relief are framed in quatrefoil niches. These reliefs portray pendant images of port cities, in dialogue with each other as well as the bronze figures of the monument. On the south face appears the image of a bustling port. Although the exact location remains unspecified, the presence of load-bearing camels suggests an attempt to render a port in the Levant, the point of departure for Ottoman subjects immigrating to Argentina. Boxes clutter the foreground as figures carry cargo and luggage to an awaiting sailboat. Like the location of the port, both the generically represented labourers and the bodies leading the burdened camels remain ambiguous. The lack of geographic specificity and the camels of the bas-relief evoke the sort of timelessness at play in stereotypical signifiers characteristic of Orientalism in the arts (Nochlin 1983). Yet the presence of port-side workers in the frieze also suggests a keen awareness by the monument's patrons and artists of discriminatory discourses circulating during the time of the Centennial. The emphasis on labouring bodies in this image visually counters stereotypical representations of so-called 'immoral idleness' permeating Orientalist representations of the Levant at the time. Alternately, the convenient ambiguity of place in the image holistically allows for diverse locational readings, permitting the work to encompass the many branches of the diasporic community that migrated to Argentina and sponsored the monument.

The northern frieze (Fig. 2.2), placed directly to the side of the Ottoman bronze figure, instead presents an idealized scene of immigration to Argentina as its main focus. On the left, the passenger boat, laden

Fig. 2.2 Detail of bas-relief, *Monumento de los Sirios a la Nación Argentina*. (Photograph by the author, Caroline Olivia Wolf, 2017)

with fez-capped immigrants rendered in detail, has arrived at the port. Unlike the panel of the Middle Eastern port, the figures disembarking from the immigrant ship are carefully individualized. Images of men, a young girl and a veiled woman carrying a baby are all readily distinguishable from the masses on the shores. At the water's edge, a gentleman in top hat and suit—representative of the ideal Argentine citizen—warmly greets the masses of immigrant arrivals with a handshake.

The right-hand portion of the scene becomes a romantic panegyric to immigration. The allegorical figure of the Republic appears once again with her trademark Phrygian cap and outstretched arms. The Republic leads a Syrian immigrant in the *ala franga* attire—still clutching his luggage—by the arm into a promising future, brightened by a sun that harkens to that of the Argentine flag, anthropomorphized with welcoming smile above the horizon. This idealized scene of migration reflects the desire of its immigrant patrons to 'custom-build' the nationalist iconography of the Centennial, which, according to Civantos (2006), later occurred with the community's literary production. This image of a hearty Argentine welcome for Eastern Mediterranean immigrants dressed in Western clothing except for the fez offers a powerful visual message of immanent assimilation.

Above the shoulder of the Argentine allegory appears the silhouette of *La Rotunda*—an early transitory structure that housed, documented and oriented immigrants at the port of Buenos Aires. Originally, the building was designed as a panorama and converted into a provisory Immigrants' Hotel (Ochoa de Eguileor and Valdés 2000; Swiderski and Farjat 2000). Its circular plan embodies Foucault's panopticon—facilitating the surveillance of the greatest number of individuals by the governing few via a centralized scopic regime. Although intended as a provisional structure, *La Rotunda* operated for 20 years from 1888 onwards, and served as the precursor to the current immigration facility (Schávelzon 2012). Following the example of North America's Ellis Island, incoming immigrants were registered upon arrival, interviewed and categorized by their ability to work; those who agreed to rural labour were given visas immediately. Those 'without means or plans' were taken to the hotel, where they were separated by gender and age, received food and lodging for five days, and could opt to be placed by the National Work Office or find work on their own (Rodriguez 2006, pp. 192–3). Railway tracks adjacent to the facilities shuttled contracted migrants to work in the pampas within days of arrival.

The representation of *La Rotunda* on the monument is fascinating as it coincides with the moment when Syrian migration was being hotly contested by government elites. The visual inclusion of *La Rotunda* upon the migrant monument reflects the desire by the diaspora to access government-sponsored immigration assistance services that were, in fact, systematically denied to Arab-speaking migrants during the sculpture's construction. While official legislation to exclude Arabic-speaking immigrants was not passed, the Ministry of Foreign Relations encouraged health inspectors to deny the entry of many Syrian and Lebanese immigrants through false diagnosis of trachoma (Di Liscia and Marrón 2009; Civantos 2006, p. 12). Such discrimination remained in practice through the wave of nationalist xenophobia known as the *Decada infama* in the 1930s when Arabic-speaking migrants were also prohibited from staying at the hotel unless they signed a contract to work as agricultural labourers in the provinces (Baycar 2008, p. 85). These measures led many Syrian immigrants to avoid the immigrant hotel, preferring to settle immediately in the closely knit ethnic enclave of the 'barrio turco' near Retiro along Reconquista Street. Other visual aspects of the Syrian monument draw strong parallels to government-sponsored Argentine monuments in the urban fabric. In addition to powerful allusions to the May Pyramid, the sculpture borrows heavily from visual formulas employed in the series of sculptures honouring the *Primera Junta* (First Council) erected for the Centennial. These bronze statues were sponsored by the local government and spearheaded by the city council under the leadership of the director of the National Historical Museum, Adolfo Carranza, along with the National Centennial Commission in 1910. The sculptural series was designed to foster historical memory in a period rife with cosmopolitan and nationalist sentiments (Gorelik 2001, pp. 200–203).[18] With the exception of the figure of Rodríguez Peña in his namesake plaza and Alberti in the northern district of Belgrano, the remaining statues of these leaders were all placed south of Rivadavia Avenue, aligned with efforts to establish a nationalist pedagogical programme and gentrify the poorer southern districts of the city. In contrast, the original site of the *Monument of the Syrian Residents* lay at a central avenue connecting the north-south sectors of the city.

All these statues, inaugurated in 1910, followed formulaic visual patterns typically employed in the late nineteenth-century media of public monuments. They featured idealized, bronze figures of the founding fathers atop granite pedestals at approximately 1.5 scale to life, frequently paired with bas-relief plaques relating a historical episode of the leader's life. The same formula applied to monumental commemorations honouring Argentine leaders duplicated throughout Argentina during the Centennial. It is no surprise then that sculptor Garibaldi Affani was employed to create the *Monument of the Syrian Residents* after producing statues of leaders General Mitre, Humberto I and Tornquist in the provinces in 1909. Affani's record of civic commissions established him as a sculptor of nationalist monuments. The Syrian monument echoes the material, composition and style of the memorials to the leaders of the May revolution. With red granite imported from Italy at the request of the Pro-Centennial Syrian Commission, the effort to employ European marble at the same scale of the state-sponsored *Primera Junta* monuments reflects academic aesthetics and materials that served as a marker of official tastes

---

[18] See *Memorandum sobre las estatuas inauguradas en 1910* and 'Comisión Nacional del Centenario', Sala 7, Legajos 18–1 to 18–6, AGN.

and cultural legitimacy at the time.[19] Inaugurated shortly after the *Primera Junta* series was raised, the Syrian monument closely adheres the formulas established to honour the Argentine leaders, suggesting an attempt to craft nationalist visual and ideological connections in this visual adherence.

A Reconstructed Memory of Migration

The allegorical figures and pendant plaques of the Syrian Centennial Monument worked together in dynamic synthesis to publically reconstruct a collective memory of Syrian migration to Argentina in the urban fabric. The monument may initially appear as a simple homage expressing gratitude to the nation, connoting its patrons as appreciative, model migrants. The figure of the ideal Syrian migrant suggests submission to the Argentine nation and shared nationalist values, while the pendant panels pictorially evoke an embrace of hard-work and convey the host nation's positive reception of its new arrivals. Yet keeping in mind the struggles of the former Ottoman subjects—now self-identifying as resident Syrians—both in their homeland and in their adopted new Argentine home, a strategic re-crafting of the memory of migration via the monument is revealed. Rather than depict the actual hurdles faced by its sponsoring immigrant community, the monument visually represents a re-imagined, curated memory of migration. By sponsoring the monument, the Syrian immigrant community can be seen as seeking to correct stereotypes and anti-immigrant discourses circulating in the public sphere at the time of its commission.

While marking its migrant patrons as Argentine residents, the monument functions as a transcultural symbolic marker visually connecting its Syrian patrons back home, to the broader diaspora, and international community. This aspect of the memorial illustrates what Landsberg (2004, p. 10) has described as the flourishing of memories and traditions in the diaspora in a manner that is far more pronounced than in the homeland, reflecting bilateral influences and transnational dialogues. This visual reshaping of memory evidenced by the memorial also evokes historian Michael Kammen's (1991, cited in Savage 2006, n.p.) claim that 'societies

---

[19] 'Exps. relativos a monumentos del centenario con intervencion del Min. de Obras Publicas', 1909–1911, Sala VII, 3646, Comision Nacional del Centenario; Iniciador Comision Siria Pro-Centenario, 1912, No Expediente 3827, Letra M, AGN. On 'polished aesthetics,' see Rosen and Zerner (1988).

in fact reconstruct their pasts rather than faithfully record them, and that they do so with the needs of contemporary culture clearly in mind – manipulating the past in order to mold the present'. The artistic programme of the Syrian Centennial Monument embodies both the forging of collective memory and an attempt to visually re-construct the history of Syrian migration to Argentina. By selectively drawing upon the visual vocabularies of both Argentina and Ottoman-ruled Syria via its gendered allegory and fez-capped immigrant figure, the monument introduced a new transnational image of exemplar Syrian-Argentine identity in Latin America. The transregional iconography embedded in the monument also echoes ideas expressed in Peter Carrier and Kobi Kabalek's (2014) examination of transcultural memory, which placed temporal and spatially relative aspects of collective identity within a larger analytical discourse interrogating the boundaries of identity.

The commemorative context of the Argentine Centennial provided the Syrian community with the perfect opportunity for the collective construction of a narrative of migration. The historic moment served as the impetus for community efforts to bolster its visibility within its Argentine host society. Monument-building initiatives have the potential to both unite and divide the immigrant communities that seek to build them (Raj 2000). Such tensions appear afoot recalling the public speech of Ottoman ambassador Emir Arslán on the date of the memorial's inauguration. Notably, the generous offering of the Syrian Centennial monument to the Argentine nation was donated at a moment when the nation was garnering global attention for its commemorative ceremonies. Therefore, it would have assisted in seeking a position of prestige and allegiance with local and national politicians for the Syrian community, bolstering the social mobility of the community in a moment rife with tensions.

The monument operated in modes that would have been visually and physically experienced. Upon its inauguration, the monument was activated as the epicentre of public commemorative practices, serving as a site where the memory of Syrian migration to Argentina would be periodically re-activated through later commemorations before the statue. According to Connerton (1989), the performative aspects of commemoration—whether experienced through ritual, habit or bodily automatisms—activate memory in a community and beyond in intergenerational modes. Just as Connerton (1989, p. 162) has shown that 'architecture is an ingredient in cultural memory', the Syrian monument for the Centennial renders a tangible, re-remembered vision of collective migration into the topography of the Argentine capital.

Building on Connerton's understanding of the performative aspects of commemorative and bodily experienced practices comprising the construction of memory, art historian Mechtild Widrich (2014) considers the symbolic function and social activation of monuments—regardless of media, permanence or grandeur—in a variety of spaces. Drawing upon a reflection of Robert Musil's (Musil 1957, pp. 480–483) work on monuments as a *Denkmal* or 'mark to think', Widrich highlights the inherent value of monuments as lying within their social—rather than material—dimension. She observes that monuments can be *any* object or event whose link to the past is socially activated, thereby maintaining a performative relationship with time. The visual representation at play in the *Monument of the Syrian Residents* reflects different aesthetic approaches and reconfigured identities, yet both works consistently held a performative function as socially activated avatars of identity via public commemorations that took place with the monument's earliest inaugurations.

Noting the historical moment in which new Syrian political movements sought autonomy from the Ottoman Empire, the visual imagery of the monument presented a new collective identity and altered historical visions of migration. As demonstrated in the pendant panels showing idealized scenes of immigration to Argentina, the monument carefully edited history at a time when the actual presence of Syrian migrants in the nation was, in fact, far from the panegyric depiction emblazoned on the bas-reliefs. In this sense, the pendant panels carry out multiple functions in the reconstruction of history and collective memories of migration. They sought to reshape and keep the memory of the transnational, transatlantic migration alive for the modern Syrian-Argentine community by presenting a romanticized, idealized vision of the Syrian immigration experience on the Syrian monument. At the same time, the visual representations imbued into the public sculpture ultimately modelled an image of what reception by the host country of these model migrants should be during one of Latin America's most intense and contentious periods of mass migration.

MONUMENTAL MOVES

The location of the statue today has been re-signified, now positioned in front of the grand former national post office building that today functions as the *Centro Cultural Kirchner*—a major cultural institution inaugurated under the government of Cristina Fernández de Kirchner, which held a strong pro-immigration stance. The position of the Syrian memorial in the plaza flanking the cultural centre accents its visual dialogue with other busts and statues of national leaders located there, in addition to new associations with national artistic production due to its physical proximity beside the recently inaugurated centre. In 1931, the monument was moved to its current location as the thoroughfare known as Leandro Alem Avenue was widened and its accompanying *plazoletas* destroyed. Correspondence between Director General de Paseos Carlos Thays, municipal official Adolfo Mugica and Dr. José Jorge Salama as representative of the Syrian-Lebanese community demonstrates that the civic and artistic value of the Syrian Centennial monument was recognized by leading figures in public works and urbanism in the capital at the time. The new site was carefully selected and approved by both municipal officials and its patron community.[20] The immigrant-sponsored monument was then placed in the plaza known as *Plaza Colón norte*, beside the architectural masterpiece that then functioned as the nation's central post office. On 29 March 2002, Buenos Aires' legislature petitioned to move the monument to the intersection of Santa Fé Avenue and *Republica Árabe Siria* Street. However, the motion was declined by the Department of Monuments and Public Works, which deemed it would 'be contrary to the conservation of social memory and urban landscape'.[21] Notably, the *Monumento a Colón*—more grandiose in scale and positioned beside the Casa Rosada—was later moved far from the city centre due to its controversial glorification of Christopher Columbus.[22] By comparison, the Syrian monument was ultimately more successful as a public memorial in the long term, by maintaining a prominent, lasting position within the urban fabric until the present day.

---

[20] *Los Sirios a La Argentina,* Inv: no 36, circumscription 14a, MOA. See 'Ubicacion del Monumento donado por la Colectividad Sirio-Libanesa', Expediente No. 119.529.D. 1931, Boletin Municipal no. 2579, June 18, 1931; Boletin Municipal no. 2546, May 16, 1931.
[21] Ibid.
[22] The statue remained in the former Parque Colon until 2013, when it was moved near the Aeroparque Jorge Newberry.

Conclusions

In the Argentine capital, the *Monument of the Syrian Residents to the Argentine Nation, 1810–1910*, served as one of the earliest examples in a later myriad of *mahjar* monuments donated by the diverse networks of former Ottoman subjects as they settled across the nation, and Latin America more broadly. Distinct branches of this immigrant community reconfigured their social networks and transnational identities over the decades that followed, using public monuments to proclaim their presence, express allegiance and draw awareness to issues affecting each community in their respective cities. These monuments and their transnational political implications signal important shifts in the construction of new collective identities and strategic mobilization of selected memories of migration in diverse *mahjar* communities. The Centennial celebrations of 1910 provided the impetus for the monument's initial commission and an opportunity for social interaction with municipal and national leaders, which essentially opened the door for social mobility. The Centennial moreover stimulated considerations of collective identities for its patrons, as well as the construction and transmission of collective memory—in this case, new Syrian diasporic identities, and memories of Syrian migration to the nation.

As Benedict Anderson (1978, p. 301) has observed, monuments were expected to outlive those that build them, 'and so partly take on the aspect of a bequest or testament… mediating between particular types of past and futures'. This allows us to consider each of these commemorations as a record of the shifting identities, social allegiances and political concerns of the diaspora performatively activated at a specific moment in time, still manifested in the urban fabric today. The Syrian monument's activation of memory via ceremonial inaugurations, public speeches and its recent relocation within the city reminds us that it is in a sense, still under construction, as Young has revealed (1993),

> monument building is a living process, and so in some sense always unfinished; no matter how much a monument may pretend to be eternal and unchanging, its meaning always evolves as its viewers bring new concerns and understandings to it. (Young, cited in Savage 2006, n.p.)

The collective patronage of the *Monumento de los Residentes Sirios* testifies to the strategic intervention of a minority immigrant community within Argentine society that engaged in transnational artistic dialogues with its newly adopted homeland, while reshaping the urban and cultural fabric of the capital as well as the memory of Syrian migration to the nation. These ideas were vocalized by Alejandro Schamún during the placement of the monument's foundational stone, as he declared,

> Emigrated from far lands, where democracy still is not ingrained … to become a part of the fusion of races in the great ideal of human brotherhood … Argentina marches toward progress … The foreigner, sirs, can be a great collaborator in progress. We bring our virility, our energies, our action, our unbreakable desire to help raise up the immense building of the material and moral greatness of this nation.[23]

In Schamún's speech, the act of collective building serves as a powerful metaphor for the construction of the Argentine nation. As the *Monument of the Syrian Residents* demonstrates, public sculpture provided a critical means of reconstructing new transnational identities for former Ottoman subjects and collective memories of Syrian migration to Argentina.

References

Anderson, B. (1978). Cartoons and Monuments: The Evolution of Political Communication under the New Order. In K. D. Jackson & L. W. Pye (Eds.), *Political Power and Communications in Indonesia* (pp. 282–321). Berkeley: University of California Press.

Astourian, S. (2012). On the Genealogy of the Armenian-Turkish Conflict, Sultan Abdülhamid, and the Armenian Massacres. *Journal of the Society for Armenian Studies, 21*, 185.

Bailey, S., & Miguez, E. (Eds.). (2003). *Mass Migration to Modern Latin America*. Wilmington, DC: Scholarly Resources.

Baycar, M. (2008). *Ottoman Emigration to Argentina, 1870–1914*. M.A. Thesis in History, Boğaziçi University Institute for Graduate Studies in Social Sciences.

Berresford, S. (2009). *Carrara e il mercato della scultura*. Milan: Federico Motta Editore.

---

[23] 'El Monumento de los Sirios—Colocación de la piedra fundamental—La ceremonia de ayer', *La Nación*, 17 Junio 1911.

Boulgourdjian-Toufeksian, N., & Toufeksian, J. C. (2012). *Inmigracion Armenia en la Argentina: Perfiles de una historia centenaria a partie de las listas de pasajeros (1889–1979)*. Buenos Aires: Fundación MGA.

Burucúa, J. E., & Campagne, F. A. (1994). Mitos y simbología de la Nación. Los países del cono sur. In A. Annino, L. Castro Leiva, & F. X. Guerra (Eds.), *De los Imperios a las Naciones: Iberoamérica* (pp. 349–381). Zaragoza: Iber-Caja.

Carrier, P., & Kabalek, K. (2014). Cultural Memory and Transcultural Memory – A Conceptual Analysis. In L. Bond & J. Rapson (Eds.), *The Transcultural Turn. Interrogating Memory Between and Beyond Borders* (pp. 39–60). Berlin: De Gruyter.

Civantos, C. (2006). *Between Argentines and Arabs: Argentine Orientalism, Arab Immigrants, and the Writing of Identity*. Albany: University of New York Press.

Connerton, P. (1989). *How Societies Remember*. Cambridge: Cambridge University Press.

Deringil, S. (1993). The Invention of Tradition as Public Image in the Late Ottoman Empire, 1808 to 1908. *Comparative Studies in Society and History*, 35(1), 3–29.

Devoto, F. (2002). Nacionalismo, fascismo y tradicionalismo en la Argentina moderna. *Una historia*. Buenos Aires: Siglo XXI.

Devoto, F. (2003). *Historia de la inmigración en la Argentina*. Buenos Aires: Editorial Sudamericana.

Di Liscia, M. S., & Marrón, M. F. (2009, November 29). Sin puerto para el sueño americano. Políticas de exclusión, inmigración y tracoma en Argentina (1908–1930), *Nuevo Mundo Mundos Nuevos*.

Fahrenthold, S. (2014). The Global Levant: Making a Nation in the Syrian and Lebanese Diaspora, 1913–1939. PhD diss., Northeastern University, Boston.

Fawaz, L. (1994). *An Occasion for War: Civil Conflict in Lebanon and Damascus in 1860*. Berkeley/Los Angeles: University of California Press.

Fawaz, L. (2014). *A Land of Aching Hearts: The Middle East in the Great War*. Cambridge: Harvard University Press.

Foote, N., & Goebel, M. (Eds.). (2014). *Immigration and National Identities in Latin America*. Gainesville: University Press of Florida.

Goebel, M. (2011). *Argentina's Partisan Past: Nationalism and the Politics of History*. Liverpool: Liverpool University Press.

Gonzalez, H. (Ed.). (2015). *Positivismo Argentino: Simuladores de la Razón*. (August–October). Buenos Aires: Biblioteca Nacional Mariano Moreno.

Gorelik, A. (2001). *La grilla y el parque*. Quilmes: Universidad Nacional de Quilmes.

Grün, R. (1996). The Armenian Renaissance in Brazil. *The Americas*, 53(1), 113–151.

Gutiérrez Viñuales, R. (2004). Hacia una geografía de lo simbólico. Escultura conmemorativa en Buenos Aires. In *Las esculturas de Buenos Aires* (pp. 1–5). Buenos Aires: Manrique Zago Ediciones.
Hyland, S. (2014). The Summit of Civilizations: Nationalisms among the Arabic-speaking Colonies in Latin America. In N. Foote & M. Goebel (Eds.), *Immigration and National Identities in Latin America* (pp. 256–280). Gainesville: University of Florida Press.
Hyland, S. (2017). *More Argentine than You: Arabic-Speaking Immigrants in Argentina*. Albuquerque: University of New Mexico Press.
Ingenieros, J. (1913). *Sociología argentina*. Madrid: Daniel Jorro.
Jozami, G. (1993). La identidad nacional de los llamados turcos en la Argentina. In *Temas de Africa y Asia 2* (p. 191). Buenos Aires: Instituto de Filosofía, Facultad de Filosofía y Letras, Universidad de Buenos Aires.
Kammen, M. (1991). *Mystic Chords of Memory the Transformation of Tradition in American Culture*. New York: Alfred A. Knopf.
Kasaba, R. (2009). The Immoveable State. In *A Moveable Empire: Ottoman Nomads, Migrants and Refugees* (pp. 123–140). Seattle/London: The University of Washington Press.
Khater, A. (2001). *Inventing Home: Emigration, Gender, and the Middle Class in Lebanon, 1870–1920*. Oakland: University of California Press.
Klitch, I. (1993). Criollos and Arabic Speakers in Argentina: An Uneasy Pas de Deux, 1888–1914. In A. Hourani & N. Shehadi (Eds.), *The Lebanese in the World* (pp. 243–284). London: Center for Lebanese Studies and I.B. Taurus.
Klitch, I., & Lesser, J. (1996). Introduction: "Turco" Immigrants in Latin America. *The Americas, 53*(1), 1–14.
Koutoudjian, A. (2015). Contexto geopolítico del genocidio armenio: estrategia de las naciones desde fines del siglo XIX hasta la Primera Guerra Mundial. *Todo Es Historia, 576*(July), 19–20.
Landsberg, A. (2004). *Prosthetic Memory: The Transformation of American Remembrance in the Age of Mass Culture*. New York: Columbia University Press.
Moore, A., & Mathewson, K. (2013). Latin America's Los Turcos: Geographic Aspects of Levantine and Maghreb Diasporas. *Nóesis. Revista de Ciencias Sociales y Humanidades, Instituto de Ciencias Sociales y Administración, 22*, 290–308.
Moya, J. (1998). *Cousins and Strangers: Spanish Immigrants in Buenos Aires, 1850–1930*. Berkeley: University of California Press.
Musil, R. (1957). *Gesammelte Werke*. Hamberg: Rowohlt.
Nochlin, L. (1983). The Imaginary Orient. *Art in America, IXXI*(5), 118–131.
Noufouri, H., et al. (1999). *Tinieblas del Crisol de Razas: Ensayos sobre las representaciones simbolicas y espaciales de la nocion del "otro"*. Buenos Aires: Editorial Calamo de Sumer.

Ochoa de Eguileor, J., & Valdés, E. (2000). *Donde durmieron nuestros abuelos: Los Hoteles de Inmigrantes de la Ciudad de Buenos Aires*. Buenos Aires: Centro Internacional para la Conservación del Patrimonio Argentino.
Payro, J. E. (1970). *Prilidiano Pueyrredón, Joseph Dubourdieu, la pirámide de mayo y la catedral de Buenos Aires*. Buenos Aires: Universidad de Buenos Aires.
Quataert, D. (1997). Clothing Laws, State and Society in the Ottoman Empire, 1720–1829. *International Journal of Middle East Studies, 29*(3), 403–425.
Raj, D. S. (2000). Ignorance, Forgetting, and Family Nostalgia: Partition, the Nation State, and Refugees in Delhi. *Social Analysis: The International Journal of Social and Cultural Practice, 44*(2), 30–55.
Rodriguez, J. (2006). *Civilizing Argentina: Science, Medicine and the Modern State*. Chapel Hill: University of North Carolina Press.
Rojas, R. (1971 [1909]). *La restauración nacionalista*. Buenos Aires: A Peña Lillo.
Rosen, C., & Zerner, H. (1988). *Romanticismo y realismo. Los mitos del arte del siglo XIX*. Madrid: Hermann Blume.
Ruggiero, K. (2004). *Modernity in the Flesh: Medicine, Law and Society in Turn-of-the-Century Argentina*. Stanford: Stanford University Press.
Savage, K. (2006). History, Memory, and Monuments: An Overview of the Scholarly Literature on Commemoration. *American Historians and the National Park Service*. www.nps.gov/parkhistory/resedu/savage.htm
Schávelzon, D. (2012). Arqueología del Hotel de Inmigrantes. *Todo es Historia, 545*, 66–77.
Scobie, J. (1974). *Buenos Aires: Plaza to Suburb, 1870–1910*. New York: Oxford University Press.
Spinetto, H. (2010). Los monumentos del centenario. *BARZON, 14*, 126–136.
Swiderski, G., & Farjat, J. L. (2000). *Los antiguos Hoteles de Inmigrantes*. Buenos Aires: Arte y Memoria Audiovisual.
Widrich, M. (2014). *Performative Monuments: The Rematerialisation of Pubic Art*. New York: Manchester University Press.
Wolf, C.O. (2017). Migrant Monuments, Monumental Migrants: São Paulo's Sculptural Homage to Syrian-Lebanese Friendship and the Crafting of Transnational Identity in Centennial Brazil. *TAREA, 4*(4), 120–152.
Young, J. E. (1993). *The Texture of Memory: Holocaust Memorials and Meaning*. New Haven: Yale University Press.

CHAPTER 3

'Columbus Might Be Dwarfed to Obscurity': Italian Americans' Engagement with Columbus Monuments in a Time of Decolonization

Laura E. Ruberto and Joseph Sciorra

On 24 September 2017, two weeks before Columbus Day, local Italian American elected officials and members of ethnic voluntary associations held a press conference in Massapequa on Long Island, New York, billed as 'Save Columbus'. The gathering was in response to almost daily calls that summer to remove public statues dedicated to fifteenth-century Genovese navigator and colonist Christopher Columbus, in cities like Detroit, New York City, St. Paul, and San Jose. The appeals were not new but voices in a decades-long debate reframing Columbus not as a heroic explorer of new lands but instead as a brutal colonizer of

L. E. Ruberto (✉)
Berkeley City College, Berkeley, CA, USA
e-mail: lruberto@peralta.edu

J. Sciorra
Queens College, City University of New York, New York, NY, USA
e-mail: joseph.sciorra@qc.cuny.edu

indigenous peoples. This particular scrutiny of Columbus statues and monuments came after outcries to remove Confederate-focused statuary in public spaces throughout the country for their celebration of white supremacist ideologies. Earlier that year New Orleans removed four Confederate monuments after an acrimonious national debate, followed by the killing of Heather Heyer during protests in Charlottesville, Virginia, around a white supremacist-led rally in defence of a monument to Confederate General Robert E. Lee. As the Columbian legacy has been increasingly contested within and beyond indigenous communities, Italian Americans have been challenged to contend with their historical affiliation with and championing of this figure. This chapter considers some of these challenges with respect specifically to the roles memory and ideology play with public monuments.

Those who gathered in Massapequa did so explicitly as Italian Americans with representatives of ethnic organizations in attendance, including the Columbus Citizens Foundation, the Italian American Action Committee, and the local lodge of the Order Sons of Italy in America. Speakers called on 'radical mayors' (Kilgannon 2017, A23) and 'misguided individuals who have no respect for history or heritage' (Thorne 2017) not to remove Columbus statues, signing a petition to that effect. For those municipalities opting to extract these statues, Supervisor Joseph Saladino offered a small park in which to house them. Speaking about New York City's Columbus monument at Columbus Circle, whose removal was also being debated at the time, Saladino categorically stated, 'Removing the Christopher Columbus statue is a slight against Italian-Americans' (Kilgannon 2017, A23).

The sentiments expressed on Long Island are similar to those made by other Italian American individuals and groups throughout the country. Representatives of local and national voluntary associations have vigorously opposed the removal of Columbus statues in the name of Italian American victimization, arguing that to critique Columbus and artefacts of his once unblemished legacy radically rewrites history and is a form of 'defamation' (Cerulli 2019, pp. 47–56). They created in 2017 the national Columbus Heritage Coalition to combat the ending of municipal, state, and national recognition of Columbus Day and the removal of Columbus statues.[1]

[1] See columbusheritagecoalition.com

These self-appointed ethnic leaders claim to speak not just for their membership, but also for a larger unspecified group of Italian Americans.[2]

Not all Italian Americans agree with these sentiments, and some have spoken out in both single and collective voices against the continued celebrations of Columbus. In 2017, largely in response to the national discussions around public commemorations of historical events, a group of scholars—including the authors of this chapter—created a 'No Columbus Day' campaign calling for 'the abolition (and/or replacement) of Columbus Day as a Federal Holiday' ('Abolition/Replacement of Columbus Day'). This campaign can be understood as part of a now-decades-old Italian American position countering Columbus, as we discuss later. We are nevertheless committed to a critical analysis, even as we are aware of the potential pitfalls in taking on a research project about which we have been actively involved in other fora.

Civic monuments are the products of specific historical moments that coalesce into the eventual design, building, and display of what is deemed of value by those with access to financial, political, and cultural resources. Such objects are never fully expressive of an all-encompassing ethos and thus are loci of tensions of competing collectives. Frictions and disagreements exist at the time of creation and have the potential to accumulate and multiply in a pluralistic society along varied lines of interpretation and affiliation (Levinson 1998, pp. 3–10). Such predicaments have occurred with Columbus monuments conceptualized, funded, fabricated, and gifted by Italian Americans to various municipalities throughout the twentieth century. Sociologist Timothy Kubal's writing on the U.S. obsession with the myth of Columbus and identity politics has done much to unpack the various stake-holders—Catholics, Native Americans, Latinos, Italian Americans, and others—who have framed the historical record 'in ways that highlight their place in American society' (2008, p. 2). This malleable and capacious mythic figure informs conflicting perspectives and retold narratives.

In this chapter we focus on two contemporary cases involving calls for removal of Columbus statues: the large monument in Manhattan's

---

[2] A full-page letter in the *New York Times* from Angelo Vivolo, president of the Columbus Citizen Foundation, stated 'As all nations do, we must continue to reevaluate our history as Americans, and whom we choose to honor …. we will state for the record that we will not allow that reflection to come at the expense of a monument that has come to represent the many achievements that Italian Americans have accomplished' (Vivolo 2017, A21).

Columbus Circle and the smaller statue in San Jose's City Hall. These two case studies—a large-scale monument and a smaller-scaled statue, situated on opposing coasts with different historical trajectories—offer a compelling comparison: each city has an Italian American mayor and Italian American voices present in the discussions, yet debates resulted in different outcomes. We hope underscoring these stories will also help shed light on the dynamic experiences and actions of Italian Americans, a white ethnic group often misguidedly defined in limiting terms.[3]

In contextualizing the two cases we review key moments in the history of Columbus commemoration in the United States and attempt to answer larger questions concerning Italian Americans' seeming embrace of Columbus and their sponsorship of monuments to him, especially in light of the recent evolution and contention of that sponsorship. We interpret the discourse supporting Italian American affiliations with Columbus especially with respect to material culture, memory, and history building. We consider how contemporary Italian Americans use memory and history as rhetorical strategies to defend or decry monuments of the past in light of mounting criticism against them in the present. In the end, the resolute stares of the respective statues belie the messy and unstable narratives of the (re)constructed past that are continually projected and challenged (Fig. 3.1).

CONSTRUCTING HISTORY AND THE 'REMEMORATION' OF COLUMBUS MONUMENTS

We understand many of the Columbus monuments in the United States as 'sites of memory' that function within a system of what Pierre Nora (1989, p. 16) referred to as *rememoration*, the act of resuscitating the past. For Nora such a site of memory could be any 'significant entity, whether material or non-material in nature, which by dint of human will or the work of time has become a symbolic element of the memorial heritage of any community' (1996, p. xvii). These symbolic, constructed memories are unique—different individuals and communities can have varying 'realms of memory'—but often they coalesce among shared ideological practices and experiences. The material world of monuments buttresses those

---

[3] See Caron's (2018) *New York Times* article depicting Italian Americans as a monolithic group categorically supporting Columbus and in opposition to Native Americans.

Fig. 3.1 Columbus Monument, Columbus Circle, New York City, November 2019. (Courtesy of Joseph Sciorra)

experiences, blending points of view and narratives into a singular collective site of memory.

Recognizing Italian Americans' rooted intimacy with Columbus monuments as sites of memory allows us to understand them historically as a strategy made by less-visible communities (Italian immigrants) to construct narratives that included them within what were otherwise dominant spaces where they were not readily represented. Historically then, as we will show, Italian immigrants' relationship to Columbus statues should be understood as a form of temporary and contextually specific counter-hegemony. However, positioning Columbus statues today as sites of memory of the subaltern histories of Italian immigrants reinterpreted by their descendants ignores other aspects of such memory work.

As views on Columbus have shifted, beginning in the late twentieth century, many Italian Americans have visibly reinforced an 'ardent, embattled, almost fetishistic "memorialism"' (Nora 2002, p. 1) of Columbus. Maurice Halbwachs (1980, pp. 128–131) convincingly argued that memory is a collective act in which individuals (operating as an active community) engage with their social environment and the 'spatial framework' as reference points of collective memories and ultimately of identities. The original intent of any monument is modified with each subsequent act of rememoration in the present. Martha Norkunas (1993, p. 6) explains, '[m]onuments and historical sites, meant to symbolize complex movements or historical events, could instead act to enshrine singular visions of the past', creating a more symbolic history for a community, when 'consciousness of a break with the past is bound up with the sense that memory has been torn' (Nora 1989, p. 7).

The current crisis of public monuments reminds us of Walter Benjamin's (1969, p. 256) discussions of memory and identity in his fragmented notes, 'On a Concept of History', that reflect on the notion that the 'cultural treasures' of the victors ('the spoils') are tied to long histories of conquest, exploitation, and violence. His words resonate with our dialogue around Columbus monuments:

> For without exception the cultural treasures he [the victor] surveys have an origin which he cannot contemplate without horror. They owe their existence not only to the efforts of the great minds and talents who have created them, but also to the anonymous toil of their contemporaries. There is no document of civilization which is not at the same time a document of barbarism. And just as such a document is not free of barbarism, barbarism taints also the manner in which it was transmitted from one owner to another. (1969, pp. 256–257)

Those who continue to favour Columbus as a positive symbol for Italian Americans rely on a view that sees history as an immutable set of experiences and exchanges. The contemporary pro-Columbus monument position includes a rhetorical strategy of evoking history to shore up the argument with logical, historically grounded sets of conclusions. Such lines of reasoning divorce themselves from the possibility of revisions of historical narratives. As Benjamin (1969, p. 255) explains, 'articulating the past historically does not mean recognizing it "the way it really was"', given that there is no single perspective on the past.

When we take into account the role of material culture in understanding the past and the present, it is imperative to consider the fluctuating ways objects are viewed over time: the changing prestige and value even as the object remains physically consistent. Nora similarly makes this kind of distinction but rather than placing it between two scholarly pursuits, as Benjamin does (between historicist and historical materialists), Nora places it within a dichotomy of memory versus history:

> Memory, insofar as it is affective and magical, only accommodates those facts that suit it; it nourishes recollections that may be out of focus or telescopic, global or detached, particular or symbolic-responsive to each avenue of conveyance or phenomenal screen, to every censorship or projection. History, because it is an intellectual and secular production, calls for analysis and criticism. (1989, pp. 8–9)

Thus we are also invested here in evaluating when and how contemporary pro-Columbus Italian Americans' continued evocation of once-counter-hegemonic sites of memory around Columbus make them complicit in dominant interpretations of the past vis-à-vis narratives of genocide as well as ongoing racism and discrimination of minority cultures. Nora's characterization of memory recognizes its emotional aspect, suggesting that emotion often pulls more strongly than the intellectual aspects.

Alongside our explicitly ideological reading of Columbus commemorations is the need to better understand Italian Americans' emotional experiences concerning Columbus. This affecting experience is perhaps most pronounced with the conflation of Columbus and immigrant ancestors, as witnessed in Joseph Tusiani's poem 'Columbus Day in New York' in which a paraded statue's eyes and hands are compared with those of the poet's grandfather (Tusiani 2000, pp. 8–9). The feelings and affiliations many Italian Americans have with Columbus play out on the ground in our case studies outlined below. The memories for both Italian

Americans and Native Americans can thus include aspects of trauma and sensory experiences gained over generations and should not be overlooked or devalued.[4]

CRAFTING COLUMBUS AS AN ITALIAN AMERICAN HERO

A popular truism claims that Italian immigrants discovered Columbus in the United States, an American mythic hero whose hagiographic narrative was first crafted in the country's earliest days (Kubal 2008, pp. 19–25; Schlereth 1992, pp. 937–945). The feminine figure Columbia, developed during the Revolutionary War as the personification of the emerging nation, would resurface in enumerable ways over the centuries (e.g. District of Columbia, Columbia University). The Columbian hero cult became a key patriotic mythos for developing a distinct non-European national character. Throughout the late eighteenth and early nineteenth centuries, Columbus was a useful symbol of the country's expansion westwards, which, grounded in the racial superiority and settler ideology of Manifest Destiny, resulted in genocidal acts of war, forced resettlement, and severe Christian conversion directed against indigenous peoples. Washington Irving's (1828) four-volume paean, riddled with inaccuracies and hyperbolic invention, further solidified Columbus as part of an American civic religion (Schlereth 1992, pp. 943–945).

In turn, statues, monuments, and other large-scale objects were crafted to glorify the positive attributes ascribed to the mythic Columbus. The first such documented monument was erected in 1792 on a private estate in Baltimore and subsequently donated to the city. Throughout the nineteenth century, the U.S. Capitol became a major site for government-sponsored depictions of Columbus—a painted frieze (1824), a marble statue (1844), bronze doors (1855–1960)—further wedding the national imaginary with the myth (ibid., pp. 946–955). The 1893 World's Columbian Fair in Chicago, a culturally and socially influential enterprise marking the quatercentenary of Columbus's landing, elevated the national hero worship to a massive scale.

Columbus was conjured to help assimilate waves of European immigrants, from the Irish onwards (Kubal 2008, p. 27). The Knights of Columbus, a Catholic voluntary association founded by Irish immigrants in 1882, was instrumental in championing Columbus as an icon for

---

[4] Klain's 2011 documentary film, *Columbus Day Legacy* explores the often conflicting positions of Native Americans and Italian Americans.

Catholic acceptance and integration (ibid., pp. 31–38). Italian immigrants arrived (1880s–1924) into this national fervour in the late nineteenth and early twentieth centuries; they saw in Columbus a way to deflect the onslaught of racial prejudice and violent xenophobia they encountered and for which they were relatively unprepared.

Italian immigrants, the vast majority coming from Southern Italy, were met with relentless anti-Italian bigotry on myriad fronts. They experienced discrimination at work, in housing, and in the Catholic Church; they were vilified and ridiculed in newspapers and on the silver screen; and were deemed unfit for citizenship. Borrowing from the pseudo-scientific theories of Italian criminologist theorist Cesare Lombroso, U.S. politicians, journalists, and other elites racialized Italians as inferior with social pathologies akin to African Americans and constructed a hierarchy of inequality that continues to reverberate (Connell and Gardaphé 2010).[5] Anti-Italian sentiment crystalized in 1891 when 11 Italian American men, mostly immigrants, were lynched in New Orleans.[6] President Benjamin Harrison issued a one-time proclamation for the first national Columbus Day in 1892, specifically in response to this act of xenophobic violence.

The symbolic linking of Italian Americans with Columbus was not a mass effort but rather the project of a small group of economic, political, and culturally elite immigrants. These *prominenti* ('prominent ones') situated themselves between the often-undereducated working poor and Italian government officials and U.S. elites but in reality 'concerned themselves almost totally with their own welfare, prestige, and public image' (Pozzetta 1971, p. 233). The rememoration of some contemporary Italian Americans often focuses on their working-class immigrant ancestors donating pennies to various Columbus projects, disregarding the reality that the few *prominenti*, self-proclaimed ethnic leaders, not the majority of working poor Italian immigrants, were driving the Columbus enterprise. Referring to New York City, Bénédicte Deschamps's (2015, p. 7) observations are equally applicable to other parts of the country in this early period, 'Memorial building was thus anything but consensual, even within the ethnic community'.[7]

---

[5] A vast literature examining Italian immigrants and race exists: see Guglielmo (2003), Guglielmo and Salerno (2003), Richards (1999), and Vellon (2014).

[6] On 12 April 2019, New Orleans Mayor LaToya Cantrell formally apologized for the lynching (Williams 2019).

[7] Italian immigrant anarchists in the newspaper *Il Grido degli Oppressi* adamantly condemned Columbus, characterizing him in 1892 as a 'pirate and adventurer ... indifferent to

Two *prominenti* stand out regarding the early Columbus–Italian American union: Carlo Barsotti and Angelo Noce. Born in 1850 in the northern city of Lucca, Barsotti immigrated to New York City in 1872 and became the founder of the influential Italian-language daily *Il Progresso Italo-Americano*. From that position, he devised a series of monument-building campaigns that solicited funds from the Italian immigrant readership and beyond. In addition to the monument at Columbus Circle (discussed below), Barsotti also spearheaded the creation of statues to Giuseppe Garibaldi (1888), Giuseppe Verdi (1906), Giovanni da Verrazzano (1909), and Dante Alighieri (1921)—in harmony with the era's ideal of the 'City Beautiful Movement'.

Noce, also a newspaper owner, was born near Genoa in Coreglia in 1847. At age three, he immigrated, first to New York City, then California, Nevada, and finally Colorado. He was central in San Francisco's first celebrations around Columbus (in 1869). The event, 'Discovery Day', featured a special mass, a banquet, and a parade with a float carrying a replica of the *Santa Maria* and 'a statue of Columbus, which was borne through the streets of the city like the figures of saints venerated in Italy during religious *festa* [sic]' (McKevitt 1992–93, p. 518). In Denver, Noce used his newspaper *La Stella* to advocate successfully for Colorado's recognition of Columbus Day as a state holiday in 1907, the first in the country.[8]

Barsotti, Noce, and other *prominenti* had definitive ideas about how and why Columbus holidays and monuments were warranted. They publicly combatted—especially as newspaper owners—the popular perception of Italian immigrants as undereducated, violent, criminally inclined, and generally unfit for U.S. citizenship (Vellon 2014, p. 2). Highlighting Columbus as an Italian progenitor of the United States was an attempt to associate with and transfer the positive attributes of this mythologized figure onto the Italian population (Battisti 2019, p. 131). But first the *prominenti* had to forge a national 'Italian' identity for Italian immigrants of different backgrounds; when the masses emigrated, Italy had only just become a nation-state and a unified Italian identity was barely in existence. Regional differences contributed to the lack of national identity. If Italian

---

massacre' and one who 'set the stage for "racial prejudices and hatreds" in America and "the martyrdom of the negroes in the South"' (Zimmer 2015, p. 74).

[8] Noce also used print media to construct his own heroism with respect to Columbus by disseminating his work in supporting Columbus, sometimes in opposition to those communities who Columbus was supposed to symbolize. Noce claimed in a self-published account that Italian immigrant labourers striking in Nevada in 1879 had distracted his efforts of confirming Columbus Day as a state holiday (Noce 1910, p. 24).

immigrants discovered Columbus in the United States, so too did many become 'Italian' in the diaspora. Thus Columbus became a key symbol for an emergent national *Italian* identity that was simultaneously linked to the confirmation of Italian Americans as whites (ibid., p. 132; Vellon 2014, p. 9).

The *prominenti*'s notion of what constituted 'Italy' and 'Italian' was, for the most part, an Italian bourgeois nationalism consisting of hegemonic narratives of *una civiltà italiana* (Gabaccia 2000, pp. 8–9), the cosmopolitan, primarily northern Italian, elite cultural–political formulation that relied on such notions as ancient Rome, the Renaissance, and institutionalized Tuscan-centric standard of the Italian language. This vision of Italy eschewed Southern Italy's history, cultures, and peoples as elements inappropriate for nation building in the diaspora. Southern Italians' racialized otherness in the United States needed to be surmounted and reconfigured if the *prominenti* were to instil their vision successfully. As Peter Vellon notes (2014, p. 3), ethnic leaders promoted a particular brand of assimilation and 'argued for full inclusion as Americans based upon an imagined "Italian" heritage of civilization and whiteness' where Italians constituted a critical and even foundational component in white European civilization.

The *prominenti's* melding of their notion of Italian national identity with the American figure of Columbus also sought to reconfigure the dominant perception of Italian immigrants by associating them with characteristics connoting formality, sophistication, and noblesse (Battisti 2019, pp. 130–132). Such characteristics also undermined and attempted to tame the vernacular knowledge, social formations, and culture of the working-class immigrant masses. By perpetuating ideas of a united Italian community based on racial hierarchies and a grand history of an invented, singular Italian civilization, ethnic leaders further disparaged already denigrated people's vernacular cultural expressions that became increasingly associated with ignorance and vulgarity—for example, Catholic street feasts characterized as pagan practices, Italian regional languages subsequently dubbed 'bad Italian' (Sciorra 2011, pp. 4–5). As Deschamps (2001, p. 13) observes, '[i]t was as if the entire community was to impersonate Christopher Columbus by appropriating his admitted virtues', attributes that opposed those ascribed to the working poor.

These tensions surrounding a conflicted and racialized group identity informed the ways Italian Americans negotiated their relationship to Columbus monuments and commemorations. Throughout the twentieth century, Italian Americans increasingly embraced the Americanized Columbian mythos, reinforced by actions the federal government took to stabilize the association between the two. They commissioned and built myriad statues, from Walla Walla, Washington in 1911, to Reading, Pennsylvania, in 1925, to Akron, Ohio, in 1938.[9] Even as Italian Americans were making headway in government and commerce, demonstrating some of the ways they experienced life in the United States with the privilege of whiteness, anti-foreign, anti-Catholic, and anti-Italian sentiments remained strong and apparent. The reconstituted Ku Klux Klan (KKK) of the 1920s repeatedly targeted Columbus Day and Columbus representations as a way to create fear and control political power. In communities like Easton, Ohio, and Richmond, Virginia, the KKK campaigned to prevent the erection of Columbus statues in opposition to Catholics and 'foreigners' (Kollatz 2014; Scheihing 2014). Despite these bigoted acts, Generoso Pope, Barsotti's successor at *Il Progresso Italo-Americano*, wielded his considerable political clout to lobby President Franklin Delano Roosevelt to proclaim an annual Columbus Day in 1934 (an effort also undertaken by the Knights of Columbus).

Italian American-driven memorial construction and holiday celebrations increased after World War II, coinciding with a new wave of Italian (mainly working-class) immigration and the post–civil rights era white ethnic revival. By 1968, lobbying efforts by politicians and businesspeople, many of them Italian American, succeeded in making Columbus Day a federal holiday (going into effect in 1971).[10] This holiday—which, significantly, has never been officially designated a day for Italian Americans—came about when national discourse around normative whiteness shifted from 'Plymouth Rock whiteness to Ellis Island whiteness' (Jacobson 2006, p. 7). Columbus Day coalesced at the moment ethnic Europeans became most invested in whiteness, in the face of civil rights movements of African Americans and other minority communities, including Native Americans. In the highly visible white ethnic revival eras of the 1970s and 1980s, the meaning of Columbus monuments and celebrations became unambiguously associated with the Americanization of European immigrants' descendants and their embrace of that privileged status together with a highly Americanized sense of Italian ethnicity. The rhetoric shifted from

---

[9] See van der Krogt for a listing of Columbus statues globally.
[10] Technically, a federal holiday is a paid day off for federal employees; Congress lacks authority to oblige individual states or local municipalities to celebrate a federal holiday.

Columbus-as-struggling immigrant towards reinforcing symbols associating him with American patriotism and a hyphenated white ethnic pride.[11]

Decolonizing Columbus

Public protest in the name of indigenous people's rights developed from the 1970s Red Power movement and surfaced just before the 1992 quincentenary of Columbus's voyage (a period when Italian Americans gifted ever more Columbus statues).[12] The American Indian Movement (AIM) attempted to create a counter-memory that deconstructed Columbus's symbolic power and therefore the acquired power of Italian Americans. Denver has been a critical place of confrontation between Italian American celebrants of Columbus Day and Native American activists. Actions by AIM protesters have been aggressive and provocative, including pouring fake blood on Denver's Columbus monument and throwing baby doll pieces along the parade route (Kubal 2008, pp. 122–123). These and other decolonizing efforts by AIM are political acts of resistance and even self-defence against genocide even as institutions label them vandalism and aggression. Italian American supporters of Columbus in Denver also have responded forcefully, according to Sam Hitchmough (2013, p. 265), becoming

> extraordinarily aggressive (and paradoxically defensive)... about the right to celebrate Columbus Day because of the historic nature of the holiday in the state and because of the way in which this symbolism and pride associates with a deep reservoir of values that Columbus is still seen to represent at the level of national narrative.

Emotions are powerful influences on all sides.

As an anti-colonial perspective has developed beyond indigenous activism (see Kubal 2008, pp. 135–165), Columbus's anti-indigenous history has become rhetorically linked with modern acts of enslavement and white supremacy, thus placing Columbus effectively in collusion with Confederate

---

[11] Harney suggests that an 'ethnic inferiority complex' is at play for those Italian North Americans looking to find Italian heroes associated with settler histories and which 'led to aggressive, ethnocentric assertions and to recitals of the group's past glories that in fact flirted with racism' (1993, p. 11).

[12] See van der Krogt's (undated) 'Columbus Monuments Pages' for information of statues donated by Italian Americans.

figures. At the same time, the anti-Columbus movement has ignited Italian American pro-Columbus efforts, especially as cities across the country debate and eliminate Columbus commemorations.[13] Confusingly, when the KKK attacked Columbus statues and celebrations during the 1920s, they were protesting both an image that would later become associated with white supremacy and also protesting Columbus because he had become associated with foreigners, Catholic Italians specifically. The National Christopher Columbus Association ('Attacks by KKK') and other pro-Columbus organizations highlight this part of the history to suggest that contemporary protests are counter to progressive politics precisely because they echo the KKK's earlier agenda. The complex contradictions in protest and action are rarely articulated from any side of the Columbus polemic.

Just before and after the 1992 quincentenary, Italian American voices were active in supporting indigenous struggles towards decolonization and attempting to remove Columbus from his heroic pedestal, often within a reclaimed legacy of radicalism and leftist ideals. These acts of rememoration do not associate these characteristics with Columbus but rather against his memory and in an effort to construct (or revitalize) historically rich narratives of Italian Americans in solidarity with marginalized groups. Such counter-Columbus activist work generally comes from an ideological position that sees Columbus celebrations as a way Italian Americans are part of a larger narrative of conquest that 'affirms the underpinning history of colonization' (Hitchmough 2013, p. 269), which in turn continues in 'defining and regenerating racial whiteness and a racially inflected vision of Americanization' (Huhndorf quoted in Hitchmough 2013, p. 269).

The New York City-based Italian Americans for a Multicultural United States (IAMUS) was founded in 1992 expressly to counter Columbus celebrations and to 'disassociate' Italian Americans from the Columbus 'myth' (Italian Americans for a Multicultural United States 1992). San Francisco's Italian American Political Solidarity Club—which grew out of a 'Dump Columbus' event organized first by gay and lesbian artists and activists on Columbus Day 1999—sponsored an annual 'Dump Columbus,

---

[13] A watershed marker of this national, ideological shift came when Berkeley became the first city to celebrate officially Indigenous Peoples Day instead of Columbus Day. Italian Americans voiced concern that removing Columbus Day was a slight to Italian Americans, a position that 'Berkeley leaders' denied (see Arnold 1992).

Embrace Humanity' event beginning in 2002 and published *Avanti Popolo: Italian-American Writers Sail Beyond Columbus* (Italian-American Political Solidarity Club 2008).[14]

Meanwhile, the Denver-based Progressive Italians Transforming the Columbus Holiday (PITCH), working with mainly indigenous groups, founded Transform Columbus Day in 2004. It publicly stated that it 'condemn[s] the celebration of Columbus as an Italian cultural icon' and recognizes the 'important[ance] that people of Italian descent are not portrayed as perpetuating racism and oppression' (Progressive Italians to Transform the Columbus Holiday; see also Calhoun 2016). As mentioned above, the national No Columbus Day group started an online petition and wrote (unanswered) letters to the Italian American Congressional Delegation urging them to abolish Columbus Day as part of 'new practices of memory inspired by the values of humanism and cultural dialogue we recognize as part of an Italian identity' ('Abolition/Replacement of Columbus Day as Federal Holiday'). In addition to these initiatives, prominent Italian American poets have offered counter-narratives, including Diane di Prima (Italian-American Political Solidarity Club 2008, pp. 13–16) and Robert Viscusi (1993).

COLUMBUS CIRCLE, NEW YORK CITY

Italian immigrants struck perhaps their most triumphal claim to the American myth in the middle of Manhattan. In 1892, to mark the 400th anniversary of Columbus's landing in the Caribbean, New York City erected a 76-foot monument to the navigator/colonist, a gift from 'the Italian residents in America' as inscribed on its pedestal. The marble figure—gazing straight ahead with his right hand on a prow handle—is perched on a granite rostral column, a curious element for a civic monument because of its references to Roman architecture commemorating naval victories. This Columbus is not the benevolent discoverer but the 'peerless conqueror of new lands' (Bradley 1990, p. 91), a vision that would garner resonance decades later as critiques of Columbus increased. Chiselled into the granite base is a message in Italian crediting the project to Carlo Barsotti, identifying him as newspaper owner and editor and employing the Italian government honorific *cavaliere*. These visual and material elements of the monument as well as others not discussed herein

---

[14] See Fachin (2012, pp. 135–139) on the group.

help convey to the late nineteenth century viewer the imagined greatness of American and Italian nationalism.

In 2017 the city's Columbus monument's appropriateness was called into question with renewed vigour. On 16 August, Mayor Bill de Blasio proclaimed on Twitter: 'After the violent events in Charlottesville, New York City will conduct a 90-day review of all symbols of hate on city property' (de Blasio, 16 August 2017). That same day New York Governor Andrew Cuomo ordered busts of Lee and another Confederate general Thomas 'Stonewall' Jackson removed from a City University of New York campus in the Bronx (Heins 2017a; Sager 2017). Calls to remove other monuments followed. On 21 August, City Council Speaker Melissa Mark-Viverito noted

> ongoing dialogue and debate in the Caribbean—particularly in Puerto Rico where I'm from—about this same conversation that there should be no monument or statue of Christopher Columbus based on what he signifies to the native population… [the] oppression and everything that he brought with him. (cited in Heins 2017b)

Puerto Rican-born Mark-Viverito, whose maternal grandfather was Italian American, asked that Columbus Circle be reviewed by the proposed Mayoral Advisory Commission on City Art, Monuments, and Markers.

Italian American politicians and representatives of volunteer associations reacted swiftly, objecting to the suggestion. On two days that week, 22 August at Columbus Circle and 24 August at City Hall, city and state elected officials, celebrities, and representatives of the National Italian American Foundation, National Council of Columbia Associations, Federation of Italian-American Organizations, and Sons of Italy in America, among others, held a press conference. Their responses reveal the ways history and public memory are selectively used and discursive strategies enacted to establish and facilitate a counter-narrative to combat the increasing and renewed attacks on Columbus commemorations.

Individuals made public pronouncements reiterating Columbus's symbolic links to contemporary Italian Americans, not only in New York but nationwide:

> The one iconic symbol for Italian-Americans was Christopher Columbus. (Comedian Joe Piscopo)

Italians are everywhere in this state. That statue in Columbus Circle does not represent the explorer, it represents the experience of the Italian immigrant population. (New York State Senator Diane Savino)

27 million Italian Americans-strong, to this day, we still hold him in a place of honour. We will continue to do so and we will continue to fight to make sure that Columbus Circle remains Columbus Circle. (New York State Assemblyperson Ron Castorina) ('Italian Americans Rally' 2017)

These brief statements evaded the messy history of the monument's origins and the ways Italian Americans had become concatenated with Columbus. Barsotti, the problematic figure, was never mentioned (Vivolo 2017). His profiting off working-class Italian immigrants as a *padrone* (labour contractor), as a landlord of low-income and 'suspicious' problematic apartments, and as a bankrupt banker that made him the richest Italian in the city is erased from the narrative (Deschamps 2015, p. 7; Luconi 2016, p. 39; Pozzetta 1971, p. 240; Vellon 2014, p. 15).[15] Missing from contemporary defences of the monument is the fact that Barsotti's self-aggrandizing drive to construct it (and other monuments in the city) was denounced by his immigrant cohorts as another form of exploitation and profiteering (Deschamps 2015, p. 7; 'Denounced' 1892, p. 3).[16] Critics said his 'mal della pietra' (illness of stone) not only made him rich but channelled Italian American donor contributions away from hospitals, schools, and libraries serving poor Italian immigrants (Deschamps 2015, p. 7; Luconi 2016, p. 48).

The historical amnesia concerning the Columbus Circle monument is particularly pronounced given its association with 1930s Fascism. Barsotti's successor Generoso Pope was an ardent defender of Benito Mussolini's Fascist regime who used his newspaper and the symbol of Columbus to foist his political agenda on his Italian American readers.[17] From 1935 to 1937 on Columbus Day, Pope, along with the representatives of the Sons of Italy, Italian and New York politicians, and thousands of ardent Fascist supporters, laid a wreath at the monument. These celebrations—well documented in the *New York Times*—mimicked Italian Fascist rallies, with

---

[15] Barsotti publicly opposed labour unions and workers aid.
[16] Barsotti 'was charged with pocketing part of the nearly $7,600' for the Verdi statue that cost approximately $8600 in 1906 (Luconi 2016, p. 48).
[17] Pope would go on to co-found the Columbus Citizen's Foundation which today organizes New York City's annual Columbus Day parade.

attendees wearing Fascist military uniforms and giving the Fascist salute. During those years the Italian Anti-Fascist Committee, led by socialist editor Girolamo Valenti, organized an alternative assembly of equal numbers (a coalition of leftist political parties and labour unions) across the street beyond the monument's police-cordoned area to protest the visibly pro-Fascist event (Pozzetta and Mormino 1998, pp. 6–7). This Fascist association, along with communists' and socialists' claims to Columbus—liberal Mayor Fiorello LaGuardia suggested Columbus was a 'radical' ('Thousands Gather' 1937, p. 3)—are inconvenient historical facts that do not jibe with contemporary Italian American rememoration.[18]

Charges of 'revisionist history' (and 'political correctness') levelled in 2017 at those seeking to discredit Columbus and to discontinue holidays and remove monuments were selective or ignorant of historical documentation (Castorina 2017; Chen 2017). Yet the early *prominenti*'s agenda in championing Columbus for Italian Americans was 'intended to rewrite history' (Deschamps 2015, p. 5) by suggesting that Italians via Columbus had been in 'America' (although not specifically the United States) well before the *Mayflower* arrived (Luconi 2012, pp. 64–65). This 'revisionist history' (Battisti 2019, p. 229) continued after World War II, when Italian Americans once again positioned Columbus as 'America's first immigrant' (ibid.) in their attempt to reform immigration laws. As Italian American Studies historians have written, the reinterpretation of Columbus and immigration has been at the core of the Italian Americans' project to position Italians as part of the U.S. origin myth, another fact conveniently forgotten by champions of Columbus Circle.

Speakers in 2017, many Republican politicians, asserted Italian Americans' support for the monument, invoking notions of 'community', that amorphous conglomeration of anonymous individuals that 'confers upon it a hoped-for alliance of interests, solidity, tradition' (di Leonardo 1984, p. 134) without any basis for collective action. They implied they had sufficient political clout to rally the Italian American 'community' through their various organizations in support of Columbus Circle in the upcoming mayoral election in which the self-proclaimed 'progressive'

---

[18] Throughout World War II, the federal government also used Columbus Day to influence Italian Americans (Pozzetta and Mormino 1998, pp. 8–11). On Columbus Day in 1942, Attorney General Francis Biddle announced that the government was lifting restrictions for Italian 'enemy aliens', the approximately 600,000 Italian nationals living in the country at the time.

Democrat de Blasio was running for a second term. Joseph Guagliardo, chairman of the Conference of Presidents of Major Italian American Organizations, stated: 'I represent over 60 organizations, over a million members, and I can promise you this, at the parade this year we will remember who our friends are, and I promise you on Election Day we will remember who is attacking Italian Americans' ('Italian Americans Rally' 2017). De Blasio addressed the Columbus monument issues during the Democratic mayoral debate:

> I'm Italian-American, and Italian-Americans have been taught to be proud of Columbus. There are things not to be proud of as well. That's going to be a part of the process, to make sense of how to handle things of a whole host of figures from our history ('Rally to keep').[19]

The intertwining of ethnic identity with politicking escalated with the approaching Columbus Day parade: a century-old Columbus statue in Central Park was vandalized; Columbus Circle saw 24/7 police protection; some Italian American representatives boycotted the mayor's annual Italian American Heritage party, and on parade day viewers lining the parade route apparently booed de Blasio for his unenthusiastic stance.

The mayor's advisory commission met for the first time the next day, holding six public hearings over three months where citizens could speak.[20] Self-defined Italian Americans from a variety of backgrounds, for and against the Columbus statue, attended these events and submitted documents to the commission. Representatives of established organizations like the Columbus Citizens Foundation, Confederation of Columbian Lawyers Association, the Christopher Columbus Preservation Coalition, and the Italian American Museum wrote letters reiterating their support of Columbus commemoration in the name of 'our ancestors' (Mayoral Advisory Commission 2018a). Several also supported the creation of Indigenous People's Day but not at the expense of Columbus Day. Other unaffiliated Italian Americans spoke

---

[19] The other Democratic mayoral candidate, Sal Albanese, an Italian immigrant, defended the maintenance of the monument ('De Blasio, Albanese' 2017). The Republican candidate, Nicole Malliotakis, questioned de Blasio's ethnicity given his non-committal stance on the monument (see Gonen 2017).

[20] The commission was made up of 18 scholars, architects, museum professionals, and visual artists. At the Manhattan meeting, Sciorra read a portion from our blog (Ruberto and Sciorra 2017b).

against Columbus, calling for the removal of the monument. Michael Madormo succinctly sums up this sentiment:

> I am a proud Italian-American who believes we need to take down the Columbus Statue and all monuments to colonization and white supremacy.
> My grandparents were poor farmers in Abruzzo in central Italy where they suffered the devastation of war. They immigrated to the United States after World War II, like so many others before and since, in search of a better life. I was raised to have pride in the tremendous sacrifices my grandparents made in my Italian-American identity.
> Rather than a celebration of my family's history and culture, the statues and day to commemorate Columbus are a symbol of this country's legacy of oppression, and the ways in which Italian-Americans have been complicit. (Mayoral Advisory Commission 2018a)

During the course of the commission's work, over 100 prominent scholars signed a public letter calling for the removal of the Columbus monument, calling it the 'most controversial' of the four sites in question (Sutton 2017). Italian American Studies scholars were largely absent from this list, more because of the letter-writers' omission rather than these scholars' position.[21] In its final report in January, the commission characterized the public comments around Columbus as 'impassioned, highly polarized arguments' (Mayoral Advisory Commission 2018b), and in the end the commission's majority concluded that the Columbus Circle monument should remain. It also called for ongoing public conversation about the statue and Columbus's legacy, suggesting the creation of new temporary art and permanent monuments 'that more fully tell our history, rooted in a nuanced recognition of the pride, trauma, marginalization, and dispossession the monument represents' (ibid.).

That would have been the final word on the subject until 8 October 2018, when Cuomo, who had strenuously advocated for the monument's preservation in August 2017, announced that the monument had been listed on the New York State Register of Historic Places (subsequently listed on the federal register), a designation that does not protect the

---

[21] Italian American Studies scholars fall across the spectrum of opinions when it comes to Columbus: some hold an anti-Columbus position (see our discussion on No Columbus Day), others have sometimes responded defensively to attacks on Columbus (ostensibly defending the established Columbus paradigm). See *The Italian American Review* (1.2, 1992) and the symposium proceedings *Columbus: Meetings of Cultures* (Mignone 1993).

monument as a city landmark ('Governor Cuomo Announces' 2018). In just over a year, the Columbus Citizens Foundation exercised its political capital and mobilized its financial resources to hire the prestigious New York Landmarks Conservancy to research and write the successful 39-page nomination ('Conservancy Helps' 2018).

The Columbus Circle example—given its age, its magnitude, the significance of the major trafficked area, the prominence of Manhattan within the national and global cultural landscape, and the large Italian American population in that metropolitan area—to a great extent shapes much of what has happened in the United States with Columbus memorialization in the twentieth century. The 2017 debate was not, for the public, informed by just the internal discussions that occurred (the fact-finding and committee work set up by de Blasio). Instead, the statue's status as a highly visible counter-hegemonic 'site of memory' for Italian Americans was a powerful reminder of memory work even as the monument has taken on different collective significations for other groups.

CITY HALL, SAN JOSE

In contrast to the Columbus Circle case, we are interested in understanding other, less visible stories of Columbus statues, and thus offer here a deep study of a smaller instance—that of San Jose, California, and a Columbus statue that was similarly debated but ultimately removed. On 30 January 2018, the San Jose's City Council, led by Mayor Samuel Liccardo, voted to remove from City Hall a Columbus statue that had been gifted to the city by Italian Americans 60 years earlier. Its elimination came after a heated 17-year span of protests and vandalism against the statue, which invigorated Italian Americans' mobilization in support of its presence.[22]

This case presents us with an example of another multi-ethnic city attempting to balance memory, emotion, and power for several communities while ultimately illuminating the role of government institutions, according to Liccardo (2019), as 'arbiters for the values of the community'. Given the statue's removal, the case also demonstrates a long-term effect of the decades of protest across the United States. San Jose's still-evolving narrative was shaped by tensions, arguments, and unsettled disputes, and although never receiving the national attention of the New York

---

[22] In addition to the cited sources, this history of San Jose's Columbus statue is also based on uncited sources listed in the bibliography's 'Archival Material'.

Fig. 3.2 Columbus Statue, San Jose City Hall, February 2018. (Courtesy of Laura E. Ruberto)

City case, illustrates the relevance of this complex history on smaller U.S. communities (Fig. 3.2).

San Jose's Columbus statue was commissioned, carved, and gifted to the city in the 1950s, an era with a steady installation of Columbus statues and markers across the country (Kubal 2008, p. 194). After World War II, Italian Americans played out class- and race-based tensions locally, again using Columbus as a way to shape group identity across accepted notions of American ideals. Italian Americans' relationship to dominant white culture remained largely provisional because as a group they retained their ethnic difference, they carried Fascism's historical baggage, they remained associated with violent organized crime, and their ranks were being filled with new needy, post–World War II immigrants from Italy (Battisti 2019, pp. 84–110; Ruberto and Sciorra 2017b, pp. 10–11). In this period, Columbus once again exemplified Italian Americans' rootedness within the United States and their articulated patriotism, showing that they belonged in the most profound way, and reaffirming their association with the epic American symbol (Battisti 2019, pp. 228–232).

By 1958, when the statue was installed, Italian Americans held political prominence in San Jose (Louis Solari was the mayor, the first Italian American to hold that office) and had made headway in the area's thriving fruit industry (Matthews 2003) even as they remained mostly part of the working and skilled labour class. As Kenneth Borelli, former president of San Jose's voluntary association, the Italian American Heritage Foundation (IAHF), has remarked, 'being Italian American did not have the appeal it has today….in attempts to promote a better image for Italian Americans the two statues were given to the city' (Borelli 2019).[23] Liccardo (2019) described this position as well:

> There's this generation of Italians who have a very distinct memory of being disregarded, maltreated, discriminated against or at least have that memory shared with them by their parents … and to them this is a symbol of the possibilities that America has offered to Italian immigrants here.

These memories are tightly connected to what Columbus symbolizes today for many San Jose Italians.

The story of how the statue came to be also includes a to-date unexplored association with Fascism. In 1957, the Columbus Monument Committee commissioned and paid for a small bronze statue of Columbus for the recently completed city hall. The statue was a smaller 3-foot replica of the 12-foot bronze statue installed outside San Francisco's Coit Tower the previous year, and their common artist was Vittorio di Colbertaldo. He had been a member of Mussolini's bodyguard and an 'artist-soldier'

---

[23] Borelli is referencing a bust of inventor Guglielmo Marconi Italian American organizations gifted in 1939.

whose work was shown in the 1942 *Prima Mostra di Artisti Italiani in Armi* (First Exhibit of Italian Artists in Arms) in Rome, Berlin, and other Fascist cities in Europe (Stone 2010). Only days before the planned 30 March 1958 unveiling, the dedication was 'postponed indefinitely', because once the statue arrived from Italy, the Columbus Monument Committee deemed it too small for the space in the newly built City Hall ('San Jose, City Hall, Columbus Statue' 27 March 1958).[24] As the *San Jose Mercury News* (ibid.) reporter described: 'Eyeing the vast expanse of wall in front of which the bronze statue was to stand, the group expressed fear that a three-foot Columbus might be dwarfed to obscurity'. This concern illustrates the interest the Italian American community had in confirming their public status. Soon after, the committee commissioned a new, larger marble statue by a different artist. However, reading the line today, the reference to the statue's diminished status poignantly reminds us of the relevance of size, proportion, and material culture in establishing a presence with public art and the monumentalizing of public heroes.

The last-minute change resulted in a statue that only slightly elevated Columbus, coming in at six feet high (with an added three-foot high engraved pedestal) and made of numerous multi-hued pieces of marble, and valued in 1958 at $3500 ('San Jose, City Hall, Columbus Statue', 10 October 1958). The Columbus monument committee arranged for Italian artist Delfo Guidi to design the statue with the assistance of the Milani Marble Company of San Jose ('San Jose, City Hall, Columbus Statue' 23 March 1958 and 13 October 1958). The new statue, with its modest design and vacuous visage, was dedicated in front of a crowd of about 300, including the Consul General of Italy, on 12 October 1958 ('San Jose, City Hall, Columbus Statue' 13 October 1958). Italian Americans' precarious position, barely a decade after a war that had pitted Italy against the United States, comes through clearly in the statue's inscription, noting it was a gift from 'Italo-American societies of San Jose as a gesture of goodwill between the two countries'.

The statue remained mostly unnoticed until 2001 when Native American activist James Cosner broke its legs and right hand with a

---

[24] The Columbus Monument Committee included: 'the Sons of Italy lodges, the Italian Catholic Federation, the Civic Club, the Italian Benevolent Society, the Tricarico Club, La Camerata, the Trabia Social Club, the Italo-American Citizens Club, the Piemonte Club, the Favalesi Club and numerous private citizens and industrial concerns' ('San Jose, City Hall, Columbus Statue' 23 March 1958).

sledgehammer ('San Jose, City Hall, Columbus Statue', 9 March 2001). The district attorney filed hate-crime charges against Cosner, and Mayor Ron Gonzales supported the statue's restoration, receiving public encouragement from local Italian Americans and criticism from Native American leaders (United Native America 2001). Reactions to the vandalism reveal how Columbus had become emotionally tied to Italian American identity: '"When I saw it", said Tony Della Monica, a member of UNICO National, an Italian-American service organization, "my eyes teared up. It's just not fair. It's just not right... Why blame Columbus?"' ('San Jose, City Hall, Columbus Statue', 10 March 2001). Eventually the statue was repaired and Cosner was held liable for the $66,000 cost.

In 2005, the restored statue was moved to the new City Hall when that building was opened, and set in an equally prominent but less majestic spot, 'in the alcove on the first floor lobby of the City Hall Tower between the public elevators and the Information Desk' (San Jose City Clerk Files, September 2017). But contention around the statue continued. In August 2017, the San Jose Brown Berets, a Chicano activist group, started a 'Relocate Christopher Columbus Statue from San Jose City Hall' petition online. A series of public actions followed. On 21 September 2017, a woman smeared paint on it and a month later a group entered the building to protest the statue (San Jose City Clerk Files, November 2017). As in the New York City case, action came quickly: A series of public events and closed-door conversations with the mayor followed. The city organized a public forum, held at nearby San Jose State University, about the statue and its meaning. Art history and Mexican American Studies professors spoke, but no speakers represented an Italian American Studies or Italian American community perspective let alone that of local Italian Americans—suggesting the event was disingenuous at best in its attempt at fair dialogue. In this same brief period, IAHF gathered over 1800 signatures in support of keeping the statue in a prominent public space, and Liccardo met with IAHF leaders and others to discuss possible outcomes.

Meanwhile Liccardo, of Italian American and Mexican American background—whose grandfather was a member of the Civic Club, the Italian American organization that led the original gift—spoke publicly against the statue and Columbus, even as he repeatedly spoke in support of the Italian American community. Italian Americans, led to a large degree by the Little Italy San Jose association and the IAHF, responded by asserting the statue's relevance as an Italian American site of memory (e.g. launching the counter-petition, speaking to the press, meeting with the mayor and other government representatives). A city council meeting on 30 January 2018, with the statue on the agenda, included dozens of speakers (pro and con): Italian Americans were overwhelmingly united in support of the statue's presence in the city (only one self-defined Italian American spoke against it), as well as in their compromise of simply moving the statue to another public location. Yet many were also cognizant of the changing values around Columbus. Joshua DeVincenzi Melander, San Jose Little Italy's executive director, said: 'I'm not here to defend Columbus. I'm not going to pretend to be ignorant to some of the questionable acts that may have happened in history' (City Council minutes). Nevertheless, the council voted to remove the statue from public space and return it to Italian American community leaders, citing the high cost of security; the symbol's contentious status in a diverse city; the lack of evidence of its cultural significance[25]; and the rather confusing idea that the statue, a gift to the city meant for permanent display, 'does not fall under the City's art and cultural material collection or under the Exhibits Policy' (San Jose City Clerk Files, September 2017).

As Liccardo understood, the issue around San Jose's Columbus statue is to a great extent 'not about history but about identity [...] because if this were a sober objective historical discussion, Columbus would be one of many complex historical figures but probably not one we'd want to put on a pedestal in a very diverse multi-ethnic city like San Jose' (Liccardo 2019). At the time of this writing the statue is in storage, slated for display in the city's future Little Italy Museum, where 'all historical accounts related to Columbus' will be housed (Little Italy San Jose Newsletter 2018). The city earmarked funds to support ways of 'honouring positive contributions of Italian American figures and contributions that have been made locally' (ibid.). Liccardo committed a line item in the city's budget to a future Italian American Museum and clarified that Italian Americans' ties to the symbol of Columbus should not be read as their association with regressive or racist politics: 'We should not allow others to conflate the history of European-led colonial oppression with Italian-Americans—even those who identify with Columbus as a symbol of ethnic pride' ('Comments from Mayor Liccardo', Little Italy San Jose Newsletter 2018). Given that some forms of rememoration make Italian Americans

---

[25] 'The statue was created by a student who never did another sculpture', said Jon Cicirelli, acting director of Public Works, 'and is not particularly valuable as a work of art' (DeRuy 2018).

complicit in narratives of genocide and racism, this declaration is significant, attempting to separate Italian Americans' emotional affiliation to Columbus from his negative legacy.

Conclusion: Memorializing in the New Millennium

The Long Island park that Italian American politicians offered as a space for unwanted Columbus statues remains vacant, possibly because the disposition of Columbus statues has occurred in just three locations, all in California: San Jose, Los Angeles, and Pepperdine University in Malibu. While municipal and state holidays for Columbus are seemingly easier to discontinue or replace with political advocacy and governmental votes, the marble and bronze objects ensconced in public spaces are permanent fixtures on the landscape that for some still embody their original collective values. For many Americans, dismantling heroic statuary and monuments is almost a foreign concept, associated with distant countries or despotic leaders' regime change. For many Italian Americans, Columbus was the one to last the ages after a long battle of acceptance into white America as the crowning glory of their assimilation and achievement. He remains a defining image for Italian Americans.

A monument is never a single thing, not upon its installation and not over time; neither is it one thing for all people, especially in a pluralistic society like the United States. History's challenges are always contested and reinterpreted. Reflecting critically on changing notions of Columbus across the country, we cannot help but consider that Italian Americans who support Columbus appear to be on the losing side of historic cultural–political battles over meaning and values.

And yet the experiences of Italian Americans cannot be reduced to Columbus. There are no commemorative sites dedicated to Italian American activists—such as Angela Bambace, Pete Panto, and Carlo Tresca, who struggled on behalf of workers' rights, and James Groppi and Vito Russo, who fought on behalf of civil rights—or victims of anti-Italian violence, such as the 11 men lynched in New Orleans in 1891, or the executed anarchists Nicola Sacco and Bartolomeo Vanzetti. This lack is a testament perhaps to suppressed histories. At the same time, statues and monuments across the United States do, quietly and without controversy, commemorate histories and experiences of Italian Americans, including inventor Antonio Meucci (Brooklyn), athlete Joe DiMaggio (Chicago), Italian fishermen (Pittsburg, CA), Italian sculptors (Barre, VT), and the anonymous 'Immigrant' (New Orleans), among others. The 'memorial heritage' (pace Nora) of Italian Americans functions within these sites and other developing public spaces (e.g. the Triangle Fire Memorial in New York City), and together with the myriad, often conflicting, acts of Columbus rememoration, remind us to be attentive to the constantly recalibrated voices of Italian Americans, which are not always easy to hear from the rigid stance of bronze or marble.

Acknowledgement We would like to thank Yiorgos Anagnostou, Siân Gibby, and Dell Upton for their suggestions on earlier versions of this article. We also received feedback from Marta Gutman and others as part of the Columbia University Seminar in Modern Italian Studies, as well as from participants of the 2019 Memory Studies Association conference. We are grateful to Melinda Riddle and Lucinda Norman of the city of San Jose for arranging an interview with the mayor and gathering some of the city's archived materials for us.

REFERENCES

Abolition/Replacement of Columbus Day as Federal Holiday (Online Petition). https://www.change.org/p/nocolumbusday. Accessed 20 May 2019.

Arnold, M. (1992, October 11). In Bay Area, Columbus Day Runs Aground: Holiday: American Indians Plan to Demonstrate at the Festivities. But Italian-Americans View the Events as a Source of Pride. *Los Angeles Times*. https://www.latimes.com/archives/la-xpm-1992-10-11-mn-456-story.html. Accessed 20 May 2019.

Attacks by KKK. http://www.truthaboutcolumbus.com/attacks-by-kkk/. Accessed 20 May 2019.

Battisti, D. (2019). *'Whom We Shall Welcome': Italian Americans and Immigration Reform 1945–1965*. New York: Fordham University Press.

Benjamin, W. (1969). *Illuminations*. New York: Schocken Books.

Borelli, K. (2019, January 17). Email Message to Laura E. Ruberto.

Bradley, C. J. (1990). Towards a Celebration: The Columbus Monument in New York. In P. A. Sensi-Isolani & A. J. Tamburri (Eds.), *Italian Americans Celebrate Life. The Arts and Popular Culture* (pp. 81–94). Staten Island: American Italian Historical Association.

Calhoun, P. (2016, October 10). Goodbye, Columbus: Happy Indigenous People's Day, Denver. *Westword*. https://www.westword.com/news/goodbye-columbus-happy-indigenous-peoples-day-denver-8390819. Accessed 20 May 2019.

Caron, C. (2018, October 5). Why Some Italian-Americans Still Fiercely Defend Columbus Day. *New York Times*. https://www.nytimes.com/2018/10/05/us/columbus-day-italians-indigenous-peoples-day.html. Accessed 20 May 2019.

Castorina Jr., R. (2017, August 28). *Attack on Columbus Statue Is An Attack on a Proud Immigrant Heritage (Commentary)*. https://www.silive.com/opinion/columns/2017/08/attack_on_columbus_statue_is_a.html. Accessed 28 May 2019.

Cerulli, S. J. (2019). *Italian/Americans and the American Racial System: Contadini to Settler Colonists?* Master's thesis at the Graduate Center, City University of New York. https://academicworks.cuny.edu/cgi/viewcontent.cgi?article=4227&context=gc_etds. Accessed 29 May 2019.

Chen, J. (2017, August 22). 'Revisionist History' at Play in Call to Remove Columbus Monument, Pol Says. *DNA Info.* https://www.dnainfo.com/newyork/20170822/columbus-circle/assemblymember-contests-speaker-request-remove-columbus-statue/ Accessed 22 May 2019.

Connell, W. J., & Gardaphé, F. (Eds.). (2010). *Anti-Italianism: Essays on a Prejudice.* New York: Palgrave.

Conservancy Helps Preserve a Piece of Italian-American History. (2018, November). *New York Landmarks Conservancy.* http://www.nylandmarks.org/advocacy/preservation_issues/conservancy_helps_preserve_a_piece_of_italian-american_history/. Accessed 29 May 2019.

De Blasio, Albanese Face Off in Final Democratic Mayoral Primary Debate. (2017, September 6). *CBS New York.* https://newyork.cbslocal.com/2017/09/06/de-blasio-albanese-mayoral-debate/. Accessed 29 May 2019.

De Blasio, Bill (@NYCMayor). (2017, August 16). After the Violent Events in Charlottesville, New York City Will Conduct a 90-Day Review of All Symbols of Hate on City Property. 2:02 PM. *Tweet.* https://twitter.com/NYCMayor/status/897926610271166464. Accessed 22 May 2019.

Denounced By His Countrymen: Italians Object To Carlo Barsotti As Their Representative. (1892, May 24). *New York Times*, p. 3. http://queens.ezproxy.cuny.edu:2048/login?url=https://search-proquest-com.queens.ezproxy.cuny.edu/docview/95026530?accountid=13379. Accessed 6 June 2019.

DeRuy, E. (2018, January 30). San Jose City Council votes to remove controversial Christopher Columbus statue. *The Mercury News.* https://www.mercurynews.com/2018/01/30/residents-pack-city-council-meeting-ahead-of-controversial-christopher-columbus-vote/. Accessed 28 May 2019.

Deschamps, B. (2001). Italian-Americans and Columbus Day: A Quest for Consensus Between National and Group Identities, 1840–1910. In J. Heideking, G. Fabre, & K. Dreisbach (Eds.), *Celebrating Ethnicity and Nation: American Festive Culture from the Revolution to the Early Twentieth Century* (pp. 124–139). New York: Berghahn Books.

Deschamps, B. (2015). 'The cornerstone is laid: Italian-American Memorial Building in New York City and Immigrants' Right to the City at the Turn of the Twentieth Century. *European Journal of American Studies, 10*(3), 1–15.

di Leonardo, M. (1984). *The Varieties of Ethnic Experience: Kinship, Class, and Gender among California Italian-Americans.* Ithaca: Cornell University Press.

di Prima, D. (2008). Whose Day Is It Anyway? In Italian-American Political Solidarity Club (Ed.), *Avanti Popolo: Italian-American Writers Sail Beyond Columbus* (pp. 13–16). San Francisco: Manic D Press.

Fachin, D. (2012). Columbus Day Legacy (film review) *Italian American Review* 2 (2), 135–139.

Gabaccia, D. (2000). *Italy's Many Diasporas*. Seattle: University of Washington Press.

Gonen, Y. (2017). GOP Candidate: De Blasio Should Use His Given German Name. *New York Post*, September 7. https://nypost.com/2017/09/07/gop-candidate-de-blasio-should-use-his-given-german-name/. Accessed 29 May 2019.

Governor Cuomo Announces Columbus Monument Listed on State Register of Historic Places and Recommended to National Register. (2018, October 8). https://www.governor.ny.gov/news/governor-cuomo-announces-columbus-monument-listed-state-register-historic-places-and. Accessed 29 May 2018.

Guglielmo, T. A. (2003). *White on Arrival: Italians, Race, Color, and Power in Chicago, 1890–1945*. New York: Oxford University Press.

Guglielmo, J., & Salerno, S. (Eds.). (2003). *Are Italians White?: How Race Is Made in America*. New York: Routledge.

Halbwachs, M. (1980). *The Collective Memory*. New York: Harper & Row.

Harney, R. F. (1993). Caboto and Other *Parentela*: The Use of the Italian Canadian Past. In N. D. M. Harney (Ed.), *From the Shores of Hardship: Italians in Canada, Essays by Robert F. Harney* (pp. 5–27). Lewiston: SOLEIL.

Heins, S. (2017a, August 17). De Blasio Announces Plan To Take Down NYC's 'Hate Symbols'. *Gothamist*. http://gothamist.com/2017/08/17/bill_de_blasio_hate_symbol_review.php. Accessed 22 May 2019.

Heins, S. (2017b). City Council Speaker Suggests Christopher Columbus Statue Is a Hate Symbol. *Gothamist*. http://gothamist.com/2017/08/22/not_so_columbus_circle.php. Accessed 22 May 2019.

Hitchmough, S. (2013). 'It's Not Your Country Any More': Contested National Narratives and the Columbus Day Parade Protests in Denver. *European Journal of American Culture, 32*(3), 263–283.

Italian Americans for a Multicultural United States. (1992). Founding Statement (flyer) January.

Italian Americans Rally to Keep Christopher Columbus Statue in Columbus Circle. (2017, August 24). *CBS New York*. https://newyork.cbslocal.com/2017/08/24/nyc-christopher-columbus-statue-rally/. Accessed 28 May 2019.

Italian-American Political Solidarity Club. (2008). *Avanti Popolo: Italian-American Writers Sail Beyond Columbus*. San Francisco: Manic D Press.

Jacobson, M. F. (2006). *Roots Too: White Ethnic Revival in Post-Civil Rights American*. Cambridge: Harvard University Press.

Kilgannon, C. (2017, September 29). Massapequa Will Take Statues of Columbus, Unwanted Elsewhere. *New York Times*, p. A23.

Klain (Navajo), B. (2011). *Columbus Day Legacy*. A TricksterFilms, LLC Production.

Kollatz Jr., H. (2014, October 13). Columbus Discovered. *Richmond Magazine*. https://richmondmagazine.com/arts-entertainment/columbus-discovered/. Accessed 20 May 2019.

Kubal, T. (2008). *Cultural Movements and Collective Memory: Christopher Columbus and the Rewriting of the National Origin Myth*. New York: Palgrave Macmillan.

Levinson, S. (1998). *Written in Stone: Public Monuments in Changing Societies*. Durham: Duke University Press.

Liccardo, Samuel. (2019, January 17). Interview with Laura E. Ruberto. Little Italy San Jose Newsletter, Email, March 2018.

Luconi, S. (2012). Columbus and Vespucci as Italian Navigators: The Ethnic Legacy of Explorations and Italian Americans' Search for Legitimacy in the United States. In *Florence in Italy and Abroad from Vespucci to Contemporary Innovators* (pp. 62–77). Florence: Florence Campus Publishing House.

Luconi, S. (2016). Opera as a Nationalistic Weapon: The Erection of the Monument to Giuseppe Verdi in New York City. *Italian Americana*, 34(3), 37–61.

Matthews, G. (2003). *Silicon Valley, Women, and the California Dream: Gender, Class, and Opportunity in the Twentieth Century*. Palo Alto: Stanford University Press.

Mayoral Advisory Commission on City Art, Monuments, and Markers Report to the City of New York (Public Testimony). (2018a). https://www1.nyc.gov/assets/monuments/downloads/pdf/monuments-commission-borough-testimony.pdf. Accessed 29 May 2019.

Mayoral Advisory Commission on City Art, Monuments, and Markers Report to the City of New York (Report). (2018b). https://www1.nyc.gov/assets/monuments/downloads/pdf/mac-monuments-report.pdf. Accessed 29 May 2019.

McKevitt, G. (1992–1993). Christopher Columbus as a Civic Saint: Angelo Noce and Italian American Assimilation. *California History*, 71(4), 516–533.

Mignone, M. B. (1993). *Columbus: Meetings of Cultures* (Symposium Proceedings). Stony Brook: Forum Italicum, Inc.

No Columbus Day. https://nocolumbusday.wordpress.com/. Accessed 28 May 2019.

Noce, A. 1910. Columbus Day in Colorado. Angelo Noce: Denver. https://archive.org/details/columbusdayincol00noce/page/24. Accessed 22 May 2019.

Nora, P. (1989). Between Memory and History. *Les Lieux de Mémoire*. *Representations*, 26, 7–24.

Nora, P. (1996). From *Lieux de mémoire* to *Realms of Memory*. In L. D. Kritzman (Ed.), *Realms of Memory. Vol. I: Conflicts and Divisions* (pp. xv–xxiv). New York: Columbia University Press.

Nora, P. (2002, April 19). Reasons for the Current Upsurge in Memory. *Eurozine*, pp. 1–9. https://www.eurozine.com/reasons-for-the-current-upsurge-in-memory/?pdf. Accessed 21 May 2019.

Norkunas, M. K. (1993). *The Politics of Public Memory: Tourism, History, and Ethnicity in Monterey, California*. New York: SUNY Press.

Pozzetta, G. E. (1971). *The Italians of New York City, 1890–1914*. Dissertation at University of North Carolina at Chapel Hill.

Pozzetta, G. E, & Mormino, G. R. 1998, January–June 17. The Politics of Christopher Columbus and World War II. *Altreitalie*, pp. 6–15.

Progressive Italians to Transform the Columbus Holiday (PITCH). *Statement in Support of a Respectful Celebration of Italian Heritage*. https://www.transformcolumbusday.org/pitch.html. Accessed 20 May 2019.

Rally to Keep Christopher Columbus Statue at Columbus Circle. (2017, August 24). *ABC7NY*. https://abc7ny.com/society/rally-to-keep-christopher-columbus-statue-at-columbus-circle/2337106/. Accessed 29 May 2019.

Richards, D. A. J. (1999). *Italian American: The Racializing of an Ethnic Identity*. New York: New York University Press.

Ruberto, L. E., & J. Sciorra. (2017a, October 4). Recontextualizing the Ocean Blue: Italian Americans and the Commemoration of Columbus. *Process: A Blog for American History*. http://www.processhistory.org/recontextualizing-the-ocean-blue/. 29 May 2019.

Ruberto, L. E., & Sciorra, J. (2017b). Introduction: Rebooting Italian America. In L. E. Ruberto & J. Sciorra (Eds.), *New Italian Migrations to the United States, Vol. 2: Art and Culture Since 1945* (pp. 1–31). Chicago: University of Illinois Press.

Sager, S. (2017). Confederate Symbols to Be Removed from Bronx Community College. *ABC7NY*. https://abc7ny.com/society/confederate-symbols-to-be-removed-from-bronx-college/2317187/. Accessed 22 May 2019.

San Jose City Council Votes to Remove Controversial Christopher Columbus Statue. (2018, January 30). *San Jose Mercury News*. https://www.mercurynews.com/2018/01/30/residents-pack-city-council-meeting-ahead-of-controversial-christopher-columbus-vote/. Accessed 28 May 2019.

Scheihing, W. (2014, October 12). Born Amid KKK Backlash, Columbus Statue Endures. *The Morning Call*. https://www.mcall.com/mc-kkk-fought-easton-columbus-statue-20141011-story.html. Accessed 20 May 2019.

Schlereth, T. J. (1992). Columbia, Columbus, and Columbians. *The Journal of American History, 79*(3), 937–968.

Sciorra, J. (2011). Introduction: Listening with an Accent. In J. Sciorra (Ed.), *Italian Folk: Vernacular Culture in Italian-American Lives* (pp. 1–10). New York: Fordham University Press.

Stone, M. (2010). Potere e spiritualità: La Mostra degli artisti italiani in armi del 1942. *Memoria e ricerca, 33*(Gennaio – Aprile), 63–79.

Sutton, B. (2017, December 1). Over 120 Prominent Artists and Scholars Call on NYC to Take Down Racist Monuments. *Hyperallergic*. . https://hyperallergic.com/414315/over-120-prominent-artists-and-scholars-call-on-nyc-to-take-down-racist-monuments/. Accessed 29 May 2019.

Thorne, K. (2017, September 25). Long Island Town Wants Discarded Columbus Statues. *New York Times.* https://abc7ny.com/society/long-island-town-wants-discarded-columbus-statues-/2452701/. Accessed 1 May 2019.

Thousands Gather To Honor Columbus. (1937, October 13). *New York Times.* (1923-Current File), p. 3. http://queens.ezproxy.cuny.edu:2048/login?url=https://search-proquest-com.queens.ezproxy.cuny.edu/docview/102281596?accountid=13379. Accessed 6 June 2019.

Tusiani, J. (2000). *Ethnicity: Selected Poems.* West Lafayette: Bordighera Press.

United Native America. (2001, April 4). *Mayor of San Jose, CA Will Rebuild Columbus Statue (Press Release).* http://www.unitednativeamerica.com/press/rebuild.html. Accessed 1 Nov 2019.

van der Krogt, P. *Undated. Columbus Monuments Pages.* https://columbus.vanderkrogt.net/. Accessed 20 May 2019.

Vellon, P. G. (2014). *A Great Conspiracy against Our Race: Italian Immigrant Newspapers and the Construction of Whiteness in the Early 20th Century.* New York: New York University Press.

Viscusi, R. (1993). *An Oration Upon the Most Recent Death of Christopher Columbus.* West Lafayette: Bordighera Press.

Vivolo, A. (2017, August 25). The Columbus Citizens Foundation Is Committed to the Preservation of the Columbus Monument at Columbus Circle (Paid Ad). *New York Times,* p. A21.

Williams, J. (2019). *Mayor Cantrell apologizes for 1891 Italian-American lynchings in New Orleans: 'What happened was wrong'. Nola.* https://www.nola.com/news/article_ebd61396-a013-5b22-8171-bd8bd7416a88.html. Accessed 21 November 2019.

Zimmer, K. (2015). *Immigrants against the State: Yiddish and Italian Anarchism in America.* Urbana: University of Illinois Press.

Archival Material

San Jose, City Hall, Columbus Statue, *San Jose Mercury News* Clipping File, California Room, San Jose Public Library.
23 March 1958.
27 March 1958.
30 September 1958.
9 March 2001.
10 March 2001.
23 December 2001.

San Jose City Clerk Files, City Hall.
17 March 1958, San Jose City Hall minutes.
13 September 2017, San Jose City Hall Memorandum.
29 November 2017, San Jose City Hall Memorandum.

CHAPTER 4

Long-Distance Nationalism: Ukrainian Monuments and Historical Memory in Multicultural Canada

Per A. Rudling

INTRODUCTION

In October 2017, a political controversy erupted, as the Russian embassy in Ottawa posted a number of images on its twitter account, purporting to depict 'Nazi memorials' in Canada. Three images of memorials to Waffen-SS veterans, a prominent Nazi collaborator, and ultranationalist insurgents were accompanied by the comment 'There are monuments to Nazi collaborators in Canada and nobody is doing anything about it'. The message was followed by the hash tags '#NeverForget #Holocaust #WorldWar2' ('Russia in Canada' 2017) (Fig. 4.1). Three years earlier, Russia had invaded Ukraine and annexed parts of its territory, an action not seen in Europe since World War II. The invasion led to a sharp deterioration of Russia's relations to the West, including Canada, the governments of which strongly and publicly denounced the aggression. The diplomatic row of 2017 should be seen in the context of this conflict.

P. A. Rudling (✉)
Lund University, Lund, Sweden
e-mail: per_anders.rudling@hist.lu.se

© The Author(s) 2020
S. Marschall (ed.), *Public Memory in the Context of Transnational Migration and Displacement*, Palgrave Macmillan Memory Studies, https://doi.org/10.1007/978-3-030-41329-3_4

There are monumets to Nazi collaborators in Canada and nobody is doing anything about it. #NeverForget #Holocaust #WorldWar2

Fig. 4.1 Tweet by Russian Embassy in Ottawa (15 October 2017). Thanks to Vasily Kultyshev of the Russian Embassy in Ottawa for the permission to reproduce. For copyright issues, the images of the Edmonton Shukhevych memorial along with the Oakville monuments to the UPA and veterans of the Waffen-SS *Galizien* have been removed. The tweet, with its images, is available online at ('Russia in Canada' 2017)

However, the controversy brings to light issues of memory, migration, and the organization of public space. Why are there monuments to Ukrainian Waffen-SS veterans and to other radical Ukrainian nationalist formations in Canada? What sort of monuments are these? Who erected them, and why? When and how did the Russian Federation become a guardian of the memory of the Holocaust? To answer these questions, we need to look closer at the political instrumentalization of history against a complex background of collaboration, displacement, and official government-sanctioned multiculturalism.

Ukrainian Long-Distance Nationalism in Canada

In the immediate post-war years, Canada received 165,000 political refugees, so-called Displaced Persons (DPs). Anti-communist applicants were favoured over others; Poles and Ukrainians constituted 39% of this group, as a total of 25,772 refugees of Ukrainian origin arrived in Canada between 1947 and 1951 through the efforts of the International Refugee Organization (IRO). Followers of Stepan Bandera (1909–1959), the leader of the radical wing of the far-right Organization of Ukrainian Nationalists, known as OUN(b), constituted the largest political party, supported by 75–80% of the West Ukrainian DPs.[1] A significant group

---

[1] A dominant force in Ukrainian émigré politics, the OUN split, in the 1940s and 1950s, into three rivalling wings, as the radical wing under Stepan Bandera, known as OUN(b), broke with the more conservative leadership of Andrii Mel'nyk, which became known as the OUN(m). In the 1950s, a smaller, CIA-funded group OUN(z), or 'OUN abroad' split off

consisted of former combatants of its paramilitary wing, the Ukrainian Insurgent Army (known under its Ukrainian acronym UPA (*Ukrains'ka Povstans'ka Armiia*). In 1950, the Ukrainian Nationalist community grew further, as Canada admitted between 1200 and 2000 veterans of the 14th Waffen Grenadier Division of the SS (1st Galician). As only a cross-section of the veterans were subjected to security screening (which was sketchy and incomplete), recurrent allegations of war criminals among them triggered intensive discussions ('Rodal Report' 1986; Margolian 2000). In Canada, the clandestine OUN(b) organized itself through front organizations, which set out to infiltrate and take control over local community networks.

While the bulk of Canadians of Ukrainian pedigree are culturally, socially, and politically integrated—if not assimilated—into the Canadian mainstream, a 'vanguard' of diaspora activists, claiming to speak on the behalf of 1.3 million Ukrainian Canadians, promotes a radical historical memory. It entails the glorification of, in particular, three Ukrainian nationalist groups, active during World War II: the above-mentioned OUN; its armed wing UPA; and the 14th Grenadier Division of the SS. The veterans of the latter, known colloquially as the Galicia Division, prefer to refer to the unit as 1 UD UNA, *Persha Ukrains'ka Dyviziia Ukrains'koi National'noi Armii*—the First Division of the Ukrainian National Army, a name adopted in the final days of World War II (Rosenberg 1945).

These intensely political refugees formed tightly knit communities around political parties, churches, schools, social organizations, credit unions, scouting groups, and charities. Recurring performances of nationalist rituals played a central role in these émigrés' collective memory and historical culture. On anniversaries, uniformed activists in folk costumes or political and military uniforms gathered to perform speaking choirs, poetry recitals, folk dances, and historical re-enactment aimed at mobilizing the community and to socialize the Canadian-born younger generation into the nationalist historical culture.

---

from the Banderites. [redacted] (1977) On the OUN émigré groups, see Markus (1992). In order to make a distinction between nationalists—that is, adherents of the idea of Ukrainian statehood, among whom all sorts of political orientations were represented—and the OUN, which subscribed to a particular, totalitarian ideology, this chapter uses capital N when referring to the ideological postulates and followers of the various wings of that organization.

From Portable Cenotaphs to Bronze

The cenotaph, the tomb to the unknown soldier, is symbolically empty. As a symbol of wartime suffering, sacrifices, and redemption it dates back to ancient Greece, but became popular across the British Empire after World War I. In 2010, in Canada alone there were over 6200 documented military memorials, and no less than 76 cenotaphs ('Cenotaphs' 2010). During the early years in Canada, the Waffen-SS veterans and the Ukrainian Nationalists performed their rituals in front of portable monuments to the unknown soldier (Rudling 2011, p.750).

War monuments place particular demands on design, material, and functionality, whereby certain materials are clearly preferred. Bronze communicates permanence; marble signifies heaviness, but also something organic of the mountains, finely sculptured by an artist. A monument of Styrofoam, plastered cardboard, or plastic—no matter how durable or heavy—simply would not do for the purpose of venerating the martyrs for the Ukrainian Nationalist cause (Abousnnouga and Machin 2013, p.219). Portable monuments were therefore regarded as an unsatisfactory, temporary solution. As the Ukrainian Nationalists established themselves in Canada, they erected new, permanent memorials in Canada, of granite, marble, and bronze.

Benedict Anderson (1991, pp.6–7) argues that the nation is imagined as a 'deep, horizontal comradeship'. The stylized depiction of the vanguard of the nation—the Nationalist insurgent and martyr, fallen for the national cause, is depicted in a highly stylized, stereotypical fashion, similar to the military men depicted on the monuments for the fallen in World War I. Abousnnouga and Machin (2013, p.111) note,

> Typically, the represented participant soldiers in the memorials share faces of perfect symmetrical proportions, square jaws, long slim noses and almond-shaped eyes, their faces can never be considered either plain or unattractive. Locks of hair are carved consistently. Bodies of the soldiers were also perfect and muscular … The figurative representations of the soldiers create physiognomic stereotypes that cause the illusion of a common ethnic identity and a race that exists within the nation that shares only desirable physical features.

The depiction of the UPA insurgents on the monuments bears little semblance to the brutal realities on the ground in Ukraine; the insurgency was often highly chaotic, a very significant part of the insurgents were former auxiliary police in German service, many of them with direct involvement in the Holocaust and accustomed to extreme political violence. The rebels were often malnourished, dirty, and—after the return of the Soviets in 1944—increasingly desperate. Their uniforms were incomplete and inconsistent. The monument design was an appropriation of established Commonwealth practices for the community's own memory culture, in which the Ukrainian Nationalist and Waffen-SS veterans depicted their heroes through Graeco-Roman aesthetics, merging antiquity with modern nationalism.

MULTICULTURALISM AND MULTINATIONALISM

According to the 2011 census, 1,251,170 people in Canada identified as Ukrainian, although only 11.5% of these could actually speak Ukrainian. The number of dedicated Ukrainian nationalists is far smaller, but well organized. In recent decades, in particular, affiliates of the OUN(b) have played important roles in the leadership of the Ukrainian Canadian Congress. During the Ukrainian crisis of 2013–2014, the Banderites dominated the leadership of the Ukrainian Canadian Congress, which claimed to speak on behalf of all people of Ukrainian ancestry in Canada. Paul (Pavlo) Grod, UCC National President between 2007 and 2018 (and currently president of the Ukrainian World Congress), has held leading positions in the Banderite youth organization SUM as well as the League of Ukrainian Canadians (Chyczij 2019).

In reality, second-, third-, and fourth-generation Ukrainian-Canadians tend to have limited interest in the increasingly distant historical homeland of grand- and great-grandparents. As the command of the Ukrainian language dissipated, the community was increasingly forged around a particular ideological rendition of history. The interpretation that the 1932–1933 famine (*Holodomor*) constituted a deliberate genocide of the Ukrainian ethnic group, along with the cult of the OUN and UPA, constituted key features of this canon. Dissent from the *Holodomor*-OUN-UPA discourse was uncommon, and often censured through ostracization or expulsion from the Ukrainian ethno-political community.

The 1971 introduction of official multiculturalism under Pierre Trudeau (1919–2000, Prime Minister from 1968–1979 and 1980–1984) was intended to defuse the issue of Quebecois nationalism and to promote good community relations in Canada.[2] People of Ukrainian heritage constituted one of the largest communities in the Canadian West. Its intensely politicized leadership was the best-organized ethno-nationalist group in Canada. Soon, Ukrainian Canadian 'ethnic activists' took the lead in this process, particularly in western Canada (Wayland 1997, p.47). 'The multiculturalist movement … began under the initiative of Ukrainian nationalists', historian Aya Fujiwara notes, 'by far the most active group in the pursuit of multiculturalism and collective ethnic rights'(2007, p.223). Canadian multiculturalism has come to underwrite long-distance nationalism financially, politically, and socially.

Ironically, Trudeau, whose policies made him one of the Ukrainian Nationalists' most prominent benefactors, not only opposed Ukrainian separatism, but nationalism as such (Kordan 2019, pp.4–5). Canadian liberalism and Ukrainian Nationalism thus made an unlikely pair. Over the years, however, they came to develop an increasingly symbiotic relationship: Canadian multicultural policies benefited and stimulated the Nationalists, strengthening their hand within the community. This, in turn, aided the organized Ukrainian Nationalists in mobilizing 'ethnic' block votes in several key ridings, not least in the Toronto area, allowing them to yield significant political influence over Canadian foreign policy vis-à-vis Ukraine (Fujiwara 2015; MacKinnon 2015; for a slightly different interpretation, see Kordan 2019, p.8). Not only the Liberals, but also the Conservatives and the leftist NDP increasingly came to cater to the Nationalists' key issues: the *Holodomor* discourse and, in the case of the Tories, the glorification of the OUN and UPA.[3]

Canadian multicultural policies were supported by 1% of the state budget. During the first three and a half years following its introduction, the Canadian government allocated CAD$ 19,160,000 to multicultural programmes, spent on 'ethno-cultural groups' and 'ethnic press'; significant resources were set aside to market its new policies (Wayland 1997, p.47). Partially as a consequence of this 'ethnic turn', in 1976 the provincial government of Alberta sponsored the establishment of a Canadian Institute of Ukrainian Studies (CIUS) with an annual grant of $350,000,

---

[2] On descriptive and normative multiculturalism, see Bauhn (1995).

[3] In 2008, Canada officially adopted the diaspora's version of the famine, recognizing, through Bill C-459, the *Holodomor* as a genocide. On the glorification of the OUN(b) and UPA by senior Tory politicians, such as Jason Kenney, formerly Minister of Citizenship, Immigration, and Multiculturalism under Stephen Harper, and currently Premier of Alberta, see Himka (2015, p. 157).

an amount later increased to $500,000 (Kravchenko 2019, p.38). In addition to direct government funding, émigré Nationalist groups were underwritten by indirect sponsorship in the form of tax rebates, reduced postage rates, and full-page government ads in their papers.

To the frustration of the Ukrainian community elites, the focus of Canadian multicultural policies changed over the 1970s and 1980s, as the funding of folklore and nationalist activism decreased in favour of sponsoring stimulating 'intercultural understanding' and anti-racism (Rudling 2011, pp.741–742). Official multiculturalism was affirmed in the Canadian Multiculturalism Act of 1988 which put increased stress on 'intercultural awareness understanding' (Wayland 1997, p.49). While the policies have shifted, multicultural funding continues to underwrite Ukrainian Nationalist activism in Canada today. For example, in 2008–2009, through the Department of Canadian Heritage and The Canada Post Corporation, the OUN(b) organ *Homin Ukrainy* received $ 23,096 in subsidies, the OUN(m)'s *New Pathway* $15,921, and the pro-nationalist *Ukrainian News* $15,751 ('Publications Assistance Program 2008-2009').

THE SHUKHEVYCH YOUTH COMPLEX, EDMONTON

The introduction of official multiculturalism was accompanied by the erection of a number of 'ethnic' memorials across Canada, particularly in the prairie provinces (Swyripa 2010, pp.172–189). Among the most impressive of all these memorials, monuments, schools, clubs, and community buildings is the enormous, partially government-funded Roman Shukhevych Ukrainian Youth Unity Complex (UYUC) (*Dim ukrains'koi molodi im. Romana Shukhevycha*) in Edmonton, Alberta. The edifice is dedicated to the wartime leader of the OUN(b) and supreme commander of its military wing, the UPA, Roman Shukhevych (1907–1950), an overside bronze bust of which stands in front of its main building (Fig. 4.2). After entering the dimly lit gates, the visitor is again greeted by Shukhevych's image, in the form of a brightly illuminated golden relief on a dark brick wall, surrounded by the acronyms, in Ukrainian, of the organizations he commanded.

Opened in 1973, the UYUC was underwritten by significant multicultural funding ($75,000) from the government of Alberta. As a non-profit charitable organization, the UYUC remains a tax exempt organization. The purpose of the complex, the OUN(b) press declared, was to 'become a blacksmith's forge, which will forge hard, unbreakable characters of the Ukrainian youth' and to 'raise and harden a new generation of fighters for

Fig. 4.2 Bust to Roman Shukhevych (pseud. Chuprynka), Ukrainian Youth Complex, Edmonton. (Photo courtesy of John-Paul Himka)

the liberation of Ukraine, ready to unite its strength with the forces of the warriors of the captive Ukraine' (Rudling 2011, p.744, 746). The Shukhevych monument was set up without much discussion or controversy. At this time, the Holocaust in Ukraine generated limited interest; the Soviet Union ignored or suppressed the memory of Jewish persecution and Soviet archives remained largely inaccessible to researchers.

It is unlikely that Pierre Trudeau had even heard of Shukhevych when he, in November 1975, visited the complex to enjoy the Nationalists' folkloristic performances before addressing them about the benefits of multiculturalism (Sinclair 1975, p.1,12). Yet, Shukhevych is controversial as a representative for Ukraine. He collaborated with Nazi Germany, as a commanding officer in the *Batallion Nachtigall*—a collaborationist subunit under the command under the *Abwehr* in 1940–1941—and thereafter in the *Schutzmannschaft* battalion 201 in occupied Belorussia from early 1942 until early 1943. In 1941, the OUN(b) enthusiastically supported a German victory in the war and supplied manpower for various collaborationist formations. *Nachtigall* soldiers partook in anti-Jewish violence in the summer of 1941, including in the Lviv pogrom and mass shootings in the Vinnytsia area. (Struve 2015, pp.354–360).

After Stalingrad, many Ukrainian Nationalists deserted the auxiliary units for the UPA, the backbone of which consisted heavily of former collaborators (Katchanovski 2019). In 1943 the OUN(b) and UPA, both under Shukhevych's leadership, launched a campaign of ethnic cleansing, which, according to the most detailed studies, claimed the lives of 91,200 Poles and several thousand Jews (Siemaszko 2011, p.341). While the UPA concluded an agreement of mutual support and cooperation with Nazi Germany in August 1944, it retained its autonomy and independence (Burds 2010; Vedeneev and Ehorov 1998). The UPA does, however, qualify as a perpetrator in the Holocaust; in 1943–1944, it killed perhaps as many as 10,000 Jews, who until then had managed to survive by hiding in the forests. The mass violence against Poles and Jews was carried out as part of the struggle for Ukrainian statehood and not—as Soviet propagandists liked to claim— by UPA members as proxies, or 'hangmen' for the Nazis (Himka 2017).

Ukrainian War Veterans' Memorial, Edmonton

The 'first wave' of Ukrainian immigrants that arrived in Canada from the Habsburg Empire at the turn of the twentieth century, and much of the 'second', interwar immigration from West Ukraine regarded cemeteries as hallowed, but rather apolitical grounds. The St. Mykhailo (Michael's) Ukrainian Cemetery in Edmonton was opened by the Ukrainian Catholic Eparchy of Edmonton in 1955 (St. Michael's cemetery n.d.). Over the years, St. Michael's started to take on more overt political characteristics. By the 1970s, as a preferred burial ground of many Nationalist activists and Ukrainian SS veterans, it had come to occupy a central place in their memory culture.

On 31 October 1976, at the centre of this cemetery, the Ukrainian War Veterans' Society in Edmonton (*Ukrains'ka Strilets'ka Hromada*, USH)— where veterans of the 14th Waffen-SS Division Galizien were the driving force—inaugurated a large memorial to their martyrs (Martynowych 2011; Bairak 1978, pp.184–185). The edifice, titled the Central Cross, still towers over the cemetery, surrounded by spruce and Manitoba maple; it carries the text 'Fighters for Ukrainian Freedom' (*Bortsiam za voliu Ukrainy*). Bronze plaques, in English and Ukrainian, explain: 'This monument was erected by the combatant organizations U.S.S., U.H.A.,

U.S.H. U.P.A. and 1-st U.D. U.N.A., it was consecrated by Patriarch Yosyf Slipyj on Oct. 31, 1976'. Incomprehensible to an outsider—and certainly to most Canadians—these are acronyms for armed Ukrainian nationalist formations of two world wars. USS is short for *Ukrains'ki Sichovi Stril'tsi*, the Ukrainian Sich Riflemen, whereas UHA stands for *Ukrains'ka Halyts'ka Armiia*, the Ukrainian Galician Army, two military formations in World War I, the latter associated with the short-lived West Ukrainian People's Republic (Fig. 4.3).

The monument was consecrated by the head of the Ukrainian Greek Catholic Church, Major Archbishop Josyf Slipyi (1893–1984), a former Soviet political prisoner. The memorial construction committee was chaired by multicultural activist Peter Savaryn (1926–2017), leader of the local chapter of the Ukrainian Waffen-SS veterans.[4] 'For whom did we erect this memorial cross?', Savaryn (2007, p.253) asked rhetorically, as he inaugurated the memorial. Answering his own question, Savaryn reeled off a long list of battles and of martyrs, 'Ukrainian Spartans' of a millennial struggle against the enemies of the nation; 'Ukrainian Thermopylians… from Poltava, Baturyn, Krut, Makivka, Bazara, Lysoni, Gleichenberg'; and heroes 'such as Petliura, Konovalets, Shukhevych, Bandera, and the nameless … who died, in order for Ukraine to live; may their eternal rest serve

Fig. 4.3 Monument 'To the Fighters for Ukrainian Freedom', Edmonton, Alberta. (Photo by Erik Visser. Thanks to Marc Turgeon, Director of Cemeteries at the Ukrainian Catholic Eparchy of Edmonton for generously allowing author to use this illustration. Image from http://www.stmichaels-rosehill-cemetery.com/st-michaels-description.html. Accessed 31 July 2018.)

[4] Volodymyr Kubijovych Fonds, Library and Archives Canada, Ottawa, (henceforth: LAC), MG 31, D 203, Vol. 10, folder 41 "Petro Savaryn."

as a call to awaken their own people'. To Savaryn, the Ukrainian nationalist struggle reaches back several hundred years, linking the present to a distant past of princely knights, Cossacks, *haidamaks*, Ukrainian Sich Riflemen, soldiers of the UHA, UNR,[5] UPA, Waffen-SS Galizien and the Carpathian *Sich*,[6] who 'laid down their exuberant heads, united, indivisible and faithful ... as members of the eternal body of the eternal Ukrainian people'. He further noted that their sacrifices were not in vain, as their children 'will take up the swords of their forefathers, to the joy of mother Ukraine' (ibid.).[7]

Monument to the Glory of the UPA, North Oakville, Ontario

Similar memorials appeared in other Canadian cities with significant Ukrainian populations. St. Volodymyr Ukrainian Cemetery, in North Oakville, Ontario, established in 1984, was owned and operated by the Ukrainian Orthodox Cathedral with the same name. The idea to erect a memorial in Oakville emerged in 1981–1982, following which a committee was formed in 1984. Inspiration came from south of the border, where Ukrainian Nationalists were erecting UPA memorials in Parma, OH, in 1982 and Bound Brook, NJ, in 1984 (Vakar 1988, p.5). The committee was pan-nationalist, bringing together representatives of the two OUN branches, the Ukrainian Free Cossack Movement, veterans of *Nachtigall* and its sister unit *Roland*, its successor, the *Schutzmannschaft* battalion 201 (euphemized as DUN, *Druzhyny Ukrains'kykh Natsionalistiv*, Units of Ukrainian Nationalists), the Waffen-SS Galizien, and the UNR in exile. By 1988, the committee had raised $88,650 for a memorial to the 'glory of the UPA'.[8] A huge granite memorial, entitled *Pam"iatnyk Slavy UPA*

---

[5] The UNR stands for *Ukrains'ka Narodna Respublika*, the Ukrainian People's Republic, a short-lived republic declared in early 1918.

[6] The Carpathian Sich (*Karpats'ka Sich*) was a paramilitary organization set up in late 1938, and which sought independence for Capatho-Ukraine.

[7] See also LAC, MG 31, D 203, Vol. 10, folders 40 "Petro Savaryn – Edmonton (1968, 1970, 1972–75)"; Peter and Olga Savaryn Family Fonds, Provincial Archives of Alberta (henceforth PAA), accession no. PR2014.0451/0003, PR0671.0005, "Information and biographies," Box 1.

[8] The list of donors read as a who-is-who of radical émigré Ukrainian Nationalism. The list of donors includes prominent OUN names such as Halamai, Stets'ko, Luciuk, Plaviuk, Kashuba, and many others (Vakar 1988, pp. 9, 14, 22, 61, 104).

('Monument to the Glory of the UPA'), designed by Volodymyr Mariian Badnars'kyi-Volod was hewn by Bronson Granite and Marble Ltd. in Kitchener, Ontario, in 1987–1988 (Vakar 1988, p.3). The monument depicts a soldier, wearing a stylized Cossack uniform hat, a so-called *mazepinka*. Behind the granite relief is a large Ukrainian trident and a black cross with a stylized symbol of the UPA, a raised sword, with the words 'Eternal glory to the soldiers of the UPA: For Ukraine, for Freedom, for the people' and the years 1942–1952. The base of the monument carries the OUN 'commandment', to which all members pledged to commit themselves: 'Achieve a Ukrainian State or Die in the Struggle for It'. Typically for these sorts of monuments, it presents death as a deliberate act of giving (Abousnnouga and Machin 2013, p.219) (Fig. 4.4).

https://commons.wikimedia.org/wiki/File:UPA_Monument_3.jpg

Inaugurated on 26 May 1988, to coincide with the commemorations of the millennial celebration of Christianity in Ukraine, the monument constitutes the imposing centrepiece of a large necropolis. The opening rituals were saturated in the rhetorical pomp so characteristic of the émigré Ukrainian Nationalists, glorifying the 'Fallen Hero Soldiers of Ukraine', specifically the USS, the OUN, and UPA, 'victims of the "Muscovite satanical machine"' (Vakar 1988, pp.5, 6, 13). Soon thereafter, the 'Monument to the Glory of the UPA' was accompanied by a cenotaph to the Ukrainian Waffen-SS veterans. It carries inscriptions in three languages. The Ukrainian text 'To the Fighters for the Freedom of Ukraine' is accompanied by 'To Those Who Died For the Freedom of Ukraine' and 'Morts Pour L'Ukraine' in the two Canadian official languages. On the top of the black marble cenotaph is a large cross with the coat of arms of the Waffen-SS Division Galizien, with the letters '1 UD UNA' (Fig. 4.5).

https://en.wikipedia.org/wiki/File:SS_Galician_monument.jpg

Beyond the Ukrainian diaspora, these monuments went largely unnoticed. The few times the St. Volodymyr's cemetery was even mentioned in the local press reflects the sleepy, peaceful Canadian suburbia that surrounded it. A fence was installed in the 1990s, 'after homeowners used to [sic] cemetery to dump yard clippings and used motor oil', reported the local newspaper, *The Oakville Beaver*. In 1996 and 1998, the *Beaver* reported cases of vandalism at the cemetery, though apparently without political motives, as the vandals made no discernment between the graves of Ukrainian veterans and that of a baby (Mozel 1998, pp.1,5).

Fig. 4.4 'Monument to the Glory of the UPA', North Oakville, Ontario. Wikipedia commons, photo by Wikipedia user 'Lvivske'

The 1990s not only saw the collapse of the Soviet Union; over the decade, interest in the Holocaust surged. The Ukrainian community, as Canada at large, meanwhile underwent significant demographic changes. As the veterans' generation aged and passed away, a 'fourth' wave of post-Soviet Ukrainian immigrants took over the management of the North Oakville cemetery, which was reflected on its web site, administered by people with a first language other than English.

Fig. 4.5 Monument 'To the Fighters for the Freedom of Ukraine', North Oakville, Ontario. Wikipedia commons, photo by Wikipedia user 'Lvivske'

Sinse [sic] its establishment St. Volodymyr Ukrainian Cemetery has developed into a [sic] largest Ukrainian cemetery in Canada. Ukrainian War Veteran's memorials of the Ukrainian Liberating Army and First Ukrainian Division marking designated burial grounds of our freedom fitters [sic]. ('St. Volodymyr's Ukrainian Cemetery' n.d.)

The cemetery's website offers 'UPA shape' tombstones, starting at $3860, with the words 'ETERNAL GLORY' [VICHNA SLAVA] (ibid.). The OUN(b) and its façade organizations regularly gather at the necropolis to perform their rituals. Yet, rather than making inroads into Canadian mainstream, this memory culture exists at the fringe of society, and the cemetery remains largely a preserve of 'frozen' immigrant culture.

Wooing the 'Ethnic' Vote

The organization today known as the Ukrainian Canadian Congress (UCC) was established in 1940 by a Canadian government concerned with the spread of communism. It has worked closely with successive Canadian governments (Fujiwara 2015, pp.208). Underwritten by official Canadian multiculturalism, since 1971 the UCC has moved its positions forward, regardless of whether Conservatives or Liberals were in power (Himka 2015, p.156). The impact of the organized Ukrainian diaspora on Canadian politics has been significant. In 1991, Canada was the first Western country to recognize Ukraine's independence, and the country has had a close relationship with Ukraine ever since (Kordan 2019, p.16). Bilateral treaties, signed in 1994, designate the relations between Canada and Ukraine as a 'special partnership' (Bessonova 2018, p.8).

During the so-called Orange Revolution of 2004–2005, Canada took an active part in promoting a peaceful solution to the conflict between an increasingly authoritarian government and pro-democracy protesters. As president, the victor of the Orange Revolution, Viktor Iushchenko (2005–2010), adopted the diaspora's memory culture and turned glorification of the OUN(b) and UPA Ukrainian into government policy. Shukhevych and Bandera were elevated to official heroes of Ukraine, posthumously awarded the highest state decorations, and their portraits appeared on postage stamps and commemorative coins. If Iushchenko's memory policies sharply polarized Ukrainian opinion, they delighted the diaspora. In Canada, the UCC felt emboldened to request recognition and pensions for OUN and UPA veterans in Canada, triggering intense discussions in the pages of the *Edmonton Journal* and the local Ukrainian press in Alberta.

Under the leadership of Grod, a successful businessman, the UCC aggressively moved its positions forward. Grod skilfully formed close relationships with top Canadian government officials, reflecting a new confidence and boldness of its mostly OUN(b)-affiliated leadership. In 2013, a satisfied UCC reported that, for the second year in a row, 'Paul Grod has been once again named as one of the top 80 influencing Canadian foreign policy by *Embassy Magazine*, a prominent Ottawa-based publication' ('Ukrainian Canadian Congress President Listed' 2012; 'Paul Grod Named...' 2013; Shane and Foster 2013). The UCC noted that this 're-affirms that the hard work of our branches, committees and member organizations ... is making a difference with Canada's top decision makers'

('Paul Grod Named…' 2013). Aside from Canadian foreign policy, in particular vis-à-vis Ukraine, historical memory constitutes a top priority for the UCC.

> During his tenure as UCC President, Paul has successfully ensured that Ukraine is a top foreign policy priority for Canada, negotiated the recognition of Canada's first national internment operations and establishment of a $10 M endowment by the Government of Canada, and ensured that Canada recognized the *Holodomor* as a genocide of the Ukrainian people. (ibid.)

The UCC's agenda is heavily focussed on historical injustices committed against Ukrainians, never on wrongs committed by Ukrainians. The UCC remains highly sensitive to matters related to the Holocaust, in particular Ukrainian involvement in atrocities. Regarding historical representations of Ukrainians, Grod stresses the importance of Ukrainians being 'viewed as victims, and not perpetrators of Nazism, during the Second World War' (Grod 2013, quote at 1:03–1:10).

The government of Stephen Harper (b. 1959, PM 2006–2015) was highly receptive to the UCC's narration of history. Harper not only affirmed the UCC's *Holodomor* discourse, but uncritically repeated its grossly inflated casualty numbers of over ten million famine deaths in the Ukrainian SSR in 1932–1933 (Himka 2015, p.157; see also Moore 2012). The Prime Minister received the OUN(b)'s revisionist historians, whereas Jason Kenney, his minister in charge of multiculturalism, visited the OUN(b)'s own Lonts'kyi Street Museum (*Tiurma na Lonts'koho*) in Lviv, Ukraine, reassuring the diaspora Nationalists back in Canada that he had paid proper tribute to 'the freedom fighters of the OUN' (Himka 2015, p.157). Aya Fujiwara (2015, p.211) cautions that

> [t]he Canadian Parliament has thus adopted the UCC's version of Ukrainian politics and history unquestionably as the most authoritative, notwithstanding its inclination towards far right political views, which hindered a balanced interpretation of the Ukrainian past.

Canada and the *Euromaidan*

Following the ouster of the corrupt Viktor Ianukovych (b. 1950, president 2010–2014) in a popular uprising in early 2014, Russia invaded Ukraine and illegally annexed parts of its territory. Ianukovych's successor,

Petro Poroshenko (president 2014–2019) resumed the glorification of the OUN and UPA. Parks and central thoroughfares in Kyiv were renamed after Bandera and Shukhevych, while 'disrespect' for 'fighters for Ukrainian statehood in the XX century' was criminalized. The Ukrainian army received new uniforms, modelled after the UPA, and adopted the OUN(b) salute. Predictably, also this round of instrumentalization of history led to protests, among other from the Jewish community, Israel, Poland, the EU, the United States Holocaust Museum, and several dozen members of the US Congress.[9]

During the 2014 crisis, the UCC further strengthened its position, all but monopolizing its position to speak on Ukrainian matters. The UCC 'was unofficially designated as a significant participant in Canadian diplomacy', and 'Paul Grod was invited to participate at every stage of Canada's action', Fujiwara notes (2015, p.210). Publicly and vigorously protesting Russia's actions, Harper adopted the diaspora's rhetoric, referring to Putin as 'evil', 'extremist', and 'imperialist', comparing him to Hitler. '[T]he government of Canada', Fujiwara argues, 'demonstrated that it would side with the UCC completely, embracing the latter's political and historical vision and incorporating UCC suggestions into its policies'. Throughout the Ukrainian crisis, 'both the UCC and Canada became active participants in the "propaganda war"' (ibid., pp.212–214). Subsequently, during his 2014 state visit to Canada, Poroshenko declared that Ukraine had 'no better friend' than Canada (Kordan 2019, p.5). In February 2015, the *Kyiv Post*, an English-language paper popular with the Ukrainian diaspora, ranked Harper among the top ten 'most influential promoters' of Ukraine in the international community, adding that 'perhaps Stephen Harper would not support Ukraine that actively if Canada did not have the world's largest diaspora community'(MacKinnon 2015).

Mykhailo Wynnyckyj, a Ukrainian Canadian diaspora political analyst, credits the diaspora community with bringing Ukraine to the attention of politicians in Ottawa. The Conservatives' support for the Ukrainian cause, he noted, has political consequences on a national scale:

> The gratitude of a community once seen as favouring the Liberal Party could tip key ridings in the Conservatives' favour, particularly in and around cities with large Ukrainian populations, such as Toronto and Winnipeg. (cited in MacKinnon 2015)

---

[9] On the Ukrainian memory laws, see Marples (2018); Israeli reactions, Sokol (2018).

Russia, which had vocally expressed its dissatisfaction with the positions of the Harper government, appears to have hoped for a new dynamic when the Liberal government of Justin Trudeau (b. 1971) took office in late 2015. At a press conference in Moscow on 26 January 2016, Russian foreign minister Sergei Lavrov criticized Canada for its stance on the conflict in Ukraine, in particular for having sided with 'rabid representatives of the Ukrainian diaspora', but expressed hopes that the relations may now improve. He was sharply rebuked by Stéphane Dion (b. 1955), the new Liberal foreign minister, reconfirming that the sway of the UCC would continue also under the new government. '[W]e will not tolerate from a Russian minister any insults against the community', Dion stated (cited in Kordan 2019, p. xiii). In response to inquiries from the media, Dion reconfirmed that 'The Ukrainian-Canadian community is a very important part of Canada's fabric. They are also experts on Ukraine. So it is natural – and beneficial for us – to consult them and take account of their views' (cited in Kordan 2019, p.151).

A similar assessment was made in the House of Commons by Liberal MP Kevin Lamoureux, who presented the work of UCC Executive Director Taras Zalusky and Paul Grod as

> excellent and wonderful ... in ensuring that whether a member or a leader of the Liberal Party [,] of the Conservative Party or the New Democratic Party, we are kept abreast of their point of view on what it actually taking place. (cited in Fujiwara 2015, p.210)

As Russia would learn, the support for the UCC's narration of history cut across the Canadian political landscape, from the Conservatives, through the Liberals, into the leftist New Democratic Party. Canadian foreign policy interests appeared conspicuously aligned with the UCC (Kordan 2019, p. xiii).

The Fascism of Others: Accusations of Nazism as Russian Foreign Policy Tool

In the 1980s, the depiction of the US and Canada as safe havens for war criminals became a staple of Soviet propaganda. Under Vladimir Putin, the legacy of the 'Great Patriotic War' has returned to the centre stage of official 'patriotic' discourse in the Russian Federation. Accusations of war criminality have similarly gained a greater prominence in Russian propaganda, as its relations with the West have deteriorated. Similarly, claims that the popular uprising against Ianukovych constituted a fascist coup became the *Leitmotif* of an intense Russian media campaign to legitimize the military aggression against Ukraine and the occupation of the Crimea (Fedor et al. 2015).

In a January 2017 reshuffle of his cabinet, Trudeau replaced Dion with the journalist Chrystia Freeland (b.1968) as Minister of Foreign Affairs. Raised in the Ukrainian community in Alberta, and with a background in the nationalist scouting organization *Plast*, Freeland works closely with the Ukrainian Canadian Congress, referring to Paul Grod as a 'friend' ('Khrystia Frilend' n.d.; Freeland 2014). Freeland appears to have become a particular irritant for the Russian government; almost immediately upon taking office, Russian-affiliated media venues portrayed her as a 'catastrophe for Canadian-Russian relations', 'a Russophobe, a hater of Putin, of Russian politics'('Ottawa's New Foreign Minister' 2017).

In an August 2016 tweet, Freeland made her own family history a public and political matter by introducing her maternal grandparents as refugees who 'worked hard to return freedom and democracy to Ukraine', adding that 'I am proud to honour their memory today' (Freeland 2016). Coming to terms with family histories of the Nazi era has often proven difficult, also in societies and communities where Holocaust awareness is a central feature of memory culture (Welzer et al. 2002). Freeland's public claims notwithstanding, her grandfather's democratic credentials are, at the very least, debatable. From 1940 to 1945, her grandfather, Mykhailo Khomiak (1905–1983) was the editor of the pro-Nazi collaborationist paper *Krakivs'ki visti* in Nazi-occupied Poland (Gyidel 2019; Markiewicz 2018). After immigrating to Canada with his family in 1948, Khomiak was active in various nationalist organizations, such as the Ukrainian War Veterans' Association in Edmonton—which played a key role in erecting the monument at St. Michael's Cemetery ('Chomiak Mychajlo' 1945; Bairak 1978, pp.147, 163). That Khomiak would end up at the centre of an international political controversy decades after his death was unexpected; he did not write anything of substance, and his private correspondence reflects a man of simple and rather pedestrian views (Gyidel 2019).

Khomiak's legacy initially became a topic of discussion on websites, blogs, and online newspapers, not least on the radical left or alternative right.[10] Soon, however, the story was picked up by mainstream media, increasingly turning into a political liability for the Trudeau government. At a press conference on 6 March 2017, Freeland dodged a direct question whether her grandfather collaborated with the Nazis, answering instead that Russia has sought to destabilize the US political system and that Canada should be prepared for the same ('Russia spreads disinformation…' 2017, quote at 5:10–5:45). An official in Freeland's office went further, denying outright that her grandfather would have been a Nazi collaborator, whereas Ralph Goodale, Minister of Public Safety, urged Canadian politicians to be alert to Russian disinformation tactics (Fife 2017).

Similar denials came from the Ukrainian community, with UCC President Grod dismissing claims originating with Russian venues as *a priori* false and 'outlandish' 'fake news' and 'disinformation' (Fife 2017).

In the *Ottawa Citizen,* Lubomyr Luciuk, a geographer at the Royal Military College in Kingston, Ontario, and a tireless promoter of the legacy of the OUN(b), UPA, and the Waffen-SS Galizien, wrote that *Krakivs'ki visti*'s 'editors had no affinity for Nazi aims but used their positions to sustain the Ukrainian resistance'. To Luciuk, not only was Khomiak's wartime past 'nothing to be ashamed of', but—quite the contrary, a source of pride (Luciuk 2017). To Canada's geopolitical adversaries, the scandal and the awkward damage control revealed a significant political potential of this undigested historical past.

Twitter Warfare

On 14 October 2017, Ukrainian Nationalists in Canada gathered for their annual commemorations of the (fictitious) 1942 foundation date of the UPA. The celebrations coincide with a Ukrainian Greek Catholic religious holiday and the anniversary of the martyrdom of Stepan Bandera at the hands of a KGB assassin on 15 October 1959. That day, the Russian embassy in Ottawa, through its official Twitter account, released its now-famous tweet, illustrated with three images: the Edmonton Shukhevych monument and the Oakville monuments to the 1UD UNA and the UPA ('Russia in Canada' 2017; Smith 2017; Sevunts 2018). The Russian Embassy tagged prominent Jewish organizations, such as the Centre for

---

[10] On the campaign, launched on *Russian Insider, Consortiumnews.com,* and *The New Cold War: Ukraine and Beyond,* see (Fife 2017).

Israel and Jewish Affairs (CIJA) and B'nai B'rith Canada. Kirill Kalinin, the Russian diplomat who managed the Twitter account, provided the following rationale for his actions:

> We wanted to let our followers on Twitter know that even today in Canada you can find monuments to Nazi collaborators that committed atrocities in the Soviet Union, Poland, etc. and fought against the heroic Red Army that was allied with Canada, U.S. and Britain during the Second World War. (Harvey 2017a)

Disbelief, Disavowal, Disinterest

To the surprise and disbelief of *The Oakville Beaver*, its sleepy suburban community suddenly found itself at the centre of an international political controversy:

> The Oakville monuments include a memorial to the Ukrainian Insurgent Army and one to the 1st Ukrainian Division. The Russian Embassy charges the latter was suspect as the 1st Ukrainian Division was created following the reformation of the 14th Waffen Grenadier Division of the SS. Both monuments have been in Oakville since the late 1980s. Neither structure features Nazi symbols and there is no reference to the SS on the memorial to the 1st Ukrainian Division. (Lea 2017)

Approached by national media, the manager, Oleg Bezpitko, appeared unprepared for the sudden interest in the cemetery. Queried by the *National Post*, Bezpitko was unable to say much about the background of the contentious monuments, other than that they were 'probably erected sometime during the 1980s, before he himself immigrated to Canada', the paper wrote. Bezpitko confirmed that several Waffen-SS men were buried in the cemetery, but added: 'Fighting on the German side doesn't mean to be a Nazi, right ...You have to understand, those were the people who were fighting communism'(cited in Smith 2017). This rather detached, matter-of-fact attitude is rather common among post-Soviet Ukrainian immigrants, many of whom are detached or disinterested in the post-World War II Galician émigrés' history and memory culture.

The largest image in the tweet, however, depicted the Shukhevych monument in Edmonton. This monument is more controversial, not only because of the far greater scope of the OUN-UPA atrocities, or because Poland, in July 2016, recognized the Volhynian massacres as genocide, but because it was set up with Canadian government funding. Contacted by the *National Post*, the Ukrainian Youth Unity complex in Edmonton reacted with defiance. Its spokesperson Taras Podilsky 'rejected any notions that Shukhevych may have been involved in war crimes', the paper reported.

> I have never heard ... about him being in any war crimes or anything we should be hiding ... He's completely seen as a hero, and respected to this day as a symbol of the fight for freedom. (Smith 2017)

Interviewed by the *Edmonton Examiner*, Ihor Broda, a leader of the Edmonton Banderites, laid out the Nationalist narration in some detail, arguing that one man's terrorist is another man's freedom fighter. He had learned about Shukhevych's fight for independence, he told the press, but 'the curriculum did not include the pogroms or controversies' (cited in Goldenberg 2017). Broda claimed that since the information flow was controlled by Nazis and Soviets, people 'did not know the Holocaust was happening', that Shukhevych's legacy 'is safe with those who understand his perspective' and that

> the people who knew him and what he was about, they support and admire him ... Others may not, the second and third generation people have drifted away. They say Nazis are bad, therefore he is bad. Most people are not that interested in getting into historical details. (ibid.)

Aidan Fishman, interim director of B'nai B'rith Canada's League for Human Rights, suggested that these monuments ought to give the Canadian public cause to pause and reflect upon history and memory. 'I think the question that Canadians really need to ask is, does the presence of these monuments in any way contribute to anti-Semitism, or to other forms of racism or bigotry in Canada today?' (cited in Smith 2017). To Fishman, the answer appeared to be 'no', since 'the intent of these monuments is not to stir up hatred or to glorify crimes against Jews'. While B'nai B'rith would not support any further such monuments, Fishman did not call for their removal.

> I think that the communities that have established these monuments, so namely the Ukrainian-Canadian community, should take a critical look at these facts and should remind themselves that many of these people were

engaged in collaboration with the Nazis ... And that may change the way that these people are portrayed and perceived in their own community. (ibid.)

To the *National Post*, Ihor Michalchyshyn, Executive Director and CEO of the Ukrainian Canadian Congress, communicated little interest in such introspection. On the contrary, he rejected outright 'any insinuation that Ukrainians collaborated with Nazi Germany during the Second World War', *National Post* reported.[11]

I think that the premise of calling them Nazi collaborators is slanderous. And our community honours our dead, and our veterans, and we're very disappointed that the story continues to be propagated in support of Russian disinformation ... I think the real story here is about the Russian Embassy and what they're trying to do to our community and how they're trying to create an issue where there isn't one. (Michalchyshyn, cited in Smith 2017)

Other UCC activists similarly dismissed Kalinin's comments as 'baseless and hav[ing] nothing to do with history'. Alexandra Chyczij, first vice-president of the UCC, dismissed the Russian claims as 'long-disproven fabrications'(Chyczij, cited in Lea 2017), whereas Lubomyr Luciuk accused the Russian embassy of provoking ethnic hatred in Canada. 'These Russian Twitterers should be reminded that the Criminal Code prohibits the public communication of statements likely to lead to a breach of the peace', he told the media (Luciuk, cited in Lea 2017).

The academic field of Ukrainian studies in Canada similarly showed little interest in the controversy. Jars Balan, interim director of the Canadian Institute of Ukrainian Studies, merely noted that Shukhevych's history is 'checkered', and that 'history in general is messy' (cited by Goldenberg 2017). He told the *Edmonton Examiner* 'I understand Shukhevych is a controversial figure, but people were not in the shoes of someone in World War II who had to make horrible decisions'. Shukhevych's legacy, Balan continued, is not an issue 'because of who brings it up', and that Russian propaganda seeks to divide the Ukrainian and Jewish communities.

[11] In a separate UCC communique to the Canadian Broadcasting Corporation, Ihor Michalchyshyn (2018) stated explicitly his claim that '[t]he veterans of the 14th Division Galicia/Halychyna joined not to fight for Germany, but to fight against Soviet Communist tyranny and for a free Ukraine'.

I don't think [the issue] is mainstream. A large part of [the] community does not lose sleep over it …The priority is to defend Ukraine and that is what they should rally around. This is all just a distraction. (ibid.)

There were, however, exceptions. Dominique Arel, the chair of Ukrainian Studies at the University of Ottawa—one of very few institutions willing to openly address these issues—noted: 'Unfortunately, the Ukrainian-Canadian organizations have not shown real readiness to discuss these issues… On the whole, there's a great deal of resistance'(cited in Smith 2017). Freeland's uncle, John-Paul Himka, a professor emeritus from the University of Alberta, was blunter:

It's about time that somebody paid attention to it … The fact is the Ukrainian government and the diaspora have been honouring Holocaust perpetrators and war criminals for a long time … You have enough corpses in the closet, it's going to start to smell. (cited in Smith 2017)

Canadian Government Reactions

The Canadian government agency tasked with handling this delicate matter appears to have been struggling to come up with an appropriate response. Documents obtained through the Access to Information Law show how the Russian tweet put the government officials in a rather difficult situation, as the Privy Council and the Prime Minister's Office requested them to counter the Russian claims about the monuments to Nazi collaborators. The initial reaction was to again dismiss the entire story as 'disinformation'. The first draft response accused Russia of 'destabilizing Western democracies', again without addressing the actual history of these Ukrainian units. Ultimately, Ursula Holland, Deputy Director for Global Affairs Canada, settled for dealing 'with the tweets as disinformation and irresponsible use of social media', arguing that 'Framing them as "destabilizing western democracies" seems a step too far' (Holland 2017). The final statement read that

Canada remains concerned by inappropriate Russian efforts to spread disinformation … [and] Canada expects all foreign representatives in Canada to act appropriately and responsibly, including their use in social media. (Harvey 2017b; Pugliese 2018a)

The reaction of the Privy Council was similar, stressing that this was hostile propaganda from an adversarial state, linking it to Canada's relatively high profile in the Ukrainian conflict. In April 2018, Canada expelled Kirill Kalinin and three other Russian diplomats from Canada. Justin Trudeau cited the campaign against Freeland, referring to it as 'efforts by Russian propagandists to discredit our minister of foreign affairs through social media and by sharing scurrilous stories about her' (Pugliese 2018b). The strategy to dodge the issue as disinformation was not very effective. On the contrary, the allegations and counter-allegations prompted the first serious discussions in mainstream media on the presence of these contentious monuments.

Conclusion

Russia is as unlikely a champion of transparency and critical inquiry as it is an awkward guardian of the memory of the Holocaust. In the Soviet Union, this memory was supressed, and the first Russian book referring to the Holocaust appeared as late as 1987. Key sites of Holocaust massacres in the Russian Federation remain neglected, and awareness is limited, not least relative to Canada (Karlsson 2013). Thus, the Russian regime's agenda was apparent enough: its alarmist messages served the political aim of discrediting an adversary by exposing and exploiting ill-conceived domestic policies. This is in line with how Russian propaganda campaigns have been conducted in recent years: rather than seeking to produce a positive image of Russia abroad, they aim at sawing doubt by focusing on shortcomings in Western political and medial cultures, thereby stimulating critical attitudes from within (Widholm 2016, p.218).

Russian propaganda reduces the complex legacy of the memory culture of the Ukrainian post-war immigration to Canada to a simplistic binary of 'Nazi' memorials, juxtaposed with the uncritical glorification of the 'heroic Red Army'. It has, however, been rather effective in putting the spotlight on some of the paradoxes of official Canadian multiculturalism, illustrating how these Canadian monuments to Shukhevych, UPA, and the Waffen-SS *Galizien* are physical manifestations of an undigested historical past. The Russian Embassy listed but a handful of these; it could easily have expanded the list with the Ukrainian War Veterans' memorial at St. Michael's Cemetery in Edmonton, the Stepan Bandera Ukrainian Black Sea Hall (*Ukrains'kyi Chornomors'ky Dim im. St. Bandery*) of St. Catharines, ON, and several other such edifices across Canada.

The presence of these monuments and community halls in Canada is neither 'fake news', nor 'disinformation'. Canadian normative multiculturalism serves as a vehicle for self-appointed community elites, facilitating access to government funds and top politicians. In underwriting multiple groups, committed to a variety of nationalist causes in ancestral homelands, it manifests itself as multi-nationalism, illustrated quite well by the Ukrainian case. The Russian Embassy identified a blind spot in Canadian historical memory, exploiting it to some effect against a geopolitical adversary. It placed the Canadian government in a difficult situation, exacerbated by its reliance on Ukrainian nationalist 'expertise' on matters of historical controversy. This episode reminds us how an undigested past can become a political liability (Colborne 2018).

Against the background of our significantly improved understanding of the legacy of Roman Shukhevych, the OUN(b), the UPA, and the Waffen-SS Galizien following the opening of the archives, it is increasingly clear that the heroic narratives of these groups would benefit from a proper *Aufarbeitung*, not only by professional historians, but also through open discussions in Canadian civic society. Media coverage in *The National Post*, CBC, and several local papers shows an increased interest in focusing on this complex set of issues. In 2018, the movie *A Monumental Secret* by Alberta filmmaker Adam Bentley sought to problematize the presence of these monuments in the form of a didactic conversation between two Edmontonians—one of whom believes the monuments ought to be torn down, the other wanting them amended (Bentley 2018). How to relate to this is ultimately a political question. As Canada is a democracy, the decision of how to allocate its tax revenues and what monuments should grace its public space is—of course—the prerogative of its citizens.

REFERENCES

Abousnnouga, G., & Machin, D. (2013). *The Language of War Monuments*. London: Bloomsbury.
Anderson, B. (1991). *Imagined Communities: Reflections on the Origin and Spread of Nationalism*. Revised Edition. London: Verso.
Bairak, M. (1978). *Ukrains'ka strilets'ka hromada v Edmontoni*. Edmonton: Ukrainian War Veterans' Association.
Bauhn, P. (1995). Normative Multiculturalism, Communal Goods, and Individual Rights. In P. Bauhn, C. Lindberg, & S. Lundberg (Eds.), *Multiculturalism and Nationhood in Canada* (pp. 85–100). Lund: Lund University Press.
Bentley, A. (2018). *A Monumental Secret – Screener Copy*. Edmonton, AB: Edmonton Arts Council and #YEGFILM. https://vimeo.com/321648828?fb

clid=IwAR0wN4tqf7PiJlNfGo0IGRon-hEhZgPgegl9J5TQvVwNCjKAq-SIq936dw6k. Accessed 5 Apr 2019.
Bessonova, M. (2018). Priorytety suchasnykh kanads'ko-ukrains'kykh vidnosyn. In H. O. Drobot (Ed.), *Ukraina-Kanada: Suchasni naukovi studii. Ukraine-Canada: Modern Scientific Studies. Knyha 1.Monohrafiia* (pp. 7–16). Lutsk: Vezha-Druk.
Burds, J. (2010). *Shpionazh i natsionalizm: Pervyi gody 'kholodnoi voiny' na Zapadnoi Ukraine (1944–1948)*. Moscow/New York: Sovremennaia Istoriia.
Cenotaphs: Monuments to Our Veterans. (2010, October 25). *CBC News*, https://www.cbc.ca/news/canada/cenotaphs-monuments-to-our-veterans-1.972283. Accessed 17 July 2019.
Chyczij, A. (2019, January 11). Thank You to Paul Grod, UCC President (2007-2018), *New Pathway/Novy Shliakh*, https://www.newpathway.ca/thank-you-to-paul-grod-ucc-president-2007-2018/. Accessed 12 Aug 2019.
Colborne, M. (2018, February 14). How a Canadian City Got Sucked Into Russia's Information War, *Coda*, https://codastory.com/disinformation/rewriting-history/how-a-canadian-city-got-sucked-into-russias-information-war/. Accessed 7 June 2019.
Fedor, J., Greene, S., Härtel A. and Makarychev A. (Eds.). 2015. Russian Media and the War in Ukraine, Special Issue of the *Journal of Soviet and Post-Soviet Politics and Societies*, 1(1).
Fife, R. (2017, March 6). Freeland Warns Canadians to Beware of Russian Disinformation, *Globe and Mail*, https://www.theglobeandmail.com/news/politics/freeland-warns-canadians-to-beware-of-russian-disinformation/article34227707/. Accessed 14 Aug 2019.
Freeland, C. (@cafreeland), Tweet of March 24, 2014., https://twitter.com/cafreeland?ref_src=twsrc%5Egoogle%7Ctwcamp%5Eserp%7Ctwgr%5Eauthor. Accessed 25 Sept 2019.
Freeland, C. (@cafreeland), Tweet of August 24, 2016. https://twitter.com/cafreeland?ref_src=twsrc%5Egoogle%7Ctwcamp%5Eserp%7Ctwgr%5Eauthor. Accessed 25 Sept 2019.
Fujiwara, A. (2007). From Anglo-Conformity to Multiculturalism: The Role of Scottish, Ukrainian, and Japanese Ethnicity in the Transformation of Canadian Identity, 1919–1971, Ph.D. dissertation, University of Alberta.
Fujiwara, A. (2015). Canada's Response to Euromaidan. In D. R. Marples & F. V. Mills (Eds.), *Ukraine's Euromaidan: Analyses of a Civil Revolution* (pp. 199–215). Stuttgart: Ibidem-Verlag.
Goldenberg, M. (2017, November 17). Critics Say Statue Immortalized Nazi Collaborator, *Edmonton Examiner*, http://www.edmontonexaminer.com/2017/11/14/critics-say-statue-immortalizes-nazi-corroborator. Link Accessed 18 Nov 2017 No Longer Active, but Screenshot Available at https://archive.ph/lJYXh, Accessed 6 Apr 2019.

Grod, P. (2013). President, Ukrainian Canadian Congress Community Townhall Meeting, Winnipeg, MB, 10 February, http://www.youtube.com/watch?feature=player_embedded&v=_zuP57u9lB0. Accessed 30 Mar 2013.

Gyidel, E. (2019). *The Ukrainian Legal Press of the General Government: The Case of Krakivski Visti, 1940–1944,* Ph.D. Dissertation, University of Alberta.

Himka, J.-P. (2015). The Lontsky Street Prison Memorial Museum: An Example of Post-Communist Holocaust Negationism. In K.-G. Karlsson, J. Stenfeldt, & U. Zander (Eds.), *Perspectives on the Entangled History of Communism and Nazism: A Comnaz Analysis* (pp. 137–166). Lanham: Lexington Books.

Himka, J.-P. (2017). Former Ukrainian Policemen in the Ukrainian National Insurgency: Continuing the Holocaust outside German Service. In W. Lower & L. Faulkner Rossi (Eds.), *Lessons and Legacies XII: New Directions in Holocaust Research and Education* (pp. 141–163). Evanston: Northwestern University Press.

Karlsson, K.-G. (2013). The Reception of the Holocaust in Russia: Silence, Conspiracy, and Glimpses of Light. In J.-P. Himka & J. B. Michlic (Eds.), *Bringing the Dark Past to Light: The Reception of the Holocaust in Postcommunist Europe* (pp. 487–515). Lincoln: University of Nebraska Press.

Katchanovski, I. (2019). The OUN, the UPA, and the Nazi Genocide in Ukraine. In P. Black, B. Rásky, & M. Windsperger (Eds.), *Mittäterschaft in Osteuropa im Zweiten Weltkrieg und im Holocaust* (pp. 67–93). Vienna: New Academic Press.

'Khrystia Frilend'. (n.d.). *Plast Kanada: Vydatni Plastuny,* https://www.plast.ca/seniory/vydatni-plastuny/freeland-khrystia.shtml. Accessed 13 Aug 2019.

Kordan, B. S. (2019). *Strategic Friends: Canada-Ukraine Relations from Independence to the Euromaidan.* Toronto: University of Toronto Press.

Kravchenko, V. (2019). The Canadian Institute of Ukrainian Studies: Foundations. *East/West: Journal of Ukrainian Studies,* VI(1), 9–49.

Lea, D. (2017, October 24). Russian Embassy Charges Monuments to Alleged 'Nazi Collaborators' in Oakville, *Oakville Beaver,* https://www.insidehalton.com/news-story/7681143-russian-embassy-charges-monuments-to-alleged-nazi-collaborators-in-oakville/. Accessed 27 July 2018.

Luciuk, L. (2017, March 9). Luciuk: Chrystia Freeland has Nothing to be Ashamed of About her Grandfather's 'Nazi' Ties, *Ottawa Citizen,* http://ottawacitizen.com/opinion/columnists/luciuk-chrystia-freeland-has-nothing-to-be-ashamed-of-about-her-grandfathers-nazi-ties. Accessed 10 Mar 2017.

MacKinnon, M. (2015, February 26). Bypassing Official Channels, Canada's Ukrainian Diaspora Finances and Fights a War Against Russia, *Globe and Mail,* https://www.theglobeandmail.com/news/world/ukraine-canadas-unofficial-war/article23208129/?utm_source=Shared+Article+Sent+to+User&utm_medium=E-mail:+Newsletters+/+E-Blasts+/+etc.&utm_campaign=Shared+Web+Article+Links. Accessed 31 July.

Margolian, H. (2000). *Unauthorized Entry: The Truth About Nazi War Criminals in Canada, 1946–1956*. Toronto: University of Toronto Press.

Markiewicz, P. (2018). *The Ukrainian Central Committee, 1940–1945: A Case of Collaboration in Nazi-Occupied Poland*, Ph.D. Dissertation, Uniwersytet Jagielloński. Kraków.

Markus, V. (1992). Political Parties in the DP Camps. In W. Isajiw, P. Boshyk, & R. Senkus (Eds.), *The Refugee Experience* (pp. 111–124). Edmonton: The Canadian Institute of Ukrainian Studies Press.

Marples, D. R. (2018). Decommunization, Memory Laws, and 'Builders of Ukraine in the 20th Century. *Acta Slavica Iaponica, 39*, 1–22.

Martynowych, O. T. (2011). Sympathy For the Devil: The Attitude of Ukrainian War Veterans in Canada to Nazi Germany and the Jews, 1933–1939. In R. L. Hinther & J. Mochoruk (Eds.), *Re-Imagining Ukrainian Canadians: History, Politics, and Identity* (pp. 173–220). Toronto: University of Toronto Press.

Michalchyshyn, I. (2018, February 28). Statement by the Ukrainian Canadian Congress, https://www.scribd.com/document/381364205/Statement-by-the-Ukrainian-Canadian-Congress. Accessed 17 Sept 2019.

Moore, R. (2012). 'A Crime Against Humanity Arguably Without Parallel in European History': Genocide and the 'Politics' of Victimhood in Western Narratives of the Ukrainian. *Holodomor, Australian Journal of Politics and History, 58*(3), 367–379.

Mozel, H. (1998, May 15). Cemetery Vandals Strike Again at St. Volodymyr, *The Oakville Beaver*, pp. 1, 5, here: p. 5.

'Ottawa's New Foreign Minister is Catastrophe for Canadian-Russian Relations, *Sputnik News*, January 14, 2017., https://sputniknews.com/europe/201701141049598262-freeland-canada-foreign-minister/. Accessed 25 Sept 2019.

'Paul Grod Named Among Top 80 Influencing Canadian Foreign Policy/Pavlo Grod nazvanyi sered 80-ty osib, iaki maiut' vplyv n zovnishniu polityku Kanady. *Konhres Ukraintsiv Kanady/Ukrainian Canadian Congress*, Press Release, 11 March 2013.

'Publications Assistance Program 2008–2009 Funding: Non-daily Newspaper', *Canadian Heritage/Patrimoine Canadien*, http://www.pch.gc.ca/pgm/pap/publctn/report-rapport/ann-rep2009/index-eng.cfm. Accessed 19 Nov 2010.

Pugliese, D. (2018a, May 17). Canadian Government Comes to the Defense of Nazi SS and Nazi Collaborators but Why?, *Ottawa Citizen*, https://ottawacitizen.com/news/national/defence-watch/canadian-government-comes-to-the-defence-of-nazi-ss-and-nazi-collaborators-but-why. Accessed 22 July 2018.

Pugliese, D. (2018b, April 6). Exclusive: Russian Diplomat Booted from Canada has Some Advise for Trudeau – It Won't Work, *National Post*, https://nationalpost.com/news/politics/russian-diplomat-calls-expulsions-over-remarks-un-canadian. Accessed 21 Jan 2020.

Rudling, P. A. (2011). Multiculturalism, Memory and Ritualization: Ukrainian Nationalist Monuments in Edmonton, Alberta. *Nationalities Papers*, *39*(5), 733–768.

'Russia in Canada@RussianEmbassyC'. The Official Twitter Account of the Embassy of the Russian Federation in Canada/Ofitsial'naia Tvitter stranitsa Posol'stva Rossiiskoi Federatsii v Kanade, 14 October 2017, 3:30 PM, https://twitter.com/RussianEmbassyC/status/919329715407736834/photo/1?ref_src=twsrc%5Etfw%7Ctwcamp%5Etweetembed%7Ctwterm%5E919329715407736834&ref_url=https%3A%2F%2Fnationalpost.com%2Fnews%2Fcanada%2Fukrainian-canadian-community-urged-to-confront-past-amid-controversy-over-monuments-to-nazi-collaborators. Accessed 19 July 2018.

'Russia Spreads Disinformation in Canada, United States & Europe', [Szuch, W.] Sign, UkeTube. 6 March 2017, quote at 5:10–5:45 https://www.youtube.com/watch?time_continue=262&v=1tvdGstGSTY. Accessed 19 Aug 2019.

Savaryn, P. (2007). *Z soboiu vzialy Ukrainu: Vid Ternopil'ia do Al'berty*. Kyiv: KVITs.

Sevunts, L. (2018, June 9). Canadian Monument to Controversial Ukrainian National Hero Ignites Debate, *RCI – Radio Canada International*, http://www.rcinet.ca/en/2018/06/09/shukhevych-monument-canada-oun-upa/. Accessed 19 July 2018.

Shane, K., & Foster, A. (2013, March 6). The Top 80 Influencing Canadian Foreign Policy, *Embassy Magazine*, http://www.embassynews.ca/top-80-influencers/2013/03/05/the-top-80-influencing-canadian-foreign-policy/43401. Accessed 30 July 2018.

Siemaszko, E. (2011). Stan badań nad ludobójstwem dokonanym na ludności polskiej przez Organizację Nacjonalistów Ukraińskich i Ukraińskich i Ukraińską Powstańczą Armię. In B. Paź (Ed.), *Prawda historyczna a prawda polityczna w badaniach naukowych* (pp. 319–344). Wrocław: Wydawnictwo uniwersytetu Wrocławskiego.

Sinclair, G. (1975, November 21). We'll Go 'Til Kingdom Come, Says Trudeau of Postal Strike, *Edmonton Journal*, pp. 1, 12.

Smith, M.-D. (2017, December 23). Ukrainian-Canadian Community Urged to Confront WWII Past Amid Controversy Over Monuments, *National Post*, https://nationalpost.com/news/canada/ukrainian-canadian-community-urged-to-confront-past-amid-controversy-over-monuments-to-nazi-collaborators. Accessed 19 July 2018.

Sokol, S. (2018). The Tension Between Historical Memory and Realpolitik in Israel's Foreign Policy. *Israel Journal of Foreign Affairs*, *12*(3), 311–324.

St. Michael's Cemetery. (n.d.). http://www.stmichaels-rosehill-cemetery.com/stmichaels-description.html. Accessed 31 July 2018.
St. Volodymyr's Ukrainian Cemetery. (n.d.). http://stvolodymyrcemetery.ca/About.aspx. Accessed 31 July 2018.
Struve, K. (2015). *Deutsche Herrschaft. Ukrainischer Nationalismus, antijüdische Gewalt: Der Simmer 1941 i der Westukraine*. Berlin: De Gruyter Oldenbourg.
Swyripa, F. (2010). *Storied Landscapes: Ethno-Religious Identity and the Canadian Prairies*. Winnipeg: University of Manitoba Press.
'Ukrainian Canadian Congress President Listed as Among Canada's Most Influential on Foreign Policy'. UCC Press Release, 28 March 2012.
Vakar, V. (Ed.). (1988). *Pam"iatnyk Slavy UPA: Propam"iatna knyha. Zvidomvlennia dilovoho komitetu na den' vidslovlennia i posviachennia 22-ho travnia 1988 r. na Oseli ,Kyiv', Okvyl, Ontario*. Toronto: The Basilian Press.
Vedeneev, D., & Ehorov, V. (Eds.). (1998). Mech i tryzub: Notatky od istorii sluzhby bezpeky orhanizatsii ukrains'kykh natsionalistiv. *Z arkhivi VUChK-GPU-NKVD-KGB*, 1/2(6/7), 368–389.
Wayland, S. V. (1997). Immigration, Multiculturalism and National Identity in Canada. *International Journal on Group Rights*, 5, 33–58.
Welzer, H., Moller, S., & Tschuggnall, K. (2002). *'Opa war kein Nazi': Nationalsozialismus und Holocaust im Familiengedächtnis*. Frankfurt: Fischer.
Widholm, A. (2016). Russia Today: En rysk röst i ett globalt medielandskap. In G. Nygren & J. Hök (Eds.), *Ukraina och informationskriget – journalistik mellan ideal och självcensur* (pp. 193–222). Karlstad: Myndigheten för samhällsskydd och beredskap.

ARCHIVAL SOURCES

LAC: Library and Archives Canada, Ottawa, Ontario.
'Petro Savaryn – Edmonton (1968, 1970, 1972–75),' Volodymyr Kubijovych Fonds, MG 31, D 203, Vol. 10, Folders 40 and 41.
Rodal, A. 'Rodal Report', prepared for the Commission of Inquiry on Nazi War Criminals in Canada (the Deschênes Commission), 1986. RG 33, Chapter XII, part 3.
Rosenberg, Alfred to Pavlo Shandruk, 12 March 1945, 'U.Ts.K. Newsletters (1940–1945).' Volodymyr Kubijovych Collection, MG 31 D 203, Vol. 18, Folder 8.
NARA: National Archives Records Administration, College Park, Maryland.
'Memorandum for the Record, Subject: CIA support of ZP/UHVR (Foreign Representation, Ukrainian Supreme Liberation Council)' [redacted], 2 August 1971, QRPLUMB, RG 263, Vol. 2, Box 59, NN3–263–02-008.

'Secret Memorandum for the Record, November 11, 1977. Major Ukrainian political organizations worldwide and in the United States. Date of Information 1971 to 1976' [redacted], QRPLUMB, vol. 1, RG 263, Vol. 2, Box 59, NN3-263-02-008.

PAA: Provincial Archives of Alberta, Edmonton, Alberta.
  Savaryn, Peter [Petro] and Olga Savaryn Family Fonds, accession no. PR2014.0451/0003, PR0671.0005, "Information and biographies," Box 1.

UAA: University of Alberta Archives, Edmonton, Alberta.
  Rudnyts'kyi, Ivan Lysiak to Ivan Kedryn Rudnyts'kyi, April 26, 1974, pp. 3–4., Ivan L. Rudnytsky Collection, 84–155, item 808.

USHMM: United States Holocaust Memorial Museum, Washington, DC.
  'Chomiak Mychajlo A.E.F. D.P. Registration Record', DP2 Card, October 28, 1945, in Central Name Index, International Tracing Service collection, 0.1, document no. 66787646.

Internal Correspondence, Global Affairs, Canada, obtained through the Access to Information Act.

Harvey, B. (2017a). URGENT OMINA REQUEST: Proactive lines – Russia tweets about 'Nazi' monuments in Canada amid ongoing concerns over political interference, 26 October. Internal correspondence, document A05502103_4-00020. (Processed under the provisions of the Access to Information Act, A201701850_2018-02-20_08-47-11.PDF).

Harvey, B. (2017b). LCFB to Catherine Fleming, IOL, 26 October, Subject: RE: URGENT OMINA REQUEST: Proactive lines – Russia tweets about 'Nazi' monuments in Canada amid ongoing concerns over political interference. (Processed under the provisions of the Access to Information Act, A0502103_1-00017, A201701850_2018-02-20_08-47-11.PDF).

Holland, Ursula. ECE, to Barbara Harvey, LCFB et al. October 26, 2017, Subject: RE: URGENT OMINA REQUEST: Proactive lines – Russia tweets about 'Nazi' monuments in Canada amid ongoing concerns over political interference." Processed under the provisions of the Access to Information Act, A0502103_1-00018, A201701850_2018-02-20_08-47-11.PDF http://uyuc.ca. Accessed 19 Nov 2018.

CHAPTER 5

Political and Social Contestation in the Memorialization of 'Comfort Women'

Mary M. McCarthy

INTRODUCTION

Memorialization, in its many forms, is integral in identity formation (Fortier 2000). It is a tool to achieve that end and a manifestation of identity. It provides a narrative that can be passed down through the generations of what a community is, what ties it together, and how it should remember its history. This is through showcasing a common past, often of struggles and overcoming those challenges together. This is true in nation building but also in the building of identity among members of an immigrant group or a diaspora more transnationally. Hoffman (2000, p. 1) describes how traumatic historical events, in particular, can become 'defining episodes whose "memory" is called upon as a guarantee of group identity and, often, its moral status'.

My thanks to the editor of this volume, an anonymous peer reviewer, and Dr Linda C. Hasunuma for their comments on previous drafts of this chapter.

M. M. McCarthy (✉)
Drake University, Des Moines, IA, USA
e-mail: mary.mccarthy@drake.edu

In order to pass these narratives down from generation to generation and, in the case of minority groups, from the communal level to the larger society, communities seek to institutionalize memory through physical markers, such as monuments. One may consider three objectives in this. First, to create or reinforce a cohesive group identity, as immigrants from a single nation may actually be quite distinct from one another (socioeconomically, religiously, ethnically, regionally) and may not have regarded themselves as sharing a common identity in the home country. In the host country, creation of a single collective may become socially, politically, economically, and, even, psychologically useful. Second, as memory transcends group memory to become part of the larger public memory of the host society as a whole, the acceptance of minority memory by the majority symbolizes the group becoming part of that larger society. Therefore, collective memory creation and recognition is part of a process of belonging at both the level of the group and the whole. Third, inserting one's communal narrative into public memory is a counter to the hegemonic power of the majority and a rejection of marginalization. It is an assertion of self and group, of pride of culture and ethnicity, within the larger whole of the host society.

Contestation may occur throughout this process, through intragroup, intergroup, and host society–group interactions. In a multicultural settler nation, where migrants bring collective memories of a past that might be integral to home country national identity, such contestations may take on particular characteristics that create intergroup tensions even as they solidify intragroup identity, and that reify the position of the host society as mediator. This is due to the fact that trauma, as described by Hoffman, often entails the existence of both victim and perpetrator. In the case of a host society, particularly one that is multicultural and diverse, immigrant groups representing both sides might be present. Therefore, an assertion of victimization and enshrining of one's higher moral status due to that experience may come into conflict with the perceived perpetrator's differing recollection of the event or rejection of that episode as one appropriate to become part of the public memory of the host society. Thus, public memorialization that may guarantee one group's identity may be seen as an attack on another group's identity. This may go so far as being seen as a means, intentional or not, to alienate the latter from fully being part of the host society.[1] Such intergroup contestation further reinforces the hegemonic power of the host

---

[1] For a discussion of contestation over collective memory and public history, see, for example, Halbwachs (1992) and Wood (2014).

society as arbiter. However, it may also undermine some of the host society's nation building or other goals, as it becomes a battleground for competing historical narratives that migrants bring from their home countries.

Contested memorialization is simultaneously a social and political process. As mentioned in the Introduction, memorials represent one simplified version of an historical event. Scholarly accounts are more complex and often blur lines between victim and perpetrator, or complicate categorization as such, as a reflection of the historical reality. Advocates of a memorial seek to simplify for the purpose of displaying a concise and predetermined message to the audience. This often exacerbates contestation because it creates a dichotomy of good and evil, or moral and immoral, in a history of trauma and tragedy. The *Holodomor* memorial in Washington, DC, described in the Introduction to this volume represents the 1930s' Ukrainian famine as a Soviet-orchestrated genocide. The role of the Soviet Union in this massive loss of life, as well as whether it constitutes genocide under international law, is debated among historians but a 'fact' in the collective memory of many in the Ukrainian diaspora (Moore 2012). The significance here is not only the content of the memorial but that it was erected by the US National Park Service (and the Ukrainian government) in the US capital, so symbolic of the host society taking sides.[2] Contestation must be negotiated in the context of the hegemonic power of the host society, as the arbiter of contested public memory. Public memorialization is an exercise of power, both power of the host society and power of the group whose version of the narrative becomes institutionalized in that society.

THE CASE OF THE COMFORT WOMEN, THE KOREAN DIASPORA, AND AREAS FOR CONTESTATION

Over time, the Korean diaspora has solidified its identity through collective memories of its relationship vis-a-vis its former colonial power, Japan, and the perpetuation of a related moral narrative.[3] 'Most Koreans have family memories or stories of the colonial era from their parents and

---

[2] For a description from the Embassy of Ukraine in the United States of America of the commemoration, see https://usa.mfa.gov.ua/en/press-center/photos/1563-u-vashingtoni-bula-vstanovlena-skulyptura-pamjatnika-zhertvam-golodomoru-1932-1933-rokiv-v-ukrajini and for an overview of the erection process from the National Park Service, see https://parkplanning.nps.gov/projectHome.cfm?projectID=39537 (Accessed August 18, 2019).

[3] For explorations of the Korean diaspora working towards independence from the Japanese colonial power, see, for example, Watanabe (1999), Lien (2001), and Chang (2016).

grandparents. Learning of their past, where they come from, and their parents and grandparents' experiences means understanding Korea was under colonial rule' (Hasunuma and McCarthy 2019, p. 149). The Korean American populace has further asserted its collective power in lobbying US national and local government bodies for institutionalization of its group memories, including those related to Japan and experiences of colonization, as public memory.[4]

In this chapter, the Korean diaspora's assertion of recognition as a group comes in the form of memorials commemorating the tragic lives of the 'comfort women',[5] a euphemism for those women and girls held in sexual servitude to the Japanese imperial armed forces during the 1930s and 1940s (Soh 2008; Yoshimi 2002).[6] Although Koreans have raised many points of injustice that occurred during the period of Japanese colonization, for which they would like to see redress and restitution, the issue of the comfort women is one that has taken on particular strength globally. This is in part due to the rise, internationally, in the notion of women's rights as human rights and greater acknowledgement of the particular vulnerabilities facing women and girls in conflict-ridden areas (McCarthy 2018).

Since the 1990s, the Korean diaspora has been active in spreading awareness of the comfort women in Europe, North America, Australia, Japan, and elsewhere, as well as at the United Nations. The movement in the United States has seen particular achievement, in the form of the successful erection of memorials commemorating the tragedy of these women's lives and this 'comfort system' of trafficking and enslavement. Nine

---

[4] A further example is the use of the term East Sea (preferred by Korea) versus Sea of Japan (preferred by Japan). The Sea of Japan is used by the US Department of State, but the state of Virginia voted in 2014 to have all new school textbooks use both names. This was seen as a victory for Korean Americans, of whom there were 82,000 living in Virginia at the time (Robertson 2014).

[5] 'Comfort women' is in quotation marks to indicate that this is a controversial term. I use it as it is the most widely accepted term for these women but utilize the quotation marks in this first mention of the term to acknowledge the controversy. See McCarthy and Kumagai (2019).

[6] Although not all victims of the comfort women system were Korean, historians suggest that the majority were, and Koreans have been at the forefront of the movement for historical justice.

comfort women memorials have been erected on public land in the United States since 2010.[7]

Whereas the erection of these memorials is viewed by the Korean American population, and some in the wider Asian American community, as a great accomplishment and an indicator of recognition and justice, these same memorials are seen by some among the Japanese diaspora, Japanese American immigrants, and Japanese nationals as an attack on their Japanese identity. Thus, we have seen a concerted push back on the erection of these memorials and the historical narrative that they seek to tell. We have also witnessed cleavages within these groups, due to historical and ideological intragroup differences.

Furthermore, this memorialization is in the context of a United States that has hegemonic power not only in terms of ethnic groups residing in the United States, but in terms of many global political post-war dynamics that resulted in the evolution of the comfort women issue. For example, the United States chose not to include the comfort women in the main post-WWII war crimes tribunal in Tokyo, although there were crimes related to sex slavery brought against Japanese officials in the smaller war crimes tribunal in Indochina (McCarthy 2018). In addition, the United States played a large role in the decolonization process on the Korean peninsula and post-war Japan–Korea relations, arguably delaying the resolution of some issues related to the colonial period (Watt 2015).

In this chapter, I look at the process of contestation (as well as collaboration) among elements of the two migrant groups, Korean Americans and Japanese Americans, and what role the host society plays as arbiter in negotiating between each group's claims to the historical narrative through political contests. I emphasize 'the importance of memory as a category of political science' (Shaery-Eisenlohr 2007, p. 272) and explore the intersection between memory studies and diaspora politics, using the theories of such to illustrate how memory works 'both as a form of continuity with the homeland and as a method of claims-staking for minority groups in multicultural spaces' (Alexander 2013, p. 590). I argue that the comfort women movement in the United States has gone through three phases, starting with little contestation, on to significant contestation with successful use of the contestation as a tool to promote the movement objectives, and then to more broad-based contestation with successes for the

---

[7] There are additional memorials on private property, but I am interested in the memorials on public land because of the different nature of contestation before a host society.

countermovement. I explain these later achievements for the countermovement through enhanced political savviness in the context of US political culture.

My research utilizes a qualitative case-study methodology and is based on extensive field research pursued since 2014. I conducted over five dozen interviews with activists, scholars, government officials, and other relevant political and social actors, in the United States, Japan, and South Korea, and visited the memorial sites in California, New Jersey, New York, Virginia, and Seoul. I have engaged with the multifaceted aspects of the issues across politics, diplomacy, activism, and community organizing while integrating analyses from multiple disciplines into a political science treatment of my cases.

THE EVOLUTION OF JAPANESE AMERICAN AND KOREAN AMERICAN COMMUNITIES IN THE UNITED STATES

Contestation between Korean Americans and Japanese Americans, as well as within the Japanese American community itself,[8] has its roots in connections with the homeland and its dominant public memories, along with different experiences of immigration and integration. Japanese immigrants were some of the first Asians to come to the United States and were the second largest group of such migrants, after the Chinese, during the late nineteenth and early twentieth centuries (Lee 2015, p. 109). Most of the Japanese came during this era as labourers and, later, as family members. In 1894, the US government signed a bilateral treaty with Japan, guaranteeing the right to immigration and the provision of citizenship-level rights to those migrants (Japanese-American Relations at the Turn of the Century 1900–1922). Discrimination in the United States, illustrated most prominently by the San Francisco Board of Education segregation policy, led to the Gentleman's Agreement, a bilateral deal that curbed labour-based immigration from Japan to the continental United States, while allowing family-based immigration to continue. This Agreement ended with the Immigration Act of 1924, which formally barred all immigration from Asia (The Immigration Act of 1924 (The Johnson-Reed

---

[8] This is not to suggest that intragroup contestation does not exist within the Korean American community as well (Chang 2016, p. 336), but there has been general consensus within the community on seeking historical justice for the comfort women since the mid-2000s.

Act)). Due to these restrictions on immigration, by 1940, 63% of people with Japanese ancestry living in the continental United States were Nisei, second-generation Japanese Americans born in the country (Lee 2015, p. 119).

Despite the purported guarantees of citizenship, in 1942, after the US entry into the war, Executive Order 9066 led to the mass incarceration of over 120,000 Japanese Americans in internment camps. More than 70% of those interned 'were American citizens, born in the United States' (Reeves 2015, pp. xv–xvi). As Kathy Masaoka of Nikkei for Civil Rights and Redress describes, 'Nisei thought they were Americans and felt betrayed' by the internment.[9]

Camp altered the lives of the internees forever. 'One government estimate was the West Coast Japanese and Japanese Americans lost 75% of their assets. The official government figure, calculated in 1982 and reported in *The Wartime Handling of Evacuee Property*, was that evacuee losses amounted to at least $250 million in real, commercial, and personal property, or approximately $3 billion 2013 dollars' (Reeves 2015, p. 258). After the war ended, serious incidents of discrimination continued and the US government encouraged Japanese Americans to relocate throughout the United States rather than return to the West Coast. For both of these reasons, the percentage of Japanese and Japanese Americans in California dropped from 88% before the war to 70% after the war (Reeves 2015, p. 258). The wartime internment broke up families and communities, some permanently. In turn, Japanese Americans 'tried to follow the instructions they had been given [by the US government] to "assimilate", "blend in", and "don't make waves"' (Lee 2015, p. 247).

The civil rights movement of the 1960s influenced young Japanese Americans, some of whom were born in the internment camps, to demand justice. The Japanese American Citizens League (JACL), the National Coalition for Redress/Reparations (NCRR) (later renamed Nikkei for Civil Rights and Redress, with the same acronym), and the National Council for Japanese American Redress (NCJAR) sought government apology and reparations (Niiya 2020; Wood 2014; Lee 2015, p. 311). Success was achieved with the Civil Liberties Act of 1988, signed by President Ronald Reagan, which provided individual compensation and federally funded public educational programmes about the internment (Wood 2014, p. 351; Reeves 2015, p. 276).

[9] Author's interview. June 8, 2015.

During this same period, the 1965 Immigration and Nationality Act ended preferential treatment for Western Europeans in US immigration policy. The Act 'liberalized the nation's immigration policy and ushered in new generations of immigrants from throughout Asia, many of whom had no connection to pre-World War II communities' (Lee 2015, p. 283). This led the composition of the Asian American community to change dramatically. Japanese Americans went from being 50% of the total Asian American population in 1960 to only 7% by 2010, reflecting both low immigration from Japan since 1924 and increases in immigration from other parts of Asia (Lee 2015, p. 287). This means that not only did Japanese Americans become a smaller population among Asian Americans, but those Japanese Americans whose families arrived pre-1924 and those who arrived post-1965 had distinct experiences in terms of their connections to Japan and their history in the United States. While internment and redress defined the Japanese American experience for many whose families were pre-1924 immigrants, these experiences had no role in the formation of post-1965 immigrants and their families.

The Korean experience was different. The Japanese empire held Korea as a protectorate from 1905 and formally annexed the peninsula in 1910. Although some emigration to the United States initially was allowed during this period, the Japanese government eventually banned it 'in order to prevent Koreans from competing with Japanese labourers already in Hawai'i and to keep an ample supply of Koreans at home to support Japanese expansionist projects' (Lee 2015, p. 138). For this reason, Koreans and Korean Americans living in the United States numbered a mere 8000 in 1924, compared to 72,000 Japanese (Park 2013, p. 181). In 1940, the US Census counted fewer than 2000 Koreans outside of Hawai'i, which became a state in 1959 after 50 years as a US territory (Park 2013, p. 177).

In 1960, Koreans were only 1.5% of the Asian population in the United States (Lien 2001, p. 44), but the 1965 Immigration and Nationality Act ushered in new opportunities for potential migrants from Asia. Ninety-five per cent of migration from South Korea to the United States began after its passage (Min 2013). Koreans and Korean Americans residing in the United States rose from 70,598 in 1970 to almost 800,000 in 1990 and 1.26 million in 2010, according to the US Census. Of this 2010 population, almost 80% were foreign born and 67% US citizens (Lee 2015, p. 299). Today the Korean American population is estimated at almost two million, making it the fifth largest Asian ethnic group (*Korea Matters for America/America Matters for Korea*). At about 1.4 million, the

Japanese American population is the sixth largest (*Japan Matters for America/America Matters for Japan*). According to US government figures (in analyses conducted 2008–2013), 40% of Japanese Americans were foreign born (half the percentage estimated for Korean Americans) and 72% US citizens (Who are Japanese Americans?).

Although all ethnic populations are heterogeneous in a diversity of ways, the differing opportunities for migration, as well as the restrictions on migration imposed by the US and Japanese governments, have produced some distinctive differences between Korean and Japanese American communities, as well as within the population of Japanese Americans. This has created varied relationships with the homeland and its historical narratives.

DIASPORA, IMMIGRANTS, AND COLLECTIVE MEMORY

Davidson and Kuah-Pearce (2008, p. 1) define diasporic communities 'as a conceptual category of community that is formed through the interplay of memories and identities'. Alexander (2013) explores how history and memory from the country both of origin and of arrival combine to constitute 'diaspora consciousness'. As described above, this consciousness creates identity, community, and belonging through an institutionalization of collective memory that ties together homeland and hostland (Halbwachs 1992). It is about the diaspora's present and future as much as it is about the past (Hall 1990).

Davidson and Kuah-Pearce further emphasize that diasporic narratives are not static or homogeneous, and Alexander describes the ritualization of diasporic memory as a dialogue. Collective memories themselves are the target and outcome of contestation (Wood 2014, p. 348). As Savage explains, 'collective memory is a product of social groups and their ever evolving character and interests; [thus] collective memory is "constructed", amidst a perpetual political battleground'.

Diaspora politics are about assertions of identity, community, needs, interests, and belonging, in the context of a host society's political system. The politics of memory involves power plays about whose narrative becomes dominant in a society, where each narrative is similarly seen as integral to one's being. Therefore, intragroup, intergroup, and group-host society conflicts are common.[10]

---

[10] Intergroup refers to conflicts between different diasporic and other identity groups within the host society.

What constitutes a 'group' is also a matter for debate. Fortier (2000) explores the differences between diaspora and immigrants, reflecting on Clifford's (1994) understanding of the latter as temporary, in the process of integration into a host society, and the former as maintaining ties with the homeland. This highlights one of many varied types of differences that may exist among members of an ethnic group residing in the same country. For Japanese Americans, one common distinction is between those who emigrated to the United States pre-1945 and post-1965. Positions taken on the comfort women issue may elucidate existing cleavages stemming from divergent experiences in the host country and disparate connections with the home country.

However, while recognition of the historical differences based on the period of emigration is important, Fujino's (2018, p. 268) analysis might be most useful as she 'frames Japanese American history not within the paradigm of ethnic assimilation and its mode of linear progress, but rather within a multiplicity of ideas, politics, and practices centred on critiques of empire'. This is the theoretical model that can most effectively explain the unified stance of Japanese American organizations led by Nisei (e.g. Nikkei for Civil Rights and Redress) along with those in which Japan-born immigrants are active (e.g. US–Japan Feminist Network for Decolonization), with the dominant Korean American position. In this way, commonality and coalition are formed through principles and ideas as much as through experience.

Thus, memory politics and diaspora politics interact to create coalitions that seek to perpetuate a historical narrative, institutionalized through memorials, that serves their needs and identity. Competing narratives put groups into conflict with one another. Both seek recognition by the host society through the formal institutions of power, through either the erection or rejection of a memorial in a public place.

The Introduction of Comfort Women Memorials in the United States

There are nine comfort women memorials in the United States on public land: in California, Georgia, New Jersey, New York, and Virginia. They were spearheaded by Korean Americans seeking to have a historical period of importance to their community publicly recognized, and to follow up on one of their first examples of national legislative success as a community, the passage of House Resolution 121. In 2007, after years of lobbying and debate, the US House of Representatives passed H.Res. 121, calling on Japan to acknowledge and apologize for the use of comfort women in the 1930s and 1940s. The US House of Representatives passed this resolution after the reframing of the debate from a bilateral (Japan–Korea), historical issue to a universal human rights and women's rights issue, with Japanese American Representative Mike Honda as the political face of the resolution. Yet, to the disappointment of some in the Korean American community, the resolution did not lead to any change in the Japanese government's position that all wartime and colonial grievances had been resolved through the San Francisco Peace Treaty and the 1965 bilateral agreement with South Korea.[11] Thus, the time was ripe for a second initiative in the movement for historical justice for the comfort women.

In 2010 the first comfort women memorial was erected in the United States. The Korean American community chose to pursue a memorial in the context of seeing other migrant communities achieve such recognition. The 'circle of freedom' outside the Bergen County Courthouse in Hackensack, New Jersey, with memorials dedicated to the Irish famine, the Armenian genocide, and the Atlantic slave trade, became a model for what they sought to achieve. Groups who migrated to the United States (including through forced migration) established themselves as communities whose histories (particularly traumatic historical events) should be publicly recognized by the host society, whether or not the host society played a role in the trauma.

As recognition by the host society was a core goal of this movement, the emphasis among advocates of comfort women memorials has been erection on public land. As Leung (2008, p. 182) describes, 'While it is logical and commonly practiced to focus on what and how migrants remember and forget in their negotiation of a sense of home in migrancy, the host society also controls the space available to the newcomers in claiming home'. In other words, the host society has rules about where and how you can erect a memorial, how it can look and what it can (and cannot) say, and, ultimately, about whether or not it will be erected at all. For each locale, the rules may differ. For example, in Virginia, the Fairfax County Chairman has control over supporting or denying a request for a memorial as a Point of Privilege. In 2014, Fairfax County Chairperson

[11] Author's interviews.

Sharon Bulova decided to offer the Comfort Women Memorial Peace Garden Committee a spot on the grounds of the County Government Center, after having been lobbied for a memorial in the local Koreatown. In San Francisco, on the other hand, there were over a dozen public hearings in addition to a vote by the city's Board of Supervisors before the memorial was unveiled.

When Chejin Park, an attorney at Korean American Civic Empowerment (KACE), based in Hackensack, New Jersey, first imagined the idea of a memorial to the comfort women in the 'circle of freedom', he reached out to the African American community that had been instrumental in securing the memorial to the Atlantic slave trade there. KACE followed the same procedures of gathering signatures, fundraising, and contacting local politicians, and was rewarded with the offer of a memorial in Palisades Park, a nearby town in Bergen County that is over 50% Korean American.[12] Phyllis Kim, Executive Director of the Korean American Forum of California (KAFC), recalled that 'KACE surprised all of us by installing a small comfort women memorial in Palisades Park. When we saw that we thought we should do the same in California. Some of us went to see how they did it, to learn from them. We formed KAFC at that time'.[13]

What drove both Park and Kim was a desire to assert community identity, needs, interests, and belonging. Although the memory was from the homeland, the assertion of all these things was in the hostland. As Kim stated in an interview with the author:

> We bring our history and culture here when we come here … Bringing this issue into the light and recognition of the American public and to be able to teach this part of history to the children in the US, is hugely important and teaching this history itself is a huge contribution to enrich our understanding of what happened in World War II … It's something we can do as Korean Americans, to contribute to the US and to the larger global community because there are still atrocities against women going on to this day.

This is what Kuah-Pearce (2008, p. 122) describes as 'transforming collective memories into diasporic community capital', which can 'contribute to the well-being of the diasporic community and the host society in general'. The community uses group memories to create a common good.

---

[12] Author's interview, April 21, 2015. Although they were initially denied their request to erect a memorial in the 'circle of freedom' in Hackensack, under new county leadership, they were able to achieve that goal as well, in 2013.

[13] Author's interview, August 8, 2017.

Grace Han Wolf, member of the Herndon Town Council in Virginia and honorary co-chair of the Comfort Women Memorial Peace Garden Committee (Fairfax County, Virginia), has emphasized the establishment of these memorials as evidence of the 'increasing influence of Korean Americans, and ability to leverage that block'.[14] McCarthy and Hasunuma (2018), however, have found that to achieve sought ends, universal messaging (women's rights, human rights, tragedies of war) and coalition building beyond one specific ethnic group were paramount. Advocates had to appeal to universal values and dismiss any argument that this was a Japan–Korea bilateral issue or purely historical matter. Instead, concrete connections needed to be made to the particular vulnerabilities that women and girls in conflict areas face to the current day, as well as evolving norms of protection, prevention, and prosecution (as seen in the Women, Peace and Security framework of the United Nations).[15] In addition, coalitions had to be built beyond the Korean American community. These coalitions included politicians, of course, but also members of the Jewish American community, the African American community, the Armenian American community, and the larger Asian American community. The common ties among these communities on issues of human rights and civil rights were emphasized.

The San Francisco memorial was a testament to pan-Asian coalition building. Although 38% of San Francisco is Asian American, Koreans only constitute a small proportion of that. Chinese Americans are the largest Asian American group in San Francisco, followed by Filipino Americans.[16] Chinese Americans, working closely with Korean Americans, were at the forefront of building a memorial in San Francisco (McCarthy and Hasunuma 2018). Unveiled in St. Mary's Square, in San Francisco's Chinatown, Fig. 5.1 displays three young women, from China, the Philippines, and Korea, respectively, whose hands are joined in a 'column of strength' and are being looked upon by a statue of Hak-sun Kim, who was the first comfort women survivor to come forward publicly.

In fact, multicultural coalitions existed in each instance of success for the comfort women movement in the United States. KACE and the

---

[14] Author's interview, July 22, 2014.
[15] In 2000, UN Security Council Resolution 1325 was passed on the basis of this agenda, and in 2017, the Women, Peace, and Security Act became law in the United States.
[16] Asia Matters for America, The East-West Center. Retrieved July 15, 2018, from https://asiamattersforamerica.org/state-district

Fig. 5.1 Column of Strength in San Francisco, California, erected 2017. (Source: Author, February 28, 2019)

Harriet and Kenneth Kupferberg Holocaust Resource Center and Archives at Queensborough Community College were jointly recognized for their work on the comfort women through a New York State Senate Resolution in 2013, on the basis of collaboration on an ongoing comfort women oral history internship course, exhibits, and other public events (Hasunuma and McCarthy 2019). This honour is commemorated on a monument at Eisenhower State Park that lists both organizations, along with the Korean

American Public Affairs Committee, and is placed next to a memorial dedicated to the comfort women that was erected in 2012. Although coalition building has its challenges, in the end, common experiences of oppression and injustice tended to expand the coalition in support of the comfort women movement. For example, Reverend Amos C. Brown, African American pastor and civil rights activist in San Francisco:

> revealed that he had been concerned by the arguments made by the opposition [to the San Francisco memorial] but, after hearing Grandma Lee [a former comfort woman who had come to a hearing to testify], he recognized the parallels between the narratives being espoused by the opposition and deniers of African American slavery. This moved him to become a supporter of the memorial. (McCarthy and Hasunuma 2018, p. 12)

This was true for elements of the Japanese American community as well, which is itself divided on the comfort women issue. As mentioned, Representative Mike Honda, who is Japanese American, was a main sponsor of H.Res. 121 and has actively championed comfort women memorials throughout the country. Nikkei for Civil Rights and Redress (NCRR), the Japan-US Feminist Network for Decolonization (FeND), and the Japanese American Bar Association are three examples of Japanese American groups that are also vocal supporters of the comfort women memorials. Kathy Masaoka, of NCRR, speaking directly of the Japanese American internment experience declared that 'We have a responsibility as Japanese Americans to support others who have gone through similar things'.[17] FeND, whose founders are 'individuals living in the US who have roots in Japan',[18] has been a staunch supporter based on their anticolonial principles. The Japanese American Citizens League (JACL) has taken different positions, depending on the chapter. While JACL supported the Glendale memorial in southern California, its San Francisco chapter came out against the memorial in that city (Koyama 2015; Sabatini 2015). The US-based Global Alliance for Historical Truth (GAHT), led by first-generation Japanese Americans and Japanese nationals, has vigorously campaigned against the memorials.

---

[17] Author's interview, June 8, 2015.
[18] Retrieved August 18, 2019, from http://fendnow.org/about/

THREE PERIODS OF CONTESTATION

Between 2010 and 2014, six memorials to the comfort women were erected in the United States on public land. Then in 2017, the above-mentioned and most high-profile memorial was unveiled, as it was in a major city, San Francisco. However, 2010–2019 actually constitutes three different periods in the comfort women memorial movement in the United States, as it relates to contestation. The first period is 2010–2012, when a single memorial existed in an arguably obscure location outside the public library in Palisades Park, New Jersey. The second period is 2012–2014, when contestation began in earnest but was met with the proliferation of memorials on public land as the host society supported the Korean American narrative. The third period is 2015–2019, when the counternarrative began to receive increased support from the host society and there began to be greater recognition of the historical narrative as disputed. These three periods do not have neat beginnings and endings without overlap, but they do indicate general trends with regard to the dynamics surrounding comfort women memorials in the United States (Table 5.1).

Table 5.1 Comfort women memorials on public land in the United States (as of July 2019)

Stage of contestation	Location	Year unveiled
First (Limited Contestation)	Palisades Park, NJ	2010
	Eisenhower Park, NY	2012
Second (Significant Contestation with Movement Momentum)	Bergen County Courthouse, NJ	2013
	Glendale, CA	2013
	Buena Park, CA	No memorial
	Union City, NJ	2014
	Fairfax County, VA	2014
	Fullerton, CA	No memorial
	Southfield, MI[a]	Private memorial
Third (Broad-based Contestation with Countermovement Success)	San Francisco, CA	2017
	Atlanta, GA[b]	No memorial
	Brookhaven, GA	2017
	Fort Lee, NJ	2018

[a]A private memorial was erected after failure to build support for a memorial on public land

[b]The memorial proposed in Atlanta was not on public land, but the public nature of the Center for Civil and Human Rights was seen by the activists as having a similar recognition and impact (Author's interviews)

First Period of Limited Contestation

When the first comfort women memorial on public land was erected outside the public library in Palisades Park, New Jersey, a majority Korean American town, it occurred without significant fanfare or opposition. Initially, the Homeowner's Association and Veteran's Association were against the memorial because there were no local victims, but support was strong enough to overcome such voices. The success in erecting this memorial was a significant step forward for Korean Americans to gain recognition by the host society of the importance of incorporating their stories into the national (and local) story through public memorials.

Still, despite its important symbolism, in daily life, one could walk by the comfort women memorial in Palisades Park a hundred times without stopping to read its inscription or perhaps even notice it. As Fig. 5.2 shows, it is an unassuming slab of stone with a plaque that reads:

Fig. 5.2 Comfort women memorial in Palisades Park, New Jersey, erected in 2010. (Source: Author, March 19, 2015)

> In memory of the more than 200,000 women and girls who were abducted by the armed forces of the government of Imperial Japan 1930s – 1945. Known as 'comfort women' they endured human rights violations that no peoples should leave unrecognized. Let us never forget the horrors of crimes against humanity. Dedicated on October 23, 2010. County of Bergen, County Executive, The Board of Chosen Freeholders, and the Borough of Palisades Park.

This modest memorial maintained a quiet presence until 2012, when the Japanese consulate and individual Japanese politicians contacted the city about removing the memorial. The Japanese officials argued that Japan had already apologized through the Kono Statement (1993) and the Asian Women's Fund (1994–2007) (e.g. Kumagai 2014), while some Japanese politicians declared that these women were well-paid prostitutes and not abducted or otherwise coerced by the armed forces of Japan. This intervention by the Japanese government into a local affair of memorialization in the United States had unintended consequences. It drew national media coverage, predominantly negative, that made the case for the universal messaging of women's rights as human rights and drew parallels between commemoration of the comfort women and US first amendment rights and national values of justice and freedom (Constant 2013; Halpin 2013).

Although not the sole reason for the proliferation of memorials in the United States, the push back from the Japanese government was a strong catalyst for local activists to seek to build more of these memorials across the United States over the next two years. Another reason was that KACE and the other promoters of the comfort women memorial in Palisades Park had become a model for what could be done in terms of garnering host society support for physical memorialization of an issue important to the Korean American community.

SECOND PERIOD OF CONTESTATION

During the first period, of limited contestation, the goal of recognition by the host society was an important feature. What distinguished the second period is that debate became more widespread. Although we first saw opposition coming from members of the Japanese government, it quickly spread to a broader range of Japanese nationals and Japanese Americans. Given the nature of diaspora and globalization in the twenty-first century, it is sometimes difficult to know if the protests originate from Japanese Americans or Japanese living in Japan. Still, some contests over public memory are clearly playing out through the domestic politics of the United States.

An additional feature of the second phase was using contestation as a tool to further the cause, which did not come into play during the first stage and only started in 2012. Public disputation could actually be used as a means to increase attention to the issue of the comfort women. The universal messaging and coalition building that preceded and accompanied advocacy to build a memorial allowed the supporters to repeatedly present their case, while highlighting the weaknesses of the other side. Advocates for the comfort women were confident that their narrative would resonate and that public contestation, preceded by appropriate preparation for the political arbiters of the likely arguments on each side, would result in a win by the movement.

Judge Lillian Sing (Ret.), of the Comfort Women Justice Coalition (CWJC), in explaining the process to erect the memorial in San Francisco, declared that 'We are never afraid of public hearings. What we are afraid of is backdoor meetings'.[19] This sentiment has been reflected by many of the advocates working in this movement, as the very process of public rivalry has been a means to increase exposure for the comfort women issue and they have often seen success as an outcome of this process.

The domestic politics of this contestation during the second period is best represented by a case study of the comfort women memorial erected in Glendale in 2013. Glendale is in Los Angeles county and is a suburb of the city of Los Angeles. It is 16% Asian American.[20] According to the 2010 US Census, there were over 10,000 Korean Americans in Glendale, only exceeded among Asian Americans by the Filipino American population at approximately 14,000. There were under 2000 Japanese Americans.

The memorial in Glendale was unveiled in 2013 next to the public library. Although in this way it is similar to that in Palisades Park, its design is much more conspicuous. As Fig. 5.3 illustrates, it is a bronze statue of a Korean girl sitting next to an empty chair, with two plaques. It is a replica of an identical statue in Seoul, located across from the Japanese embassy site.

---

[19] Author's interview. August 18, 2017.
[20] This is according to the 2017 US Census Bureau American Community Survey.

Fig. 5.3 The Peace Monument in Glendale, California, erected in 2013. (Source: Author, June 10, 2015)

The first plaque reads:

'I was a sex slave of Japanese military' – Torn hair symbolizes the girl being snatched from her home by the Imperial Japanese Army – Tight fists represent the girl's firm resolve for a deliverance of justice – Bare and unsettled feet represent having been abandoned by the cold and unsympathetic world – Bird on the girl's shoulder symbolizes a bond between us and the deceased victims – Empty chair symbolizes survivors who are dying of old age without having yet witnessed justice – Shadow of the girl is that of an old grandma, symbolizing passage of time spent in silence – Butterfly in shadow represents hope that victims may resurrect one day to receive their apology.

The second reads:

Peace Monument. In memory of more than 200,000 Asian and Dutch women who were removed from their homes in Korea, China, Taiwan, Japan, the Philippines, Thailand, Vietnam, Malaysia, East Timor and

Indonesia, to be coerced into sexual slavery by the Imperial Armed Forces of Japan between 1932 and 1945. And in celebration of Proclamation of "Comfort Women Day" by the City of Glendale on July 30, 2012, and of passing of House Resolution 121 by the United States Congress on July 30, 2007, urging the Japanese Government to accept historical responsibility for these crimes. It is our sincere hope that these unconscionable violations of human rights shall never recur. July 30, 2013.

The first section describes how each physical element of the statue represents some aspect of the narrative of a young girl taken forcibly and now seeking justice in her elderly years or even beyond the grave. Across both sections, the emphasis is coercion and the normative framework of human rights. Unlike the Palisades Park memorial, it explicitly notes the multinational element of this tragedy, fitting with the strategy of the movement to be universal rather than Japan–Korea specific.

The choice of the design came from the local politicians in Glendale. Although KAFC had suggested a different design, when the local officials saw pictures of the memorial in Seoul, unveiled in 2011, they suggested this would be an appropriate design for Glendale as well. This replica of Seoul's Statue of Peace is known in Glendale as the Peace Monument. It is officially a donation from Glendale's Korea Sister City Association. Local donations in California paid for the advocacy and erection of the memorial.

KAFC was founded with the explicit mission of erecting a comfort women memorial in California. The movement to build the memorial in Glendale was a grassroots one. As mentioned earlier, KAFC received assistance from KACE in strategizing for their own California memorial. The location of the memorial was not predetermined; KAFC reached out to numerous cities and universities to gauge interest.[21] Although not part of the consideration in choosing Glendale, according to this author's interviews, the fact that 30% of Glendale residents are of Armenian descent (US Census) seems fortuitous in retrospect. Armenian Americans have long sought greater recognition within the United States, and transnationally, for the Armenian genocide. In fact, at the same time that H.Res. 121 was being debated in the US House of Representatives, a similar resolution calling for recognition and apology from Turkey was tabled, presumably

---

[21] Author's interview with Phyllis Kim, KAFC, August 8, 2017.

due to US foreign policy concerns. Therefore, the issue of contestation over recognition of the past was well known by Armenian Americans.

At the unveiling ceremony of the comfort women memorial, Councilmember Zareh Sinanyan, the grandson of an Armenian genocide survivor, said:

> I understand the pain, I understand the horror that the victims [sic] ... The best way to resolve conflicts ... the best way to heal wounds ... is to acknowledge them ... My people, my grandfather, were subjected to a horrible, horrible crime ... To this day, because no apology has come, no proper acknowledgement has come ... the wound is deep, it's festering, and there can be no moving forward without it.[22]

Other speakers at the ceremony included a former comfort woman who flew in from South Korea (Bok-dong Kim), Japanese American Kathy Masaoka of NCRR, and representatives of the Glendale City Council. Statements of support from Representative Adam Schiff (Congressional district 28) and Representative Ed Royce (Congressional district 39) were read aloud.

Yet the path to this memorial was not smooth or assured. The Glendale City Council received hundreds of letters and emails from Japanese nationals and Japanese Americans in Japan and the United States in opposition to the memorial. This included a letter from the mayor of Higashiosaka, Glendale's sister city in Japan. There were also words of resistance voiced at the public hearing prior to the erection of the memorial. Glendale Councilmember Dave Weaver was against the memorial; the only councilmember to be so. At the time, he stated that he opposed the memorial due to other plans for the area, including the possibility of a parking lot. Later he also said he thought the memorial was a local city becoming involved in an international dispute, which was not appropriate (Kim 2013; Levine 2013).

After the unveiling, opponents continued to protest. Japanese Americans living in the area, as well as Japanese in Japan, cited reports, unsubstantiated by police or school officials, that Japanese American

---

[22] Quoted in Yamamoto, J.K. and Culross, M.H. (2013, August 2). Comfort Women Monument Unveiled in Glendale. *The Rafu Shimpo*. Retrieved February 5, 2019, from http://www.rafu.com/2013/08/comfort-women-monument-unveiled-in-glendale/

children were being bullied because of the memorial (Schreiber 2014). They also argued that the memorial was anti-Japanese.[23]

In 2014, the Global Alliance for Historical Truth (GAHT) and two individuals, Koichi Mera (President of GAHT) and Michiko Shiota Gingery, brought a lawsuit against the city of Glendale. Mera was a resident of Los Angeles and Gingery a resident of Glendale (Poulisse 2014). Their goal was to have the Glendale memorial removed. The lawsuit contended that 1) the comfort women memorial and accompanying plaque constitute foreign policymaking, which, according to the US Constitution, can only be conducted by the federal government, and 2) the caption on the plaque was not presented to the city council during its deliberation over the memorial and, thus, was a violation of city code (Mera 2015). The lawsuit has gone through a series of stages in different courts, including initial dismissal and then a preliminary finding in favour of Glendale. In 2017 the US Supreme Court declined to hear the case. This ended the dispute from the legal perspective. What Mera had called a 'test of the US legal system' ended in what he saw as a failure of that system.[24] With a very different interpretation, Judge Julie Tang (Ret.), of the Comfort Women Justice Coalition (CWJC), celebrated the ruling and stated that 'Essentially, the US Supreme Court has given a green light for comfort women peace memorials to be built anywhere in the US' (cited in Constante 2017).

Third Period of Contestation

In the same year, of 2017, we simultaneously saw this legal 'green light' and the advent of the third stage of contestation of comfort women memorials. While the countermovement lost in court, it had gained in political savvy. Its failures were also learning experiences.

One of the complaints raised by opponents to the Glendale memorial was that they did not have sufficient time prior to the public hearing to prepare their position in order to sway the local politicians.[25] Another weakness may have been the approach they took. Mera discussed one strategy as contacting Japanese politicians and newspapers. This

---

[23] Author's interviews.
[24] Author's interview with Koichi Mera. June 9, 2015.
[25] Author's interview with Mera. Interestingly, Phyllis Kim made the same argument as to why Buena Park voted against a memorial—lack of time to prepare and organize before the vote (Author's interview, August 8, 2017).

overlooked the hegemony of the host society as arbiter and the political culture of that society where there is a history of localities determining local memorials and other physical markers. While continuing to target first-generation Japanese Americans through Japanese-language newspapers and web sites (Koyama 2015), the countermovement transitioned away from GAHT as its centre. It began to engage more explicitly with US political culture, in recognition of the hegemony of local governments in the host society as arbiters of contestation on this issue (when it comes to the erection of memorials on public land).

In 2014, the Fullerton City Council in California voted to endorse H.Res. 121 in a 3–2 vote and approved the Fullerton Museum Center Association's consideration of erecting a comfort women memorial (Fullerton council approves 'comfort women' resolution). Although the museum held a comfort women exhibit in 2015, no memorial has been built by the time of this writing, which has been attributed by some to waning political support in the face of opposition (Kandil 2016). Nearby Buena Park considered a memorial in 2013 but the City Council voted down the measure. Japanese Americans in the area worked closely with local politicians with the goal of addressing the larger interests of those politicians, while emphasizing the controversies over the comfort women issue. Comfort women memorials began to be discussed more widely as representing a history that was contested, as opposed to a definitive narrative based on clear, indisputable historical fact.

In 2016, the Korean American community in Atlanta and its suburbs approached the Center for Civil and Human Rights in that city to erect a memorial outside the museum. The Atlanta Comfort Women Memorial Task Force thought that an agreement was in place when the Center pulled out of the deal. The Center officially cited rules not to erect anything on the exterior grounds and offered to have an exhibit inside. But accompanying statements indicated that representatives from the Center were concerned with getting involved in a Japan–Korea dispute (Emerson 2017; Park 2017). A short time later, the Atlanta suburb of Brookhaven agreed to accept the memorial, upon the sponsorship of John Park, a Korean American member of the Brookhaven City Council (Brookhaven Makes History to Memorialize WWII 'Comfort Women'). That memorial has moved from one park to another since being unveiled in 2017, as community concerns arose, ostensibly about parking (Bagby 2017).

So what changed? I argue that the nature of contestation changed as Japanese Americans (and the Japanese government) became more focused on basing their arguments on a foundation of US political culture and engaging more with local political and economic interests. Glendale was a battleground, and the comfort women movement won that battle. But it was a battleground where the countermovement learned how to engage on the issue and how not to. GAHT was not a successful face for the countermovement. The ultra-conservative and historical revisionist comments that it advanced were easy to dispute. In addition, after emotional appeals from comfort women who came to speak before the Glendale City Council or the San Francisco Board of Supervisors, public comments that the women were liars and this story was fabricated by Koreans were deemed offensive. This can be seen in the repeated cries of 'shame on you' levelled at the opposition for their denier rhetoric by San Francisco Supervisor David Campos at a public hearing where a former comfort woman had just spoken.[26] The shift for the countermovement has been in working behind the scenes, serving the interests of local politicians and businesses by nurturing good relationships.

An argument that can be made against my three phases is the success of the San Francisco memorial, which was during the third phase of contestation, and is the first large city in the United States to have a comfort women memorial. However, the broad-based contestation in that case was apparent. For example, Judy Hamaguchi, president of the San Francisco chapter of the Japanese American Citizens League, one of the major Japanese American organizations in the country, actively spoke out against the memorial, arguing that it 'projects hate towards a specific nationality' (quoted in Sabatini 2015). And Campos, even while supporting the memorial, acknowledged that there could be reasonable arguments to oppose it.[27] Therefore, it was only the strong, multicultural coalition, steeped in decades of experience working within the US political system, that brought about the memorial's successful unveiling in San Francisco (McCarthy and Hasunuma 2018).

CONCLUSION

The political space in the United States (the host society) for public memorialization for diasporic causes created opportunities for Korean Americans. The experience of successfully passing H.Res. 121 and decades of civil rights and political work by many of the memorial supporters led them to understand US political culture. The countermovement has now

---

[26] Retrieved on August 18, 2019, at https://www.youtube.com/watch?v=dqFFvyq0vaI
[27] Ibid.

learned how to take advantage of a different type of political space. The comfort women movement in the United States is benefitted by public exposure; the countermovement by behind-the-scenes interactions; both require personal connections beyond ethnic and other distinctions.

In this chapter, I examined the process of US-based political contests over the erection of comfort women memorials, with a focus on Korean Americans and Japanese Americans, and what role the host society plays as arbiter. Diaspora politics has introduced a continuity between historical narratives dominant in the homeland and those being promoted by ethnic groups in the United States. Yet diverse experiences of migration and immigrant or ethnic group experience in the host society, as well as differing perspectives and principles on empire, has made memory coalitions defy purely ethnic categorization. Identity politics and staking one's claim, in terms of interests, needs, and belonging, in the host society goes beyond ethnic identification, even when a particular memory has its origins in a specific homeland.

Today rivalry between the movement to memorialize the comfort women and the resulting countermovement continues. After periods of limited contestation and then significant contestation with momentum on the side of the comfort women movement, we are now in a period of broad-based contestation with successes seen for a countermovement that is promoting the idea that this is a disputed history. Given the nature of this third stage, I expect to see few if any new memorials on public land in the United States in the immediate future. Still, as one of the defining features of diaspora is its mobile territoriality and transnational mobility, both collaboration and contestation will continue to evolve in form and location.

Recently, the comfort women movement in the United States has been working in more transnational ways, including becoming involved in efforts to build memorials in Germany and Australia. Advocates have also expanded their work to focus more on education (Hasunuma and McCarthy 2019). Due to the lobbying of groups such as KAFC and CWJC, the state of California now includes the comfort women in its approved curriculum. As the largest textbook market in the country, the formal introduction of the comfort women into the California curriculum is likely to have an impact on the probability that school children throughout the United States will learn about this period in history and the tragic stories of these women's lives.[28]

---

[28] Daniel C. Sneider, associate director of research at Stanford University's Shorenstein Asia-Pacific Research Center, quoted in Kim, V. (2016, February 7). "Comfort Women" and a lesson in how history is shaped in California textbooks. *Los Angeles Times*.

References

Alexander, C. (2013). Contested Memories: The Shahid Minar and the Struggle for Diasporic Space. *Ethnic & Racial Studies, 36*(4), 590–610.
Bagby, D. (2017, September 20). Brookhaven Relocates 'Comfort Women' Memorial to Main Blackburn Park. *Reporter Newspapers*. Retrieved October 1, 2017 from http://www.reporternewspapers.net/2017/09/20/comfort-women-memorial-relocatedmainblackburn-park-brookhaven/
Brookhaven Makes History to Memorialize WWII 'Comfort Women.' (2017, May 23). *Reporters Newspapers*. Retrieved May 24, 2017, from www.reportersnewspapers.net/2017
Chang, G. (2016). Asian Americans, Politics, and History. In D. K. Yoo & E. Azuma (Eds.), *Oxford Handbook of Asian American History* (pp. 331–344). Oxford: Oxford University Press.
Clifford, J. (1994). Diasporas. *Cultural Anthropology, 9*(3), 302–338.
Constant, L. (2013). 'Comfort Women' Statue Memorializes Local and Global Human Rights Issues. *HuffPost The Blog*. Retrieved August 15, 2013, from https://www.huffpost.com/entry/comfort-women-statue-memorializes_b_3684584
Constante, A. (2017, March 31). Supreme Court Declines Case Over Lawsuit to Remove 'Comfort Women' Memorial. *NBC News*. Retrieved February 5, 2019, from https://www.nbcnews.com/news/asian-america/supreme-court-declines-case-over-lawsuit-remove-comfort-women-memorial-n740996
Davidson, A. P., & Kuah-Pearce, K. E. (2008). Introduction: Diasporic Memories and Identities. In K. E. Kuah-Pearce & A. P. Davidson (Eds.), *At Home in the Chinese Diaspora: Memories, Identities and Belongings* (pp. 1–11). London: Palgrave Macmillan.
Emerson, B. (2017, March 3). Civil Rights Center Cancels 'Comfort Women' Memorial. *The Atlanta Journal Constitution*. Retrieved May 24, 2017, from http://www.ajc.com/news/civilrights-center-cancels-comfort-women-memorial/VrjGHYMBiu218jYZDdJWjI/
Fortier, A. (2000). *Migrant Belongings: Memory, Space, Identity*. London: Berg Publishers.
Fujino, D. (2018). Cold War Activism and Japanese American Exceptionalism: Contested Solidarities and Decolonial Alternatives to Freedom. *Pacific Historical Review, 87*(2), 264–304.
Halbwachs, M. (1992). *On Collective Memory*. Chicago: University of Chicago Press.
Hall, S. (1990). Cultural Identity and Diaspora. In J. Rutherford (Ed.), *Identity: Community, Cultural Difference* (pp. 222–237). London: Lawrence & Wishart.
Halpin, D. (2013, May 29). Palisades Park and the First Amendment. *U.S.-Korea Institute at SAIS Policy Brief*.

Hasunuma, L. C., & McCarthy, M. M. (2019). Creating a Collective Memory of the Comfort Women in the USA. *International Journal of Politics, Culture, and Society, 32*(02), 145–162.

Hoffman, E. (2000). Complex Histories, Contested Memories Some Reflections on Remembering Difficult Pasts. Retrieved August 20, 2018, from http://townsendcenter.berkeley.edu/sites/default/files/publications/OP23_Hoffman.pdf

Japan Matters for America/America Matters for Japan. (2019). Asia Matters for America. Washington, DC: East-West Center. Retrieved July 25, 2019, from https://asiamattersforamerica.org/uploads/publications/2019-Japan-Matters-for-America.pdf

Japanese-American Relations at the Turn of the Century. (1900–1922). *Milestones in the History of US Foreign Relations.* Office of the Historian. US Department of State. Retrieved June 21, 2019, from https://history.state.gov/milestones/1899-1913/japanese-relations

Kandil, C. Y. (2016, January 1). 'Comfort Women' Debate Continues in Conflicted O.C. *Los Angeles Times.* Retrieved August 18, 2019, from https://www.latimes.com/socal/daily-pilot/tn-wknd-et-0103-comfort-women-20160101-story.html

Kim, J. S. (2013, October 3). Glendale Mayor Regrets Erecting Comfort Women Memorial. *KoreAm.* Retrieved January 28, 2014, from http://iamkoream.com/glendale-mayor-regrets-erecting-comfort-women-memorial/

Korea Matters for America/America Matters for Korea. (2018). Asia Matters for America. Washington, DC: East-West Center. Retrieved July 25, 2019, from https://asiamattersforamerica.org/uploads/publications/2018-Korea-Matters-for-America.pdf

Koyama, E. 2015. The U.S. as "Major Battleground" for "Comfort Woman" Revisionism: The Screening of Scottsboro Girls at Central Washington University. *The Asia-Pacific Journal, 13*(22), 2.

Kuah-Pearce, K. E. (2008). Collective Memories as Cultural Capital: From Chinese Diaspora to Emigrant Hometowns. In K. E. Kuah-Pearce & A. P. Davidson (Eds.), *At Home in the Chinese Diaspora: Memories, Identities and Belongings* (pp. 111–127). London: Palgrave Macmillan.

Kumagai, N. (2014). Asia Women's Fund Revisited. *Asia-Pacific Review, 21*(2), 117–148.

Lee, E. (2015). *The Making of Asian America: A History.* New York: Simon and Schuster.

Leung, M. (2008). Memories, Belonging and Homemaking: Chinese Migrants in Germany. In K. E. Kuah-Pearce & A. P. Davidson (Eds.), *At Home in the Chinese Diaspora: Memories, Identities and Belongings* (pp. 164–186). London: Palgrave Macmillan.

Levine, B. (2013, November 5). Glendale's "Comfort Women" Memorial Still Stirs Controversy. *Los Angeles Times.* Retrieved October 1, 2015, from http://

articles.latimes.com/2013/nov/05/local/la-me-ln-glendales-comfort-women-sex-slave-20131105

Lien, P. (2001). *The Making of Asian America through Political Participation.* Philadelphia: Temple University Press.

McCarthy, M. M. (2018). The Power and Limits of the Transnational 'Comfort Women' Movement. In M. M. McCarthy (Ed.), *Handbook of Japanese Foreign Policy* (pp. 366–380). London/New York: Routledge.

McCarthy, M. M., & Hasunuma, L. C. (2018). Coalition Building and Mobilization: Case Studies of the Comfort Women Memorials in the United States. *Politics, Groups, and Identities, 06*(03), 411–434.

McCarthy, M. M., & Kumagai, N. (2019). *The Rhetoric of the "Comfort Women" in the Context of Changing Global Norms.* Memory Studies Association Annual Meeting. Madrid.

Mera, K. (2015). *Comfort Women Not "Sex Slaves": Rectifying the Myriad of Perspectives.* Private publication through Xlibris.

Min, P. G. (2013). The Immigration of Koreans to the United States: A Review of Forty-Five Year (1965–2009) Trends. In P. G. Min (Ed.), *Koreans in North America* (pp. 9–34). Lanham: Lexington Books.

Moore, R. (2012). 'A Crime Against Humanity Arguably Without Parallel in European History': Genocide and the 'Politics' of Victimhood in Western Narratives of the Ukrainian Holodomor. *Australian Journal of Politics & History, 58*(3), 367–379.

Niiya, B. (2020). National Coalition for Redress/Reparations. *Densho Encyclopedia.* Retrieved June 21, 2019, from http://encyclopedia.densho.org/National_Coalition_for_Redress/Reparations/

Park, L. S. (2013). Authenticity Dilemma Among Pre-1965 Native-Born Koreans. In P. G. Min (Ed.), *Koreans in North America: Their Twenty-First Century Experience* (pp. 173–194). Lanham: Lexington Books.

Park, J. (2017, June 25). Commentary: "Comfort Women" Memorial Belongs in Brookhaven. *Reporter Newspapers.* Retrieved July 19, 2019, from https://www.reporternewspapers.net/2017/06/25/commentary-comfort-women-memorial-belongs-brookhaven/

Poulisse, A. (2014, April 18). Glendale Comfort Women Statue Controversy Goes to US District Court. *Los Angeles Daily News.* Retrieved May 28, 2015, from http://www.dailynews.com/general-news/20140418/glendale-comfort-women-statue-controversy-goes-to-us-district-court

Reeves, R. (2015). *Infamy: The Shocking Story of the Japanese American Internment in World War II.* New York: Henry Holt and Co.

Robertson, G. (2014). Virginia Vote on Sea of Japan Hands Victory to Koreans. *Reuters.* Retrieved July 25, 2019, from https://mobil.reuters.com/article/amp/idUSBREA150SB20140216

Sabatini, J. (2015, September 15). Supervisors' Support of a 'Comfort Women' Memorial in San Francisco Sparks Debate. *San Francisco Examiner.* Retrieved

October 1, 2015, from http://www.sfexaminer.com/supervisors-support-of-a-comfort-women-memorial-in-san-francisco-sparks-debate/

Savage, K. History, Memory, and Monuments: An Overview of the Scholarly Literature on Commemoration. *US National Park Service*. Retrieved April 6, 2014, from http://www.nps.gov/history/history/resedu/savage.htm

Schreiber, M. (2014). Tracking Southern California's Elusive "Bullies." *Number 1 Shimbun*. The Foreign Correspondents' Club of Japan, September 30. Retrieved July 6, 2019, from http://www.fccj.or.jp/number-1-shimbun/item/471-tracking-souther-california-s-elusive-bullies/471-tracking-souther-california-s-elusive-bullies.html

Shaery-Eisenlohr, R. (2007). Postrevolutionary Iran and Shi'i Lebanon: Contested Histories of Shi'i Transnationalism. *International Journal of Middle East Studies*, 39(2), 271–289.

Soh, C. S. (2008). *The Comfort Women: Sexual Violence and Postcolonial Memory in Korea and Japan*. Chicago: The University of Chicago Press.

The Immigration Act of 1924 (The Johnson-Reed Act). *Milestones in the History of US Foreign Relations*. Office of the Historian. US Department of State. Retrieved June 21, 2019, from https://history.state.gov/milestones/1921-1936/immigration-act

Watanabe, P. (1999). Asian American Activism and U.S. Foreign Policy. In E. Hu-DeHart (Ed.), *Across the Pacific: Asian Americans and Globalization* (pp. 109–128). Philadelphia: Temple University Press.

Watt, L. (2015). Embracing Defeat in Seoul: Rethinking Decolonization in Korea, 1945. *The Journal of Asian Studies*, 74(1), 153–174.

Who are Japanese Americans? (2015). Center for American Progress. Retrieved August 18, 2019, from https://cdn.americanprogress.org/wp-content/uploads/2015/04/AAPI-Japanese-factsheet.pdf

Wood, A. L. (2014). Rebuild or Reconcile: American and Canadian Approaches to Redress for World War II Confinement. *American Review of Canadian Studies*, 44(3), 347–365.

Yoshimi, Y. (2002). *Comfort Women: Sexual Slavery in the Japanese Military during World War II* (S. O'Brien, Trans.). New York: Columbia University Press.

CHAPTER 6

Contested Memory in an Eponymous City: The Robert Towns Statue in Townsville, Australia

Rodney Sullivan and Robin Sullivan

INTRODUCTION

This chapter examines the development of public memory in Townsville, an Australian settler-society coastal city in tropical Queensland. It focuses on two major sources of public memory: versions of the past propagated by official, settler-dominated narratives and minority interests. Following Bodnar (1992) and, more recently, Mihelj (2013), we define official memory of a city as that sponsored by its municipal government, business and other elites. Official memory is anchored in the city's foundation, underpins its identity and develops over generations, tending towards continuity and inertia, though also susceptible to evolution. Contrasting with this, we examine the content and impact of the counter-memory of a particularly potent Townsville minority which '…looks to the past for the hidden histories excluded from dominant narratives' (Lipsitz 2001, p.293). Counter-memory, while potentially problematic in its own right, is here

---

R. Sullivan (✉) • R. Sullivan
The University of Queensland, Brisbane, QLD, Australia
e-mail: r.sullivan2@uq.edu.au

© The Author(s) 2020
S. Marschall (ed.), *Public Memory in the Context of Transnational Migration and Displacement*, Palgrave Macmillan Memory Studies, https://doi.org/10.1007/978-3-030-41329-3_6

understood as a revisionist mix of history and myth, anchored in personal experience, dismissive of official history, yet determined to reformulate its vision of the past.

Urban public memory evolves dialectically, frequently propelled by friction between elites and minorities (Loughran et al. 2016, p.198). Townsville provides a case study not only on the dialectics of memory, but also on the 'jagged borders' between collective memory and group identity, a focus of Michael Rothberg's *Multidirectional Memory*. Memory in Townsville has been shaped by 'negotiation, cross-referencing and borrowing' (Rothberg 2009, p.3) across the porous borders of three societal groups and their visions of the past: white settlers, Indigenous Australians and Australian South Sea Islanders[1] (Islanders). The focus here is on the last, descendants of migrants who, despite their relatively small numbers, have formed a potent reciprocal mnemonic alliance with the Indigenous minority.

Robert Towns (1794–1873), Townsville's eponym, is a strikingly mobile memory commodity. With mobility comes entanglement (Conrad 2003, pp.86–7), a feature of the officially endorsed memory and minority-driven counter-memories attached to the British-born settler and the city's foundational financier. We explore the consequences of Townsville's eponymity and Robert Towns' memorialisation, including his manifestations as a symbolic figure in multiple memory communities. Memory contestation marked the genesis, execution and reception of his public statue, unveiled in Townsville in 2005. The furore triggered by the statue had implications for further development of Townsville's memorial landscape.

We approached Robert Towns' statue as historians, seeking answers to controversy generated by its unveiling. This led us to investigate multiple pasts, extending over 150 years, of the city and its residents, including South Sea Islander and Indigenous minorities. We examined Townsville's historiographies and primary sources including oral testimonies, newspaper reports, a library exhibition, photographs, government records and city council minutes. Our historian's toolkit was supplemented by memory studies theory, especially Rothberg's concept of multidirectional

---

[1] 'South Sea Islander' is the term preferred by the community. Historically, the names Polynesians, Kanakas and Pacific Islanders have been loosely applied to Melanesians in Australia. Torres Strait Islanders, from the group of islands in the Strait between continental North Australia and Papua New Guinea, are Indigenous Australians and, in this chapter, will be designated Torres Strait Islanders, their preferred term.

memory. We sought to balance the weight of documentary evidence against the power of Australian South Sea Islander intergenerational memory. Australian South Sea Islanders used the statue's unveiling as an opportunity to gain visibility for their challenge to Robert Towns' official memory. They were also seeking admission to a memorial landscape nationally resistant to migrant recognition, particularly for communities without numerical heft (Hamilton and Ashton 2001, pp.27–8; Ashton and Hamilton 2008, p.19). In the twenty-first century, Australian Islander memory travelled back across the Coral Sea to Melanesian homelands and, certainly in the case of Vanuatu, was deployed to boost national cohesion. Robert Towns, embodying past foreign exploitation, was accorded symbolic status, serving the cause of unity in the culturally and linguistically diverse Pacific Island state (Hunt 2016; Lawson 2016, p.390). Such exchanges validate Astrid Erll's (2011, p.9) observations on 'travelling memory', at least in regional contexts—its capacity, even necessity, to traverse time, space, cultural boundaries and generations.

The emphasis of this chapter is the Islanders' impact on memory in the Australian city of Townsville. Although present-day Islander residents are relatively few, their engagement with Townsville's sites of memory, including its name, has been amplified by compatriots elsewhere in Australia, who also use Robert Towns, not only as a symbol of the exploitation of their Pacific ancestors, but also as a rallying cry against present-day disadvantage. The chapter will first examine the city's nineteenth-century origins and the role of Robert Towns in its foundation. This is followed by a focus on the Pacific Island labour trade, entangled in the city's past, present and future. We also examine how Robert Towns came to dominate Townsville's memorial landscape. Such an historical perspective reveals the deep roots of Islander resentment and anger, expressed so forcibly during the statue's unveiling and subsequent public controversy (Hunt 2006, pp.805–6; Moore 2015, p.168). The Robert Towns statue is a catalyst, helping extend the reach of Townsville's public memory beyond its historical white-settler preoccupation.

Townsville: Foundation and Eponymity

With over 190,000 people, Townsville is Australia's largest tropical city. Encircling the distinctive ochre rock monolith of Castle Hill, the city's symbol, it stands on Cleveland Bay, named in 1770 by British navigator,

Captain James Cook, the first European to observe the locality and evidence of Aboriginal occupation (Cook 2014, p.271). In the early 1860s, impelled by land hunger, pastoralists advanced overland from the south. Funding them, and eventual beneficiaries of their land claims, were city capitalists. Among these was Sydney-based financier and entrepreneur, Robert Towns, who, from 1859, acquired extensive grazing lands in Townsville's hinterland. Born in England, with little formal education, he used seafaring as a stepping stone to wealth, his influence extending throughout Eastern Australia into Melanesia and as far as China (Shineberg 1976).

Naming Townsville after Robert Towns, who only visited Cleveland Bay briefly in 1866, was historically dubious. His North Queensland agent, Scottish pastoralist John Melton Black (1830–1919), had much greater claim to eponymity. By 1863 Black had acquired conditional leases on more than 1000 sq. km including frontage to Cleveland Bay. The following year, Andrew Ball and Mark Watt Reid, following Black's instructions, established a settlement on the banks of Ross Creek. Black joined them to supervise the town's foundation. Work proceeded under the gaze of Aboriginal people, kept at bay by a detachment of Native Police, a mounted force of Indigenous troopers commanded by European officers, noted for their brutal suppression of Aboriginal resistance to European expansion. Frontier conflict was excluded from the town's official narrative which took an 1863–1864 injection of civilisation into a wilderness as its starting point (Black 1864; Clarke 1913, pp.23, 29; Gibson-Wilde 1984, pp.20–25; Griffin 2014, pp.12–14, 22, 59; Richards 2010). In February 1865, the Queensland government, eager for further Northern investment, proclaimed the municipality of 'Townsville' (*Queensland Government Gazette* 1866, p.211; Clarke 1913, p.29) in honour of the entrepreneurial and influential Robert Towns, a far more prominent figure in colonial society and politics than Black.

SOUTH SEA ISLANDERS AND THE LABOUR TRADE

Towns was hungry for not only land but also cheap labour. In 1863 he pioneered the labour trade between Australia and Melanesia when the *Don Juan* brought the first contingent of South Sea Islanders from the New Hebrides (Republic of Vanuatu from 1980). Soon 260 Islanders were employed on his Logan River cotton plantation, Townsvale, in southeast Queensland. Labour and race relations on Townsvale could be considered progressive for that era. Robert Towns' 1863 instructions stipulated that Islanders were to be contracted for up to 12 months, paid ten shillings monthly, with food and accommodation supplied. They had the right of repatriation upon request (Kennedy 2004, p.65). Helga Griffin examined Townsville's Indigenous and immigrant minorities, as well as Robert Towns, and deemed Townsvale 'a showcase for happy race relations…[reflecting] Towns' benevolent paternalism' (2014, p.26). The apparent success of Towns' experimental use of South Sea Islanders for heavy manual work underpinned the rapid expansion of the labour trade, conducted in some cases by far less scrupulous men, and the development, through the remainder of the century, of the pervasive ideal of a 'White Queensland quietly served by Melanesians' (Megarrity 2006, p.3).

In January 1865 Towns transferred ten Islanders from Townsvale to Cleveland Bay. These were foundational workers, and early Townsville was built on their toil:

> Nearly all labour was done by kanakas, imported from the islands, who worked almost completely nude, with a small band around the waist; they were strong, tall and shapely "boys", as called, and very intelligent, quick and ready to learn. (Clarke 1913, p.26)

Their arduous tasks included the preparation of anchorages, working in waist-deep water to clear mangroves from the banks of Ross Creek, a crocodile habitat. In 1868, 127 South Sea Islanders were living in Townsville when its population was estimated at 760. Between 1865 and 1884, a total of 1703 disembarked at Townsville, though many travelled further afield for employment (Griffin 2014, pp.26–7, 32, 129, 138, 141). An image of plantation labourers and their overseers near Townsville ca. 1870 (Fig. 6.1) epitomised the fateful interaction between European colonialism and Melanesian societies on Australia's eastern seaboard in the second half of the nineteenth century: it spoke of labour migration between two worlds, buttressed by power disparity and racial hierarchy.

Immigrant labour from Melanesia, particularly Vanuatu and the Solomon Islands, changed Australia's racial composition and underpinned the economically crucial sugar industry in coastal Queensland (Megarrity 2018, pp.23–4). Some 50,000 Islanders, predominantly young males, were recruited between 1863 and 1904. Most came voluntarily, but there were instances, particularly in the early phase, of kidnappings and deceit, giving rise to the labour trade synonym 'blackbirding', connoting illegality

Fig. 6.1 South Sea Islanders outside overseer's hut, John Melton Black's plantation, Townsville, ca. 1870. State Library of Queensland.

and slavery. Historians estimated that this might apply in up to 15% of cases (Moore 2015, p.159). The majority were recruited legally and came voluntarily. About half sought further engagements after their contracts expired. Over a quarter of newly arrived Islander migrants in the 1890s were re-enlistees. In 1901, around one half of Queensland Melanesians were men whose contracts had expired. Many were employed or had become farmers or small business people. This cohort owned their own homes and was largely accepted in communities (Corris 1970, p.54; Lake 2013, pp.554–5; McCreery and McKenzie 2013, pp.580–582).

In 1901 the new Commonwealth Government attempted to legislate a White Australia with its Immigration Restriction and Pacific Island Labourers Acts. Particularly for Islanders, the spectre of deportation loomed as rank injustice. In 1901, a South Sea Islander Kanaka Association in Mackay, a sugar-growing district south of Townsville, sought to prevent 'the deportation of civilised Islanders back to their savage homes' (*Morning Bulletin* (Rockhampton), 28 November 1901, p.6).

The Commonwealth Government attempted to deport all Melanesians in 1906 and 1907. The draconian measure was softened after resistance from Islanders themselves, evangelical Protestants, sugar growers and the Queensland Government. Nevertheless, over 4000 were returned to their home Islands, some 1200 were granted exemptions and a further 1000 evaded deportation. Most remaining in North Queensland lived in sugar-growing districts north and south of Townsville. By 1947 there were only 25 South Sea Islanders in Townsville's population of 17,464 (Mercer 1995, pp.69–70; *Census* 1947, pp.250, 253).

AUSTRALIAN SOUTH SEA ISLANDER IDENTITY, HISTORY AND MEMORY

Identity has been a vexed issue for Australian South Sea Islanders. Uprooted from Melanesia, they lacked the moral and territorial claims of the Indigenous dispossessed, yet shared with them the consequences of exploitation and embedded racism. Islanders took pride in their ancestry. They were also prone to regard Aborigines as racial inferiors, despite the prevalence of intermarriage between the two groups (Moore 2001, pp.172–173). Australia's unhappy racial history took a turn towards reconciliation in 1967, when, by referendum, the federal government acquired the power to legislate for the benefit of Aboriginal people and include them in the census.

The 1967 referendum outcome confronted South Sea Islanders with an identity dilemma. The substantial benefits that flowed from the Commonwealth's entry into Indigenous affairs, such as education and health subsidies, were not available to them unless they claimed Aboriginal or Torres Strait Islander identity. While in many cases they were entitled to make such a claim through intermarriage, this denied them their preferred identity and heightened tension between the two groups. Some Indigenous people resented descendants of immigrants receiving the same welfare benefits as the continent's original inhabitants. Further, the three criteria for Aboriginality—Aboriginal descent, Aboriginal identity and acceptance by the Aboriginal community—could force South Sea Islanders into an invidious position. Some Islanders found that their claims to Aboriginal identity, even with Aboriginal ancestry, were blocked by Indigenous gatekeepers, leaving them with a sense of doubled victimhood, discriminated against by both white and black (Evatt Foundation 1991, pp.12–15).

By the 1980s, heightened identity consciousness among Indigenous people placed South Sea Islanders at an increased disadvantage. Moreover, the task of South Sea Islander identity construction and maintenance required a distancing from Aboriginality. The Human Rights and Equal Opportunity Commission (HREOC) took up their cause in the early 1990s. It called for recognition of South Sea Islanders as a distinct racial group, separate from the Indigenous population, and one which had contributed to national development. The Australian Government finally recognised Islander descendants as a distinct and disadvantaged community in 1994, and the Queensland State Government afforded similar recognition in 2000. In the second decade of the twenty-first century, Australian South Sea Islanders number some 40,000, concentrated in Queensland. This estimate is based on self-classification and complicated by the high rate of intermarriage—some 50%—between Islanders and Indigenous Australians (Corris 1970, p.54; HREOC 1993, pp.66–70; Lake 2013, pp.554–555; Moore 2000, p.23; 2016).

Despite historical evidence that most South Sea Islanders came voluntarily, many remaining or returning for second contracts, Islander memory traces their Australian origins to kidnappings and slavery. The slavery allegation was as old as the labour trade itself and a favourite weapon wielded by humanitarians and other campaigners against imported coloured labour. In the second half of 1889 the Queensland Legislative Assembly debated the contentious issue at length. Supporters, such as Mackay's representative David Dalrymple, pointed to Islanders returning after completing initial contracts. He declared 'proof that this is not slavery lies in the fact that one-third of the Polynesians return after having completed their term of service' (*Queensland Parliamentary Debates (QPD)* 30 August 1889, p.1340). Jean Isambert, from southeast Queensland, offered the contrary view, insisting 'coloured labour is slavery in every respect but name' (*QPD* 26 September 1889, p.1828). The debate re-emerged, with even greater vehemence, in the second half of the twentieth century. Second-generation Islander memory tended towards hereditary victimhood. This involved the sacralisation of memories to 'effectively block the sceptical and critical gaze of outsiders' (Lim 2010, p.140). Faith Bandler (1993) emphatically expressed her preference for oral memory over documented history and rejection of outside scrutiny:

> So I don't want historians, and I don't want anthropologists telling me how my father got here and how he worked, because he told me and that's good enough. So he worked for nothing for years and years and years. It wasn't indentured labour, he'd signed no papers, he was enslaved.

A wave of decolonisation swept through Melanesia from the mid-1970s, with Papua New Guinea winning independence in 1975, followed by the Solomon Islands in 1978 and Vanuatu in 1980. This coincided with a 'memory boom' in the societies of former colonial powers responding to a collapse of faith in grand narratives of progress. Their populations, including minorities, turned from the future to the past in quests for legitimacy and identity (Olick et al. 2011, p.3). Previously repressed identities resurfaced, many bearing an 'historical wound' (Chakrabarty 2007, p.166) which, as a fusion of history and memory, lay outside historians' capacity for verification or refutation. Such newly activated identities, many charged with a grudge, triggered the emergence of multiculturalism as a coping and management mechanism for the plethora of new claims on the state.

The postcolonial priority accorded to racial equality and minority rights generated an upsurge in transnational memory of slavery in many places with pasts entangled in the slave trade. Eponymous New World cities, including Washington DC and Columbus, Ohio, were subject to identity shaming. Once their eponym's connection to slavery was publicised, there were calls to jettison their names, along with monuments to their founders (Schuman et al. 2005; Gunderman 2015). Eruptions of slavery memory were not confined to cities which had directly participated in or benefitted from the trans-Atlantic slave trade. Slavery rhetoric seeped into Australian popular culture. It can be detected in Edward Docker's influential, if not particularly scholarly, account of the Queensland–Melanesian labour trade, *The Blackbirders*. The first edition, published in 1970, was subtitled, '*The Recruiting of South Seas Labour for Queensland, 1863-1907*'. Eleven years later, a second edition bore the more emotive subtitle, '*A Brutal Story of the Kanaka Slave Trade*' (Docker 1970, 1981).

Rothberg's notion of multidirectional memory, of 'dynamic transfers that take place between diverse places and times' (2009, p.11), has Australian resonances. Townsville is a city of cohabiting memories: white-settler-oriented official memory jostles with Indigenous and South Sea Islander perspectives on the past. Their reactions to Robert Towns' statue exemplify Rothberg's emphasis on productive interaction and exchange between minority collective memories. Moreover, Robert Towns' early twenty-first-century insertion in Townsville's central memorial landscape illustrates memory's multidirectionality, with Indigenous Australians joining him to Captain Cook as an additional icon of dispossession. The image of Towns has travelled well beyond the city named after him, acquiring symbolic salience throughout Australia and the Oceanic homelands of

South Sea Islander immigrants, exhibiting what Rothberg (2009, pp.3, 5, 11) terms memory's anachronistic and creative character, its ability to cross time, continents and oceans.

The convergence of Robert Towns and slavery in Islander memory, both in Australia and Pacific island states, followed the widespread trend, from the late twentieth century, to use 'innocent victimhood' (Lim 2010) in the construction of collective memories. The South Sea Islander embrace of slavery origins is primarily a post-1980 phenomenon. The slavery paradigm has since infiltrated Government documents and institutions. The Queensland Government's *Recognition Statement* claimed that many Islanders were 'tricked into coming, others were kidnapped or "blackbirded" …. [and] were treated like slaves' (Queensland Government 2000). A 2018–2019 Exhibition, *Plantation Voices*, mounted by the Queensland State Library (QSL) also appears to endorse the kidnapping and slavery paradigm, asserting that many Islanders brought to Australia were 'kidnapped, tricked or blackbirded' (QSL 2018–2019).

A circular feedback loop thus strengthened the conviction of most present-day Australian South Sea Islanders that they were descendants of kidnapped sugar slaves (Moore 2015, p.171). Oral evidence collected by historians Clive Moore and Patricia Mercer in the 1970s from Islander descendants living in North Queensland included recollections of force, deception and kidnapping but not the slavery preoccupation of later decades (Moore 2015, p.160). In an earlier work, *Kanaka*, Moore (1985) showed how Islander memory, in the last two decades of the twentieth century, was influenced by popular literature and media narratives drawing on the imagery and vocabulary of American slavery. After a detailed investigation of Melanesian experiences in Mackay, he concluded that the kidnapping myth was deeply entrenched and revealed as much about the present as the past. The myth spoke of an immigrant group's quest for identity and recognition, its sense of past injustice, need for psychological solace and determination to enjoy the promise of Australian citizenship, 'a fair go' (Moore 1985, pp.337–40).

An Australian South Sea Islander historian, writing in the twenty-first century, Tracey Banivanua Mar, of Fijian, British and Chinese ancestry, further embedded kidnapping and slavery motifs. She rejected cultural explanations for the divergence of settler history and Islander memory, validating the latter with insistence that, for South Sea Islanders, a sojourn in nineteenth-century Queensland was confined to 'the traumas of, at worst, kidnap and years of abuse, and, at best, alienation and exploitation'

(Mar 2000, p.34; Lester 2017). Waskam Emelda Davis, President of the nationally prominent Australian South Sea Islanders (Port Jackson) organisation, received government funding to support historical research on a project entitled 'Children of the Sugar Slaves'. Her communications included the assertion that the South Sea Island labour trade was underpinned by trickery, kidnapping and coercion (Davis 2018).

Historians cannot help but be impressed by the apparent integrity and consistency of the memory which underpins the identities of the Australian South Sea Islanders. Historian Doug Hunt (2016) argued not only that the blackbirding narrative was integral to their twenty-first-century identity but also that its potency was functional. It strengthened the community's collectivity, underpinning attempts at national organisation and enhancing lobbying power with governments. Moreover, it helped restore their homeland links to Melanesia, where the kidnapping and slavery saga found a place in nationalist mythologies.

Two Australian historians, Moore (2015, p.168) and Hunt, were invited by the Vanuatu Government to speak at the commemoration of the 150th anniversary of the labour trade in the capital, Port Vila, in June 2013. Some 150 Australian South Sea Islanders also flew there for the occasion. The highlight, though possibly not for the two Australian historians, was re-enactment of brutal blackbirding scenes which attracted a large assembly of ni-Vanuatu, including Prime Minister, Moana Carcasses Kalosil. The commentary singled out Robert Towns for censure, revealing diasporic memory transfer to the homeland. The Prime Minister led a chorus shouting 'Shame on You!', condemning Australia for its role in blackbirding and failure to mitigate its legacy (Hunt 2016).

Despite Mar's (2000, pp.15–21) rejection of cultural explanations for discrepancies between Islander memory and documented history, other Australian historians, particularly Clive Moore (2016), have attempted to account for the divergences with reference to trauma. Australian South Sea Islanders suffered the geographical and cultural displacement of immigration, whether voluntary or otherwise, and the shock of moving to a racially stratified society in which they were at, or near, the bottom of the hierarchy. The death rates for Islanders, particularly in their first year of indenture, were far higher than the Australian average, as they had no immunity to common diseases. Their labour was arduous and poorly paid by European standards. Their disadvantage was compounded in the early twentieth century by the humiliation of actual and threatened arrest and deportation. Moore interpreted this Islander experience as 'cultural

kidnapping', involving enticement, displacement, exploitation and racial discrimination similar to that experienced by Indigenous Australians.
There is, perhaps, also a broader explanation. Australian South Sea Islanders were not the only immigrant group to incorporate involuntary homeland departures into their new hybrid identities. The Irish and Highland Scots, most of whom emigrated for opportunistic reasons, constructed New World collective identities incorporating a romanticised homeland from which they were banished by cruel external agencies. Such mythologies absolved immigrants from any suspicion of family and homeland desertion to escape constrictive local circumstances or pursue personal advancement. They also provided a conduit through which they, or their descendants, might reconnect with the homeland on honourable terms. Moreover, diasporic communities found, in misery narratives of this kind, persuasive unifying scripts for memory and identity performances (Miller 1990, pp.91–92; Basu 2005, pp.140–144).

TOWNSVILLE: OFFICIAL MEMORY AND EPONYMITY IN THE TWENTIETH CENTURY

Urban official memory may appear as solid as the public monuments that so often house it. Yet its foundations can prove unstable. Such is the case with Townsville where its Indigenous dimension, European founders, Islander presence and even the establishment year have eluded the certainty memory agents crave. The primary custodians of official memory until Townsville's 1913 Jubilee were first-generation historians, Englishmen Dodd S. Clarke (1847–1918) and Edmund Banfield (1852–1923). The former sponsored Townsville's celebration of regional pre-eminence with a Separation Carnival in 1890, when the fever for Northern self-determination was most intense. It was a proclamation of the town's exceptionality and civic cohesion. A procession and pageant, attracting 6,000 onlookers, presented a story of white civilisation's conquest of the tropical North. Aboriginal people featured as comic props, relics of a doomed race. A float contained four Indigenous men, two with garishly whitened faces and two others being continuously shaved, an illustration of the cleansing power of a local manufacturer's 'Separation soap' (*Townsville Herald*, 18 October 1890, p.14).

Banfield, Clarke's protégé, wrote an early history of his adopted city, nominating it as 'the chief of the North'. Unable to fully acknowledge prior Indigenous habitation, his vision of the first residents focussed on the 1864 party from Woodstock Station: Andrew Ball, Mark Watt Reid and their guides, two anonymous 'black boys'. Banfield's narration was above all a salute to the enterprise, energy and local patriotism of pioneers and the prosperity they unlocked for the future. Indigenous people occasionally appeared, but only as features of the natural landscape, anonymous as the rocks and mangroves of Ross Creek and similar obstacles to progress (Banfield 1906, pp.1, 3, 10).

In 1913, Townsville celebrated its Jubilee, an opportunity for leading citizens to align the past with the present and project a preferred future. After 50 years Townsville's European population had grown to 14,000, and many children were third-generation North Queenslanders. W. Lloyd Warner (1959, pp.107, 110) showed how urban commemorative events, such as jubilees and centenaries, were secular rites intended to bind the population into a unified community. Townsville's civic leaders orchestrated a presentation of the past which honoured European founders and fabricated a history in accordance with what they wished it had been. Indeed, the commemoration itself was envisaged as a didactic pioneer memorial. Organisers proposed:

> making the occasion a salient feature in local history — such an historical monument to the efforts of the early pioneers of our prosperity as will tend to stimulate coming generations to emulate their efforts. (*Townsville Daily Bulletin (TDB)* 7 June 1913, p.10)

The prior and continuing presence of Aboriginal people was largely ignored. Their camps on Townsville's periphery were matched by their marginal status in the city's European identity narrative (Reynolds 2003, p.9). According to the *Jubilee Souvenir*, the civic mission was to fill the 'empty spaces' of tropical Australia with 'imported Britons and Europeans' (Clarke 1913, p.26). Townsville was proof that 'our North European race can...live and thrive in tropical Australia' (*TDB* 9 July 1913, p.7). Also denied any place in foundational mythology were South Sea Islanders and Chinese. Each comprised only 3% of the Townsville census district population in 1881, yet both made significant contributions in the city's early decades (*Census* Queensland 1881, pp.06–8, 12).

A dissenting voice challenged this presentation of official memory. English-born salesman, Charles Hughes, who had arrived in the 1870s, pointed out Townsville was the outcome of a 'White Man's Invasion', and that there were still Aborigines alive who witnessed the overland arrival of the first intruders. He called for them to have a place in the Jubilee Carnival (*TDB* 22 August 1913, p.7). They did indeed, but in an ironic fashion that denied their existence. An award-winning float in the procession, 'The Founders of Townsville', featured an Aboriginal bush hut mounted on a truck against a background of a campfire and shadowy figures among trees. Marching alongside were 'blacks with all the implements of olden savagery' (*TDB* 26 August 1913, p.5). However, the marchers were not Aborigines, but blackened Europeans.

During the interwar and depression years, Townsville's official memory was largely dormant. A 1941 stimulus from Sydney increased Robert Towns' stature, at the expense of John Melton Black's, and led to the former's domination of Townsville's memorial landscape. Towns had been buried in Sydney's Balmain Cemetery with an imposing obelisk over his grave. The cemetery was closed in 1912 and converted to a public park (King 1940, p.9). Those charged with dispersal of headstones offered the obelisk to the northern city, which, they believed, Towns founded. Townsville's newspaper editor hoped that it would trigger 'history consciousness' in a city with a scarcity of records, few monuments and 'a forgotten past' (*TDB* 23 December 1941, p.4). The Council acceded, though the populist and parochial alderman, Tom Aikens, unconsciously illustrated the editor's complaint about historical apathy when he ridiculed the offer of Towns' obelisk as an attempt by Southerners to palm off a dilapidated tombstone on naïve Northerners. Nevertheless, the gift triggered a resurgence of memory of Towns and debate over whether he was a worthy foundational figure or an unscrupulous pioneer of blackbirding (Townsville City Council Minutes (TCCM) 1941, p.1591; *TDB*, 20 December 1941, p.4; 19 January 1942, p.4; 21 January 1942, p.2).

The offer of Towns' monument coincided with the outbreak of the Pacific War (1941–1945) when the Northern city was a forward and vulnerable base. The obelisk languished in open air storage from 1943 until 1947, when the Council again turned its attention to the city's impoverished memorial landscape. With advice from the Royal Australian Historical Society, the summit of Castle Hill was selected as the obelisk site, because it would enable the city founder's memory marker to preside over Townsville and its surroundings (TCCM 1947, p.2301). Another two years passed before the Council raised the monument. There was no unveiling ceremony, and its inscription was terse, noting its Sydney origin and Towns as the city's eponym.

Nevertheless, its prominence and visibility intensified the city's identification with Towns, both in official memory and subsequent Australian South Sea Islander counter-memory. While it is true that memory shapes monuments, the reverse is also true, for in this case, the erection of the obelisk intensified official memory's attachment to a man who was only briefly in the city and whose reputation was inextricably linked to the Pacific Island labour trade.

Townsville celebrated its 100th anniversary in 1964, sparking an upsurge of settler memory, bolstered by the presence of Dr RA Douglas, grandson of 1864 founder, Andrew Ball. Indigenous antecedents were no longer absent, though still peripheral, compared to principal contenders for civic paternity: Robert Towns, Andrew Ball, Mark Watt Reid and John Melton Black. Celebrations included re-enactment of Ball and Reid meeting an Indigenous man in 1864. Yet the dominant historical metaphor remained transformation of a wilderness into a modern tropical city (*TDB*, 2 November 1964, pp.1, 2, 12).

The Queensland Governor, Sir Henry Abel Smith, unveiled a plaque, set in Cape Cleveland rock, less than 150 metres from the site of the first European encampment. He also forgot prior Aboriginal occupation in his description of the past 100 years as a story of progress in which a swamp had been transformed into one of the world's most beautiful and healthy tropical cities. The plaque honoured a quartet of European founders. Towns was allocated first place as the entrepreneur, while pioneer John Melton Black occupied the last. The second and third places were occupied by explorers, Andrew Ball and Mark Watt Reid, who preceded Black to Cleveland Bay in 1864. Indigenous guides were forgotten.

The Development of Townsville's Twenty-First-Century Landscape of Memory

With the closing of the twentieth century, Indigenous Australians secured a significant presence in Townsville's landscape of memory with the dedication, in 1999, of the ambitious Hambeluna Spirit Rising environmental sculpture on The Strand. It attempted to integrate early 1860s' white appropriation of the site with its prior Aboriginal occupation. Nevertheless, the new millennium began with confrontation between the majority of Townsville's residents and the interlinked Indigenous and Australian South Sea Islander minorities. The city brand was collateral damage in a cultural collision between official memory and South Sea Islander counter-memory, anchored in kidnapping and slavery. Islander memory insurgency had potency in Townsville because of its relatively large Indigenous population, more than 5%, and the high rate of intermarriage between the two groups (Australian Bureau of Statistics 2002; Australian Human Rights Commission 2003). Australian South Sea Islanders, in Townsville and across Australia, had adopted Robert Towns as the embodiment of their kidnapping and slavery origins in much the same way Indigenous Australians used Captain Cook to symbolise dispossession.

Aboriginal Captain Cook narratives placed the navigator all over the Australian continent, at places he could not have visited and at times when he was not in the southern hemisphere. As Indigenous historian John Maynard pointed out, the phrase 'Captain Cook' entered multiple Aboriginal languages as a synonym for personal and collective disasters and, 'from an Aboriginal perspective Cook remains the scapegoat for white invasion' (Maynard 2018, p.3). Public statues and other monuments to James Cook, scattered throughout Australia, are sources of controversy, with intensifying demands from Indigenous and other groups that they be removed, or, more commonly, have inscriptions adjusted to recognise the fatal consequences of his voyage for Indigenous people (Maynard 2018 p.1; Grant 2017).

Captain Cook and Robert Towns played parallel symbolic roles in Indigenous and Australian South Sea Islander collective memories. By virtue of its eponymity, Townsville was, for both, a kidnapping and slavery memory site. Local James Cook University academic, Gracelyn Smallwood, of South Sea Islander and Indigenous ancestry, wryly noted that Townsville was named after a slave trader, hosted a university whose name honoured 'an imperialist colonising navigator' and, in the twenty-first century, celebrated the slave trader with a public statue (Smallwood 2018).

The city deepened Islanders' estrangement with commemorations of its founder. Disaffection among Townsville Islanders was further intensified by their exclusion from its landscape of memory when other Queensland towns with whom their history was intertwined had prominent memorials to South Sea Islanders. Two such notable South Sea Islander memorials, both erected in 2001, occupy central locations in the southern Queensland sugar centres of Maryborough and Childers. Mackay, a sugar city some 400 km south of Townsville, completed a memorial precinct honouring its South Sea Islander minority. The complex includes an arresting statue of an Islander cane-cutter, dedicated in 2005, the same year Townsville placed Robert Towns on a pedestal.

TOWNSVILLE'S CENTENARY CITY CELEBRATIONS, 2003

In *Eddie Mabo and Others* vs *The State of Queensland (1992)*, the High Court of Australia ruled that native land title existed throughout the nation. The chief plaintiff was Townsville resident, Eddie (Koiki) Mabo, a Torres Strait Islander, married to Bonita, an Australian South Sea Islander and activist. He discovered that, legally, he did not own his ancestral land on Mer, part of the Murray group of islands in the Torres Strait. This was an epiphany and part of his motivation in initiating the historic legal challenge. By the early twenty-first century, invasion, rather than settlement, had been established, nationally and locally, as the more accurate description of the arrival of Europeans. This destabilised official memory discourse and partly explained Townsville's sharpened appetite for commemoration. It also emboldened South Sea Islanders, both Townsville residents and from across the country, to pit their hereditary memory of Robert Towns against the official version (Reynolds 1982; Loos 1982; Loos and Mabo 1996).

An early trigger for these memory hostilities was a 2001 proposal from Tony Hogan, chairman of CBD Promotions, an inner-city business lobby closely linked to the Townsville Council, to install a public statue of Robert Towns. He was armed with research from local historian and newspaper manager Jim Manion, who had reformulated, for a twenty-first-century audience, the settler-oriented narrative of Townsville's genesis. Bolstered by documentary evidence, it acquitted Towns of kidnapping and slavery. The published report on the eponym's innocence was accompanied by a photograph of Manion and Hogan paying homage at Towns' obelisk on the summit of Castle Hill (Anderson 2001, p.9). Such exoneration infuriated the Islander community. One of the more outspoken gatekeepers of their memory was Robert Cole, president of the Australian South Sea Island Corporation and of South Sea Islander and Indigenous ancestry. He responded by reiterating Towns was a slave trader who paid his workers in treacle and flour. The very name of Robert Towns was anathema to Islanders, whose ancestors, Cole asserted, were whipped, killed and thrown off boats to drown (Anderson 2001, p.9). The statue proposal acquired additional momentum two years later when Townsville celebrated the centenary of its gazettal as a city.

In 2003 Townsville re-enacted its 'First City of the North' identity (Barr 2003, p.2). The Centenary City celebrations intersected with a larger scheme to rejuvenate its run-down central business district and increase the city's appeal as a destination for tourism and mobile capital. Renewal projects included privatisation of a portion of Hanran Park, a controversial inner-city recreational area abutting Ross Creek. The park was frequented by itinerants, alcoholics and homeless people, many of them Indigenous. Townsville attracted unwelcome attention in the 1990s as the Council and State Government attempted to move occupants, in some cases with the help of private security guards, into alternative accommodation and reclaim space for public use. That the majority of the 'parkies' were Indigenous people led to claims of Council racism. This intensified Townsville's deep-north image already sullied from installation of its eponym in Islander counter-memory as a kidnapping and slavery symbol (O'Malley 1996, p.8; Estimates Committee G 1996, 1997).

Remarkable for their duration and intensity, the Centenary City Celebrations included 26 events over five months (TCCM 2003, p.22982). Grappling with globalising neo-liberalism, Townsville was changing rapidly and used commemoration as a tool for place marketing, wooing investment capital, inner-city revival and urban redevelopment (Crinson 2005, p.ix; Bélanger 2002, pp.69–76). Official memory was deployed with renewed vigour to promote shared civic identity, values and economic aspirations for the future. Settler determination and enterprise were invoked and embodied in the appearance at the grand finale of Robert Badgery, Robert Towns' great-great-great-great grandson. Mayor Tony Mooney and the *Townsville Daily Bulletin* capitalised on his visit by identifying the city's twenty-first-century businesspeople and entrepreneurs with Robert Towns, albeit with aspirations outstripping those of their eponymous predecessor (*TDB*, 19 September 2003, p.2; 20 September 2003, p.8).

A Centenary City play, *Towns' Town*, commissioned by CBD Promotions, sought to cleanse the reputation of Robert Towns, and Townsville, of blackbirding tarnish. The drama, written by theatre manager, John du Feu, was didactic, seeking to present Towns as an exceptional achiever, confronting denigrators with historical evidence that refuted kidnapping and slavery charges. It also sought to explain the origin of Townsville's name, as its tautology had also attracted unwelcome attention. The script was empirically defensible; du Feu consulted Islanders during the writing of the play and included their perspectives on the labour trade and stereotype of Robert Towns. The latter, however, was represented, in accordance with documentary evidence, as an ambitious, puritanical, ethical, self-made entrepreneur, with Townsville as his namesake and legacy. Towards the conclusion, after Towns had been established as the city's visionary founder, the narrator attempted to close the argument about whether he was a saint or sinner: 'He's dead and gone. Build him a monument and forget him...' The play opened on the Mall's semi-circular centre stage before an invited audience of notables. Surrounding them was a phalanx of mostly Indigenous and South Sea Islander demonstrators, waving flags and signs of protest. Jonathan Brown, who played Towns, found it one of his most unsettling roles. Actors remained in dressing rooms until the crowd dispersed (du Feu 2003; Brown 2015; Fleming 2015; Reitmajer 2003, p.3).

THE ROBERT TOWNS PUBLIC STATUE: CONTROVERSY AND CONSEQUENCES

The City Council was undeterred by the failure of *Towns' Town* to rehabilitate the memory of its subject among Islanders and Indigenous people. On 18 May 2004 it approved CBD Promotions' commission of North Queensland sculptor Jane Hawkins to execute, at a cost of $40,000, a life-sized bronze statue of Robert Towns on Pioneers Walk near the Mall (TCCM, 18 May 2004, p.23679) (Fig. 6.2). Regarding historical accuracy as important, and aware of unsavoury memory attached to Towns, Hawkins suggested John Melton Black as a possible alternative subject. This was dismissed because of eponymity. The city needed to explain and defend its name. Treading the porous line between history and memory, Hawkins tried not to judge Towns but concentrated on his achievements, including his role as foundational financier. She cast him in heroic pose, wearing period costume and grasping a telescope, a widely used feature of Australian explorer statuary (TCCM 18 May 2004, p.23679; *Townsville Bulletin*, (*TB*) 19 June 2004, p.29; Hawkins 2015).

A faction of the white community shared Islander indignation at the proposal. These included Ian Fleming (2015), a Mall business owner and vehement critic of both Robert Towns and his further memorialisation. Many other residents appeared apathetic. A poll conducted in the Mall in late May found that 6 out of 15 passers-by were unable to say who Robert Towns was, with one identifying him as a serving politician. Another

Fig. 6.2 Robert Towns statue, Pioneers Walk, Townsville, unveiled 2005 (Authors' photograph)

respondent, a woman of Aboriginal and Islander ancestry, was far from apathetic, declaring: 'Towns was the founder of Townsville and had been involved with a lot of naughty things with South Sea Islanders....South Sea Islanders always spoke badly about Towns. They don't like him' (Anderson 2004, p.6).

Responding to evidence of continuing hostility to Towns and his proposed statue, the Council, in early July, commissioned retired history professor, Kett Kennedy, to investigate the relevance of blackbirding to the city's foundation and naming. His report, presented at the end of August, cleared Towns of any personal connection to illegal or unethical behaviour. It considered the case for Blacktown or Blackville as alternative names but concluded that Towns was a worthier eponym than John Melton Black because his financial contribution was crucial to the survival and eventual prosperity of the northern outpost (Kennedy 2004, pp. iv-v, 58–9). In December, public opinion was measured in the annual *Townsville Bulletin* Survey. Drawing responses from 659 residents, it showed a small majority in favour of a Towns' statue: 45.1% supported the project, 39.5% rejected it and 15.4% offered no opinion (*TB* 28 December 2004, p.6).

The statue was unveiled on 18 May 2005 by Jack Wilson, Chairman of the Council's Lifestyle and Community Development Committee and staunch defender of Towns. Its inscription, drafted by Kett Kennedy, and attached to the plinth, identified Jane Hawkins as the sculptor and CBD Promotions as its funding source. Interpretative signage, also drafted by Kennedy, was placed near the statue. It acknowledged criticism of Towns and included two sentences detailing the crucial heavy labour undertaken by Islanders in establishing the town. A paragraph headed Visionary or Villain? alluded to Towns' blackbirding reputation. It dismissed this as an unfounded allegation, describing his attitude to Islander workers as 'paternalistic but well intentioned'.

Exhibiting the opportunities afforded by multidirectionality, memories of Islander slavery and Aboriginal dispossession converged during the unveiling ceremony, bearing out Rothberg's (2009, p.311) assertion that memory is not a zero-sum game. Rather, the joint activation of Indigenous and Islander memories of disparate European aggressions and intrusions increased the political firepower of both groups. Such convergence was a strategic advantage for Australian South Sea Islanders in particular, who lacked the numbers, and purchase on the national conscience of Indigenous people. The formalities of the unveiling ceremony were overshadowed by Islander and Indigenous protestors. Wilson had barely begun to speak when an Islander activist shouted, 'You worship a blackbirder, you ought to be ashamed of yourself'. Other interjections included 'Give the land back to Aboriginal people'. A particularly vocal demonstrator, a woman of South Sea Islander and Indigenous ancestry, was removed by police. Despite the commotion, Wilson persisted with his case for official memory. He cited the acquittal of Towns by Kennedy but was howled down by cries of 'slave trader'. Pastor Alan Johnson, an elder in both Indigenous and Islander communities, was rebuffed when he sought to speak with Wilson after the ceremony. Johnson's grievance was exclusion of Islander perspectives from the unveiling ceremony, including an opportunity for forgiveness (Johnson 2018).

The unveiling of Towns' statue manifested the friction between Islander and Indigenous shared understandings of the city's past and official memory. It also showed the two versions of the past were dialectical, their interaction shaping public memory. In a vain attempt to placate protestors at the Towns' statue unveiling, Councillor Wilson suggested the next public statue might be that of Torres Strait Islander land rights hero Eddie Mabo (Mortison 2005, p.3). This was an indication that contestation over Towns and his statue helped make the city's central landscape of memory more inclusive. The Council's subsequent blueprint for the future of Castle Hill included relocation of the dominant Towns obelisk and reworking the Hill's landscape of memory to recognise its rich Indigenous past (Castle Hill Concept Plan 2018, pp.30, 42). Yet the city's small Islander community, less than 600 in 2018 (Multicultural Affairs Queensland, p.29), still hungers for monumental recognition. It is an appetite shared by their national diaspora. A leader, Emelda Davis (2018), called for an additional memorial to acknowledge her community's contribution to Townsville's foundation and development. She proposed a sculpture of a South Sea Islander warrior or cane-cutter in the city centre, opposite Towns' statue. Such a gesture would not only bring further healing to a historical wound but align Townsville's memorial landscape more closely with its early history.

Mabo Memorial, Townsville

In October 2006 the Council added an Indigenous Australian to the city's pantheon of pioneers, commissioning a monument to Eddie Mabo in Pioneers Walk (TCCM 2006, pp.3872–3) (Fig. 6.3). Matthew Harding, a nationally renowned artist, executed the work. The Mabo Memorial featured a bronze Warup drum modelled on a traditional instrument carved by its subject. It resembled a cannon aimed at Towns' statue across Ross Creek. A fingerprint, signifying the bond between people and their land, was inscribed on an adjacent boulder. It was unveiled on Mabo Day, 3 June 2007, by Townsville Mayor Tony Mooney and Bonita Mabo. The Mayor recalled Mabo's commitment, courage, drive into uncharted legal territory and value as a Townsville resident (Sharrat 2007, p.6).

This unveiling demonstrated the multidirectionality of urban memory with Eddie Mabo, and Indigenous Australians, winning a place in central

Fig. 6.3 Eddie Mabo Memorial, Pioneers Walk, Townsville, unveiled 2007. (Authors' photograph)

Townsville's memorial landscape. Collective memories were in dialogue with each other, acknowledging mutual and antagonistic pasts in the present. The contrast with the unveiling of Towns' statue was stark. There was a far larger crowd, Indigenous, Islander and non-Indigenous. Celebration and harmony, rather than controversy and rancour, marked the ceremony (Wilson 2007, p.11), exemplifying the transformative power of symbolic gestures, underpinned by fundamental reform. Moreover, the perpetrator–victim vocabulary that dominated the unveiling of Robert Towns' statue was absent, replaced by the rhetoric of shared citizenship and mitigation of historical injustice. This development bears out Rothberg's optimism, expressed in *The Implicated Subject: Beyond Victims and Perpetrators* (2019, pp.19–20) that the cul-de-sac of perpetrator–victim discourse can be replaced by a new vocabulary of responsibility and recognition.

The memorial bore no inscription, but adjacent interpretative signage began with Mabo's impact on Australian history and Indigenous land claims: 'Eddie Koiki Mabo was a fundamental figure in the fight for recognition of Aboriginal and Torres Strait Islander Native Title'. It likened the Warup drum to the continuum of Eddie's voice, bridging past, present and future. Now a location for commemorations of the Mabo land rights victory, the sculpture is a memory site for Townsville's Indigenous community, particularly Torres Strait Islanders, and a counterpoint to Robert Towns' statue. It is also emblematic of interlinked Indigenous and Australian South Sea Islander communities, exemplified in the marriage of Eddie and Bonita (Turner 2017).

CONCLUSION

Across Ross Creek, Robert Towns still stands in bronze, embodying the collision of traditional officially endorsed memory with oral memory and minority interests. His statue is far from moribund, operating as a forge for public memory, where settler memory intersects with those of South Sea Islander and Indigenous communities. It is a negotiating platform, allowing divergent memories to converge, interact, bargain and borrow (Rothberg 2009, p.3). In 2013, Islander and Indigenous people, including Bonita Mabo, assembled in front of the statue to mark the 150th anniversary of the beginning of the Pacific Island labour trade in Queensland. They had invested Towns' statue not only with counter-memory of migrant abuse and Indigenous dispossession, but also hope for the future. There was a note of healing, with expressions of appreciation for government recognition and compensation (Wilson 2013, p.7). As Chakrabarty (2007, pp.77–78) observed, historical wounds, such as those sustained by Australian South Sea Islanders, are not permanent. To be able to speak of the wound is an early sign of recovery.

This case study of Robert Towns' statue illustrates the salience of multidirectional memory in migratory settings. The movement of labourers from Oceania to Northern Australia led to an accretion and thickening of memory. This process accelerated in the twenty-first century as cheap airfares and digital communications facilitated the urge of Islander descendants, third generation in many cases, to reconnect with homeland relatives and ancestral villages. The movement of Island migrant labour to Australia has produced at least four new forms of cultural memory: for immigrants and their descendants in the country of destination, for those who remained in their Oceanic homelands and for both Indigenous and non-Indigenous Australians.

The efforts of Townsville City Council and business leaders to harness settler history in defence of their city's name culminated in the installation of Robert Towns' statue. However, this attempt to perpetuate, in bronze, the eponym's white-settler-oriented official memory failed. Nevertheless, his statue maintains its vitality, not as a guardian of official memory, but as a focal point for Islander and Indigenous counter-memory. The image of Robert Towns crossed the cultural border between Indigenous and Islander communities, serving both in their joint challenge to official memory of a foundational figure. In similar fashion, Islander memory of Towns has crossed the geo-political border between Australia and Melanesia, a mnemonic export serving as an identity-building commodity on a national scale in Vanuatu. This paralleled his role in Australia, where leaders among the Islander diaspora used his memory to craft a common mainland identity, distinct from that of Indigenous and non-Indigenous Australians.

In the city named after him, the statue weakened the grip of eponymity and diminished Towns' place in public memory. It increased the visibility of Islander and Indigenous memory and helped turn Towns into a unifying symbol of colonialist intrusion, exploitation and dispossession. Such productive convergence vindicates one of the core claims for the value of multidirectional memory: that it 'provides a critical resource…for contesting the unequal distribution of attention' (Rothberg 2009, p.311).

Robert Towns is entangled in multiple memory traditions (Conrad 2003). The controversy over his statue exemplifies the successful deployment of converged memories and innocent victimhood in acts of civic, transcultural and transnational (in the case of Vanuatu) remembrance. The unveiling of the memorial activated a mnemonic alliance between Islanders and Indigenous people. It showed that the articulation of collective memory by these minorities was not necessarily a competitive enterprise; rather it augmented the capacity of both groups to 'advance their claims for recognition and justice' (Rothberg 2011, p.524).

REFERENCES

Anderson, J. (2001). Monster or Man of Vision. *Townsville Bulletin (TB)*, 2 June, 9.

Anderson, J. (2004). Hero or Villain? City Founder a Mystery to Most. *Townsville Bulletin (TB)*, 29 May, 6.

Ashton, P., & Hamilton, P. (2008). Places of the Heart: Memorials, Public History and the State in Australia Since 1960. *Public History Review, 15*, 1–29.
Australian Bureau of Statistics. (2002). *2001 Census: Further Analysis of Aboriginal and Torres Strait Islander Population Distribution*, Media Release, 26 June.
Australian Human Rights Commission. (2003). *Australian South Sea Islanders: A Century of Race Discrimination Under Australian Law*. https://www.humanrights.gov.au/our-work/race-discrimination/publications/australian-south-sea-islanders-century-race-discrimination. Accessed 27 Jan 2019.
Bandler, F. (1993). Interviewed by Robin Hughes. Recorded 24 March 1993, Australian Biography Project, www.australianbiography.gov.au/bandler/interview1.html. Accessed 5 Jan 2019.
Banfield, E. (1906). *Townsville Illustrated: Together with a Short Historical Sketch of the City from its Earliest Days*. Townsville: G.H. Pritchard.
Barr, T. (2003). The First City of the North. *TB*, Centenary Supplement, 3 May, 2.
Basu, P. (2005). Roots- Tourism as Return Movement: Semantics and the Scottish Diaspora. In M. Harper (Ed.), *Emigrant Homecomings: The Return Movement of Emigrants, 1600–2000* (pp. 131–150). Manchester: Manchester University Press.
Bélanger, A. (2002). Urban Space and Collective Memory: Analysing the Various Dimensions of the Production of Memory. *Canadian Journal of Urban Research, 11*(1), 69–92.
Black, J. (1864). Letter, 21 November Cleveland Bay to Robert Towns. In W. J. Doherty (Ed.), *The Townsville Book: A Complete Sketch of the History, Topography, and Prominent Early Settlers of Townsville* (p. 33). Brisbane: Edwards, Dunlop.
Bodnar, J. (1992). *Remaking America: Public Memory, Commemoration, and Patriots in the Twentieth Century*. Princeton: Princeton University Press.
Brown, J. (2015). Interviewed by Rodney Sullivan and Robin Sullivan, 25 September.
Castle Hill Concept Plan. (2018). https://www.townsville.qld.gov.au/data/assets/pdf_file/0026/59804/Castle-hill-masterplan_w.pdf. Accessed 24 Jan 2019.
Census of Queensland. (1881). http://hccda.ada.edu.au/pages/QLD-1881-census_01-06_12. Accessed 18 Feb 2019.
Census of Australia. (1947). *Vol. 1, Part III*. Canberra: Commonwealth Statistician.
Chakrabarty, D. (2007). History and the Politics of Recognition. In K. Jenkins et al. (Eds.), *Manifestos for History* (pp. 77–87). London/New York: Routledge.
Clarke, D. (1913). Fifty Years in Townsville, 1863 to 1913: Half a Century's Progress. In *Townsville Bulletin Jubilee Souvenir, 1863–1913* (pp. 23–32). Townsville: North Queensland Newspaper Co..
Cook, J. (2014). In W. Wharton (Ed.), *Cook's Journal During his First Voyage Round the World, made in H.M. Bark Endeavour, 1768–7*. Cambridge: Cambridge University Press.

Conrad, S. (2003). Entangled Memories: Versions of the Past in Germany and Spain, 1945–2001. *Journal of Contemporary History, 38*, 85–99.
Corris, P. (1970). Pacific Island Labour Migrants in Queensland. *Journal of Pacific History, 5*(1), 43–64.
Crinson, M. (2005). Urban Memory: An Introduction. In M. Crinson (Ed.), *Urban Memory: History and Amnesia in the Modern City* (pp. xi–xx). New York: Routledge.
Davis, E. (2018). Email to Robin Sullivan, 18 December.
Docker, E. (1970). *The Blackbirders: The Recruiting of South Seas Labour for Queensland, 1863–1907.* Sydney: Angus and Robertson.
Docker, E. (1981). *The Blackbirders: A Brutal Story of the Kanaka Slave Trade.* Sydney: Angus and Robertson.
Du Feu, J. (2003). Towns' Town, Script.
Erll, A. (2011). Travelling Memory. *Parallax, 17*(4), 4–18.
Estimates Committee G. (1996, 1997). Queensland Parliament. Transcript, 26 September 1996 and 19 June 1997, https://www.parliament.qld.gov.au/global/search. Accessed 17 Feb 2019.
Evatt Foundation. (1991). *Australian South Sea Islanders: A Report on the Current Status of Australian South Sea Islanders.* Sydney: The Evatt Foundation.
Fleming, I. (2015). Interviewed by Rodney Sullivan and Robin Sullivan, 25 September.
Gibson-Wilde, D. (1984). *Gateway to a Golden Land, Townsville to 1884.* Townsville: History Department, James Cook University.
Grant, S. (2017, August 25). Between Catastrophe and Survival: The Real Journey Captain Cook Set us on, ABC News, http//www.abc.net.au/news/2017-08-25/stan-grant-captain-cook-indigenous-culture-statues-history/8843172. Accessed 4 Aug 2019.
Griffin, H. (2014). *Frontier Town: A History of Early Townsville and Hinterland, 1864–1884.* Townsville: North Queensland History Preservation Society.
Gunderman, R. (2015). Should We Change the Name of Washington, DC Because He Owned Slaves? Newsweek.com/should-we-change-name-washington-because-heowned-slaves-367268. Accessed 27 Oct 2015.
Hamilton, P., & Ashton, P. (2001). On not Belonging: Memorials and Memory in Sydney. *Public History Review, 1*, 23–36.
Hawkins, J. (2015). Interviewed by Rodney Sullivan and Robin Sullivan, 15 October.
Human Rights and Equal Opportunity Commission (HREOC). (1993). *The Call for Recognition: A Report on the Situation of Australian South Sea Islanders.* Canberra: Australian Government Printing Service.
Hunt, D. (2006). Bye Bye Blackbirder: The Death of Ross Lewin. *Journal of the Royal Historical Society of Queensland, 19*(5), 805–823.

Hunt, D. (2016). Robert Towns and the Pacific Labour Trade. Paper Presented to the 6th Biennial Conference of the Australian Association for Pacific Studies, James Cook University, Cairns, 1–4 April.
Johnson, A. (2018). Interviewed by Robin Sullivan, 18 and 19 August.
Kennedy, K. (2004). *Robert Towns' Townsville and the "Blackbirding" Controversy*. Townsville: Townsville City Council.
King, G. (1940). "Bobbie" Towns. His Grave will Soon be in a Park. *Sydney Morning Herald*, 19 October, 9.
Lake, M. (2013). Colonial Australia and the Asia-Pacific Region. In A. Bashford & S. Macintyre (Eds.), *The Cambridge History of Australia, Vol. 1: Indigenous and Colonial Australia* (pp. 535–559). New York: Cambridge University Press.
Lawson, S. (2016). Regionalism, Sub-regionalism and the Politics of Identity in Oceania. *The Pacific Review, 29*(3), 387–409.
Lester, A. (2017). Tracey Banivanua Mar 1974–2017. *The Journal of Pacific History, 52*(4), 518–523.
Lim, J. (2010). Victimhood Nationalism in Contested Memories: National Mourning and Global Accountability. In A. Assmann & S. Conrad (Eds.), *Memory in the Global Age: Discourses, Practices and Trajectories* (pp. 138–162). London: Palgrave Macmillan.
Lipsitz, G. (2001). *Time Passages: Collective Memory and American Popular Culture*. Minneapolis: University of Minnesota Press.
Loos, N. (1982). *Invasion and Resistance: Aboriginal-European Relations on the North Queensland Frontier, 1867–1897*. Canberra: Australian National University Press.
Loos, N., & Mabo, K. (1996). *Edward Koiki Mabo: His Life and Struggle for Land Rights*. Brisbane: University of Queensland Press.
Loughran, K., et al. (2016). Urban Spaces, City Cultures and Collective Memories. In L. Tota & T. Hagen (Eds.), *Routledge International Handbook of Memory Studies* (pp. 193–204). New York: Routledge.
Mar, T. (2000). *Buliman and Hard Work: Indenture, Identity and Complexity in Colonial North Queensland*. PhD thesis, Department of History, University of Melbourne.
Maynard, J. (2018). I'm Captain Cooked: Aboriginal Perspectives on James Cook, 1770–2020. In J. Maynard et al. (Eds.), *Cook and the Pacific* (pp. 1–13). National Library of Australia: Canberra.
McCreery, C., & McKenzie, K. (2013). The Australian Colonies in a Maritime World. *The Cambridge History of Australia, 1*, 580–582.
Megarrity, L. (2006). White Queensland: The Queensland Government's Ideological Position on the Use of Pacific Island Labourers in the Sugar Sector, 1880–1901. *Australian Journal of Politics and History, 52*(1), 1–12.
Megarrity, L. (2018). *Northern Dreams: The Politics of Northern Development in Australia*. Melbourne: Australian Scholarly Publishing.

Mercer, P. (1995). *White Australia Defied: Pacific Islander Settlement in North Queensland*. Townsville: Department of History and Politics, James Cook University.
Mihelj, S. (2013). Between Official and Vernacular Memory. In E. Keightley & M. Pickering (Eds.), *Research Methods for Memory Studies* (pp. 60–75). Edinburgh: Edinburgh University Press.
Miller, K. (1990). Emigration, Capitalism and Ideology in Post-Famine Ireland. In R. Kearney (Ed.), *Migrations: The Irish at Home and Abroad*. Dublin: Wolfhound Press.
Moore, C. (1985). *Kanaka: A History of Melanesian Mackay*. Port Moresby: Institute of Papua New Guinea Studies and University of Papua New Guinea Press.
Moore, C. (2000). Good-bye, Queensland, Good-bye White Australia, Good-Bye Christians: Australia's South Sea Islander Community and Deportation. *The New Federalist*, 4 December, 22–29.
Moore, C. (2001). The South Sea Islanders of Mackay, Queensland, Australia. In J. Fitzpatrick (Ed.), *Endangered People of Oceania: Struggles to Survive and Thrive* (pp. 167–181). Westport: Greenwood Press.
Moore, C. (2015). Australian South Sea Islanders' Narratives of Belonging. In F. Gounder (Ed.), *Narrative and Identity Construction in the Pacific Islands*. Amsterdam: John Benjamins Publishing Company.
Moore, C. (2016). Australian South Sea Islanders in Queensland, Stories from the Archives. 27 May, https://blogs.archives.qld.gov.au/2016/05/27/australian-south-sea-islanders-in-queensland/. Accessed 5 Jan 2019.
Mortison, D. (2005). Protestors go to Town Over Statue. *TB*, 19 May, 3.
Multicultural Affairs Queensland. (2018). *Multicultural Diversity Figures*. https://www.dlgrma.qld.gov.au/multicultural-affairs/multicultural-communities/multicultural-diversity-figures.html. Accessed 13 Mar 2019.
Olick, J., et al. (2011). Introduction. In J. Olick et al. (Eds.), *The Collective Memory Reader* (pp. 3–62). Oxford: Oxford University Press.
O'Malley, B. (1996). Mooney Withdraws Security Guards from City Parks. *Courier-Mail* (Brisbane), 21 June, 8.
Queensland Government. (2000). *Australian South Sea Islander Recognition Statement*. https://www.dlgrma.qld.gov.au/resources/multicultural/communities/assi-recognition-statement.pdf. Accessed 25 Aug 2019.
Queensland Government Gazette. 1866.
Queensland Parliamentary Debates. 1889.
Queensland State Library. Plantation Voices. www.slq.qld.gov.au/showcase/ASSI. Accessed 25 Aug 2019.
Reitmajer, E. (2003). New Play Delivers Answers on City Founder. *TB*, 23 September, 3.

Reynolds, H. (1982). *The other Side of the Frontier: Aboriginal Resistance to the European Invasion of Australia*. Townsville: History Department, James Cook University.
Reynolds, H. (2003). *North of Capricorn: The Untold Story of Australia's North*. Sydney: Allen & Unwin.
Richards, J. (2010). Native Police. *Queensland Historical Atlas*. https://www.qhatlas.com.au/content/native-police. Accessed 20 Jan 2019.
Rothberg, M. (2009). *Multidirectional Memory: Remembering the Holocaust in the Age of Decolonization*. Stanford: Stanford University Press.
Rothberg, M. (2011). From Gaza to Warsaw: Mapping Multidirectional Memory. *Criticism, 53*(4), 523–548.
Rothberg, M. (2019). *The Implicated Subject: Beyond Victims and Perpetrators*. Stanford: Stanford University Press.
Schuman, H. et al. (2005). Elite revisionists and popular beliefs: Christopher Columbus, hero or villain? *Public Opinion Quarterly, 69* (1), 2–29.
Sharrat, S. (2007). A Fitting Tribute. Mabo Sculpture Marks Memory of Native Title Legend. *TB*, 4 June, 6.
Shineberg, D. (1976). Towns, Robert (1794–1873). In B. Nairn (Ed.), *Australian Dictionary of Biography* (Vol. 6, pp. 294–296). Melbourne: Melbourne University Press.
Smallwood, G. (2018). Interviewed by Robin Sullivan, 11 October.
Townsville City Council (TCCM). (1941; 1947; 2003; 2004; 2005; 2006). Minutes of Proceedings.
Turner, R. (2017). *SBS*. New Push for Day of Recognition on 25th Anniversary of Mabo Victory. https://www.sbs.com.au/nitv/nitv-news/article/2017/06/05/townsville-celebrates-mabo-day-amid-calls-national-public-holiday. Accessed 31 Jan 2019.
Warner, W. (1959). *The Living and the Dead: A Study of the Symbolic Life of Americans*. Westport: Greenwood Press.
Wilson, A. (2007). Honouring Koiki. *Koori Mail* (Lismore), 20 June, 11.
Wilson, A. (2013). Protesters Want Statue Removed. *Koori Mail*, 25 September, 7.

PART II

Refugees, Informal Memorials and the Dissolution of the Monument

CHAPTER 7

Tracing Paths of Transcultural Memory: The Usage of Monuments in Guided Tours by Refugees

Michal Huss

On a pleasant day in May 2019, as part of a two-hour tour of Berlin for a group of international students, we visit the *Memoria Urbana Berlin* (see Fig. 7.1). Yasmin, a Syrian refugee and our tour guide, allows time for participants to take selfies with the memorial, designed by Spanish artist Juan Garaizabal in June 2012. Next, she explains that the memorial commemorates the Bohemian Bethlehem Church ruined during the Second World War. The memorial is a reconstruction of the destroyed church silhouette in its exact location and size, consisting of lines made out of steel tubes. Yasmin tells us that Bohemian refugees persecuted due to their religion built the original Church in 1732 to thank the Prussian King Frederick William I for welcoming them in the district. By referencing this memorial, Yasmin articulates an ongoing history of movement inherent to Berlin's development. In her words: 'I think this mirroring is a good way to show, this is nothing new, this is part of history, part of human development, people move'.

M. Huss (✉)
Architecture Department, University of Cambridge, Cambridge, UK
e-mail: mrh64@cam.ac.uk

© The Author(s) 2020
S. Marschall (ed.), *Public Memory in the Context of Transnational Migration and Displacement*, Palgrave Macmillan Memory Studies,
https://doi.org/10.1007/978-3-030-41329-3_7

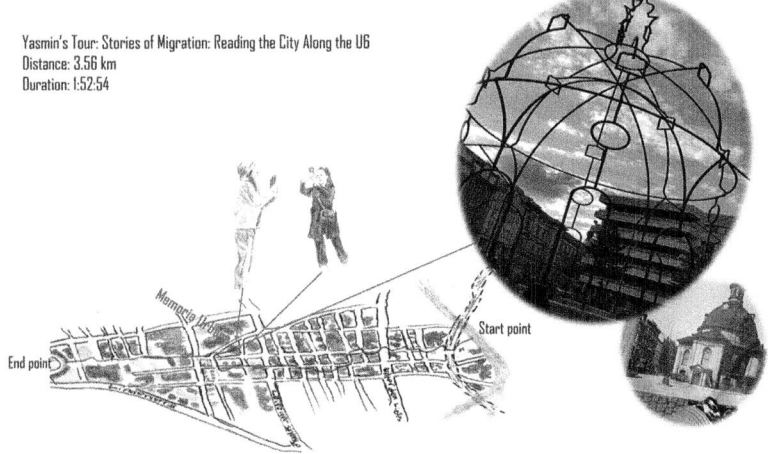

Fig. 7.1 Map of Yasmin's tour, Berlin, and images of memorials along route, drawn or photographed by author

In much of the discussion around the arrival of refugees into European cities, especially relating to their integration, Europe is understood as homogenous, erasing long-existing ethnic, cultural and religious diversity (Balibar 2009). Yasmin deconstructs this assumption by emphasising that Berlin has always been a transit station for waves of migrants. That it took so long to commemorate the destroyed church sparked Yasmin's interest in this memorial, since it raises the issue of whose heritage is perceived as worth commemorating in the public arena and why. Yasmin adds a transcultural relevance to this local memorial, adding that the issue has great application to Syria's process of reconstruction.

This is an example of tours guided by refugees (mostly Syrian as well as Iraqi and Kurdish) in Berlin, available in German and English.[1] The tours, facilitated by a German NGO *Querstadtein* ('off the beaten track' in German) since 2015, are open for the public on a weekly basis or can be booked privately. The audience is a mixture of tourists and locals, the

---

[1] The term 'refugee' is itself nebulous as it is difficult to draw a clear border between voluntary and involuntary migrants (Čapo 2015). Shifting public opinions and political agendas further determine the language used to describe refugees (Sigona 2018). In light of this, I use the word refugee to describe those who proclaim to be refugees, asylum seekers, forced migrants or displaced, regardless of their official status.

majority young professionals and students. Each of the six tour guides designs the tours in a complex process that involves multiple walks around the city.[2] This chapter focuses on the refugee tour guides' usage of memorials to mediate and represent the trails of collective memory of other places and times, and to form an attachment with the city. I propose a theoretical shift in thinking about memorials, from indexing national memory to enabling transcultural memories. The scars of twentieth-century tragedies are visibly present within the urban landscape of Berlin; it is both a German and global site of remembrance (Till 2005; Huyssen 2003b). As the capital, official state-commissioned memorialisation is especially present in the city. As highlighted by Huyssen (1995), monuments play a crucial role in the negotiation of a society's memories, beliefs and values. By referencing these important cultural sites within guided tours, the refugee tour guides insert their narratives into the local memory culture. Therefore, I contextualise the tours as a type of transnational memory activism, deploying memory-mixing to open up a space of recognition and interchange, and assign new meanings to dominant memory narratives.

This chapter is based on extensive 'walk-along' ethnography conducted between 2017 and 2019 on over a dozen refugee-guided and other relevant tours in Berlin. Existing literature suggests walking interviews are useful for generating richer data prompted by meanings and connections to the surrounding landscape (Evans and Jones 2011; Macpherson 2016). I utilised several different observational and ethnographic strategies to study the tours; conducted informal interviews with participants; documented my own participant-researcher experience; recorded questions asked by participants; created a series of behavioural maps sketching participants' bodily activities; photographed sites and materials the tour guides used as mnemonic tools; and used a GPS app to map the tours' route, pace and weather conditions. To supplement this, I conducted oral semi-structured thematic interviews with refugee tour guides and NGO workers. As noted by Aoki and Yoshimizu (2015), social entanglements of walking ethnographers interfere with, and construct, the research. Accordingly, my positionality—as a researcher, female and a Jewish Israeli—has an effect on the research process and on participants. Encounters with participants had to be navigated with sensitivity in order to establish trust, especially important with an 'overly researched'

[2] Tours are now also operating in another city, Dresden, with three additional tour guides.

population such as refugees. For instance, Amir, an Iraqi refugee and tour guide, described to me an unpleasant encounter with journalists, concluding: 'my story is not for sale and I tell it my way, to who I want'. Therefore, it was important to avoid direct questions about my informers' traumatic memories and focus instead on their agency as tour guides. I hope this chapter's focus on refugees' self-expression and protest avoids the risk highlighted by hooks (1990) of further marginalising participants in the study.

After highlighting the importance of memory and movement to studies on the experience of displacement, I situate the tours within the larger context of Germany's ambivalent hospitality towards refugees. Following this, I contextualise the tours as part of a larger trend of alternative guided tours in Berlin that act as an embodied counter monument and compare them with other relevant examples. I analyse the tours' usage of commemorative monuments as a setting to address recent traumas of war and dictatorship from elsewhere as a transcultural memory activism. I then expand the analysis of the tours' activism by looking at the affective attributes of the testimonies voiced throughout, and the role shift enacted through the tours, from refugees to tour guides—experts on the city and its heritage.

REFUGEES' TRAILS OF COLLECTIVE MEMORY

Pierre Nora (1989) uses *lieux de mémoire* (sites of memory) to describe the material reconfigurations of memory at specific sites. His work has influenced many scholars in examining the function of objects and places for the cultural storage of the past. A strand within this literature focuses on the usage of memorials as tools to communicate selective national histories (Dickinson et al. 2010; Macleod 2013) and how such national sites foster public debate and negotiation (Dwyer 2000; Till 1999). Refugees and their memories travel within or through nation states and complicate the assumed bond between collective memory, nationality and place. As noted by Breckenridge and Appadurai (1989, p. i), 'Diasporas always leave a trail of collective memory of other places and times, and create new maps of desire and of attachment'. Therefore, experiences of diaspora and displacement allude to the importance of place in the identities of individuals and groups. Yet among refugees, their sense of place is often attached to remembered sites that may have vanished or been destroyed by war (Bender and Winer 2001). As such, remembered and imagined places charged with emotional and symbolic attributes serve as anchors for individual and collective longing and commemoration. However, simultaneously, refugees form multifaceted attachments to new, unfamiliar and often hostile landscapes (Malkki 1992).

Thus, displacement involves an amplified painful awareness of 'places that are not', as well as complex and contradictory relations to 'homeland', 'home' and 'host land' (Mandel 2008). Within these complex maps of temporal and spatial undercurrents, memory holds a crucial role for the formation and perseverance of cultural identity. Memory further plays a crucial role in refugees' struggle for acceptance, safety and freedom within host countries (Tirosh 2018; Ram and Yacobi 2012; Butler 2017). At the primary level, the acceptance of a legal status in countries such as Germany is dependent on the approval of refugees' life memories as part of a comprehensive and strict inspection (Coffey 2003; Griffiths 2012). Beyond official recognition, host societies are more welcoming to refugees when their stories are acknowledged by the public as legitimate (Tirosh and Klein-Avraham 2017). Yet this attempt to be included or incorporated within more established memory groups is often met with resistance (Dolff-Bonekamper 2011). Evoking local memory discourses can serve as a source of incorporation or exclusion of migrants, depending on the socio-political context (Glynn and Kleist 2012). Therefore, what strategies should refugees deploy to interlace their life stories into the host society's shared collective memory and negotiate their legal and cultural inclusion? The largely unexplored practice of refugee-guided tours provides one answer to this crucial question, as they attempt to weave refugees' memories into the host countries' physical landscape of collective memory.

This chapter contributes to the 'transcultural turn' in memory studies that shifts the focus from Nora's 'Lieux de Mémoire' to the 'travels of memory' across and beyond territorial and social borders (Erll 2011, p. 11). The 'transcultural turn' provides a useful framework for studying issues around refugees' memories and their interactions with other cultural or national memories (Crownshaw 2016; Carrier and Kabalek 2014). For instance, Rothberg and Yildiz (2011) examine the formation of migratory archives of Holocaust Remembrance in Contemporary Germany. Instead of 'archives of remembrance', this chapter focuses on the less examined repertoires (performative and embodied acts) of remembrance (Taylor 2003). Nora (1989 p. 8) distinguishes between the 'lieux' (mediations, reconstructions that are distant and incomplete variations) of memory and 'milieux' of memory (primordial and unmediated gestures, habits or skills). The first appearing at the disappearance of the latter. Thus, as Taylor (2003) observes, a problematic sequenced binary is formed between memory and history, the archive and the repertoire. Yet, with memorials, performative practices around *lieux* of memory are inseparable aspects of the mnemonic experience. For instance, Edensor (2016) closely observes the range of performative styles that occur within the Bannockburn and the Wallace Monuments in Scotland. Edkins (2003) further demonstrates how bodily practices around memorials, such as placing flowers or using these sites for a protest, can further create an alternative narrative that refuses to refer to trauma in the past tense.

Hence, studying the repertoire of transcultural memory requires a close attention to the body as a vital tool of memory (Strathern 1996, p. 26). It further requires attention to the 'agency' of buildings and infrastructure (such as monuments) as opportunities and provocations of memory (Legg 2007, p. 258). Finally, it involves a receptivity to the significance of movement within mnemonic performances. The practice of pilgrimage is an example of the significance of bodily movements in ritualised commemoration (Legassie 2017; Connerton 2009, pp. 7–40). In a similar vein, Kuusisto-Arponen (2009) examines a walking commemoration of the Karelian evacuation in Eastern Finland, the 'Trail of the Displaced', within one of the main roads used in the evacuation. Her research demonstrates that mobility has a crucial role in the formation of bodily memories, as well as within processes of healing and a shared construction of a sense of place. Therefore, as Till (2008, p. 105) points out, places are themselves 'porous and mobile', transformed by the 'movements of memory through landscape, story and ritual', in linkage with other places and times. Till further suggests that looking at activists' place-based practices highlights the important linkage between place, body, mobility and collective memory; refugee-guided tours provide an additional place-based activism that stresses this linkage.

The motifs of travel and movement run throughout this chapter; they are significant to defining the experience of taking refuge, as well as the experience of guided walking tours. These motifs are also markers of the inequality at the heart of globalisation: the technological advances and increasing accessibility of mass transport enables travel on an immense and unprecedented scale, yet the restriction of mobility of 'undesirable identities' is emerging as a new transnational form of governance (Rygiel 2011). The mobilities paradigm provides a much-needed perspective from which to theorise the realities faced by refugees, through its focus on movements and their broader socio-political implications (Cresswell 2006; Sheller and Urry 2006). The paradigm situates the movements of people as important sites of analysis (Cresswell 2006). The mobilities paradigm enables the exploration of different scales of movements, from crossing nations to walking, to be addressed together (Sheller and Urry 2006). Studies linking memory, tourism and displacement examine roots-seeking or home-longing journeys and 'dark' tourism to sites of atrocity (e.g. Marschall 2017; Hirsch and Miller 2011; Araujo 2018; Schramm 2004). This chapter further advances these themes through focusing on the role of refugees as tour guides. Before providing a more detailed account of the tours, I briefly address the context in which they operate—Germany's ambivalent attitude to refugees.

GERMANY'S AMBIVALENT HOSPITALITY

The ongoing Syrian civil war continues to cause displacement within the country and across the region, with a majority of refugees resettled in neighbouring nations. Within the EU, German Chancellor Angela Merkel's publicly pledged 'open arms' policy towards Syrian refugees stands out in comparison to the increasingly restrictive policies towards refugees and the closing of borders elsewhere (Sigona 2018; Orchard and Miller 2014). The large number of refugees has been politically polarising for Germany, and several parties have openly challenged Merkel's decisions.[3] Yet, in the wake of the so-called refugee crisis, collective practices of solidarity—including Germans cheering newly arrived refugees at train stations—were widely celebrated as part of Germans' *Willkommenskultur* (culture of welcome). In August and September 2015, around 10% of Germany's adult population were involved in welcoming initiatives (Ahrens 2017). Local traumatic collective memories hold an important role in raising a sense of responsibility for welcoming those fleeing war and persecution. Politicians, intellectuals and volunteers reference the collective memory of the *Vertriebene* (post-war German expulsions) to form a sense of proximity and compassion, comparing German refugees with Syrians; this comparison also rearticulates the experience of the *Vertriebene*

---

[3] Parties such as the Bavaria-based *CSU*, sister party to Merkel's *Christliche Demokratische Union (CDU)* and the new right-wing party *Alternative für Deutschland (ADF)*.

within German public discourse (Karakayali 2019).[4] Additionally, as Borneman and Ghassem-Fachandi (2017, p. 117) note, reports on police shootings of refugees crossing borders are reminders of the East German border guards' 'shoot to kill' policy in the 1980s. They suggest that *Willkommenskultur* towards refugees serves as a symbolic compensation for historic crimes.

This *Willkommenskultur* has its limitations, involving a hierarchy of victimhood between 'deserving' refugees and 'undeserving migrants', and between 'grateful' and 'ungrateful' refugees or those reluctant to learn German and assimilate (Holmes and Castañeda 2016). Furthermore, since the initial enthusiasm, public perceptions of refugees have been subjected to 'mood shifts' swinging from indifference to ambivalence, xenophilia and xenophobia (Borneman and Ghassem-Fachandi 2017). The 2017 elections gave an indicator of the hostility towards Merkel's policy. Her *Christian Democratic Union/Christian Social Union* won, yet suffered a large swing against it. The far-right *Alternative für Deutschland* became the third largest party in the Bundestag, after calling for stronger borders and promising to 'take back our country'. Anti-refugee sentiments are currently gaining political popularity, translating into legislation such as the attempt to limit refugees' family reunifications (Vollmer and Karakayali 2018). Additionally, xenophobic violence against refugees has been on the rise since 2015 (Benček and Strasheim 2016; Jäckle and König 2017). Muslim migrants and refugees are particularly subjected to a process of 'othering', and deemed harder to integrate because of 'cultural differences' (Borneman and Ghassem-Fachandi 2017). Hence, present-day xenophobic fears and hierarchies of victimhood conflict with the morality formed by traumatic memories (of the Nazi regime and the Holocaust, war and displacement) to shape Germany's ambivalent hospitality. Germany has long been a home for many non-citizens and those with so-called '*Migrationshintergrund*' (migration background); yet, the 'refugee crisis' has intensified debates about coexistence, integration, national identity and belonging (Bock and Macdonald 2019).

In Berlin the *Willkommenskultur* has been especially prominent, notwithstanding a reduction in the initial enthusiasm (Selim et al. 2018). Since 2015, a vast number of residents have supplemented, or substituted,

---

[4] The post-war expulsions refer to the ethnic Germans who fled Central and Eastern Europe after the Second World War, who were subsequently settled as refugees in West Germany.

the state's welcoming efforts, providing refugees with healthcare, translation services, bureaucratic assistance and housing (Holmes and Castañeda 2016; Karakayali and Kleist 2016; Bochow 2015). Several years after the first wave of refugees entering the city, the numbers of new arrivals are declining, refugees are more settled and emergency volunteer work has declined. Many grassroots initiatives now focus on collaborative action such as making music, dialogue, story-telling or cooking with refugees (Selim et al. 2018). Grassroots organisations such as *Querstadtein* are no longer newsworthy yet remain an integral part of the urban landscape. *Querstadtein* formed as a platform to facilitate tours guided by homeless people, utilising city tours to foster dialogue, political education and fight prejudice (tour-guiding in Berlin does not require formal training and registration). In 2015, the NGO decided to develop another strand of tours, *Refugees Show Their Berlin*, to voice refugees' perspectives, hitherto largely unheard within German public discourse. The tours' autobiographical approach also aims to show the multifaceted and varied perspectives of refugees instead of depicting them as one homogenous group.

Berlin's Heritage Trails

The refugee tour guides are paid, yet the majority of them have other jobs, and they all emphasise that money was not their main reason to become a tour guide. For instance, Amir observes:

> For me it is about passing a message, not a job… I help in this way, raising awareness to the topic, giving people an understanding…at least the majority, it touches them, and they will tell friends, and so I do something. It gets big.

The tours cost 13.00 € per individual (an optional 'support' price costs around 30.00 €), or around 175 € for a group booking; the NGO aims to function as a sustainable social enterprise instead of depending on governmental funds, and this allows for greater freedom of expression during the tours.

To recruit tour guides, the NGO approaches various networks that engage with refugees to find individuals who are eager to become active and gain public visibility. The next stage is to assess whether these individuals' stories or perspectives can be expressed through the city's urban fabric. Subsequently, the complex process of designing the tour—which can take up to a year—begins. First, each guide identifies certain locations in the city that are meaningful to him or her. It is challenging to find such sites within walking range. One NGO worker tells me, refugees' mobility in the city is scattered and dispersed: 'they get their registration at one part of the city, and then language learning in a completely different part, and another where they have to work and so on'. The next step includes multiple visits to the area in order to identify other potential stops for the tour, taking into account constraints of time and scale. The tours are designed to last two hours, and the stops need to be within walking distance.

The strand of tours I focus on in this chapter are in the central touristic Mitte district and include various cultural and mnemonic sites such as churches, governmental buildings, museums and monuments. Refugees learn about these sites in their German courses, yet during the tours they charge them with their personal perspectives. Walking is a powerful embodied, sensory and material engagement with the city (Middleton 2010, 2009). The tours involve a mixture of two types of walking practices identified by Wunerlich (2008): the spontaneous 'discursive walking' that focuses on the journey itself; and 'conceptual walking', which is planned and reflective. This process of reflection and immersion within the city enables tour guides to form an attachment to the city. As Amir describes, 'the tour made me feel closer to the city'. Mobility is embedded in the construction of a sense of place through the tour, since the tour is developed and communicated by walking, and as it involves the bodily memories from other places that impact refugees' perception of the city.

Refugees Show Their Berlin operates within Berlin's vast and varied array of walking heritage tours. Heritage trails serve as an invitation to 'walk down memory lane', a means for an all-encompassing memory experience triggered through sounds, smells and sensations. As Nora (1989, p. 17) observes, 'Never have we longed in a more physical manner to evoke the weight of the land at our feet, the hand of the devil in the year 1000, or the stench of eighteenth-century cities'. Much can be learned about a city's public memory by looking at the heritage tours it offers. Especially popular are tours that highlight Berlin's history as divided city and bridge in a divided continent, such as '*A neighbourhood walk: Living at the Wall*' and '*A Tale Of Two Cities: Exploring Life In East & West Berlin*'. Also popular are Jewish history tours, as one website highlights (*The Jewish Berlin*):

Most frequently booked are our Jewish Berlin tours, focusing on the history and current life of Jews in Berlin. Who were the Jews of Berlin that made this community so successful before the Holocaust?

Here the once-thriving Jewish district serves as a phantasmagoria. The high visibility of the traces of this absent community directly contrasts with the more hidden or ignored culture manifestations of contemporary marginalised groups such as Turkish Berliners (Mandel 2008).

To supplement my research, I join a four-hour Jewish heritage tour in Mitte, available in English three times a week at the cost of 20 €. The tour guide leads us through some of the canonical memorials in the city related to the *Shoah* (Holocaust in Hebrew). Hence, despite the promise to teach us about Jewish life in Berlin, the tour caters to touristic obsession and fetishisation of Nazi history. All the memorials addressed in this tour are highly visible, easy to locate and within the centre of the city. Numerous other guided walking tours follow the same paths, and at each memorial, many others surround us. Thus, the tours engage in 'preservation and conservation: keeping what already is' (Hall 1999, p. 3). In contrast, *Refugees Show Their Berlin* guides trace less visible heritage trails and less canonical memorials, such as the *Memoria Urbana Berlin*, which mark the often-overlooked multicultural history of Berlin. These tours enable participants to experience the city and its rich history from a viewpoint that heritage tours largely ignore—that of newcomers. As one tour participant observes, 'I think it is nice to see the city from the perspective of someone not from here, like myself. I can relate to what he says because I come from a similar situation'. Thus instead of using walking to preserve the city's canonical landscape of memory, the tours deploy walking to expand it.

Walking as Counter Monument

Refugees Show Their Berlin is part of a larger trend that Fabian, an experienced German tour guide in Berlin, describes to me, by which an increasingly diverse audience seeks more versatile perspectives and marginalised memory discourses.[5] As part of this trend, Fabian observes that instead of

---

[5] This further links to border emerging urban truism in Berlin that seeks 'off the beaten track areas' and 'authentic experiences', often contributing to processes of gentrification (Füller and Michel 2014).

merely focusing on 'what is', tour guides point participants' attention to what is missing, overlooked or silenced. Other notable examples of this trend are the *Drag Queen* tours of Berlin where participants are required to wear high heels, and the post-colonial tours in Wedding, Mitte and Neukölln districts. These tours enable visitors to experience Berlin's visible and invisible traces of history as layered, multiple and entwined within the city's urban fabric. These heritage tours often act as an embodied version of what James E. Young (1992) refers to as a 'counter monument', describing a diversion by artists in Germany in the '90's from traditional memorials. Similarly, the tours form 'counter' practices within the site of dominant monuments. For instance, during a post-colonial tour in Neukölln, our tour guide points our attention to the placement of a far smaller memorial for Herero and Nama victims on the grounds of a memorial for the very soldiers who committed the genocide.[6] Such tours' temporality, performativity and the critical discourse they prompt about memorials can be argued to resemble the counter monument makers described by Young: in their attempt to replace memorials' indexing impulse with ever-changing, ever-vanishing and interactive gestures that question the very premise of a memorial.

Another type of tour that addresses migrants' perspectives of Berlin is the *Route 44 Tour* in the Neukölln district, which has a long history of migration, housing various groups of refugees, guest workers and their descendants. The district is known for its large Turkish and Arab minorities, high welfare dependency and low level of education and income; Neukölln is often used to exemplify a 'failed integration' that is blamed on migrants themselves who maintain a 'parallel society' (Tize and Ries 2019).[7] Female immigrants from the district who have studied Neukölln's history (as part of an initiative by the district's museum) guide the tours. As the website highlights, participants discover the 'unknown' and 'get a different picture of Berlin's "notorious" district' (Route 44 website). Some of *Refugees Show Their Berlin* tours also take place in Neukölln and similarly focus on translating the traces of the Arabic culture in the district; for example, by explaining why a shisha bar is named after Umm Kulthum,

---

[6] German military forces committed a genocide of the indigenous Herero and Nama in their colony in Southwest Africa (present-day Namibia) during 1904–1907 (for more information, see Conrad 2012).

[7] Contributing to Neukölln's bad reputation is a book by Heinz Buschkowsky (2012), *Neukölln ist überall* (*Neukölln is Everywhere*), published by the district Mayor (at the time of publication) that criticizes integration and multiculturalism.

the famous Egyptian singer. Such tours enable 'Germans'—the 'locals'—to visit and learn about a migrant neighbourhood. This is a promising avenue for fostering dialogue and understanding between host communities and migrants. However, it also risks perpetuating cultural stereotypes and divisions: by orientalising and exoticising the district or reducing its inhabitants to their identities as Muslims or Arabs, neglecting more complex and layered identities (O'Brian 2018; Tezcan 2012).

A somewhat reversed gesture is enacted as part of the *Multaqa* (meeting point in Arabic) project that provides Arabic-speaking refugees free tours of museums in Berlin and trains refugees to be volunteer tour guides. The tours started in December 2015 with over 6500 participants and over 670 guided tours; the project receives significant media attention and governmental support. On 21 May 2016, the German Ministry of Culture awarded the project a €10,000 grant. Bernadette Lynch's (2019, p. 119) research captures both the potentials and limitations of this project. On the one hand, she notes that the tours use 'collections to open up dialogue and understanding between refugees and local communities'. On the other, her interviewees, *Multaqa* coordinators, are weary of 'limiting the stories to people's own cultural backgrounds'. The coordinators are also aware that 'having tours by refugees simply for other refugees, risks keeping people in "their bubble"'. They further suggest to her that the state support for the project hinders the tours' role as 'a small part of a 'drip-drip' integration process', and that the rigid training by the museum service solidifies a 'controlled corporate message'.

In sum, *Route 44*, *Multaqa* and *Refugees Show Their Berlin* tours are productive examples of an evolving significant role for museums (and NGOs), described by Lynch (2019, p. 123) as 'upskilling people as researchers' to foster their individual and collective activism. This comes across in Yasmin's account on being a tour guide during our interview (her tour described in the beginning of this chapter):

> Doing the tour felt like putting this researcher glasses [on] and looking at things with a different depth and it gives me a lot of extra knowledge and I like to brag about it all the time.

This is a greatly promising avenue to replace such institutional acts of speaking for these populations or using them as objects of representation, curating exhibitions about their struggles. It further undermines a simplistic understanding of marginalised groups as silenced 'subalterns' (Spivak

1985), or as 'removed from political life' (Arendt 2017). Nonetheless, the tours also risk perpetuating divisions and binaries between Western and Eastern cultures or between locals and migrants in the city. Additionally, the lines between empowerment and 'integration' are blurred, as seen in the example of *Multaqa*. The inherent inequality at the heart of 'integration' is its positioning of immigrants as responsible for adapting to German society, both culturally and bureaucratically. As Samar, another Syrian refugee and tour guide, tells us during his tour, 'the Germans say you need to become German. But this is not true; we need to integrate both cultures'. This raises the question, as posed by Selim et al. (2018, p. 40), 'when does welcoming stop and living together start?' For refugees whose legal protection is temporary and requires frequent renewal, integration is further complicated by Germany being a temporary home and by the constant fear of being expelled. As Amir observes:

> It is not nice to have the idea in the back of my mind that I will need to leave at some point…don't ask me why I don't learn the language, why I don't work- and when I do all these things you still send me back.

A promising avenue for undoing the one-way rhetoric of assimilation/integration and for constructing a meeting point between cultures is evident in a gesture enacted in a newer strand of *Refugees Show Their Berlin* tours in the central district of Mitte: using official memorials as a site for memory-mixing.

Borrowing, Mixing and Referencing Trauma

The starting point of another tour (see point 1 on Fig. 7.2), booked by a group of 15 German youths and guided by Wael, a Syrian refugee, is the *Memorial of the Book Burning*. The bitter cold on this Sunday morning in March 2018 seems to me a fitting atmosphere for the memorial. Much like the countless tour guides in that area, Wael begins by providing us with a brief description of the monument, which commemorates an event that took place in the very same square on May 1933, when Nazis burned the works of hundreds of authors and academics. The memorial's features, designed by artist Micha Ullman in 1995, include an underground room with empty bookshelves and two bronze plates inscribed with the following:

7 TRACING PATHS OF TRANSCULTURAL MEMORY: THE USAGE...   203

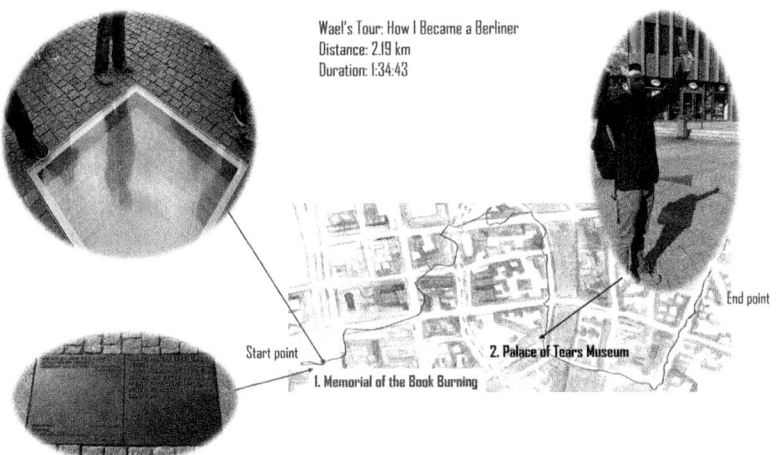

Fig. 7.2 Map of Wael's tour and sights along route, drawn or photographed by the author

> *That was but a prelude;*
> *where they burn books,*
> *they will ultimately burn people as well.*
> Heinrich Heine *1820* (Translated from German by the author)

This is a highly symbolic setting for what Wael tells us next: he describes how gradually Syria became a dictatorship, and protesters, opposition parties and intellectuals were tortured and killed. He also tells us that the Syrian government imprisoned and tortured his brother. Monuments 'aid in the establishment of memory, by materializing history and linking familiar landscapes, times, and selective memories in an inextricable embrace' (Mitchell 2003, p. 445). Site-specificity is often a significant feature of the memorial that enhances its symbolic and affective attributes. In the attempt to testify to trauma, the multisensory engagement with sites is valuable in providing a non-linguistic affective presence or sensation (Till 2008). For example, in his study on the popular Israeli youth trips to Poland, Feldman (2002) describes the testimony of a Holocaust survivor performed at the sites of his suffering. Feldman (2002, p. 90) observes that the students' sensory experiences of the site and the sensations and emotions it ascends are 'important means by which experiences become imprinted on students imaginations'. In contrast, our tour guides cannot access the sites of their traumatic memories.

Instead, they deploy local site-specific memorials as an affective setting for their testimony. This mixing of histories indexes similar themes in a non-competitive manner while maintaining the uniqueness of each history. Thus, the tours are a transcultural performance that is local and site-specific. Memorials often serve as a means for forgetting trauma by sealing it in a coherent linear narrative. For instance, Michael Landzelius (2003) sees the assignment of a monumental form as political ammunition; it involves the cleansing of the fragmented, multiple meanings of the past for the sake of self-affirming notions of the truth. In the case of Holocaust memorial sites, as Marianne Hirsch (2012) highlights, presubscribed haunting 'postmemories' provoked by mediated images, objects, stories and ceremonies further solidify a selective universal memory narrative. This undermines any site-specific authentic qualities. Till and Kuusisto-Arponen (2015) observe how the Westerbork Camp Memorial Museum in the Netherlands, for instance, communicates a singular universal Holocaust narrative at the expense of other site-specific silenced stories. For them, a more ethical form of remembrance is one that uses the material landscape to articulate a complex understanding of place as layers and linkages of 'translocal' meanings. The example of refugee-guided tours offers a possibility for such 'ethical remembrance' since it opens up a fixed and singular spatial memory by transforming local memorials into transnational sites, relevant to other similar experiences. This offers a fragmented and heterogeneous transcultural memory narrative instead of a singular or universal one (Huyssen 2003b).

This complex memory-mixing also creates a temporary space of recognition and dialogue between self and other, local and foreign or citizen and non-citizen. By referencing the memory of the Holocaust, the tour makes a direct appeal to local collective memory and its focus on guilt, seeking recognition as similar victims. Within national host cultures that are intensely oriented towards traumatic history, diasporic communities can feel marginalised from the collective memory discourse (Huyssen 2003a). For instance, Germany's collective past serves as a form of reference for belonging through the rejection of the Nazi past; this excludes newcomers, such as Turkish Germans (Diner 1998; Huyssen 2003a). Together with this exclusion, migrants, especially those identified as Muslims, are often blamed for their alleged indifference to this topic (Rothberg and Yildiz 2011).

Thus, paradoxically, the focus on guilt within Germany's collective memory disseminates key elements of this past. Namely, it reinforces the self-conception of German identity as ethnically based, thereby neglecting a more universal lesson of the Holocaust (Senocak 2000). Yet, the tours appeal to the memory of the Holocaust by physically visiting Holocaust memorials and by mimicking the ritual of the survival testimony. As Astrid Erll (2011) advises, studying memory from a transcultural perspective points to the travelling of commemorative practices. Within the post-Holocaust era, the survival testimony has emerged as a powerful tool to document and protest various human rights violations across the globe (Gutman 2017). The tours deploy this ritual of testifying and witnessing to voice the marginalised traumatic memories of refugees in the public sphere. This resonates with Rothberg's (2009) notion of 'multidirectional memory' that demonstrates how the Holocaust is a vehicle through which other histories of suffering are articulated.

However, the tours' memory-mixing also undermines German canonical memory narratives since they deem the crimes committed in Nazi Germany as less unique, given that atrocities are continually committed across the world. This gesture further challenges the entire discourse of commemoration and the pretence of keeping memory alive in order to prevent the reoccurrence of atrocities. Hence, the tours enable a form of transcultural memory activism. The transcultural perspective on memory is inherently subversive as it undermines hegemonic terms, such as nation state or globalisation (Mageo 2001). However, memory activism refers to a more deliberate and future-oriented political action, an alternative commemorative performance that intends to enrich the dominant collective memory and reframe public debate (Gutman 2017). Accordingly, this spatial performance appropriates existing landscapes of memory to produce a memory that challenges current politics of forgetting in the form of reconciliation, silencing or overlooking. The ethical dimension of this memory activism is that it opens new opportunities for protesting sufferings and injustices, and offers new possibilities for living with each other, and with each other's traumatic memories (Margalit 2009).

Affective Reproduction of Memory

Crucial to the tours' memory activism is the testimonial event. Testimony is a broad and nebulous label, referring chiefly to a personal witness account of a truth, anchored by both personal and collective experiences

(Butler 2017). The testimonial event is a process founded on power difference that can produce an 'ethical encounter' (Rose 2004). This comes across in the repetitive type of questions participants ask during the tours; they seek to understand more about refugees' lives in their new locality, why they chose Berlin and how they arrived. For instance, one person asks Samar: 'How long did it take you to get here? What was the hardest part?' He answers:

> 3 months. I took a train, plane, car, everything. The hardest part was crossing the sea. We are at the mercy of smugglers. We are sent to sea alone and it is very easy to get lost. The journey on the boat lasted maybe 3 days but it felt like 3 years. It's like the judgment day, people cry, shit on themselves. Everyone was sure this is the last day of their life.

Samar's self-narrated story stresses his agency in arriving, in crossing against all odds. He emphasises the body itself as integral to the experience of migration. This type of personalised perspective challenges the focus on borders and governments. Instead, it shifts the focus onto the body, and the in-between of the penetration of borders, the life before, the journey itself and the difficulties of building a life in a new location. Thus, the tours enable a type of memory work: the act of collective witnessing in which the primary eyewitness is paired with the listener who is part of the testimonial exchange (Felman and Laub 2013). In terms of the testifier, this event can be experienced as a moral responsibility that allows others to become second-hand witnesses. All refugee tour guides that I interviewed exemplify this and describe their participation in the tours as a moral obligation, crucial in spite of the difficulty in testifying to their traumas that they all note. In this type of witnessing, the linkage between the testifier and second-hand witness relies on modes of empathy and identification, and, significantly, *agency*. For instance, one tour participant notes:

> Hearing a personal story that you can identify with, instead of theoretical information about refugees' makes it easier to understand the situation. We all know the reasons for the arrival of refugees here, but less about their experience of the city.

Hence, the tour functions as what Fredric Jameson (1990) names 'cognitive mapping', through which a phenomenological subjective perspective, such as a refugee's experience of the city, anchors a situational representation of the vaster un-representable totality of socio-political structures.

Critical to this collective witnessing is physical presence that enables a direct participation in and transmission of the production and reproduction of memory (Taylor 2003). As one participant observes, 'you participate ... it is not just about thinking and learning about facts, but more about going deep in another level'. This proximity also enables what Massumi (1987, p. xvi) describes as 'an ability to affect and to be affected'. As another participant says, 'it's gone to the heart. I feel it, I feel with her'. This participation is enhanced by walking collectively around the city from one monument to the next, as an NGO worker highlights, 'I think walking is a connecting element, we do something together'. Walking is an inherently mnemonic experience that involves mobility through the real, imagined, experienced and remembered (Ingold 2010). The tours are a collaborative exercise in commemoration and imagination. Indeed, heritage tour guides' agency lies in their ability to elicit feelings and affect in order to create historical empathy (Modlin et al. 2011). *Refugees Show Their Berlin* guides deploy this historical empathy in conjunction with the affective power of personal testimonies to raise awareness of the present-day struggles of refugees.

Looking at tour guides of the Nazi Party Rally Grounds in Nuremberg, Macdonald (2006) advances the understanding of their complex mnemonic work in what she names 'difficult heritage sites'. She closely observes how guides lead tourists through layers of different ways of seeing the rally grounds, enacting a type of 'façade peeling'. This involves seeing past the actual site and its beauty, and instead imagining the grounds in use during rallies in the 1930s and 1940s. I identify an additional temporal gesture enacted in *Refugees Show Their Berlin* tours that further contributes to this multiplying gaze: the tour guides show images of the sites we visit in Berlin during the War or the East–West division and images of their home countries. For instance, during Wael's tour, we stand by the Palace of Tears museum (see point 2 on Fig. 7.2), a former border crossing point between East and West Berlin at Friedrichstraße station. Wael explains that the name symbolises the tearful partings that occurred in the site, showing us an image of the station before and after the formation of the wall. Next, Wael shows us images of his home, the Syrian city Aleppo, before and during the civil war. He describes the checkpoints in Aleppo and how people who try to cross are shot from both sides. This gesture temporally collapses the distance between the past and the present *and* between this site and other troubled sites. Thus, the tours create a highly complex *felt* space through the overlapping of sensual experiences provoked by the memorial in the present and multiple histories and memories of the past. The tours deploy this emotional and bodily sensitivity for political purposes.

THE RIGHT TO BERLIN'S MEMORY

An important aspect of the tour's political performance is the role-shift it entails, through which non-citizens or newcomers embody the role of heritage tour guides and city exports. Amir alludes to the humorous nature of this role-shift, 'it is strange to tell Germans about places they know, it is funny that I am doing this, I have only been here a few years … It is nice to tell them about *their* capital'. As theorists of gender, race and sexuality demonstrate, parodic performances threaten the stability of racial, sexual and class categorisation, and disrupt fixed identity formulations (Butler 2011; Bhabha 2012). The tour's role-shift is similarly subversive as it calls into question restrictive categorisations of city-dwellers, as 'locals' and 'foreigners', or citizens and non-citizens. Roy (1998) further captures the agency at the heart of colonial mimicry: 'to be seen and to be seen as one wishes to be seen'. Similarly, through the tours, refugees gain visibility and, more crucially, they control (to some extent) *how* they are seen.

To elaborate, philosopher Marieke Borren (2008) coins the phrase 'harmful visibility' to describe surveillance technologies that monitor refugees' bodies and movements, or represent them in mediated and political discourses as merely victims. Additionally, such discourses frame refugees as a threat to national security or social cohesion (Holmes and Castañeda 2016). As Amir tells me, in contrast to mediated depictions of refugees, the tours create a controlled and intimate environment where he can say *what* he wants to say, *how* he wants to say it. Thus, in a Rancièrean (2004b) sense, the tours provide an avenue for refugees, whose public image and political subjectivity are abstracted to protest their exclusion, thereby asserting their political subjectivity. More so, by performing as tour guides, refugees protest their marginalisation from society and from the city's public memory and assert their claim over Berlin's heritage.

Tour guides direct tourists' gazes, provide vocal narration and choreograph their movements along prescribed paths (Edensor 2000). Tour guides are also important memory agents that hold a cultural authority over the past and its interpretation; they reconstruct historical narratives, focus gazes on particular memorials and influence participants' interpretations and experiences of these sites (Hanna et al. 2004; Baum et al. 2007). The refugees' tour guides deploy this 'aesthetic control' and the role of Berlin's memory agents to form auto-representations of their experiences. By representation, rather than a fixed image, I refer to a performative composition occurring through movement within space (Dewsbury 2000). This act of representation involves working with and around the 'materiality of the tour', such as weather conditions or required distance and pace (MacDonald 2006). The practice of walking and the role of a tour guide allow refugees to weave their own memories and perspectives, as localised to the city, anchored in its urban past and present. A tour participant succinctly captures the importance of the tours as a tactical appropriation of the city:

> For me it is very interesting the way she found a way to appropriate the city; it is my city, my story and I know about these places. All that is very powerful. It is always such a struggle; I am an immigrant myself in another country. It is a special moment when you feel that the place you are living is also your place.

Thus, by acting the role of city experts, refugees assert their 'right to the city' (Harvey 2012), and their 'right to its memory' (Tirosh 2017).

Conclusion

Mobility is integral to *Refugees Show Their Berlin* tours: the movement of eyes, of walking bodies, of sound, and the circulation of historical and more recent traumatic memories in relation to a singular memorial. Equally integral are refugees' memories of forced movement and the capacity to be affectively moved through this tour. This focus on movement and the travelling of memory challenges the understanding of site-specific memory or place-based agency as static or restricted to permanent residence of the city. Instead, this chapter has closely examined how the tours localise transcultural memory by addressing its historical presence in the city and by weaving refugees' memory in the fabric of Germany's official memorial landscape.

As suggested by Carter (2009, p. 13), 'footsteps are also footprints, our wanderings are also designs'. By focusing on refugees' auto-generated spatial designs, this chapter contributes to discussions on how those whose public image is abstracted counter this abstraction, asserting their political subjectivity (Rancière 2004b). Public political performances by refugees that receive academic attention include subjection to self-harm to stress the voicelessness of being labelled a refugee, such as hunger strikes (Cordeiro 1999), or lip-sewing (Edkins and Pin-Fat 2005). It also includes marches and demonstrations (Monforte and Dufour 2013; Ataç 2016). In contrast, the tours' performance involves a mixture of walking genres, notably linking walking framed as march to articulate a political message through the public domain with the performative touristic walking style. By focusing on a less traditional type of protest, the guided walking tour, I expand the repertoire of refugees' resistance. More so, this chapter has demonstrated the importance of memory, space and performativity within refugees' struggles and provided one avenue for the much needed research into memory activism by refugees.

Opening memorials designated for the recollection of particular historical events to reinterpretation by others has crucial implications for identity and belonging. First, it suggests the appropriation of these imperative cultural mnemonic sites as a resource for protesting suffering and injustices by linking them with more recent wars and conflicts. Second, this appropriation is also a means of place making. As Lefebvre poises (1992, p. 143), space lays down the law because it implies a certain order—and hence also a certain disorder. By complicating monuments' syntax, the tours not only open new possibilities for reading a city's mnemonic signs, but also recreate place. Through the tours, refugees marginalised in mainstream German society and memorialisation culture create temporal sites that speak to multidirectional plural interpretations of historical events. Hence, the tours are a form of aesthetic politics, of making space within the space of official representation (Rancière 2004a, 1999).

Finally, this appropriation disrupts notions of cultural purity and undermines the concept of assimilation as a one-way-street where newcomers learn the local culture. For Senocak and Tulay (2000, p. 6), immigrating to Germany means entering the realm of German's recent past. As discussed throughout this chapter, the presence of the past in contemporary German culture and politics has both negative implications for refugees, as well as being a positive resource for seeking solidarity. Instead of visiting this memory realm as outsiders, the tour guides add their own perspectives to German public memory, expanding and problematising it. Thus, the tours' memory activism opens up potentials of hybridity, of comparing, mixing and performing shifting positions, speaking from within and without.

REFERENCES

Ahrens, P. (2017). *Skepsis und Zuversicht: wie blickt Deutschland auf Flüchtlinge?* Hannover: Creo Media.
Aoki, J., & Yoshimizu, A. (2015). Walking Histories, Un/Making Places: Walking Tours as Ethnography of Place. *Space and Culture, 18*(3), 273–284.
Araujo, A. L. (2018). Tourism and Heritage Sites of the Atlantic Slave Trade and Slavery. In, *A Companion to Public History* (pp.277–88). Wiley Blackwell.
Arendt, H. (2017). *The Origins of Totalitarianism*. London: Penguin.
Ataç, I. (2016). 'Refugee Protest Camp Vienna': Making Citizens Through Locations of the Protest Movement. *Citizenship Studies, 20*(5), 629–646.
Balibar, Étienne. (2009). *We, the People of Europe?: Reflections on Transnational Citizenship*. Princeton University Press.
Baum, T., Hearns, N., & Devine, F. (2007). Place, People and Interpretation: Issues of Migrant Labour and Tourism Imagery in Ireland. *Tourism Recreation Research, 32*(3), 39–48.
Benček, D., & Strasheim, J. (2016). Refugees Welcome? A Dataset on Anti-Refugee Violence in Germany. *Research & Politics, 3*(4), 1–11.
Bender, B., & Winer, M. (2001). *Contested Landscapes: Movement, Exile and Place*. London: Bloomsbury Academic.
Bhabha, H. K. (2012). *The Location of Culture*. Abingdon: Routledge.
Bochow, A. (2015). We Are Only Helping! Volunteering and Social Media in Germany's New Welcome Culture. *Medizinethnologie.* https://www.medizinethnologie.net/volunteering-and-social-media-in-germanys-new-welcome-culture/. Accessed 7 July 2019.
Bock, J., & Macdonald, S. (2019). *Refugees Welcome?: Difference and Diversity in a Changing Germany.* New York: Berghahn Books.
Borneman, J., & Ghassem-Fachandi, P. (2017). The Concept of Stimmung: From Indifference to Xenophobia in Germany's Refugee Crisis. *HAU: Journal of Ethnographic Theory, 7*(3), 105–135.
Borren, M. (2008). Towards an Arendtian Politics of In/Visibility. *Ethical Perspectives, 15*(2), 213–237.
Breckenridge, C., & Appadurai, A. (1989). On Moving Targets. *Public Culture, 2*(1), i–iv.
Buschkowsky, H. (2012). *Neukölln ist überall.* Berlin: Ullstein Verlag.
Butler, J. (2011). *Gender Trouble: Feminism and the Subversion of Identity*. New York: Routledge.
Butler, K. J. (2017). *Witnessing Australian Stories: History, Testimony, and Memory in Contemporary Culture.* Abingdon: Routledge.
Čapo, J. (2015). The Security-Scape and the (In)Visibility of Refugees: Managing Refugee Flow Through Croatia. *Migracijske i Etničke Teme, 3*, 387–406.

Carrier, P., & Kabalek, K. (2014). Cultural Memory and Transcultural Memory – A Conceptual Analysis. In L. Bond & J. Rapson (Eds.), *The Transcultural Turn: Interrogating Memory Between and Beyond Borders* (pp. 39–60). Berlin: Walter de Gruyter.
Carter, P. (2009). *Dark Writing: Geography, Performance, Design*. Honolulu: University of Hawaii Press.
Coffey, G. (2003). The Credibility of Credibility Evidence at the Refugee Review Tribunal. *International Journal of Refugee Law, 15*(3), 377–417.
Connerton, P. (2009). *How Modernity Forgets*. Cambridge: Cambridge University Press.
Conrad, S. (2012). *German Colonialism: A Short History*. Cambridge: Cambridge University Press.
Cordeiro, A. (1999). Johanna Siméant La cause des sans-papiers Presses de Sciences Po, Paris. 1998. *Hommes & Migrations, 1219*(1), 130–132.
Cresswell, T. (2006). *On the Move: Mobility in the Modern Western World*. Abingdon: Taylor & Francis.
Crownshaw, R. (2016). *Transcultural Memory*. Abingdon: Routledge.
Dewsbury, J. D. (2000). Performativity and the Event: Enacting a Philosophy of Difference. *Environment and Planning D: Society and Space, 18*, 473–496.
Dickinson, G., Blair, C., & Ott, B. L. (2010). *Places of Public Memory: The Rhetoric of Museums and Memorials*. Tuscaloosa: University of Alabama Press.
Diner, D. (1998). Nation, Migration, and Memory: On Historical Concepts of Citizenship. *Constellations, 4*(3), 293–306.
Dolff-Bonekamper, G. (2011). Memorable Moments – Chosen Cultural Affiliations. In M. Blaive, C. Lindenberger, & T. Gerbel (Eds.), *Clashes in European Memory: The Case of Communist Repression and the Holocaust* (pp. 123–153). New Brunswick: Transaction Publishers.
Dwyer, O. J. (2000). Interpreting the Civil Rights Movement: Place, Memory, and Conflict. *The Professional Geographer, 52*(4), 660–671.
Edensor, T. (2000). Staging Tourism: Tourists as Performers. *Annals of Tourism Research, 27*(2), 322–344.
Edensor, T. (2016). National Identity and the Politics of Memory: Remembering Bruce and Wallace in Symbolic Space. Environment and Planning D: Society and Space, November.
Edkins, J. (2003). *Trauma and the Memory of Politics*. Cambridge: Cambridge University Press.
Edkins, J., & Pin-Fat, V. (2005). Through the Wire: Relations of Power and Relations of Violence. *Millennium, 34*(1), 1–24.
Erll, A. (2011). Travelling Memory. *Parallax, 17*(4), 4–18.
Evans, J., & Jones, P. (2011). The Walking Interview: Methodology, Mobility and Place. *Applied Geography, 31*(2), 849–858.

Feldman, J. (2002). 'Marking the Boundaries of the Enclave: Defining the Israeli Collective through the Poland "Experience"'. *Israel Studies, 7*(2), 84–114.
Felman, S., & Laub, D. (2013). *Testimony: Crises of Witnessing in Literature, Psychoanalysis and History.* Abingdon: Routledge.
Füller, H., & Michel, B. (2014). 'Stop Being a Tourist!' New Dynamics of Urban Tourism in Berlin-Kreuzberg. *International Journal of Urban and Regional Research, 38*(4), 1304–1318.
Glynn, I., & Kleist, J. O. (2012). The Memory and Migration Nexus: An Overview. In I. Glynn & J. O. Kleist (Eds.), *History, Memory and Migration: Perceptions of the Past and the Politics of Incorporation* (pp. 3–29). Basingstoke: Palgrave Macmillan.
Griffiths, M. (2012). 'Vile Liars and Truth Distorters'; Truth, Trust and the Asylum System. *Anthropology Today, 28*(5), 8–12.
Gutman, Y. (2017). *Memory Activism: Reimagining the Past for the Future in Israel-Palestine.* Nashville: Vanderbilt University Press.
Hall, S. (1999). 'Whose Heritage?'. *Third Text, 13*(49), 3–13.
Hanna, S. P., Del Casino, V. J., Selden, C., & Hite, B. (2004). Representation as Work in 'America's Most Historic City'. *Social & Cultural Geography, 5*(3), 459–481.
Harvey, D. (2012). *Rebel Cities: From the Right to the City to the Urban Revolution.* London: Verso Books.
Hirsch, M. (2012). *The Generation of Postmemory: Writing and Visual Culture After the Holocaust.* New York: Columbia University Press.
Hirsch, M., & Miller, N. K. (2011). *Rites of Return: Diaspora Poetics and the Politics of Memory.* New York: Columbia University Press.
Holmes, S. M., & Castañeda, H. (2016). Representing the 'European Refugee Crisis' in Germany and beyond: Deservingness and Difference, Life and Death. *American Ethnologist, 43*(1), 12–24.
Hooks, B. (1990). *Yearning: Race, Gender, and Cultural Politics.* Boston: South End Press.
Huyssen, A. (2003a). Diaspora and Nation: Migration into Other Pasts. *New German Critique, 88*, 147–164.
Huyssen, A. (2003b). *Present Pasts: Urban Palimpsests and the Politics of Memory.* Stanford: Stanford University Press.
Huyssen, A. (1995). *Twilight Memories: Marking Time in a Culture of Amnesia.* Psychology Press.
Ingold, T. (2010). Ways of Mind-Walking: Reading, Writing, Painting. *Visual Studies, 25*(1), 15–23.
Jäckle, S., & König, P. D. (2017). The Dark Side of the German 'Welcome Culture': Investigating the Causes behind Attacks on Refugees in 2015. *West European Politics, 40*(2), 223–251.

Jameson, F. (1990). 'Cognitive Mapping.' In: C. Nelson and L. Grossberg (Eds). *Marxism and the Interpretation of Culture*. Urbana: University of Illinois Press.
Karakayali, S. (2019). Solidarity with Refugees. In J. Bock & S. Macdonald (Eds.), *Refugees Welcome?* (pp. 191–213). New York: Berghahn Books.
Kuusisto-Arponen, A. (2009). The Mobilities of Forced Displacement: Commemorating Karelian Evacuation in Finland. *Social & Cultural Geography*, 10(5), 545–563.
Landzelius, M. (2003). Commemorative Dis(Re)Membering: Erasing Heritage, Spatializing Disinheritance. *Environment and Planning D: Society and Space*, 21(2), 195–221.
Lefebvre, H. (1992). *The Production of Space*. London: Wiley.
Legassie, S. A. (2017). *The Medieval Invention of Travel*. Chicago: University of Chicago Press.
Legg, S. (2007). Reviewing Geographies of Memory/Forgetting. *Environment and Planning A: Economy and Space*, 39(2), 456–466.
Lynch, B. (2019). I'm Gonna Do Something. In R. R. Janes & R. Sandell (Eds.), *Museum Activism* (pp. 115–126). Abingdon: Routledge.
Macdonald, S. (2006). Mediating Heritage: Tour Guides at the Former Nazi Party Rally Grounds, Nuremberg. *Tourist Studies*, 6(2), 119–138.
Macleod, J. (2013). Britishness and Commemoration: National Memorials to the First World War in Britain and Ireland. *Journal of Contemporary History*, 48(4), 647–665.
Macpherson, H. (2016). Walking Methods in Landscape Research: Moving Bodies, Spaces of Disclosure and Rapport. *Landscape Research*, 41(4), 425–432.
Mageo, J. M. (2001). *Cultural Memory: Reconfiguring History and Identity in the Postcolonial Pacific*. Honolulu: University of Hawaii Press.
Malkki, L. (1992). National Geographic: The Rooting of Peoples and the Territorialization of National Identity among Scholars and Refugees. *Cultural Anthropology*, 7(1), 24–44.
Mandel, R. (2008). *Cosmopolitan Anxieties: Turkish Challenges to Citizenship and Belonging in Germany*. Durham: Duke University Press.
Margalit, A. (2009). *The Ethics of Memory*. London: Harvard University Press.
Marschall, S. (2017). *Tourism and Memories of Home: Migrants, Displaced People, Exiles and Diasporic Communities*. Bristol: Channel View Publications.
Massumi, B. (1987). 'Notes on the Translation and Acknowledgments'. In G. Deleuze and A. F. Guattari (Eds). *Thousand Plateaus: Capitalism and Schizophrenia*. Minneapolis: University of Minnesota Press.
Middleton, J. (2009). Stepping in Time': Walking, Time, and Space in the City. *Environment and Planning A: Economy and Space*, 41(8), 1943–1961.
Middleton, J. (2010). Sense and the City: Exploring the Embodied Geographies of Urban Walking. *Social & Cultural Geography*, 11(6), 575–596.

Miller, N. K., & Tougaw, J. D. (2002). *Extremities: Trauma, Testimony, and Community*. University of Illinois Press.

Mitchell, K. (2003). Monuments, Memorials, and the Politics of Memory. *Urban Geography, 24*(5), 442–459.

Modlin, E. A., Alderman, D. H., & Gentry, G. W. (2011). Tour Guides as Creators of Empathy: The Role of Affective Inequality in Marginalizing the Enslaved at Plantation House Museums. *Tourist Studies, 11*(1), 3–19.

Monforte, P., & Dufour, P. (2013). Comparing the Protests of Undocumented Migrants Beyond Contexts: Collective Actions as Acts of Emancipation. *European Political Science Review, 5*(1), 83–104.

Nora, P. (1989). Between Memory and History: Les Lieux de Mémoire. *Representations, 26*, 7–24.

O'Brian, P. (2018). 'Islamophobia & Europhobia: Expanding Rhetorics of Exclusion. *Bulletin of the Transilvania University of Brașov, Series IV' Philology & Cultural Studies, 11*(1), 9–26.

Orchard, C., & Miller. A. (2014). Protection in Europe for refugees from Syria. RSC Forced Migration Policy Briefing 10.

Ram, M., & Yacobi, H. (2012). African Asylum Seekers and the Changing Politics of Memory in Israel. In I. Glynn & J. O. Kleist (Eds.), *History, Memory and Migration: Perceptions of the Past and the Politics of Incorporation* (pp. 154–170). Basingstoke: Palgrave Macmillan.

Rancière, J. (1999). *Disagreement: Politics and Philosophy*. Minneapolis: University of Minnesota Press.

Rancière, J. (2004a). *Partage Du Sensible*. New York: Continuum.

Rancière, J. (2004b). Who Is the Subject of the Rights of Man? *The South Atlantic Quarterly, 103*(2), 297–310.

Rose, D. B. (2004). *Reports from a Wild Country: Ethics for Decolonisation*. Sydney: University of New South Wales Press.

Rothberg, M. (2009). *Multidirectional Memory: Remembering the Holocaust in the Age of Decolonization*. Stanford: Stanford University Press.

Rothberg, M., & Yildiz, Y. (2011). Memory Citizenship: Migrant Archives of Holocaust Remembrance in Contemporary Germany. *Parallax, 17*(4), 32–48.

Route 44 Tours. http://www.route44-neukoelln.de/. Accessed 7 July 2019.

Roy, P. (1998). *Indian Traffic: Identities in Question in Colonial and Postcolonial India*. Berkeley: University of California Press.

Rygiel, K. (2011). *Globalizing Citizenship*. Vancouver: University of British Colombia Press.

Schramm, K. (2004). Coming Home to the Motherland: Pilgrimage Tourism in Ghana. In S. Coleman & J. Eade (Eds.), *Reframing Pilgrimage: Cultures in Motion* (pp. 133–149). London: Routledge.

Selim, N., Abdalla, M., Alloulou, L., Halli, M. A., Holmes, S. M., Ibiß, M., Jaschke, G., & Martín, J. G. (2018). Coming Together in the So-Called

Refugee Crisis: A Collaboration Among Refugee Newcomers, Migrants, Activists and Anthropologists in Berlin. *Anthropology in Action*, 25(3), 34–44.

Senocak, Z. (2000). *Atlas of a Tropical Germany: Essays on Politics and Culture, 1990–1998*. Lincoln: University of Nebraska Press.

Senocak, Z., & Tulay, B. (2000). 'Germany- home for Turks? A plea for overcoming the crisis between Orient and Occident'. In Z. Senocak (Ed.). *Atlas of a Tropical Germany: Essays on Politics and Culture, 1990–1998*. Lincoln: University of Nebraska Press.

Serhat, K., & Olaf, K. J. (2016). 'Volunteers and asylum seekers'. *Forced Migration Review*, 51(1), 65–67.

Sheller, M., & Urry, J. (2006). The New Mobilities Paradigm. *Environment and Planning A: Economy and Space*, 38(2), 207–226.

Sigona, N. (2018). The Contested Politics of Naming in Europe's 'Refugee Crisis'. *Journal of Ethnic and Racial Studies*, 41(3), 456–460.

Spivak, G. C. (1985). Three Women's Text and a Critique of Imperialism. *Critical Inquiry*, 12(1), 243–261.

Strathern, A. (1996). *Body Thoughts*. Ann Arbor: University of Michigan Press.

Taylor, D. (2003). *The Archive and the Repertoire*. Durham: Duke University Press.

Tezcan, L. (2012). Das muslimische Subjekt. Verfangen im Dialog der Deutschen Islamkonferenz.

The Jewish Berlin Heritage Tours. http://www.berlinjewish.com/jewish-berlin-tour. Accessed 7 July 2019.

Till, K. E. (1999). Staging the Past: Landscape Designs, Cultural Identity and Erinnerungspolitik at Berlin's Neue Wache. *Ecumene*, 6(3), 251–283.

Till, K. E. (2005). *The New Berlin: Memory, Politics, Place*. Minneapolis: University of Minnesota Press.

Till, K. E. (2008). Artistic and Activist Memory-Work: Approaching Place-Based Practice. *Memory Studies*, 1(1), 99–113.

Till, K. E., & Kuusisto-Arponen, A. (2015). Towards Responsible Geographies of Memory: Complexities of Place and the Ethics of Remembering. *Erdkunde*, 69(4), 291–306.

Tirosh, N. (2017). Reconsidering the 'Right to Be Forgotten' – Memory Rights and the Right to Memory in the New Media Era. *Media, Culture & Society*, 39(5), 644–660.

Tirosh, N. (2018). Dominant News Frames, Society's Memory, and the African Asylum Seekers' Protest in Israel. *American Behavioral Scientist*, 62(4), 405–420.

Tirosh, N., & Klein-Avraham, I. (2017). Memorless. *Journalism Studies*, 20(3), 1–20.

Tize, C., & Ries, R. (2019). Neukollen Is Where I Live, It's Not Where I'm from: Children of Migrants Navigating Belonging in a Rapidly Changing Urban Space In Berlin. In J. Bock & S. Macdonald (Eds.), *Refugees Welcome?* (pp. 121–141). New York: Berghahn.

Vollmer, B., & Karakayali, S. (2018). The Volatility of the Discourse on Refugees in Germany. *Journal of Immigrant & Refugee Studies, 16*(1–2), 118–139.

Wunerlich, F. M. (2008). Walking and Rhythmicity: Sensing Urban Space. *Journal of Urban Design, 13*(1), 125–139.

Young, J. E. (1992). The Counter-Monument: Memory Against Itself in Germany Today. *Critical Inquiry, 18*(2), 267–296.

CHAPTER 8

From Here because from Abroad? Migrants and Grassroots Memorials in Paris in the Aftermath of 13 November 2015

Sarah Gensburger and Gérôme Truc

INTRODUCTION: MAKING MIGRANTS VISIBLE AT GRASSROOTS MEMORIALS

On the night of 13 November 2015, three gunmen rushed inside the Bataclan, a concert hall located on Boulevard Voltaire in the 11th arrondissement of Paris, only one block away from Place de la République. They opened fire on the crowd. On this same night, other gunmen shot people in several other cafés and restaurants around the same area, as well as in the nearby 10th arrondissement, leaving a total of 130 people dead and almost 500 wounded. Immediately, the affected neighbourhoods became a stage for the memorialization, tributes and homages to the victims.

On 9 January 2016, one of us was conducting fieldwork, observing the areas around the Bataclan which had turned into a huge memorial. While there, we met a man wearing a yellow baseball cap, carrying two large

S. Gensburger (✉) • G. Truc
French National Centre for Scientific Research (CNRS), Paris, France
e-mail: sarah.gensburger@cnrs.fr; gerome.truc@cnrs.fr

© The Author(s) 2020
S. Marschall (ed.), *Public Memory in the Context of Transnational Migration and Displacement*, Palgrave Macmillan Memory Studies,
https://doi.org/10.1007/978-3-030-41329-3_8

bags. He was from Mali, and he talked to us informally, in broken French.[1] He was used to walking this way, he said; he had come to look for the photograph of a man who volunteered in distributing free food 'for the hungry' at the Place de la République (a site for the distribution of free meals for a long time), and who had always been very nice to him. He had not seen the man since 13 November and had been told that he had been killed in the Bataclan. He didn't know his name but had wanted to come and pay his respects to him. For several months, well before the attacks, this man had passed along the Boulevard Voltaire and the Bataclan every day to go to the Place de la République, where hot lunches were served to the needy. Now, every time he passes, he looks to see if the man's photograph has been added. He was very upset when he talked about it, just as he was when he described his own experiences of the night of 13 November, a night without sleep, talking endlessly with his fellows on the street. This witness lives on the street and is an undocumented migrant. Yet he is no less a resident of the neighbourhood and was clearly touched by the events. It is highly unlikely, however, that his experiences will be preserved among the testimonies being collected in the oral history programmes which, as it was the case in New York after 9/11, have been flourishing in France since the end of 2015.

During the past two decades, many researchers have paid attention to the 'spontaneous shrines' or 'temporary memorials' which tend to flourish in the streets after terrorist attacks or other traumatic events (Santino 2006; Doss 2008; Magry and Sánchez-Carretero 2011). These are most often now conceived as parts of a 'grassroots memorialization' process, understood as

> the process by which groups of people, imagined communities, or specific individuals bring grievances into action by creating an improvised and temporary memorial with the aim of changing or ameliorating a particular situation. (Magry and Sánchez-Carretero 2011, p. 2)

---

[1] Unlike what happens in the English-speaking world, social science research in France does not have to be approved by a university ethics committee to proceed and no formal agreement is needed to reproduce interviews quotations. However, French researchers have, of course, also some ethical principles. In the present case, firstly, we made sure that the anonymity of anyone we spoke with was protected. Secondly, we tried hard to find writing style that was as free as possible from any moral or judgemental perspectives, in order to really give a voice to everyone we interviewed, encountered, interacted with or simply observed.

As it appears these singular types of immediate commemorative monuments, which are a prominent form of social responses to terrorist attacks in Western societies (Truc 2018), systematically articulate local, national and cosmopolitan expressions of grief and concern (Guisan 2009).

However, so far, and strangely enough, the migrants' relationships to these memorials have been relatively neglected by those who study the social reactions to terrorist attacks, except a few exceptions (Chulilla 2005; Yocom 2006; Doving 2018; Lödén 2018; Sanchez-Carretero 2019). They have been of no more interest to the broader literature on collective and public mourning (Elliott 1999; Kear and Steinberg 1999; Walter 1999, 2001; Ben Amos 2000; Fureix 2009). While some migrants are socially invisible, as in the case of the one mentioned above, this lack of research contributes to the double disappearance (Edkins 2011) of migrants as participants in collective mourning and commemoration after terrorist attacks. In the Paris case, paying attention to these social actors is crucial and urgent since in September 2018, the French president announced the creation of a national memorial museum for terror victims, in which, with no doubt, this popular expression at the grassroots memorial will play a central role (Gensburger 2019). Giving voice to the migrants' practices at and views of these memorials is part of a larger ongoing reflection on the best way to 'create the conditions for an inclusive or exclusive memorial site' after terrorist attacks (Délano and Nienass 2014, p. 403). It might also enable us to better grasp how Muslim people living in France reacted to the 2015 Islamist attacks, beyond public discourses criticizing their so-called 'silence' in the immediate aftermath of the event and demanding that they dissociate themselves from the perpetrators (Geisser et al. 2017).

Beyond the opening encounter of this chapter, migrants, in legal or illegal situations, in transit or settled in France, appeared at several occasions in our fieldwork while studying social responses to Paris attacks and their memorialization. The current text takes stock of three groups of data. First, being both a sociologist of memory and an inhabitant of the Bataclan neighbourhood, one of us conducted daily ethnographic fieldwork for a period of one year in this new memory landscape, taking observation notes, conducting interviews and listening to ordinary conversations (Gensburger 2018, 2019).[2] Secondly, since the end of this in-depth

---

[2] Thanks to Sylvain Antichan and Brian Chauvel for their participation in some of these fieldwork observations.

research period and together with a group of colleagues and students, we have conducted additional research on site for the annual anniversaries of the attacks, in November 2016, 2017, 2018 and 2019 (Antichan et al. 2017). Indeed, and beyond the spontaneous grassroots memorials, several commemorative plaques have been inaugurated in 2016 for the first anniversary of the events. They offer a starting point for conducting fieldwork on commemorative practices, as has been done in the case of previous terrorist attacks in other European centres (Tota 2003, 2004, 2005; Truc 2011, 2012; Allen and Brown 2016). Finally, starting in December 2015, the Paris Archives progressively collected the tributes left at the grassroots memorials for the 13 November attacks. These archival documents have been studied and coded, adding a quantitative dimension to the qualitative material of our study.[3]

These diverse data reveal that, even if migrants have mostly remained uninvestigated so far, they were definitely part of the memorialization process that took place in the immediate aftermath of the Paris attacks. In doing so, they participated fully in the overall post-attacks consensus, and relied on the local level, the one of Paris as their city, to identify with the event. However, as the time from the event passes on, the migrants' situation regarding the commemoration of 13 November appears to be problematic, particularly in the case of those originating from North Africa and Muslim countries. The construction of a shared collective memory through the planned permanent memorial museum will have to take care of this dimension in order to be inclusive and not to add yet another dimension of exclusion to the current public memory of terrorist attacks in France.

Local Dynamics, Inclusiveness and Migrants' Participation in the Grassroots Memorials

At the time of the attacks, the 11th arrondissement was populated by almost 150,000 inhabitants. It has been a place of immigration since the 1960s, mostly of people coming from North Africa. Since the beginning of the twenty-first century, however, new inhabitants, from French and wealthy backgrounds, have been settling there. The 11th arrondissement is considered as one of the few areas of genuine and balanced social

---

[3] These three groups of data have been collected in the framework of the REAT research cluster, supported by the CNRS (https://reat.hypotheses.org)

diversity that still exist in the French capital. Nineteen per cent of its population are migrants coming from a diversity of origins (INSEE 2017). During the fieldwork conducted at the grassroots memorials in the Bataclan neighbourhood, we had many encounters with migrants passing by, stopping for a few minutes or more, on rare occasions leaving a picture or a piece of paper with a handwritten message on the site. In most cases, they expressed themselves as being from abroad and living here, in Paris. Several messages were phrased as referring to groups of migrants, such as 'the Paris Sri Lankan People', 'the Tamil community' or 'the Kabyle people in Paris'. In several documents, the message even contains the word 'here' as in this example, 'That our children live in peace here and everywhere else', written in Spanish and French (translated by the authors).

The materials collected by the Paris Archives enable us to move beyond these idiosyncratic remarks to draw a more systematic picture. About 7700 paper documents were collected on the Parisian sites of the attacks, from 8 December 2015 to 1 March 2016. They are now available online.[4] They enable us to produce some statistics about the content of the post-November attacks' memorialization. It turns out then that 6.4% of the messages left at these grassroots memorials refer to a foreign country or city and that 32 different languages other than French were used in them. Most frequently occurs English, in 20% of the messages, while all the other languages represent between 1.6%, for Italian (the second most frequent after English), and 0.4%, for Chinese. However, it is difficult to distinguish among these messages between those coming from migrants versus tourists. The overrepresentation of documents in English and of people quoting the USA or European countries may signify than tourists were more numerous than migrants in this process. Paris is indeed the most touristic city in the world.

Whether migrants or tourists, what these foreigners expressed in their messages left at the grassroots memorials in Paris is most often a sense of solidarity without specific identification with the victims. They speak on behalf of their country to express their support for Paris or, more often, France. For instance: 'USA stands with Paris', 'Turkey are in solidarity with the people of France' or 'Russia is with France'. Messages addressed to France, in particular, systematically follow this pattern—'we are *with* you', meanwhile messages expressing a sense of direct identification with the victims—we *are* you—are almost always formulated at the local level

[4] http://archives.paris.fr/r/137/hommages-aux-victimes-des-attentats-de-2015/

of the city of Paris (emphasis added). The formula 'Je suis Paris' (I am Paris), inspired by the famous 'I am Charlie', that emerged and quickly gained international currency after the Charlie Hebdo attack in Paris on 7 January 2015, can be found in nearly 5% of the messages collected by the Paris Archives on the sites of the November attacks. But only 0.3% of them contain something like 'I am France/French'. This result is perfectly congruent with what was already observed in similar documents, namely those taken from the grassroots memorials that were established in Madrid after the train bombings on 11 March 2004, collected through the 'Archivo del Duelo' research project (Sánchez-Carretero 2011). The anthropologist Cristina Sánchez-Carretero, who leads this project, remarks indeed:

> While many examples of complete identification with Madrid or the train are found in the materials of the project, there are no similar examples with respect to Spain. For instance, messages saying 'Belgians are also Madridians' or 'we are all Madridians' were frequently found at the stations. At the same time, there is not evidence of even a single similar message stating that 'We are all Spain' or 'Ecuador is Spain'. (…) The level of the nation-state is employed to express solidarity among countries or to express shared sentiments, but it is not used to express total identification. (Sánchez-Carretero 2019, p. 82)

This recurrent observation refers to the fact that, except in the case of people with dual nationality, identification with a nation is exclusive, while identification with a city can be inclusive: modern cities, especially metropolises like Madrid or Paris, are, by nature, places of social mixing, open to all, cosmopolitan (Simmel 1950). Thus, being the inhabitant of a city is not the same as being member of a nation, and so the two do not come into conflict. Thus it is possible to say, 'the Turks are Paris' or 'I am Algerian, but I am also Paris'. However, declaring that 'the Turks, or the Algerians, are also French', or 'I am Algerian, but I am also French'— except, once again, in the specific case of people with dual nationality— would strike many people as a logical contradiction (Truc 2018, p. 151). It is worth noting that the messages left at the grassroots memorials by people from the overseas French territories (DOM-TOM) follow exactly the same pattern. Even if the Réunion island (or the Guadeloupe, but less cited) is indeed French territory and their inhabitants have French nationality, one can find in the messages left in front of the Bataclan sentences like 'La Réunion is with you' or 'La Réunion is Paris'.[5] Such messages often appear next to the historic flag of the island along with the French flag, exactly as if their inhabitants were foreigners to the country attacked by the terrorists, like migrants or tourists.

Therefore, here is precisely what can allow us to identify messages specifically left by migrants within the grassroots memorials among all the foreigner's messages. Contrary to the tourists who do not live in Paris and therefore express their support to the victims as a solidarity of their country with France, the migrants settled in Paris, whether for days or years, express a direct identification with the victims at the local level of the city, building then an inclusive relation to the events. This direct identification is sometimes expressed in long messages, taking the shape of a personal narrative, as in the case, for instance, of this Chilean person, who tells his own migrant trajectory to explain why, although a foreigner, he is so sensitive to what is happening to his adopted city (translated from Spanish by authors):

> To the French people, to Paris, I am writing in my native language as I did not learn yet to do it in French, hoping that some of you will understand what I am saying here. The first time I discover Paris was a long time ago. It was not for tourism. I left my country because I didn't have the right to live there with my ideas and convictions. I knew very closely the cruelty and arrogance of people pretending to say what is the true and the best for our country, Chile. Today, so many years later, I am overwhelmed to be here, knowing what is happening, without being able to do anything else than writing this.[6]

But messages of this kind require narrative and linguistic skills, as well as a social disposition, to publicly expose one's life; not all migrants have such skills. Most of the messages of migrants expressing a sense of identification with the victims at the level of Paris are much shorter, using symbols, like flags, the Eiffel Tower and the 'Pray for Paris' logo, as well as ready-made formulas such as 'I am Paris'. In this way, some of them could also have been written by tourists. These are generally adapted to provide evidence of the migrant's origin—for instance, in the case of migrants from Algeria: 'Alger is Paris' or 'The Kabylia is Paris' (Fig. 8.1).

---

[5] See for example, in the Paris Archives, documents 3904 W71–107 to 114.
[6] Paris Archives, document 3910W8-8.

Fig. 8.1 'Kabylia is Paris'. (© Paris Archives, document 3907W1-109)

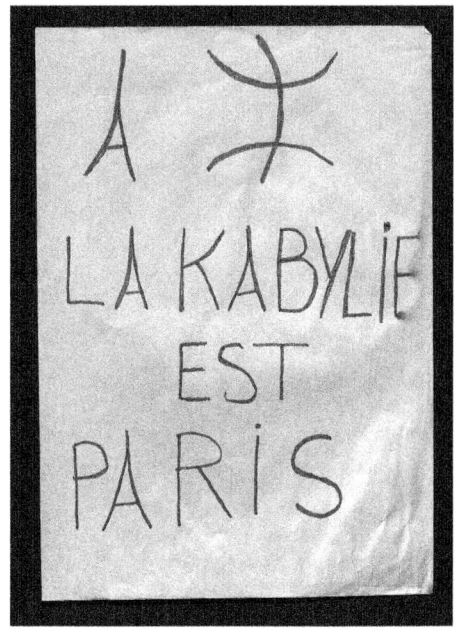

After the 11 March 2004 attacks in Madrid, messages written by migrants were mainly from countries of South America—Ecuador, Peru, Colombia, Argentina and so on (Sánchez-Carretero 2011). Given the history of migration in France, it is not very surprising to note that in the case of the post-13 November grassroots memorials in Paris, countries of Africa, and more precisely former French colonies of North Africa prevail—particularly Algeria, but also Morocco and Tunisia. It must also be taken into account that the perpetrators of the November attacks were from families originating from these countries and that these Islamist attacks, consequently, were particularly difficult to live with for French citizens born in these same countries and of Muslim faith or culture (see Geisser et al. 2017; Beaud 2018, cpt. 10).

Another group of people who can be identified among the migrants who left messages at the grassroots memorials, although a small minority, are refugees from Syria. The war in Syria and the 'refugee crisis' appears as one of the relevant geopolitical contexts of the 13 November attacks. Some 30 messages mention Syria, and several of them in particular were left on the different sites of the attacks in the name of the 'Free Syrians of

France', along with Syrian flags (Fig. 8.2). The presence of these Syrian messages in the grassroots memorials can be interpreted as a means to raise awareness and solidarity with the Syrian cause among French people. One of these messages says for instance: 'Parisians, stay on your feet! The Syrians of France are with you. The blood flowing is the same in Syria and in Paris'. The Syrians are not the only ones to establish such links between the Paris situation and that of other cities or countries outside the Western world struck by terrorism. Some Kurds, for example, left this message at the Bataclan: 'Yesterday Kobane, today Paris. We are all Kurds, we are all

Fig. 8.2 Messages left by the 'Free Syrians of France' in front of the Bataclan, 11 January 2016. (© Gérôme Truc)

Paris'.[7] Here, migrants appear as a key factor in the transnationalization of the post-November grassroots memorials in Paris.

This observation is consistent with the transnational turn taken by memory studies in the recent years (e.g. Assmann 2014). The imbrication between local feelings of belonging and global identification with extra-national groups confirms the importance of the 'glocal' in this transnationalization of memory (Erll and Rigney 2018). Since migrants took active part in the immediate memorialization which followed 13 November 2015, it is now important to take a closer look at the kind of narratives they referred to when visiting the sites of the attacks. Did migrant participation in grassroots memorialization contribute to the construction of cosmopolitan memory that is so often called for (Levy and Sznaider 2010) or did it illustrate the multidirectional nature of any evocation of the past (Rothberg 2009)? In other words, on whose 'travelling memories' (Erll 2011) did this transnationalization dynamic rely?

MIGRANTS' ROLE IN THE TRANSNATIONALIZATION OF GRASSROOTS MEMORIALS

On 13 November 2015, almost 20% of the victims were foreigners, this proportion would be even higher when including those who were both French and foreign nationals, but who are more difficult to identify as such in public data. This proportion results of course from the status of Paris as cosmopolitan metropolis. It explains that some of the first flags, flowers and messages to be left on the sites came from other countries, from Portugal to Tunisia, as occurred previously in London after the bombings on 7 July 2005 (Truc 2018). From the start, the (bi)nationality of the victims and some of their close friends and relatives staged the memorial as a transnational symbolic space. But beyond this first dimension, the transnationalization of the grassroots memorials also relied on the frequent inclusion of other terrorist attacks in the scope of the events to be mourned and memorialized on these sites. In December 2015, it was someone from Turkey who attached a message to the metal fence in front of the Bataclan, paying homage to the victims of the attack in Ankara on 10 October 2015.[8] Again in January 2016, a man who identified him-

---

[7] Paris Archives, document 3904 W43–15.

[8] On 10 October 2015, an attack in Ankara left 102 people dead and more than 500 wounded. A double explosion targeted a pacifist demonstration organized by left-wing forces. This occurred in a context of political tensions in Turkey.

self as coming from Africa pasted a short but clear message on a pre-existing pink poster speaking of love, 'I am Ouagadougou! with all my heart' (Fig. 8.3), the Burkina Faso capital having just been hit by a terrorist attack.[9]

Even more than the Bataclan site, it was the Place de la République where the transnationalization of the memory of the Paris attacks was most visible. Unfortunately, the materials collected by the Paris Archives in the grassroots memorials are of no help to highlight this since they include nothing from this site. This requires some explanation. Immediately after the Charlie Hebdo attack in January 2015, people spontaneously gathered around the Place de la République due to a combination of three

Fig. 8.3 'I am Ouagadougou! with all my heart'. Bataclan, Paris, 18 January 2016. (© Gérôme Truc)

[9] On the evening of 15 January 2016, a bar, a restaurant and a hotel in Ouagadougou, the capital of Burkina Faso, all primarily frequented by foreigners, were attacked by members of Al-Qaeda in the Islamic Maghreb.

factors. Firstly, it is one of the most important plazas in Paris, with a strong symbolic significance and a long story of public gatherings for celebrations and mass demonstration around its central monument—an allegoric representation of the French Republic. Secondly, it is very close to the scene of the Charlie Hebdo attack, just a few blocks away; and thirdly, it had just been renovated and declared a pedestrian area at the time of the attack. Thus the most important grassroots memorials in Paris for the victims of the January 2015 attacks took shape there, and the Place de la République and its central monument internationally became the iconic place of memory for these attacks, even if no bullets were fired and nobody was killed right there. A few weeks after the attacks, when the city authorities started to remove tributes and clean the place, people protested. A group that baptized itself '17 never again' (in reference to the number of dead) emerged through social media organization, notably Facebook, to take charge of the maintenance of the memorials and take care of the tributes in memory of the victims (Truc and Bazin 2019). Thanks to their action as 'guardians of memory', the grassroots memorials stayed on the Place de la République throughout the summer of 2015 and were still there when the 13 November attack took place. After these new attacks, people went to the sites to pay tribute to the victims, as well as coming back to the Place de la République, to revitalize the grassroots memorials there. When the Paris Archives started to collect the content of the informal memorials on each site of the attacks (Bataclan and café terraces), they decided to leave the Place de la République aside to avoid any conflict with the '17 never again' group who, meanwhile, has come to act as custodian and quasi-owner of the grassroots memorials there (Truc and Bazin 2019). That is why researchers can in this case only rely on site observations, such as the following one we made in June 2016.

On 12 June 2016, a shooting took place in a popular gay nightclub in Orlando, Florida.[10] Immediately, the grassroots memorial on the Place de la République echoed this new massacre. A gathering was held in tribute to the Florida victims, and new drawings and messages were left on the base of the statue. One young couple left a banner made in paper that read 'The more you kill us, the more we will love each other'. The man, aged 26, and the woman, aged 23, were both philosophy students and had

---

[10] During the night of 12 June 2016, the day of Gay Pride, a man opened fire in a crowded nightclub in Orlando, Florida, popular with the LGBT community. Fifty people were killed; Islamic State later claimed responsibility for the attack.

arrived in Paris from Portugal in September 2015. She was Portuguese and he was Belgian-Portuguese; both lived in the 18th arrondissement at the time. They reported being particularly sensitive to issues around LGBT rights. That night they had come in response to the attack in Orlando and brought a banner [*The more you will kill us, the more we will love each other*], which they proceeded to hang with great care. The man wanted it to be displayed next to a Franco-Belgian tribute already left there in honour of the victims of the attacks that occurred in Brussels in March 2016, as though this location was an echo of his own national belonging. This was the first time that either of them had come to this site to participate in grassroots memorialization efforts after a terrorist attack. For the Brussels attacks, the young man said he had been 'too involved'; he 'called people' and 'didn't even think' of coming here. For the Paris attacks in November 2015, however, they 'had just arrived' in the capital. The symbolic meaning of their tribute to the victims was hence linked simultaneously to Orlando, Brussels and Paris.

The scholarly literature on the memorialization of terror attacks has stressed the cosmopolitan dimension without always identifying the concrete actors and vectors which make this transnationalization possible (Brown and Hoskins 2010; Milosevic 2017). Through these examples, outcomes of an in-depth ethnographic fieldwork process on the sites of grassroots memorials, the migrants appear as important actors in this transnationalization of solidarity and immediate commemoration after the attacks. As mentioned earlier, both migrants and tourists participated in this transnational memorialization dynamic, yet their responses differ. When tourists contributed to the informal memorials at the sites, it was generally a ready-made, individual and anonymous message, such as 'Pray for Paris'. When migrants left messages, on the contrary, they were more often in the form of a type of manifesto, collective and signed.

Moreover, in recent years, some scholars have rightly denounced the fact that this cosmopolitan solidarity only manifests itself when terror strikes cities in the Western world (Brassett 2008, 2010; Bond 2015; Heath-Kelly 2016). For example, Jouan (2017) comments critically on the difference in reactions following the attacks in Beirut on 12 November and in Paris on 13 November 2015, although Islamic State claimed responsibility for both. During our fieldwork, however, some migrants took advantage of the grassroots memorials to move beyond this North-South divide and claim visibility and solidarity for victims of terrorism in non-Western countries in the global South. On 16 July 2016, a minute of silence was organized around the grassroots memorials on the Place de la République to mourn the victims of the massive attack which had taken place two days before, on Bastille Day, in Nice, a touristic city in the South of France. Once the ceremony was over, a large group of 50 men, visibly migrants from the Indian subcontinent, circled the main side of the memorial. After a few minutes, they displayed two large banners saying 'Bangladesh Buddhist Association, Paris France' and 'No place for terrorism in Bangladesh'. Jack Santino (2011) highlights the tension between apolitical commemoration and political activism, which lays at the very core of grassroots memorials. In the present case, migrants as a largely invisible and under-researched group of social actors turn out to participate as much as anyone in this social dynamic of informal memorialization. In fact, they even appear as major actors of the commemorative processes taking place at the grassroots memorials following the 2015 terrorist attacks in Paris.

Commemoration, Monuments and Exclusion of the Migrants

The grassroots memorials discussed above were eventually doomed to disappear. The collection of the artefacts and documents that make up these informal memorials by the Paris Archives is unprecedented in France,[11] but the social uses of this heritage are yet to be explored. In any case, we can already see how the heritagization of these artefacts makes it impossible to distinguish between a 'pre-memorial era' (Simpson and Corbridge 2006) and a subsequent era of 'memorial mania' (Doss 2010). The immediate responses to the attacks on the one hand, and the commemoration of the events on the other, form a continuum (Truc 2017; Gensburger 2019)—stages in the ongoing process of memorialization that begins in the very first hours after the attacks and demonstrates the 'restlessness of events' (Wagner-Pacifici 2010).

This cyclical temporal framing, the time map, as Eviatar Zerubavel (2003) puts it, is associated with a memorial topography. At the time of writing, four years after the terrorist attacks, several sites in the Parisian

---

[11] Although such archival collection was unprecedented in France, this is not true for the set-up of grassroots memorials or collective gatherings after terror attacks, which were observed in Paris as early as the nineteenth century (Salomé 2010) and which have occurred more regularly since the twentieth century (Salomé 2015).

public space still bear witness to their memory. In November 2016, for the first anniversary of the events, the Paris City Council and the French government made the decision to have the memorial topography reflect the cartography of the attacks. Commemorative plaques were inaugurated in each of the sites affected (cafés, concert hall and football stadium[12]). Each year on 13 November, the families of survivors and victims, individually or as part of victims' associations, return to these sites one after the other. These ceremonies are attended by the Mayor of Paris, Anne Hildago, and a state representative, the French President, François Hollande in 2016, Emmanuel Macron in 2017 and the Prime Minister, Edouard Philippe, in 2018. They each lay an official wreath in turn, but none speaks; the ceremonies are completely silent. There is only the reading of the names of the dead, a now global ritual (Laqueur 2016), to break the silence. This litany, alternating feminine and masculine voices, was pre-recorded for the first anniversary and has been replayed every year since. Both before and after the reading of the names and the one minute of silence that follows, members of the audience are generally engaged in intense discussion. Their comments are political, for example, critically reflecting on the fact that the president and other ministers remain silent. Ethnographic observation of these ceremonies clearly demonstrates that there is no consensus around the meaning of the attacks (Who is to blame for these attacks? Were they parts of a 'war' or not? A consequence of French foreign policy? Or of some laxity in immigration policy?). There is also little agreement on how and which memories should be preserved (Are commemorative plaques enough? Do we need something else, like a monument or a memorial museum? If so, where should it be set up? Should the Bataclan indeed be the main *lieu de mémoire* for the 13 November attacks?). Behind the commemorative consensus that characterizes much of the grassroots memorials, and beyond the questions around resilience that run through French society as a whole, the multiplicity of meanings given to the attacks and their memory are clearly visible here. They also demonstrate the symbolic weakness of the contemporary political representation on this issue (Boussaguet and Faucher 2017). Within this audience, balancing between consensus and conflict in front of the commemorative plaques during commemorations, migrants occupy a singular position.

---

[12] The night of 13 November 2015 started with the attack of the Stade de France in Saint-Denis, in the suburbs of Paris.

A one-week full time fieldwork process was conducted in 2016, 2017, 2018 and 2019 respectively in front of the commemorative plaques and former sites of grassroots memorials during the commemorative period.[13] This research material enables us to investigate the migrants' relationship to the permanent memorials in memory of 13 November. It appears that the distance to the events on the one hand, and the institutionalization of collective remembering, from grassroots memorials to permanent memory markers, on the other, have created tensions within the migrants' position, particularly in the case of people coming from North Africa and Muslim countries.

The commemoration ceremonies in front of the plaques take place on a consensual basis and refer mainly to a national scale, embodied by the presence of either the French President or the Prime Minister. The audience adopts a ritualistic mourning behaviour, and for this occasion, the grassroots memorials come back to life. People leave messages of 'peace', 'love' and 'togetherness'. Some flags appear again at the sites, but this time they are only French ones. However, once the ceremony ends or if the observer moves a few metres away, the scene changes radically and the staged impression of national unity fades drastically. One can observe, for instance, small groups of people criticizing government policy from multiple perspectives. Some regret that the attacks did not lead to changes in terms of foreign affairs; they call for a stop to French military interventions in Africa and the Middle East. Others adopt a domestic affairs perspective and would have liked the terror attacks to create more collective awareness about ethnic discrimination in France. At the opposite end of the scale, some prefer the French State to be more repressive of Muslim religious extremism in France.

Beyond the ritualistic expression of pain, sadness and concern, discussions between people who did not know each other before the commemoration ceremony are very uncommon. On 15 November 2016, the remembrance cycle of the first anniversary was still ongoing. We stood in front of the commemorative plaque recording the names of the dead at the Bataclan concert hall. When we arrived, a man called out to us: 'Please can you hold a minute of silence with me'. During the ensuing one minute, he silently read the names and concluded with 'shall they rest in peace'. The discussion began while he lighted some candles. From the

---

[13] These observations were conducted with Sylvain Antichan, Delphine Griveaud and Solveig Hennebert.

outset, he declared that he was more empathic and in shock than the 'native-born French people' and went on to spontaneously identify himself as 'Arabic' ('it shows on my face right?') and a Muslim. He told us about his personal history and the role played by the wake of terrorism in Algeria that motivated his family's migration to France. He concluded his speech on a very angry tone, one that we rarely witnessed in the vicinity of the memorials and commemorative plaques: 'these terrorists they should go and be fucked by horses'.

Everything took place as if the presence of this man was socially necessary but at the same time in tension, between social pressure and illegitimacy, reflecting the unmanageable position of Muslims in France, following the new wave of Islamic terrorism which has started in 2015 (Geisser et al. 2017). As it happens, and without any deliberate choice on our part, a large part of the people we managed to speak with on the memorial sites during the commemorations were migrants from North Africa. Some of them even reached out to us and other members of our research group spontaneously as if they wanted their presence to be noted and acknowledged.

Moreover, most of the open conflicts and occasionally vicious arguments we witnessed during the annual commemorations involved migrant people, usually arguing with each other. On 13 November 2016, around 7 pm on the Place de la République, in front of the central statue, a violent dispute started. For several hours, a man wrapped in a huge French flag had been selling French flags and candles for a handful of euros, a few metres away from the statue. He had a strong North African accent, and his face was typical of the labour migrants who came to France in the 1960–1970s. A black man, around 50 years old and very neatly dressed, came closer to the statue and left a note about peace. On his way back, he stopped in front of the man with the flags and aggressively shouted at him, in French, with a clear African accent: 'you should be ashamed of yourself! Making money out of pain and grief. Go back home! Please just go back home!',[14] in a mix of anger and pity. If the expression 'go back home' could be understood literally, it was not in this way that the people witnessing the scene made sense of it and neither did the man with the flags.

---

[14] In the French language, two different pronouns exist for the English 'you'. It may be noted that the black man used the familiar 'tu' when addressing the migrant, which is usually reserved for people who know each other quite closely. The migrant equally responded by using 'tu'.

He replied vividly, in French and also with a strong accent, 'This is my home, France is my home sir!'. The argument went on for a few more minutes, the first one repeating 'But go home! Leave, please leave. You make me ashamed' and the other replying 'I am home as much as you are'.

Two years later, on 13 November 2018, another public dispute took place in front of the statue on the Place de la République, the main site of the former grassroots memorials. During each commemoration since 2015, we had noticed a 20-metre-long banner, demonstratively brought back each time by its creator (Fig. 8.4). The concept underpinning this commemorative piece involves the collection of handprints; people were asked to print their hand and colour it in one of the thousands of squares designed on the long piece of fabric and write a message inside the print. This banner is possibly the most important participatory commemorative memorial to exist so far in relation to the Paris attacks. This year (2019) we decided to contribute to it ourselves. A young man, around 25 years, was signing it at the same time, writing 'Kabylia' in his print, referring to a region in northern Algeria. That was not surprising. After more than three years of fieldwork, we had already noticed how many people in the 11th arrondissement, and in Paris more generally, had connections with Kabylia.[15] Kabyle flags were very frequent on the grassroots memorials. On 11 January 2015, during the enormous demonstration that had followed the Charlie Hebdo attacks of 7 January,[16] we had already been struck by the number of these blue and yellow flags among the crowds that had visited the neighbourhood, which ten months later would be known as the 'Bataclan neighbourhood'.

While we were hence little surprised at the man's inscription, a woman in her fifties almost jumped on the young man, challenging him, 'Why did you write that?! I created this piece of fabric for people to share a common humanity and not for you to bring back here the causes of civil wars and conflicts that I left behind me in Algeria'. The woman who had initiated this participatory banner turned out to be a migrant from Algeria who had been married to a man from Kabylia and felt that her husband's family resented her non-Kabyle origin. Quickly approximately 30 people

---

[15] Kabylia is a northern region of Algeria whose people have been claiming autonomy first from the French state and, after 1962, from the Algerian one.

[16] On 11 January 2015, 2 million people demonstrated in Paris, in protest against the attacks that had occurred the week before. Several commentators described this march as 'republican'.

Fig. 8.4 The recurring banner. (© Sarah Gensburger)

gathered around the woman and the young man who started to speak alternatively in Kabyle's vernacular language and Arabic. Most of the people seemed to understand the verbal exchanges. Here again, migrant people from North Africa seemed to be defining their place in and belonging to French society, through the participation in the commemoration and their relationship to the memorials. Arguing that we and three other people close to us were unable to understand the conversation in Arabic, we asked the woman and the young man to skip to French: 'It is not fair that we cannot participate'. The woman turned to us and said, in French and in a friendly manner, 'You are right, I made this banner to include everyone'. The conversation then opened to other participants and quickly focused on the legitimacy for people from North Africa and of Muslim origin to take part in this commemoration on the one hand, and on the discrimination and racism they had to cope with since the event, on the other. At this point, the migrants' relationship to the commemorative monuments of 13 November appeared both inclusive and exclusive.

* * *

As a conclusion, we can say that if migrants have mostly remained neglected in the study of the societal response to the Paris terrorist attacks, they were definitely part of the memorialization process that took place in the immediate aftermath. In doing so, they participated fully in the overall dynamic of remembering and commemorating, and relied on the local level, Paris as their city, to identify with the event. However, when we move away from the event, the migrants' situation regarding the commemoration of 13 November appears to be problematic, especially in the case of those originating from North Africa and Muslim countries, moving from inclusiveness to exclusion. In the Paris case, paying attention to migrants as actors of commemoration is crucial and urgent since, in September 2018, the French president announced the creation of a national memorial museum for victims of terrorism, which will, with no doubt, give special attention to the popular expression of grief at the grassroots memorials (Gensburger 2019). Giving voice to the migrants' practices at these memorials must definitely be part of a larger ongoing reflection on the best way to preserve the past as a way to build the future.

These empirical conclusions highlight furthermore the ongoing theoretical reflections on the transnational dimension of contemporary memory dynamics in Paris. If the transnational scale is central to the current literature in the field of memory studies, so far, few works have managed to resolve the 'tension between the production of remembrance through transnational processes and its grounding in concrete locations', as Jenny Wüstenberg (2019, p. 1) has rightly acknowledged in a recent journal special issue on *Locating transnational memory*. One of the ways to resolve this tension has been to pay attention to travelling memory (Erll 2011) and to the circulation of memory actors who work at obtaining official recognition of past offences and commemoration of difficult pasts (Hasunuma and McCarthy 2019). However, this chapter suggests that the transnationalization of memory can also rely on the grounding of migrants in concrete locations who, far from being memory entrepreneurs, invest monuments, memorials and sites of commemoration with contemporary issues which have no real links with the public evocation of the past. A new question arises then: how have monuments, memorials and commemoration sites become a relevant place for migrants to speak publicly? This chapter calls for not only studying the transnationalization of memory, but also, symmetrically, the memorialization of the transnational (Dybris McQuaid and Gensburger 2019).

References

Allen, M., & Brown, S. D. (2016). Memorial Meshwork: The Making of the Commemorative Space of the Hyde Park 7/7 Memorial. *Organization, 23*(1), 10–28.

Antichan, S., Griveaud, D., & Gensburger, S. (2017). La mémoire en ses lieux. Essai de topographie de la première commémoration du 13 novembre 2015 à Paris. *Mémoires en jeu, 4,* 50–60.

Assmann, A. (2014). Transnational Memories. *European Review, 22*(4), 546–556.

Beaud, S. (2018). *La France des Belhoumi: portraits de famille (1977–2017)*. Paris: La Découverte.

Ben, A. A. (2000). *Funerals, Politics and Memory in Modern France 1789–1996*. Oxford: Oxford University Press.

Bond, L. (2015). *Frames of Memory After 9/11. Culture, Criticism, Politics and Law*. Basingstoke: Palgrave Macmillan.

Boussaguet, L., & Faucher, F. (2017). The Politics of Symbols: Reflections on the French Government's Framing of the 2015 Terrorist Attacks. *Parliamentary Affairs, 71*(1), 169–195.

Brassett, J. (2008). Cosmopolitanism Vs. Terrorism? Discourses of Ethical Possibility Before and After 7/7. *Millennium: Journal of International Studies, 36*(2), 121–147.

Brassett, J. (2010). Cosmopolitan Sentiments After 9–11: Trauma and the Politics of Vulnerability. *Journal of Critical Globalisation Studies, 3,* 12–29.

Brown, S. D., & Hoskins, A. (2010). Terrorism in the New Memory Ecology: Mediating and Remembering the 2005 London Bombings. *Behavioral Sciences of Terrorism and Political Aggression, 2,* 87–107.

Chulilla, J. L. (2005). Presencia de las comunidades inmigrantes en los Santuarios Populares del 11-M. In J. L. Chulilla & P. Azagra (Eds.), *Espacios urbanos e immigracion en el Madrid del s. XXI* (pp. 364–403). Madrid: La Casa Encendida.

Délano, A., & Nienass, B. (2014). Invisible Victims: Undocumented Migrants and the Aftermath of September 11. *Politics and Society, 42*(3), 399–321.

Doss, E. (2008). *The Emotional Life of Contemporary Public Memorials. Towards a Theory of Temporary Memorials.* Amsterdam: Amsterdam University Press.

Doss, E. (2010). *Memorial Mania. Public Feeling in America.* Chicago/London: University of Chicago Press.

Døving, C. A. (2018). Homeland Ritualised: An Analysis of Written Messages Placed at Temporary Memorials After the Terrorist Attacks on 22 July 2011 in Norway. *Mortality, 23*(3), 231–246.

Dybris McQuaid, S., & Gensburger, S. (2019). Administrations of Memory: Transcending the Nation and Bringing Back the State in Memory Studies. *International Journal of Politics, Culture and Society, 32*(2), 125–143.

Edkins, J. (2011). *Missing: Persons and Politics.* Ithaca: Cornell University Press.

Elliott, A. (1999). *The Mourning of John Lennon.* Berkeley: University of California Press.

Erll, A. (2011). Travelling Memory. *Parallax, 17*(4), 4–18.

Erll, A., & Rigney, A. (2018). Cultural Memory Studies After the Transnational Turn. *Memory Studies, 11*(3), 272–273.

Fureix, E. (2009). *La France des larmes: Deuils politiques à l'âge romantique (1814–1840).* Paris: Champ Vallon.

Geisser, V., Marongiu-Perria, O., & Smaïl, K. (2017). *Musulmans de France, la grande épreuve: face au terrorisme.* Ivry-sur-Seine: Les Éditions de l'Atelier.

Gensburger, S. (2018). Beyond Trauma. Researching Memory on My Doorstep. In D. Drozdzewski & C. Birdsall (Eds.), *Doing Memory Research: New Methods and Approaches* (pp. 109–128). London: Palgrave.

Gensburger, S. (2019). *Memory on my Doorstep. Chronicles of the Bataclan Neighbourhood (Paris, 2015–2016).* Leuven: Leuven University Press.

Guisan, C. (2009). Of September 11, Mourning and Cosmopolitan Politics. *Constellations, 16*, 563–578.

Hasunuma, L., & McCarthy, M. (2019). Creating a Collective Memory of the Comfort Women in the USA. *International Journal of Politics, Culture and Society, 32*(2), 145–162.

Heath-Kelly, C. (2016). *Death Security: Memory and Mortality at the Bombsite.* Manchester: Manchester University Press.

INSEE. (2017). *Une mosaïque sociale propre à Paris.* Insee Analyses Ile-de-France, n°53.

Jouan, M. (2017). Politique du deuil: entre reconnaissance et invisibilisation. *Raison publique, 21*(1), 113–152.

Kear, A., & Steinberg, D. L. (Eds.). (1999). *Mourning Diana: Nation, Culture and the Performance of Grief.* London: Routledge.

Laqueur, T. (2016). *The Work of the Dead. A Cultural History of Mortal Remains.* Princeton: Princeton University Press.

Levy, D., & Sznaider, N. (2010). *Human Rights and Memory*. University Park: Pennsylvania State University Press.

Lödén, H. (2018). 'It's Difficult to Be a Norwegian': Minority Voices in the Memorial Messages After the Terror Attacks in Norway 2011. *Nordic Journal of Migration Research, 8*(1), 56–64.

Magry, P., & Sánchez-Carretero, C. (Eds.). (2011). *Grassroots Memorials: The Politics of Memorializing Traumatic Death*. Oxford: Berghahn Books.

Miloševic A., (2017). Remembering the Present: Dealing with the Memories of Terrorism in Europe. *Journal of Terrorism Research, 8*(2), 44.

Rothberg, M. (2009). *Multidirectional Memory: Remembering the Holocaust in the Age of Decolonization*. Stanford: Stanford University Press.

Salomé, K. (2010). L'attentat de la rue Nicaise: l'émergence d'une violence inédite ? *La Revue d'histoire du XIXe siècle, 40*(1), 59–75.

Salomé, K. (2015). La France, scène du terrorisme international – 1982–2015. In E. Laurentin (Ed.), *Comment en sommes-nous arrivés là ? Histoire d'une République fragile* (pp. 171–176). Paris: Fayard.

Sánchez-Carretero, C. (Ed.). (2011). *El Archivo del duelo: análisis de la respuesta ciudadana ante los atentados del 11 de marzo en Madrid*. Madrid: CSIC.

Sánchez-Carretero, C. (2019). Emotions, Neighbors and Nation-State Identifications at the Grassroots Memorials of the Madrid Train Bombings. *Ethnologie Française, 173*, 77–88.

Santino, J. (2006). *Spontaneous Shrines and the Public Memorialization of Death*. New York: Palgrave Macmillan.

Santino, J. (2011). Between Commemoration and Social Activism: Spontaneous Shrines, Grassroots Memorialization, and the Public Ritualesque in Derry. In P. Magry & C. Sánchez-Carretero (Eds.), *Grassroots Memorials. The Politics of Memorializing Traumatic Death* (pp. 97–107). New York: Berghahn Books.

Simmel, G. (1950). The Metropolis and Mental Life. In K.H. Wolff (Ed., Tr.), *The Sociology of Georg Simmel* (pp. 409–424). New York/London: The Free Press.

Simpson, E., & Corbridge, S. (2006). The Geography of Things That May Become Memories: The 2001 Earthquake in Kachchh-Gujarat and the Politics of Rehabilitation in the Prememorial Era. *Annals of the Association of American Geographers, 96*(3), 566–585.

Tota, A. L. (2003). *La città ferita. Memoria e commucazione pubblica della strage di Bologna, 2 agosto 1980*. Bologna: Il Mulino.

Tota, A. L. (2004). Ethnographying Public Memory: The Commemorative Genre for the Victims of Terrorism in Italy. *Qualitative Research, 4*(2), 131–159.

Tota, A. L. (2005). Terrorism and Collective Memories: Comparing Bologna, Naples, Madrid 11 March. *International Journal of Comparative Sociology, 46*(1–2), 55–78.

Truc, G. (2011). Le politique aux marges de la commémoration: une ethnographie des cérémonies de commémoration officielle des attentats du 11 mars 2004 à Madrid. In M. Berger, D. Cefaï, C. Gayet-Viaud, & J. Stavo-Debauge (Eds.), *Du civil au politique: ethnographies du vivre- ensemble* (pp. 205–227). Bruxelles: Peter Lang.

Truc, G. (2012). Memory of Places and Places of Memory: For a Halbwachsian Socio-Ethnography of Collective Memory. *International Social Science Journal, 62*(203–204), 147–159.

Truc, G. (2017). Mémorialisations immédiates. *Mémoires en jeu, 4,* 47–49.

Truc, G. (2018). *Shell Shocked: The Social Response to Terrorist Attacks.* Cambridge: Polity Press.

Truc, G., & Bazin, M. (2019). Guardians of Memory: Mobilizations and Conflicts of Appropriation Surrounding Post-Terrorist Attack Memorials in Madrid, London, and Paris. *Ethnologie Française, 173,* 63–75.

Wagner-Pacifici, R. (2010). Theorizing the Restlessness of Events. *American Journal of Sociology, 115*(5), 1351–1386.

Walter, T. (Ed.). (1999). *The Mourning for Diana.* Oxford/New York: Berg.

Walter, T. (2001). From Cathedral to Supermarket: Mourning, Silence and Solidarity. *The Sociological Review, 49*(4), 494–511.

Wüstenberg, J. (2019). Locating Transnational Memory. *International Journal of Politics, Culture and Society.* https://doi.org/10.1007/s10767-019-09327-6.

Yocom, M. R. (2006). We'll Watch Out for Liza and the Kids: Spontaneous Memorials and Personal Response at the Pentagon, 2001. In J. Santino (Ed.), *Spontaneous Shrines and the Public Memorialization of Death* (pp. 57–97). New York: Palgrave Macmillan.

Zerubavel, E. (2003). *Time Maps. Collective Memory and the Social Shape of the Past.* Chicago: University of Chicago Press.

CHAPTER 9

Walter Benjamin in Fortress Europe: Refugees and the Ethics of Memory in an (Ex)Border Town

Garikoitz Gómez Alfaro

INTRODUCTION

Some sites feel more 'historical' than others. This is not to suggest or deny the historical nature of every location, but to query why some places seem to draw more attention from heritage professionals or tourists of history and to interrogate the temporal imaginaries elicited in them. In 'On the Concept of History' (2007) one of his most renowned writings, German philosopher Walter Benjamin (1892–1940) argued for a historical sensibility that prioritises the study of dispersed fragments dismissed by larger historical discourses. Seemingly banal, neglected traces of the past were for Benjamin the most productive resource for historians attempting to 'brush history against the grain' and unleash the fragment's potential to reveal, albeit in a fleeting manner, history's kaleidoscopic entirety (Buck-Morss 1989; Hamacher 2005; Schwartz 2001). Now celebrated as one of the most important philosophers of the twentieth century, both his condition

G. Gómez Alfaro (✉)
University of Brighton, Brighton, UK
e-mail: G.GomezAlfaro@brighton.ac.uk

© The Author(s) 2020
S. Marschall (ed.), *Public Memory in the Context of Transnational Migration and Displacement*, Palgrave Macmillan Memory Studies,
https://doi.org/10.1007/978-3-030-41329-3_9

of stateless migrant and his death in a small border town between France and Spain trying to flee from the horrors of Fascism posit interesting questions with regard to the tightening of Europe's borders.

Today a declining town on an obsolete border, Portbou has been linked over the last decades to a series of experiences, concepts and names that echo the violence that marked the European twentieth century. Not only was it the last station for Benjamin, but it was also a witness of the Retirada—the retreat or flight of hundreds of thousands of soldiers and civilians to France, following the defeat of the Spanish Republic during the Spanish Civil War (1936–1939). Far away from the great museum corridors, where a celebratory history of 'strategic Europeanization' (De Cesari 2017) is presented, Portbou—the fragment which this chapter is devoted to—allows us to interrogate the hidden face of progressive narratives of Europe.

Similar to other towns associated with 'dark tourism' (Lennon and Foley 2000; Tumarkin 2005), many visitors refer to Portbou's 'heavy atmosphere', which conjures up a sense of melancholic unfinishedness. This affective and symbolic capital has been used as a platform to institute a narrative that characterised wider trends in modern European memory—more specifically, the marriage between European identity and the sacralisation of the memory of the Shoah. The central point of the chapter is that, through the figure of Walter Benjamin, a combination of local, national and international agencies has projected an imaginary of victimhood, defeat and trauma onto the town's landscape which allegorically connects past and present border violence.

This has in turn attracted a number of Benjaminian 'pilgrims' drawn by the 'auratic qualities' of the place itself. However, the decadent atmosphere of the town means different things for the dwellers, who experience their environment not as a Benjaminian allegory, but as an abandoned border town stranded in the present. Here different forms of experiencing time play into wider debates about the relationship between memory and space. In fact, many of the town's residents regard this symbolic inscription of Benjamin into the local imaginary as a top-down process that has failed to engage with the cultural memory of Spain or Catalonia, which in the last decades has been preoccupied with the redress of the victims of Francoist Spain and the vindication of the Spanish Republican exiles. The estrangement of some long-term residents tends to concentrate on the memorial to Benjamin commissioned to Israeli artist Dani Karavan in 1989. At the same time, the memorial has proven to be central to the rearticulation of the memory of the millions of forced exiles produced by the Second World War (1939–1945). As we shall see, annual non-scripted walks function as embodied acts of commemoration which challenge the linearity of progressive time upon which official commemorations are often predicated.

While some early commemorative initiatives attempted to reclaim the disruptive potential of Benjamin's writings, such attempts remained discursively tied to Holocaust memory, thus constructing his as a passive victim of a past regime. The inauguration of the memorial to Benjamin was one of the key scenarios of this discursive operation, but other commemorative practices have contested a politics of time that considers, explicitly or implicitly, the catastrophe that befell Benjamin as existing (only) in the past. The annual re-enactment of Benjamin's crossing of the Pyrenees allows participants to collectively draw parallels between Benjamin and other past and present catastrophes. As an example of how a memorial can be negotiated, I will reconceptualise temporal experience in political terms by looking at how heterogeneous regimes of temporality emerge in encounters with the memorial and its surroundings. Can Benjamin reveal something about the Spanish state's long history of repression, and the resistance to it?

My understanding of Portbou's commemorative landscape is informed by a hybrid engagement with recent work on temporality, historiography, cultural geography and new materialist studies. Sites associated with violent events allow us to explore the continuity and the discontinuity of time contained within these spaces (Gordillo 2014; Harrison 2005; Hetherington 2008). This material relationship between landscapes, objects and history is not the result of social projection, but rather a dialectical relationship between bodies, which reminds us that not only human beings have a history. Benjamin too aimed to expose objects and texts in such a way that the resultant montage would expose the entanglement between temporalities. The commemorative landscape of Portbou works as an ecology of memory, that is to say, as a material and symbolic space between 'the public and the private, between larger histories and those of families and individuals, between memory functions, material, texts, images and senses' (Jones and Garde-Hansen 2012, p. 5).

Methodologically speaking, this signals a distancing from an engagement with memorials or urban spaces as 'texts' that are authored, negotiated and contested (Duncan 1990). While this is surely an important part of what goes on in Portbou, such metaphors tend to render space as passive and it focuses on the symbolic, thus ignoring the materiality of the spaces and the practices that inform, sustain and contain such discursive practices (Lorimer 2005; Waterton and Watson 2015).

The chapter is structured as follows: I will start by contextualising the town as well as the process through which it was mnemonically articulated during the 40 years of Francoist dictatorship that followed the Spanish Civil War. I will then turn to the uncanny geography produced by the coalescence of Benjamin's afterlife and Portbou's material landscape. As I will argue, the inauguration of a memorial to Benjamin in 1994 consolidated the framing of Benjamin's death as the epitome of a European tragedy, that of totalitarian violence during the Second World War. Finally, the chapter will explore the changing narratives around Walter Benjamin and the politics of a shared European memory.

The Origins of Portbou: The Storm We Call Progress

Portbou is a small seaside border town on the eastern end of the Pyrenees, south of the border between France and Spain. Shelley Hornstein describes it as a place that 'has shifted from being a border town to one that no longer has a frontier function, but carries the formidable weight of being both a fishing village with a quiet beach, and the place of Walter Benjamin's death' (Hornstein 2011, p. 15). Actually, Portbou owes its origin to the railway station that dominates the town's skyline. The first train arrived in 1878, although the modern station was built in 1929 on the occasion of Barcelona's International Exposition (Gubert i Macias 1990). Border administration and trade, rather than fishing or tourism, structured the social and economic life of Portbou until the mid-1980s and early 1990s, when the dissolution of the European Union's internal borders due to the Schengen Agreement brought the city's development to a standstill.

On 10 February 1939, Portbou—the Republic's last remaining bastion in Catalonia—was conquered by the Francoist rebel army. Ernesto Giménez Caballero, a Falangist soldier who arrived with the rebel troops, scornfully refers to the town in his chronic of the Rebel Army's 'heroic deed': '[a]ll those border towns seem to be for the Jews. In fact, it is where Jews usually hide themselves' (1939, p. 63 emphasis mine). Located between at least two homelands, the border is depicted as a threat for the very idea of nationhood insofar it serves as a cradle for the stateless—a word that for the Francoist regime was equivalent to the term 'judío' [Jew] or 'rojo' [red]. The conquest was consecrated through a catholic baptism and flag-raising ceremony, followed by a solemn mass the day after. Only a few days before, thousands of republican refugees had fled Spain through Portbou. Amongst these was the celebrated poet Antonio Machado, who died that very February. In 2009, an ensemble of commemorative boards with explanatory texts and archival photographs of the Republican retirada was inaugurated. Situated next to the now empty custom office, the inscription on the main panel reads:

> Homage to the 100.000 men, women and children, Spanish republican and Internationalist that embarked on the path towards exile after 3 years of war against Francoism. They crossed this border of Portbou-Cerbère in February 1939 and were the precursors to antifascist struggle in Europe.

The set of boards is located in front of a currently derelict monolith installed in 1940 to honour the memory of los caídos [the fallen] from the Navarre 4th Division on the day. The rhetoric of this memorial monolith echoed the commemorative narrative of the Francoist Regime, which only recognised the casualties on its side (Aguilar and Humlebaek 2002). In an attempt to redress the uneven grievability (Butler 2009) the monolith signalled, it was both signposted and contextualised by the Memorial Democràtic de Catalunya, the same institution which funded the boards vindicating the legacy of Spanish Republican refugees.[1] The monolith was not the only means through which Portbou's landscape symbolically reflected the new regime. The streetscape changed to commemorate, for example, the military heroes (Generals Mola and Sanjurjo), as well as the events of the Nationalist coup (18th July), while the very name of the town, following a decree that prohibited the use of any language but Castilian, was Hispanicised.[2]

---

[1] The *Memorial Democràtic de Catalunya* is an institution created in 2007 by the Spanish autonomous community of Catalonia to safeguard and promote the 'democratic memory' of the Republican Government and the victims of state repression until the approval of the new Spanish constitution. Its inception occurred at a time when Spanish society was revisiting the Spanish 'Pact of Forgetting' sanctioned by the 1977 Amnesty Law (Vinyes 2004, 2009; Messenger 2017).

[2] The change in the name, which went from 'Portbou' to 'Port-bou', was reverted 40 years later, during the long transition to a parliamentary democracy. Ironically, the English use of 'Port Bou', still widely used, borrows from this earlier act of linguistic violence carried out by the Francoist regime.

Walter Benjamin arrived in Portbou a year after the end of the Spanish Civil War. He embodied the paradigm of the stateless Jew as described by Giménez Caballero after abandoning his home country in 1933 with the rise of Hitler's National Socialist Party; not only was his application for French citizenship unsuccessful but he also saw his German citizenship revoked in 1939. Having wandered across Europe, during his last years, Benjamin worked in Paris in order to finish The Arcades Project, a book which remained incomplete. Reluctant to leave a city that seemed essential for his project, Benjamin headed southwards with the intention to leave France for New York only when the German troops were about to enter Paris (Hutton 2010). Unable to obtain the documents to legally leave France, Benjamin decided to cross the Pyrenees in order to reach Lisbon. Helped by Lisa Fittko and accompanied by others who tried to escape, both from the Gestapo and French collaborators, Benjamin arrived in Portbou, where border guards denied his group entry into Spain. Caught between two fronts, Benjamin is thought to have committed suicide on 26 September 1940. From this point, what we know about Benjamin has merged with the myth about the man, fuelled by what has been labelled the 'Benjamin industry' (Greenberg 2008). A disappeared suitcase containing the last manuscript, a transcribed letter of suicide, the missing body and, finally, an empty grave are only some of the ingredients that are often present within the chronicles of those who visit or write about Portbou in relation to Benjamin.[3]

In his last work 'On the Concept of History', Benjamin offered an understanding of history as open and ever-present (Löwy 2005). In these pages, he set out to 'displace, by questioning the boundaries between past and present, the notion of linear historical time which was sustained by narrative form' (Savage 2000, p. 40). According to Benjamin's formulation, historiography should not concern itself with 'historical truth', as it is neither a matter of facticity nor objectivity. On the contrary, it has to do with both an ethical and a political standpoint for, as Benjamin put it, 'only that historian will have the gift of fanning the spark of hope in the past who is firmly convinced that even the dead will not be safe from the enemy if he wins. And this enemy has not ceased to be victorious' (Benjamin 2007, p. 255). It is therefore urgent, argued Benjamin, to pick

---

[3] Benjamin's remains were moved to niche 503 in the local cemetery, but it is believed they were moved to a mass grave in the same cemetery before the end of the lease (Scheurmann 1992; see also Taussig 2006).

up all the fragments, all the defeats, and compose with them a new revolutionary moment. His approach to remembrance (Eingedenken) is not as much a practice of repetitive mourning as a redemptive endeavour (Fritsch 2006). In this sense, memory becomes laden with utopian possibilities offering a way out of teleological or catastrophic thinking. 'To go to Portbou now', in the words of John Payne (2007, p. 102), 'is to remember'. But what should be remembered? Which fragments would help us in the task Benjamin pointed to? What is it in this space that pulls out our memories?

A Memorial for Benjamin: Pan-European Uses of Memory in Global Cosmopolitanism in the 1990s

Today's visitor is likely to ignore both the monolith in honour to the Francoist troops that conquered the town and the memorial plaques in honour of the republican exiles. At the tourist office, however, the staff speaks of dozens of tourists coming to walk in Benjamin's footsteps. To be sure, one of the main incentives for this pilgrimage is Passages, the above-mentioned memorial. Composed by different elements, the most well-known of which is the tunnel with a staircase that runs aground on the same cliff as the town's cemetery, Passages chimes with the aesthetics of the self-reflective counter-monuments that emerged in the late 1980s in Germany as an attempt to come to terms with the challenges of memorialising the Nazi genocide (Osborne 2017; Young 1993). The tradition of the counter-monument embodied a scepticism towards the sacred aura of former national monuments privileging 'the educational over the commemorative and representative functions of memorials', while also promoting the 'view of historical education as dependent upon active, critical engagement with the past' (Harjes 2005, p. 143).

Almost at the end of the staircase in Passages, when the tunnel gives way to the sky, one faces a thick glass panel where the following quote from Benjamin can be read: 'It is more arduous to honour the memory of the nameless than that of the renowned. Historical construction is devoted to the memory of the nameless'. Was the project intended as a veiled homage to the Spanish Republicans buried, like Benjamin, in mass graves? Did the German authorities—which provided most of the funding—rather want to pay tribute to those who lost their lives while trying to escape from the violence of the Second World War? Did Karavan have in mind the anonymous Jews murdered in Nazi camps? Or did he seek to draw visitors' thoughts to the contemporary refugees that keep crashing against new walls and borders across Europe? To be sure, these options are not mutually exclusive. Lupu (2003, p. 132) has argued that '[w]hile surely all monuments are subject to audience reception and interpretation, countermonuments depend almost entirely on their audience to interpret their intent, making the artist a sort of prisoner of his/her audience'. In this particular case, the 'nameless' operates as an empty signifier which hinges on the historical consciousness of the visitor. Yet, while the nature of the solidarity emanating out of the encounter with the memorial in Portbou can never be determined, the act of interpreting the ambiguity of this formulation is both constrained and enabled by a larger, historically contingent framework. As demonstrated below, this always incomplete 'hermeneutic circle' (Jenkins 2003) more often than not gravitates towards the crimes of Nazism as the master code of reference (Fig. 9.1).

If we contextualise the construction of the memorial within the debates it generated in Germany, as well as within Catalonia's political landscape,

Fig. 9.1 Glass panel in Karavan's Passages (1994). (Photograph by Caterina Nicolau Oliver 2012)

we may offer some answers to those questions, for it was Richard von Weizsäcker, then president of a recently reunited Germany, who promoted the project, following discussions on how to mark the 50th anniversary of Benjamin's death in 1990. Inevitably, then, we are confronted here with what Weizsäcker himself coined *Vergangenheitsbewältigung* or 'coming to terms with the past'—the German past (Berg 2003). However, the issue at stake was actually how to pay homage to those who, like Benjamin, Carl Einstein or Ernst Weiss, lost their lives in exile (Palmier 2006). The choice of Benjamin, himself an émigré, as an epitome of the exile needs to be clarified—not only because he supposedly committed suicide, but because his political profile was covered up by a sense of 'political ambiguity' that made him suitable for rearticulation (Greenberg 2008). Karavan's Passages thus participates in what Koselleck terms the semantic shift of the victim's ontology, as the institutional discourse of Weizsäcker's reunited German government rendered the victims as subjects without agency, that is to say, as 'victims of unfortunate circumstances' (Kattago 2011, p. 139) rather than members of the resistance. The project wasn't without its own conflicts, where there was much criticism about the funding, the purpose of the memorial and the tombstone laid in 1992 (Protzman 1992, 20 August). The supporters highlighted Benjamin's victimhood as well as the debt of Germany to his intellectual stature—some of them even argued Portbou is a place 'where German culture meets its fate'(Schneckenburger 1992, 6 June).

The project was initially commissioned by the Federal Republic of Germany's Ministry of Foreign Affairs via the Arbeitskreis selbständiger Kultur-Institute (AsKI), but it was also funded by the Catalan government and a series of private donors (Scheurmann and Scheurmann 1995). At the opening of the memorial on the 15th of May 1994, attended by Lisa Fittko—Benjamin's guide—the Spanish Ministry of Culture and other authorities from Germany and Spain, connections were drawn between 1940 and the Balkan War, as well as with the rise of the new far right in Germany. No words, however, for the Spanish exiles nor the Francoist regime, as Spain's own critical engagement with the past was at a standstill. In fact, local authorities seemed more interested in the economic boost, memory tourism could bring to the border region than in the symbolic significance of such a monument.

While Hans Eichel, Essen's Ministerpräsident, spoke of Germany's obligation to 'grant refuge to the persecuted and the threatened', a note sent by the President of Catalonia, Jordi Pujol, merely referred to humanity's need for 'moral values'. On the one hand, Benjamin was being praised as a figure that symbolises pacifism in a depoliticised fashion while, on the other hand, the monument was expected to bring new options to a depressed economy, as the borders that once structured the town's economy were eradicated. In fact, within the last 15 years, a number of initiatives, each as unsuccessful as the next, have tried to capitalise on Benjamin's popularity to attract visitors. As a local councillor put it years later, Portbou saw an opportunity to turn its 'decay, pessimism and grayness [la grisor]' into a 'profitable heritage value' (Vancells 8 June 2007), thus developing a place-making strategy along the lines of other dark tourism destinations[4] (Fig. 9.2).

Fig. 9.2 Portbou's Cemetery. Stone laid in 1992 to commemorate the 100th Anniversary of Benjamin's birth. (Photograph by Caterina Nicolau Oliver, 2012)

[4] The promises associated with Benjaminian tourism were met with increasing apathy by the residents after a multi-million project for a 'casa Benjamin' endorsed by star architect Norman Foster failed to secure the required funding. As one resident told Sonia and Alexander Alland, while: '[t]he monument to Benjamin is a wonderful work of art [...] it does not really play a role in the community. It has been a bit of a disaster' (Alland Jr. 2011, p. 97).

The opening ceremony also revealed the role of the memorial as an incentive towards the construction of Europe's cultural memory (Pakier and Stråth 2010). Benjamin's tragic fate was described by Hans Eichel (1994) as a 'collective trauma', whereas the support of the Catalan government was seen as proof of its 'European cultural identity'. Even more striking was the language used by the Minister President of Baden-Württemberg, Erwin Teufel, who seized the opportunity to note that the border, at the time, was 'not an obstacle any longer but a free crossing-place within a Europe that (...) will soon have grown together in all aspects' (Scheurmann and Scheurmann 1995, p. 150). The strategic relevance of Spain's participation in a European memory couched within the traumatic tropes derived from the Holocaust was also registered by the likes of Spanish intellectuals Marta Pessarrodona and Mª Àngels Anglada. The former situated Portbou at the forefront of 'Catalan Europeanism', whereas the later complimented the local authorities for 'cultivation and divulgation' of both Benjamin's oeuvre and 'the memory of the Holocaust' (Pessarrodona, 18th May 1994). Despite being a relatively epiphenomenal episode, Benjamin's death became a comfortable opportunity for Spanish authorities to contribute to the establishment of the Holocaust's 'normative status' (Poole 2010) as an almost transhistorical shorthand for the systematic violation of human rights, without engaging in a meaningful exploration of Spain's own history of antisemitism (Baer 2011). Thanks to such an ironic quirk of fate, a memorial in honour of a stateless migrant handed the 'European entry ticket' (Judt 2006) to Spain, providing its access to European cultural memory.

After Benjamin's Suitcase: Embodied Encounters of 'Being in the Past'

Martínez Bachrich (2011, p. 48), a Venezuelan writer who stopped by Portbou looking for Benjamin, described the village as follows: 'anyone who circulates through the streets, beaches or mountains of this town cast in stone and water between Costa Brava and the Pyrenees will sooner or later notice its strained atmosphere'. Bachrich is just one amongst many visitors accounting for the spectral shroud surrounding the Catalan town. This affective encounter between landscape and the 'memory pilgrims' must, however, be understood within a particular historical context. To a certain extent, the melancholy of Portbou is a contemporary condition.

Take, for example, the victorious imagined geography of the conquest of Portbou as imagined by Giménez Caballero in 1939. In his description, the Pyrenees turned the same colour as the Francoist flag immediately after the flag raising ceremony: 'again a mountain of fire' (Giménez Caballero 1939, p. 23, emphasis mine). Albeit shattered by the indiscriminate bombing and virtually empty of its residents, the material geography of Portbou operated as a crucial locus for the National Catholic 'July revolution' of 1936 in terms of both its military role as strategic point of defence and its symbolic role as the threshold separating Francoist Spain from European liberal democracies. It is important to note, however, that the ideological role performed by imagined geographies rarely remains unchallenged. Even dominant spatial readings can be contested in various, sometimes unexpected ways (Kelly and Mitchell 2012).

Already in 1940, when Germany occupied France, Portbou embodied hope for those refugees who, like Benjamin, were trying to escape Fascism. In the first years of the Spanish democracy, after Benjamin's plaque was unveiled in 1979 and, especially, following Passages´ inauguration, the hegemonic perception of the space changed again. In addition to the aforementioned awakening of an esoteric Benjaminian industry and the wider implications of the transnational memory boom (Berliner 2005), it is important to consider other issues. At a local level, the economic depression brought by the reordering of the transport networks resulted in the isolation of Portbou. The disappearance of the border, which was to be celebrated by EU politicians in Brussels as a triumph for Europe, altered the economic infrastructure and the sociality of the town. The effects are still felt. 'Portbou', recently wrote a local journalist, 'has slipped into a depressive cycle which, I am afraid, [it] won't be able to leave' (Martos, 14 September 2014). At a national level, the reorientation of Spanish cultural memory away from a 'pact of silence' towards the re-evaluation of the Republican exiles' significance (Gemie 2006; Graham 2004; Labanyi 2008) made it easier for Benjamin's fate to resonate within the discursive frame of the Spanish Republic's defeat. Another conditioning factor for the reorientation in the reading of the memorial, this time at a global level, was the rise of an imperative to remember closely linked to the Shoah (Levy and Sznaider 2006).

Since its opening in 1994, the memorial has operated as a powerful semiotic anchor for the imagination of those who write about Portbou. Art critic Pierre Restany, for example, praised the 'congruence between the site, Benjamin's biography, and the artistic form' of the memorial.

Facing the glass wall at the end of the staircase, Restany had the impression that '[t]o some extent the world seems to come to an end here' (cited in Scheurmann and Scheurmann 1995, p. 163). In a similar vein, anthropologist Michael Taussig (2006, p. 29) has related how his experience of the town changed once he visited the memorial: '[t]he cold atmosphere of the town now made sense. Right or wrong, there was this feeling, this social fact, that secrets like nameless graves lay everywhere and that the border town had probably been the scene of much brutality and certainly of unbearable anxiety'.

The memorial also drew the attention of a number of fiction writers, whose work has contributed to Portbou's profile as a particularly fertile ground for the constant refashioning of the politics of memory. For example, in both Jaume Benavente's (2003) *Portbou's Nightrain* [Nocturn de Portbou] and Carme Riera's (2004) *The Center of My Soul* [La meitat de l'ànima], the space is key for the narrative structure as it is presented as characterised by its relationship with a troubling past. The first novel takes place in Portbou's railway station, from which the narrator recalls his own life story while also making connections to other characters, including Walter Benjamin. Already from the beginning, Portbou appears as a contemplative stage for the revisiting of existential emptiness and human tragedies. The narrator of *Portbou's Nightrain* is able to come to terms with his past the moment he leaves the town. Riera's novel traces the quest of a woman to find her mother, disappeared in Portbou in unknown circumstances. In a Sebaldian move, Riera then builds up a narrative device based around the impossibility to faithfully capture the past beyond the flashes that we are afforded by dispersed and unreliable fragments (Dubow 2007). One such fragment is Portbou, where her mother stayed at the same hostel as Benjamin. Both novels establish connections between Benjamin's life and the narrator's personal memories, further enlivening the ecology of memories embedded in Portbou's geography. Thus, Portbou serves not only as the locale where the 'remembering' takes place, but also the very material condition that enables such forms of nostalgic remembrance (Dora 2006).

These accounts indicate that while the memorial functions as the nerve centre of a semantic constellation that underwrites the metonymic relationship between the town and the horrendous violence of displacement, it certainly necessitates other spatial elements to secure its effect. The importance of Passages' ambiguous inscription in terms of punctuating the moral economy of the visitor can easily be overstated. Other sites, bodies and objects ought to be brought into the equation, too. Simultaneously affective and imagined, the material surface of the landscape is as much a prisoner of historical contingency as the visitor's body, whose voice coexists with that of non-human agents (Drozdzewski et al. 2016). This 'embodied imagination' (Dawney 2014) arises out of a co-constitutive process, where the production of subjects and objects is always already knotted together in a deeply heterogeneous assemblage of temporal layers. Although there are those who note its wild beauty (not least the remarkable aesthetic qualities of Karavan's design), the decaying town is generally perceived as a heartless and standoffish place, haunted by the spectres of those forced to cross the border, as well as those who lost their lives trying. Moreover, its isolated location—almost stranded at the foot of the mountain—together with its pebble beach and the windy conditions, all seem to underline Karavan's reading of the environment as a natural echo of Benjamin's story.

Crossing the Border, Crossing Time: Annual Re-Enactments and the New Refugees

What else lingers on the landscape? Perhaps the views of the surrounding mountains, which outline the imagined line of the border serve as a reminder of something else. As John Payne (2007, p. 105) puts it, 'the borders may be open within Europe, but they remain largely closed to refugees and asylum-seekers from beyond Europe's borders'. Walking around the town in the presence of the border, the abandoned customs office, the derelict Guardia Civil headquarters or the train station, can turn such spaces into potential mnemonic devices eliciting reflection upon the technologic-political dispositive that produce the very category of the migrant. Given that the conditions that enabled the well-known tragedy of Benjamin are still in place—after all, the border of Fortress Europe has only been externalised (Akkerman 2018)—Portbou's liminality has the potential to act as a useful reminder of the violent nature of borders and the perpetual catastrophe facilitated by 'the inequality of the global border regime' (Jones 2016, p. 179).

Through the Memorial Democràtic, the Catalan Government has promoted the signposting of various sites of 'democratic memory' in the past decade, including the route taken by Benjamin and fellow refugees on September 1940. Every year, towards the end of the summer, dozens of hikers walk the old smuggler's path, a 17-kilometre-long route over the Pyrenees starting in Banyuls-sur-Mere. The march is currently organised by the university chair Col.loqui Walter Benjamin and the Nau Côclea Centre for Contemporary Creation with the support of regional authorities. Over the last decade, the Nau Côclea has offered a Walter Benjamin grant to support a performance inspired by the work and life of the German author. Appart from this performance, which does not always require the participants' active engagement, there are no commemorative scripts, official speeches or old photographs to mediate the walker's experience of the landscape, yet as Rosenberg (2007, p. 60) points out, this does not necessarily equate a more 'direct link to an otherwise inaccessible past'.

The hiker's haptic experience is usually focused on securely placing her feet in what still is a treacherous route. Contrary to the introspective experience facilitated by the memorial in Portbou, during the walk, once the walker's body is attuned to the group's pace, conversation flows. The affective encounter with the landscape of memory mobilises both retrospective and anticipatory imagination: walking the Benjamin path immediately activates a communion between those present, and those temporally and geographically distant. Memory scholars contend that 'memory and its association with a particular past are not an impediment for the future but a prerequisite to enunciate a narrative (bridge) over the present' (Levy 2010, p. 16). During the walks, the shared private and family memories speak to the legacy of Republican exiles and the victims of Fascism, but parallels with the predicament of refugees who travel to Europe from the Global South are regularly drawn, too.

The inclusion of the victims of Fortress Europe in the pantheon of 'the nameless' is only a recent and, thus far, rather informal phenomenon. The current migrant crisis is more often than not mentioned as an appendix to the reassessment of a Republican diaspora, which figures prominently in current debates about the past in Spain (Cate-Arries 2004; Font Agulló 2010). Moreover, the haunting spell the town casts upon its visitors, the ethical demands it places on those who are attracted by the one name, is not only tied to the village's troubling past, as mentioned earlier, but also to the current economic downturn this border region has suffered since EU's internal borders were abolished in 1995.

Karavan's memorial is only one of the material elements that mediate the experience of both visitors and locals. This is perhaps what draws so much attention to the town: not only the so-called authenticity of a

Benjaminian experience the town itself seems to safeguard, but also the potential to open up what Marita Sturken (2011, p. 292) calls a 'space of compassion for others'. However, the ethical demands cannot be perceived equally by every visitor. The different commemorative practices and discourses that centre on Portbou mark the difference between individual empathy and collective solidarity. Portbou has an interesting potential to become a space for various kinds of engagement with a past that spills over into the present. It is precisely that temporal dimension—whether the tragedy is narrated using the past tense or recognised as still happening—what determines the extent to which contemporary refugees are invoked in this place of European memory (Bevernage 2015).

The multiple conjunctions of spaces and times conjured up at Portbou, in turn, inform the reading of the memorial to Benjamin. The choice of what to highlight amongst the many layers that form part of his biographical constellation (the obscure writer, the persecuted Jew, the frustrated lover, the committed intellectual or the helpless refugee) matters as much as the spatiotemporal references used to locate today's nameless. 1939, the end of the Spanish Civil War, can become 2005, the year Frontex—the European Border and Coast Guard Agency—was established; Portbou can appear alongside Calais, Ceuta and Melilla, Cape Town's District Six, Auschwitz, Gorée, Lesbos, Lampedusa, Rivesaltes, Ferguson or Ciudad Juárez. Although the town is not listed amongst the central scenarios of Europe's twentieth century history, it does have a great say in the afterlives of that past; despite the initial purposes of the agencies that funded the memorial to Benjamin, the place avoids symbolic over-determination. It refrains from proscribing either a closed interpretation of the past or a particular affective response. It has, however, the ability to foster, if not a sense of identification, then at least an abstract, though emphatic connection with an event that is associated with wider structural violence engendered by a border that has only been relocated.[5]

Thus, the task to link the struggles of the past to the struggles of the present—the project of underscoring the continuities in what is often seen a progressive line—can find a space in this tiny town. As Rothberg and

---

[5] France has in fact temporarily introduced Border Controls on a number of occasions in the last years due to 'terrorist threats and situation at the external border'. Only in 2017 they 'intercepted' 24 minors who were attempting to reach France. The network UNITED for Intercultural Action does an excellent work tracing these 'estates of exception' as well as the effects of 'Fortress Europe' ('UNITED for Intercultural Action. The Fatal Policies of Fortress Europe,').

Yildiz (2011, p. 41) argue, it is not a matter of prescribing a shared past; 'traumatic histories do not always intersect harmoniously; yet the conflicts that arise can lead to – and indeed may be the necessary grounds for – new forms of solidarity'. In Portbou, the commemorative landscape punctuated by Karavan's memorial invites visitors to ask themselves what and where the borders are in our time. Or, perhaps, it raises questions about who are the refugees without a name and, more importantly even, who is responsible for their predicament?

By taking part in the annual re-enactment of Benjamin's crossing, the participants are able to complete a journey Benjamin never came back from. In these walks, the border is experienced in all its ambiguity as an anachronism of today's European Union. On the one hand, its presence remains conspicuous, even though its latent power does not threatens the majority of the (regular) citizens who travel to Portbou on purpose. During my fieldwork between 2012 and 2018, I never heard any conversation that considered the 'uneven economy of citizenship' (Gikandi 2009) afforded to different travellers, yet on very rare occasions did participants dwell on tropes of 'banal Europeism' (Kaasik-Krogerus 2019), that so often featured in official speeches celebrating Portbou as a minor capital of European memory in the 1990s.

On the other hand, the conversations and the recollections that emerged out of an engagement with Benjamin's story allowed participants to collectively draw on other 'historical parallels' beyond the ambivalence of the inscription on Karavan's memorial, which lends itself to an actualisation of the meaning behind such a declaration of mnemonic justice. One of the regular participants of the march, A.S.G, a local woman in her 60s, described her long-term engagement with the afterlives of Benjamin in non-hagiographic terms. Her participation was meaningful to her insofar as it was 'an homage to all those who suffer'. During an interview in 2014, Edna (not her real name) put it this way: 'When I walk I always think: shit [about] those who are leaving Syria'. Despite the limits to this empathy and the virtual absence of actual refugees in these re-enactments, the march allows participants like A.S.G. to establish historical links with the new dispossessed, with the sans-papiers, with those who are being prosecuted by a novel form of low-intensity fascism (Méndez Rubio 2015).

The slow violence enacted by these less spectacular, less eventful forms of violence is embodied by agencies such as Frontex—yet another example of that enemy 'that has not ceased to be victorious' (Benjamin 2007, p. 255). This, as pointed out by others, does not mean that the relationship between the refugee crisis and the memory of the Holocaust is a matter of arrhythmic or competitive concurrence (Stone 2018). Her experience suggests that the multidirectionality of the memory (Rothberg 2009) of the German and Austrian Jewish refugees of the Second World War, as well as that of the Spanish exiles, can indeed play a productive role in animating responsibility in the face of Europe's new (refugee) camps. It is in this sense that the anachronicity of the border reveals itself like a 'battered historical survivor' that can serve as witness to expose the constellations of 'concrete, historical referents' (Buck-Morss 1989, p. 7) that contaminate the seemingly innocent present.

Conclusion

In this chapter, I have contended that by examining Portbou's commemorative landscape we can recast the construction of post-1989 European cultural memory as based on a selective mobilisation of empathy. As the commissioning of a memorial and the subsequent series of initial official commemorations of Benjamin's death became synecdochal with the commemoration of the experience of German-Jewish exiles, the town of Portbou was constructed as a European site of memory—in line with the fruitful alliance between human rights discourses and the flourishing of a mnemonic culture around the Holocaust. However, while European politicians gathered to pay homage to Benjamin's intellectual figure in the early 1990s, the European Union was reconfiguring the concept of border security through the Schengen Agreement. The destitution, deportation and death this policy would subsequently enforce on non-EU citizens ought to be juxtaposed with the expressions of cosmopolitan tolerance offered in memory of Walter Benjamin at a time when the Balkan Crisis threatened Europe's idea of itself as a continent finally free from conflict.

As argued above, Portbou remains a place ridden with mnemonic ambivalence, where residents and visitors constantly negotiate the spatial and temporal reverberations of its past. This is a healthy reminder that memorials ought to be understood as being both continually rearticulated by its visitors and in constant dialogue with its material and discursive environments. The presence of idle passengers that wait for a train connection, the sounds emanating from the station or the precarious security fences around the derelict police headquarters also participate in the incantation that speaks of the politics of mobility and, ultimately, the bodies that are the subject of the violence effected by national borders. This corner of Europe, I have argued, works as a memory theatre, which can strongly invoke or draw upon troubling memories. It thus creates a magnetic field where the afterlives of the displacement of civilians after the Second World War and the persecution of Jews and other minorities can interpellate current debates about state violence and, more concretely, our complicity in it.

References

Aguilar, P., & Humlebaek, C. (2002). Collective Memory and National Identity in the Spanish Democracy: The Legacies of Francoism and the Civil War. *History & Memory, 14*(1–2), 121–164.

Akkerman, M. (2018). *Expanding the Fortress. The Policies, the Profiteers and the People Shaped by EU's Border Externalisation Programme*. Amsterdam: Transnational Institute and Stop Wapenhandel.

Alland, A., Jr., & Sonia, A. (2011). *Catalunya, one Nation, Two States: un estudi etnogràfic de la resistència no violenta a l'assimilació*. Barcelona: Pol·len edicions.

Bachrich, R. M. (2011). Memoria de Portbou. *Revista Universidad de Antioquia, 303*, 44–49.

Baer, A. (2011). The Voids of Sepharad: The Memory of the Holocaust in Spain. *Journal of Spanish Cultural Studies, 12*(1), 95–120.

Benavente, J. (2003). *Nocturn de Portbou*. Barcelona: Random House Mondadori.

Benjamin, W. (2007). *Illuminations* (Harry Zohn, Trans. H. Arendt Ed.). New York: Schoken Books.

Berg, N. (2003). *Der Holocaust und die westdeutschen Historiker: Erforschung und Erinnerung*. Göttingen: Wallstein Verlag.

Berliner, D. C. (2005). The Abuses of Memory: Reflections on the Memory Boom in Anthropology. *Anthropological Quarterly, 78*(1), 197–211.

Bevernage, B. (2015). The Past is Evil/Evil is Past: On Retrospective Politics, Philosophy of History, and Temporal Manichaeism. *History and Theory, 54*(3), 333–352.

Buck-Morss, S. (1989). *The Dialectics of Seeing: Walter Benjamin and the Arcades Project*. Cambridge/London: MIT Press.

Butler, J. (2009). *Frames of War: When is Life Grievable?*. London: Verso.

Cate-Arries, F. (2004). *Spanish Culture Behind Barbed Wire: Memory and Representation of the French Concentration Camps, 1939–1945*. Lewisburg: Bucknell University Press.

Dawney, L. (2014). "Feeling Connected". Practising Nature, Nation and Class Through Coastal Walking. In P. Gilchrist, T. Carter, & D. Burdey (Eds.), *Coastal Cultures: Liminality and Leisure* (pp. 87–101). Eastbourne: Leisure Studies Association.

De Cesari, C. (2017). Museums of Europe: Tangles of Memory, Borders, and Race. *Museum Anthropology, 40*(1), 18–35.
Dora, V. D. (2006). The Rhetoric of Nostalgia: Postcolonial Alexandria Between Uncanny Memories and Global Geographies. *Cultural Geographies, 13*(2), 207–238.
Drozdzewski, D., De Nardi, S., & Waterton, E. (2016). Geographies of Memory, Place and Identity: Intersections in Remembering and Conflict. *Geography Compass, 10*(11), 447–456.
Dubow, J. (2007). Case Interrupted: Benjamin, Sebald, and the Dialectical Image. *Critical Inquiry, 33*(4), 820–836.
Duncan, J. S. (1990). *The City as Text: The Politics of Landscape Interpretation in the Kandyan Kingdom*. Cambridge: Cambridge University Press.
Eichel, H. (1994). *Letter to Jordi Pujol*. Archive Sala Walter Benjamin, Portbou.
Font Agulló, J. (Ed.). (2010). *Reflexionant l'exili. Aproximació a l'exili republicà: entre la història, l'art i el testimoniatge*. Catarroja: Afers.
Fritsch, M. (2006). *The Promise of Memory: History and Politics in Marx, Benjamin, and Derrida*. Albany: SUNY Press.
Gemie, S. (2006). The Ballad of Bourg-Madame: Memory, Exile, and the Spanish Republican Refugees of the Retirada of 1939. *International Review of Social History, 51*(1), 1–40.
Gikandi, S. (2009). Between Roots and Routes: Cosmopolitanism and the Claims of Locality. In J. Wilson, C. Şandru, & S. L. Welsh (Eds.), *Rerouting the Postcolonial. New Directions for the New Millenium* (pp. 36–49). London/New York: Routledge.
Giménez Caballero, E. (1939). *¡Hay Pirineos! Notas de un alférez en la IV^a de Navarra sobre la conquista de Port-bou*. Madrid: Editora Nacional.
Gordillo, G. n. (2014). *Rubble: The Afterlife of Destruction*. Durham: Duke University Press.
Graham, H. (2004). The Spanish Civil War, 1936–2003: The Return of Republican Memory. *Science & Society, 68*(3: Special Issue), 313–328.
Greenberg, U. E. (2008). The Politics of the Walter Benjamin Industry. *Theory, Culture & Society, 25*(3), 53–70.
Gubert i Macias, J. (1990). *Portbou, segle XIX. Inicis i engrandiment d'un poble*. Barcelona: Ajuntament de Portbou / Diputació de Girona.
Hamacher, W. (2005). 'Now': Walter Benjamin and Historical Time. In A. Benjamin (Ed.), *Walter Benjamin and History* (pp. 38–68). New York: Continuum.
Harjes, K. (2005). Stumbling Stones: Holocaust Memorials, National Identity, and Democratic Inclusion in Berlin. *German Politics and Society, 23*(1), 138–151.
Harrison, R. (2005). Dreamtime, Old Time, This Time: Archaeology, Memory and the Present-Past in a Northern Australian Aboriginal Community. In J. Lydon & T. Ireland (Eds.), *Object Lessons: Archaeology and Heritage in Australia* (pp. 243–264). Melbourne: Australian Scholarly Publishing.

Hetherington, K. (2008). The Time of the Entrepreneurial City: Museum, Heritage and Kairos. In A. H. Cronin & Kevin (Eds.), *Consuming the Entrepreneurial City: Image, Memory, Spectacle* (pp. 273–294). New York/Abingdon: Routledge.

Hornstein, S. (2011). *Losing site: Architecture, Memory and Place*. Farnham: Ashgate.

Hutton, P. H. (2010). Walter Benjamin: The Consolation of History in a Paris Exile. *Historical Reflections/Réflexions Historiques, 36*(1), 76–94.

Jenkins, O. (2003). Photography and Travel Brochures: The Circle of Representation. *Tourism Geographies, 5*(3), 305–328.

Jones, R. (2016). *Violent Borders. Refugees and the Right to Move*. London: Verso.

Jones, O., & Garde-Hansen, J. (Eds.). (2012). *Memory and Geography. Place, Identity and Becoming*. London: Palgrave.

Judt, T. (2006). *Postwar: A History of Europe Since 1945*. London: Penguin.

Kaasik-Krogerus, S. (2019). Identity Politics of the Promotional Videos of the European Heritage Label. *Contemporary Politics, 26*, 1–16.

Kattago, S. (2011). *Ambiguous Memory: The Nazi Past and German National Identity*. Westport: Praeger.

Kelly, L., & Mitchell, A. (2012). 'Walking'in North Belfast with Michel de Certeau. In O. P. Richmond & A. Mitchell (Eds.), *Hybrid Forms of Peace. From Everyday Agency to Post-Liberalism* (pp. 277–292). New York: Palgrave Macmillan.

Labanyi, J. (2008). The Politics of Memory in Contemporary Spain. *Journal of Spanish Cultural Studies, 9*(2), 119–125.

Lennon, J., & Foley, M. (2000). *Dark Tourism. The Attraction of Death and Disaster*. London: Continuum.

Levy, D. (2010). Changing Temporalities and the Internationalization of Memory Cultures. In Y. Gutman, A. Brown, & A. Sodaro (Eds.), *Memory and the Future. Transnational Politics, Ethics and Society* (pp. 15–30). London: Palgrave Macmillan.

Levy, D., & Sznaider, N. (2006). *The Holocaust and Memory in the Global Age*. Philadelphia: Temple University Press.

Lorimer, H. (2005). Cultural Geography. The Busyness of Being 'More-Than-Representational'. *Progress in Human Geography, 29*(1), 83–94.

Löwy, M. (2005). *Fire Alarm: Reading Walter Benjamin's On the Concept of History*, (C. Turner, Trans.). London: Verso.

Lupu, N. (2003). Memory Vanished, Absent, and Confined: The Countermemorial Project in 1980s and 1990s Germany. *History and Memory, 15*(2), 130–164.

Martos, M. (2014, September 14). Las claves de la maleta de Portbou, *El País. Catalan edition*. Retrieved from https://elpais.com/ccaa/2014/09/14/catalunya/1410649277_270674.html

Méndez Rubio, A. (2015). *Fascismo de Baja Intensidad*. Santander: La Vorágine.

Messenger, D. A. (2017). Contemporary Memory Politics in Catalonia: Europeanizing and Mobilizing the History of the Spanish Civil War. In C. Kraenzle & M. Mayr (Eds.), *The Changing Place of Europe in Global Memory Cultures: Usable Pasts and Futures* (pp. 49–62). Cham: Palgrave Macmillan.

Osborne, J. F. (2017). Counter-Monumentality and the Vulnerability of Memory. *Journal of Social Archaeology, 17*(2), 163–187.

Pakier, M., & Stråth, B. (Eds.). (2010). *A European Memory? Contested Histories and Politics of Remembrance.* New York/Oxford: Berghahn Books.

Palmier, J.-M. (2006). *Weimar in Exile: The Antifascist Emigration in Europe and America.* London: Verso.

Payne, J. (2007). 'An Expensive Death' Walter Benjamin at Portbou. *European Judaism: A Journal for the New Europe, 40*(2), 102–105.

Pessarrodona, M. (1994, May 18). Repensar Europa, *Avui*.

Poole, R. (2010). Misremembering the Holocaust: Universal Symbol, Nationalist Icon or Moral Kitsch? In Y. Gutman, A. Brown, & A. Sodaro (Eds.), *Memory and the Future. Transnational Politics, Ethics and Society* (pp. 31–49). New York: Palgrave Macmillan.

Protzman, F. (1992, 20 August). Dead-end Memorial to Nazi Victim, *The New York Times*.

Riera, C. (2004). *La meitat de l'ànima*. Barcelona: Proa.

Rosenberg, E. (2007). The Geography of Memory: Walking as Remembrance. *Hedgehog Review, 9*(2), 54.

Rothberg, M. (2009). *Multidirectional Memory: Remembering the Holocaust in the Age of Decolonization*. Stanford: Stanford University Press.

Rothberg, M., & Yildiz, Y. (2011). Memory Citizenship: Migrant Archives of Holocaust Remembrance in Contemporary Germany. *Parallax, 17*(4), 32–48.

Savage, M. (2000). Walter Benjamin's Urban Thought: A Critical Analysis. In M. T. Crang & Nigel (Eds.), *Thinking Space* (pp. 9–33). London: Routledge.

Scheurmann, I. (1992). *Neue Dokumente zum Tode Walter Benjamins.* Bonn: AsKI e.V.

Scheurmann, I., & Scheurmann, K. (Eds.). (1995). *Dani Karavan. Homage to Walter Benjamin. "Passages", Place of Remembrance at Portbou.* Mainz: Philipp von Zabern.

Schneckenburger, M. (1992, June 6). Kleinmut siegt. Ein Denkmal für Walter Benjamin wird gekippt, *Frankfurter Allgemeine Zeitung*.

Schwartz, V. R. (2001). Walter Benjamin for Historians. *The American Historical Review, 106*(5), 1721–1743.

Stone, D. (2018). Refugees then and now: Memory, History and Politics in the Long Twentieth Century: An Introduction. *Patterns of Prejudice, 52*(2–3), 101–106.

Sturken, M. (2011). Pilgrimages, Reenactment, and Souvenirs: Modes of Memory Tourism. In M. Hirsch & N. K. Miller (Eds.), *Rites of Return. Diaspora Poetics and the Politics of Memory* (pp. 280–293). New York: Columbia University Press.

Taussig, M. T. (2006). *Walter Benjamin's Grave*. Chicago: University of Chicago Press.

Tumarkin, M. (2005). *Traumascapes: The Power and Fate of Places Transformed by Tragedy*. Carlton: Melbourne University Press.

UNITED for Intercultural Action. The Fatal Policies of Fortress Europe. (2019). Retrieved 12 April 2019 http://www.unitedagainstracism.org/campaigns/refugee-campaign/fortress-europe/#_8. Accessed 21 May 2019.

Vancells, S. (2007, June 8). La decadencia com a encant, *Diari de Girona*.

Vinyes, R. (Ed.). (2004). *Un futuro para el pasado. Proyecto de creación del Memorial Democrático*. Barcelona: CEFID.

Vinyes, R. (Ed.). (2009). *El Estado y la memoria. Gobiernos y ciudadanos frente a los traumas de la historia*. Barcelona: RBA.

Waterton, E., & Watson, S. (2015). A War Long Forgotten. Feeling the Past in an English Country Village. *Angelaki. Journal of the Theoretical Humanities, 20*(3), 89–103.

Young, J. E. (1993). *The Texture of Memory: Holocaust Memorials and Meanings*. New Haven/London: Yale University Press.

CHAPTER 10

Augmented Reality: Memorializing Deaths of Migrants Along the US-Mexico Border

Jessica Auchter

The physicality of lands and landscapes draws on a history of border-creation that is integral to modern statecraft. As Mark Salter (2006, p.168) says, 'sovereignty and boundary maintenance are inextricable'. The border is thus the site of a multiplicity of boundary-making practices that are repeated throughout society to 'state' the state. Bordering is not solely geographical, but is oriented towards subject production. As Roxanne Doty (1996, p.180) puts it, 'regaining control of our borders conjures up a mythic past, an age of purity, when the inside was clearly and unambiguously differentiated from the outside'.

Yet, as Prem Kumar Rajaram (2004, p.220) states, 'sovereign territoriality is always being constituted and challenged …each response to the stranger reinforces the sense of what it is to be part of the normal community'. This critique of territoriality emphasizes that borders are constantly being produced and reproduced. The unattached, non-territorial condition of the stranger, as Rajaram puts it, reminds us that our identity need not be bound up with sovereign territoriality and that the state

---

J. Auchter (✉)
The University of Tennessee at Chattanooga, Chattanooga, TN, USA
e-mail: Jessica-Auchter@utc.edu

© The Author(s) 2020
S. Marschall (ed.), *Public Memory in the Context of Transnational Migration and Displacement*, Palgrave Macmillan Memory Studies, https://doi.org/10.1007/978-3-030-41329-3_10

operates through bio-political power and the production of bare life at the border. In this vein, migrant deaths are the effect of the exercise of sovereign territoriality, and their memorialization is inherently political, because it forms the memorialization of bare life. The main empirical context I address in this chapter, migrant deaths along the US-Mexico border, attends to lives and deaths that are deemed unworthy in some ways: unworthy of global attention, unworthy of memorialization, as a result of them being deaths of the stranger, deaths of the Other. The artistic projects I discuss in this chapter memorialize the deaths of migrants who are narrated by the state as threatening to its authority.

New technologies of surveillance and tracking have been mobilized in the service of statecraft along the border, but at the same time, new technologies are also being utilized by artists to resist these totalizing narratives of statecraft. In particular, such artists seek to draw attention to the vulnerabilities and deaths of migrants in border areas and to the precarity of refugees. There is much global attention on human migration, most of which focuses either on states managing this movement (techniques of governance), or on the work of non-governmental organizations (NGOs) to raise awareness about the human toll. Less attention has been paid to virtual and augmented reality (AR) technologies, their use in memorialization of migrants and how they shape the narratives surrounding migrants and refugees.

This chapter focuses on two key questions: how has new media shaped the way migrant experiences, particularly hardship and death, are depicted and accessed? What political and ethical problems and opportunities arise from engaging with migrant deaths in new ways, via monuments that are virtual rather than physical? I answer these questions by examining two different memorial projects. Drawing on James Young's (1994) theorization of the counter-monument, a monument which disappears over time or with which viewers must interact in order to perform the work of memory, I consider how new technologies reshape our interactions with sites of death and remembrance.

First, the augmented reality project *Border Memorial: Frontera de Los Muertos* by visual artist John Craig Freeman allows users of mobile devices to 'witness' the death of undocumented immigrants attempting to cross the US-Mexico border; this is achieved by marking with a virtual object each location where human remains have been recovered. Via a mobile app, viewers aim their cameras at the landscape along the border and the surrounding desert, and, using geolocation software to superimpose individual augments at the GPS coordinates of each recorded death, one can see renditions of *Dia de Los Muertos* skeletons integrated into the physical location as if they existed in the real world. It thus acts as a memorial to dead undocumented migrants, but also encourages us to reimagine our visual fields and our encounters with these ghostly figures. In this vein, unlike static memorial projects, it requires direct engagement by the user in order for the memorial project to succeed and in fact even materialize. Second, American artist Andrew O'Brien's work *Drift Alignment* uses astronomical mapping technology and big data to produce art that images the night sky on the day migrant remains were found in the Arizona desert. This work focuses on placing the viewer in a new space and place of interaction with the space of death through use of new technologies.

These projects, which I will discuss in detail later in this chapter, use technology to widen the empathetic community by drawing our attention to lives that have been largely deemed cursory to the functioning of global politics. In this way, they are both memorials that commemorate the deaths of vulnerable individuals, and part of a larger story of how awareness and memorialization of particular marginalized deaths is itself a political act.

During and after a traumatic event, traditional schemas of identification and representation are ruptured and fractured. This is widely agreed to be a key aspect of trauma, perhaps best articulated by Cathy Caruth (1995, 1996). More recent approaches to trauma have focused on the inability to describe the traumatic event through language, and sought to move beyond the national level of memorialization. Resende and Budryte, for example, have advocated challenging nation-centred accounts of memory construction and argued that

> memory is pluralistic, multidimensional and multilayered, and to study memory means to be ready to explore various (including non-territorial) spaces of memory and to construct various memory communities. (Resende and Budryte 2014, pp.9–10)

This chapter follows with the impetus to examine non-territorial forms of memory as a way of thinking about the formation of memory communities. Beyond this, the chapter draws on the growing scholarly engagement with public debates about border deaths (Squire 2017; von Bieberstein and Evren 2016) as a way to engage with the larger politics of border fatalities and their commemoration. I shall return to this point in the discussion of the two projects, while moreover proposing some conclusions.

Counter-Memory: Themes of Absence in Memorial Technologies

Traditional discourses of memorialization often focus on physical sites of memory. However, increased attention recently has been paid to what Andrew Hoskins (2017) has referred to as 'digital memory'. While others began to notice the influence of media and memory as early as the mid-1990s (Sturken 1997; Urry 1995), the internet age led to sustained examinations of electronic media. The projects I discuss in this chapter offer news ways of considering the intersections between technology and memorialization, including the use of augmented reality and smartphone apps, as well as the use of big data combined with photography to map migrant deaths as a form of memorialization. In other words, this chapter is firmly enmeshed within this turn towards exploration of new media and memory.

This section brings together traditional literature on memorialization practices with emerging forms of new media to offer a theoretical context for considering the use of virtual and augmented reality technologies. It argues that such technology should be considered as a form of counter-monument, one which plays with the trope of material reality through technological adaptation, and which places the burden of memorialization on the viewer. Such counter-monumentalization invokes the play of presence and absence that captures the precariousness and vulnerability of the migrant experience in unique ways that—it is argued—cannot be represented by physical monuments.

James Young theorized the idea of the counter-monument as a form that disrupts time-honoured conventions of memorials. Young, in *The Texture of Memory,* describes (among others) the Harburg Monument Against Fascism, designed by Jochen Gerz and Esther Shalev-Gerz (1986–1993), as a key example of this concept. The monument is a lead column 12 metres high where people can inscribe their names with a special writing implement. The nearby plaque informs visitors that as they sign their names on the monument, as a pledge against fascism, it will be lowered into the ground. The column has been graffitied extensively, including with swastikas and racial epithets. This troubled many members of the surrounding community. Young describes it as doubly troubling both because it recalls what happened in the past and because it is a social mirror reflecting to the community their own complex responses to the past. The monument thus sheds lights on the community's memorial projections and preoccupations.

The monument is constantly being written, both literally and in the sense that the meaning of monumentalizing against fascism is constantly shifting and being performed. The inscription on the memorial encourages visitors to think through their own roles in memorializing. It reads: 'In the end it is only we ourselves who can rise up against injustice'. The vanishing monument will have returned the burden of memory to the visitors, and to all of us. Young (1994, p.31) finds this apropos, asking 'how better to remember a vanished people than by the perpetually unfinished, ever-vanishing monument?'. The best monument, he concludes, might be no monument at all, but rather the memory of an absent monument, a monument to absence itself. 'All that remains is the memory of the monument, an afterimage projected onto the landscape by the rememberer' (Young 1994, p.32). Indeed, the current 'monument' as of this writing is simply a plaque that describes the project in an empty plaza, as the final pieces of the column were lowered in 1993. The plaque is accompanied by images of the progressive lowering to tell the story of the process.

Young refers to this phenomenon as a counter-monument, not because it negates memory, but because it negates the illusion of permanence traditionally expressed by monumentalization. Stevens, Franck and Fazakerley (2012) distil Young's conceptualization into four key features of distinction from conventional monuments: Counter-monuments 'express a position opposing a particular belief or event rather than affirming it; they eschew monumental forms (indeed, in their inversion of form, both of Young's exemplary case studies became nearly invisible); they invite close, multisensory visitor engagement; and, rather than being didactic, they invite visitors to work out the meanings for themselves' (2012, p.954). Similarly, Strakosch (2010) has noted the political resistance posed by such memorials:

> Counter-monuments aim to challenge and invert the nation-building agenda of traditional state memorials. Instead of presenting a simple story of triumph or martyrdom, they confront the nation-state with its own crimes and exclusions. (2010, p.68)

As Lupu (2003) similarly notes, counter-monuments, first emerging in Germany, counteract the perceived normalization of the German past, seen to be concretized in physical monuments of traditional forms. McGeough (2011, p.1-2) also notes that virtually all existing literature on counter-monuments describes them as performative contradictions insofar as the monuments refuse all elements of monumentality...their refusal to remember a single metanarrative in favor of simultaneously representing multiple voices.

Conventional monuments are often situated within a narrative that solidifies one story or one way of engaging with a traumatic event. Commemoration ultimately privileges certain kinds of experience and excludes others (Sherman 1996). 'Memorials provide the sites where groups of people gather to create a common past for themselves, places where they tell the constitutive narratives, their "shared" stories of the past' (Young 1994, pp.6–7). 'Memorials can realize individual and commemorative impulses, assuage postponed demands for justice, and (re) assert political identity' (Hite and Collins 2009, p.379).

Memorials serve to, as James Mayo (1988) argues, create 'an ongoing order and meaning'. In the aftermath of a traumatic event, people want to reorder society in some way; they want exact facts and settled limits (Andrieu 2009, p.12), and political elites often respond to trauma by reimposing order (Hutchison and Bleiker 2008, p.386). The physical memorial site is often an attempt to do so by making concrete the memory of the event, and in the process firmly placing the traumatic event in the past (Hite and Collins 2009, p.380). In other words, conventional monuments, particularly war memorials, are often designed to serve a function of coming to terms with loss, and to restore or normalize society after trauma, as other chapters in this volume examine. The Harburg Monument Against Fascism and the border memorial cases I will explore later in this chapter offer a way of rethinking the structure and function of monuments. They reference space and place with their absence, but they also focus on alternative ways to commemorate trauma and death that resist the traditional materiality of monuments and offer new opportunities for enlarging empathetic communities.

According to Lupu (2003), the time in which counter-monuments emerged is one characterized by the over-proliferation of monuments; it was also a time of reckoning with the idea of collective blame and the beginning of a backlash experience against this. He notes:

> countermonuments would be memorial spaces conceived to challenge the very premise of the monument—to be ephemeral rather than permanent, to deconstruct rather than displace memory, to be antiredemptive. (Lupu 2003, 131)

Ultimately, it is the notion of absence in Holocaust counter-monuments that frames the exploration of memorial forms in this chapter. Still, it bears asking not only how to think about counter-monuments in the case of migrant deaths, but also how to reckon with the criticisms that have been made of counter-monuments and their effects. Lupu, for example, notes that those who engaged with the Harburg monument against fascism, whether they were supporters or critics, did not engage with the monument as a counter-monument, but rather 'responded to the monument as a traditional representation of the experience of fascism' (Lupu 2003, p.136). In this vein, while the monument was designed to intrude into everyday space by being built in the hustle and bustle of central Harburg, rather than in a quiet park, Lupu traces the way its banality rendered it part of bureaucratic and logistical discussions about budgets and traffic management in the centre of the city. Similarly, Strakosch (2010) has emphasized the way in which counter-monuments are often built by the perpetrators (colonial states) in an attempt to atone for their own historical crimes, which can further marginalize the victims by speaking for them rather than inviting them to represent themselves.

Similarly, the disappearance of the monument, while a key feature of its role as a counter-monument, implied to the community the 'archiving of its content' (Lupu 2003, p.140). Lupu takes the example described by Young of one Harburg resident asking 'What kind of monument disappears?' to be exemplary of the silencing of the remembered experience of fascism through the disappearance of the monument (Lupu 2003, p.140). Lupu also takes the sentiments of the public to be evidence for the failure of the counter-monument: in the case of another case study, Aschrott's Fountain in Kassel, he notes that those opposed to it did not want such an 'abysmal' monument in the centre of their town (Lupu 2003, p.151). Yet, this is precisely the intent of a counter-monument: to thrust memory upon us in ways and places that do not allow it to be conceived of cleanly and positioned only in spaces set aside for reflection.

Counter-monuments make us question the very notion of memory and memorialization by blurring what constitutes legitimate memorialization; by forcing us to ask 'what kind of monument disappears?', and to reckon with the answer; and by forcing us to encounter both the banality of memory and the lack of traditional memorial forms and perhaps memorial forms at all. It is in these gaps, these interstitial spaces, that political questions about the role of memory can be explored.

Lupu (2003) argues that the problem with counter-monuments, and the Harburg monument in particular, is that they claim to be about absence but are in reality about an 'invisible presence'. Even as the monument has disappeared into the ground, the top part of it can still be seen through a viewing window and there are photographs displayed of the stages of disappearance, making the 'nonsite' an 'archive of the physical history of the monument itself' (2003, p.146). However, I would argue that this is precisely what counter-monuments can achieve. Contrary to Lupu's claim that these monuments resemble conventional memory markers by remaining partially present, I argue that they hover between absence and presence; they leave traces and frame themselves as archives through—and of—their disappearance. They are not the same as absent monuments, which have their own politics (the choice not to memorialize, or the lack of attention given to memorialization of an event), but rather are monuments to absences, as I have traced elsewhere (Auchter 2014). In this sense, it is precisely the idea of invisible presence that I seek to explore in this chapter.

To sum up, the counter-monument resists traditional memorial forms. As DeTurk (2017, p.83) notes, 'counter-monuments can be read as complicating the act of remembering'. She characterizes the 9/11 memorial *Reflecting Absence* as part of the same genre, offering a framework to broaden the applicability of counter-monuments beyond Holocaust memorialization. DeTurk focuses almost entirely on how counter-monuments force visitors to grapple with the burden of memory themselves and how they disrupt traditional memorial forms. My own use of the term, however, engages three main components drawn from the wider literature around counter-monuments: first, the way in which they resist traditional forms of memorial representation, putting into question what memorialization means; second, the way in which they have a specific focus on absence that reflects not only on the loss they commemorate but also on the way in which physical place and space may be imperfect ways to represent such loss; and third, the way they place the burden of memory on the viewer.

I take up this framework to examine the following cases of migrants and monuments—cases where there have been few conventional structures aimed at memorialization. Deaths of undocumented migrants in the deserts are political, and as a result, tangible memorials to these deaths have been vandalized or removed, often in the name of securing these border spaces, as I have detailed elsewhere (Auchter 2013). Yet there have been efforts to reckon with these experiences, these lives and deaths. New technologies of the virtual and the augmented arguably disrupt traditional memorial forms in ways similar to the counter-monument. They not only negate the illusion of permanence, traditionally a key characteristic and in fact the very objective of a monument, but they also embrace the ambiguity of such a lack. They draw out the importance of monumental forms that change, adapt with the landscape or are ephemeral. In doing so, they lead us to reflect on the intersections between bodies and spaces, and in the necessity of monuments in the first place.

I should note that while the framing of counter-monuments has become a global one in its application to contemporary cases, the emergence of the form in post-Holocaust Germany is a significant historical point of reference. The very idea emerged in a context where Germans were reckoning with guilt and its larger politics, while the historical record of what had occurred had largely been settled and was on display in other memorial sites. In the context I address in this chapter, the debate about the politics behind the migrant deaths is still ongoing. As a result, the aesthetic intervention comes before the record of the connections between the border policy and these deaths is settled. In other words, the aesthetic representation is part and parcel of how we understand these deaths, rather than simply a way to represent them. I would argue that this is one of the reasons why virtual reality technologies (VR) are key to situating these projects as counter-monuments, something I take up in the next section.

Virtual and Augmented Reality

Virtual and augmented reality technologies are recently becoming part of the memorial toolkit. Augmented reality technologies are available at sites ranging from cave paintings in France to Italian archaeological sites, from the 9/11 Memorial (Cocciolo 2014), to the museum at the Intrepid in New York City, the US Natural History Museum, and even interacting directly with the stories of survivors at the US Holocaust Memorial Museum (Pardes 2018). Indeed, the use of such technologies is widespread, as Cocciolo (2014) demonstrates: one-third of all American museums planned to introduce a mobile technology platform in 2011, in 2012, 29% of museums were using mobile technologies, with a further 27% planning to do so in the near future (Tallon 2012).

While some argue that these technologies are just the next iteration of previous museum technologies, such as audio guides (Pardes 2018), I argue here that there is a meaningful difference in their use. They do represent the next horizon in the ability to actively engage with exhibits, but they also represent a shift in ways of thinking about space and how we interact with it, raising many of the same questions as migration itself: what is the purpose of space? How does space become territorialized? Who is included or excluded from particular spaces and territories? How do bodies interact with spaces? What might it mean for such spaces to be rethought? Steve Sullivan, who as head of Microsoft's Mixed Reality Capture Studios programme works on many of these museum programmes, notes, 'It's getting museums to think outside of their physical confines' (cited in Pardes 2018, unpaginated).

Yet, such augmented reality technology has typically been used in the context of memorialization as a tool *in situ*. One visits the US Holocaust Memorial Museum and then this technology turns it into an alive space where one can interact directly with the exhibits and the humans they concern: the purpose is generating a more tactile experience at these museums. The examples I address in this chapter, on the contrary, are not space-bound in the same way. They both traverse space in allowing us to interact with one who is not there, as these exhibits do, but they are also 'monuments' where the interaction can take place outside of the physical spaces of museums. This is one of the main reasons why I characterize these cases as new manifestations of the counter-monument: they problematize the very idea of physical space.

This also allows us to examine the impact of new media on the way we think about migration and monuments. Garde-Hansen, Hoskins and Reading (2009, p.1) have emphasized this in their volume on digital memory, noting that 'the digital suggests that we may need to rethink how we conceive of memory; that we are changing what we consider to be the past; that the act of recall, of recollection and of remembering is changing in itself'. Hess (2007) similarly argues that online memorials can be rhetorically material even as they are not physically material, and that digital monuments allow us to reckon with the ephemeral nature of the monument. We often assume that because monuments tend to be physical, they are imbued with some sort of permanence. Yet, digital monuments and their impermanence remind us that even physical monuments decay, and that the burden of memory in the larger community often determines what memories linger and which disappear.

Digital memory, then, returns us to exploring questions about memory and forgetting. As Hoskins (2017, p.1) notes, we have seen an ontological shift in what memory is and what memory does, liberating it from the traditional bounds of the spatial archive, the organization, the institution, and distributed it on a continuous basis via a connectivity between brains, bodies, and personal and public lives.

Yet much of this work has explored the use of the digital to resuscitate history, focused on the memory of the past (Pogacar 2018). In the next section, I take up these concepts in a contemporary case where the deaths being memorialized are in fact still ongoing, to examine the role of public space and bodies in the context of alternative forms of memorialization.

Augmented reality technologies are suitable for the cases I explore precisely because we begin with absences: with absent bodies; with individuals and groups who are absent from the stories we tell about global politics; who are absent from the boardrooms where policies that determine whether they live or die are being hashed out; lastly, with the absence of formal monuments and memorials commemorating their death. The following sections will examine the two selected artistic projects with a focus on the counter-monument framing, to think through virtual memorialization as a form of counter-monumentalization. In this sense, I hope to trace the way these new forms of technology related to migrant memorialization impact the way we think, both about migration and about monuments, or as Hoskins put it in the quotation above, about an ontological shift in our thinking about memory and memorialization.

Placing Migrant Deaths Along the US-Mexico Border

Despite the general decrease in border crossings over time,[1] border deaths rose in 2017, compared to 2016, partly because increased enforcement by US Border Patrol forces migrants into more remote areas that are substantively more dangerous (Romero 2018). Yet the bulk of attention has been paid to the mechanisms of securitization at the border: walls, border patrol, policies and laws. Recently, scholars are beginning to pay increased attention to border deaths themselves (Squire 2017; von Bieberstein and Evren 2016; Alonso and Nienass 2016). Kim Rygiel (2016), for example, has called attention to the way political activism surrounding migrant

---

[1] See, for example, https://www.nytimes.com/2018/06/20/us/politics/fact-check-trump-border-crossings-declining-.html

death can transgress the logic of modern statecraft and citizenship. The projects I discuss in this section follow this argument, focusing on how augmented reality and new media projects blur the state's claim to governance over territoriality, inaugurating new ways of thinking about place and space in border politics.

Recent scholarship has also examined some of the failings of empathy: Rygiel (2016) notes that dead migrants often count more than the living, in terms of the attention they get from state actors, and Squire (2016) has focused on the shortcomings of efforts to make border deaths visible, particularly in the framing of dignity. In this context, while the projects below do widen the possibility of the community of empathy, they also offer new ways of thinking about migrant memorialization. I argue in this section that virtual and augmented reality technologies offer innovative ways of memorializing migrants. In this way, they form monuments to deaths which cannot be otherwise monumentalized and begin to move us beyond the framing of empathy that has not been very successful at spurring policy change.

Some of the other chapters in this volume take up the question of place in memorialization. While memorials could and have been erected in the migrants' places of origin, what makes this chapter's case study an interesting one is that the memorials I describe function not only to memorialize individuals and their deaths. They also act as forms of resistance to the larger political structures that led to these deaths in the first place, and to resist the stories told by the state about these landscapes. They humanize these deaths for an audience external to the origin communities of these migrants, and in doing so, enlarge the community of empathy beyond one that adheres to national borders and identity. I should also note the limitations of border memorial projects more generally here: while humanitarian organizations often seek to draw attention to death toll and to humanize dead migrants as a means to generate policy change, such change has not been forthcoming. As Anne McNevin (2016) has suggested, while border deaths are political, the narrative of the state is that such deaths are necessary as part of the enactment of border security politics. She asks,

> what if the state and its citizens were to confront that violence in its full reality and be able to live with it? What if that violence was rationalized not as an unfortunate side effect of compelling policies but as a necessary feature of liberal democracy itself? What if states and citizens, in other words, were able to incorporate that violence into their own self-understanding? (2016, unpaginated)

These questions shed new light on the larger politics of border memorials, because it becomes insufficient to simply draw attention to the deaths of migrants. In other words, while I articulate these two projects as initiatives that have the potential to widen empathetic communities, more attention should be paid to whether empathy is a productive tool for policy change. In the analysis of the specific projects below, I address this potential critique more substantively.

As mentioned in the Introduction, this section examines two projects that utilize augmented reality to memorialize the deaths of migrants in the spaces and places in which they died. One focuses on using virtual technology to place migrant deaths, while the other seeks to map migrant deaths onto the stars. Both use alternative technologies that move beyond the standard physical monument to propose new ways of interacting with border deaths in this region, and to interrogate the complex connections between bodies and spaces. Due to the nature of border crossing along the US-Mexico border, a highly securitized zone, and the fact that migrants by nature move across landscapes, traditional monumental forms may not apply. As a result, augmented and virtual technologies offer ways to engage with bodies and spaces that allow us to embrace the ambiguity of the crosser: one with intimate ties to the landscape and the land, but which throws traditional conceptions of territoriality into flux.

Border Memorial: Frontera de los Muertos

John Craig Freeman's project *Border Memorial: Frontera de los Muertos* seeks to rethink the intersections between space and body, via the medium of technology. It is an augmented reality public art project and memorial dedicated to the thousands of migrants who have died along the US-Mexico border in recent years (Freeman and Auchter 2015). Using a smartphone and an app, users travel to the border area and surrounding desert, launch the app and aim their phone camera at the landscape surrounding them. The application uses geolocation software to superimpose individual augments in the form of *calacas*, which are representations of *Dia de los Muertos* skeletons (as seen in Fig. 10.1) at the GPS coordinates of each recorded death of a migrant, enabling the public to see the objects integrated into the physical location as if they existed in the real world (Freeman and Auchter 2015) (Fig. 10.1). Freeman uses the information about placement of deaths and discovery of sets of remains to spur the viewer to consider what it might mean to memorialize the undocumented

Fig. 10.1 *Border Memorial: Frontera de los Muertos*, John Craig Freeman, augmented reality public art, Three Points, Arizona, 2015, courtesy of John Craig Freeman

migrant. In other words, his project acts as a counter-monument because it plays with the idea of presence and absence using augmented reality: the remains are not there in the landscape around us, but we see them presenced through the *calaca* image on our smartphone screen. Then, when we put our phone down, the burden of memory, as with the Harburg monument against fascism, falls on us. We are left with the knowledge that the landscape around us may carry secrets that remain invisible to us, and so the commemorative purpose lingers in the questions it drives us to consider about how we interact with these landscapes, placing the burden of memory on us rather than on a specific physical memorial.

One of the significant components of the project that I have discussed elsewhere (Auchter 2014) is the necessity for one to be in the space itself to aim the smartphone camera and experience the augment. As Freeman notes in a personal interview (28 July 2013, electronic communication),

> One must travel, often to very remote locations, to experience such work first hand…most people will never have a first hand encounter…but just knowing that they are out there, that they exist, makes them significant.

The requirement to be physically present in the landscape hence places a limit on the type of engagement one can have with this memorial project. Interestingly, virtual reality is typically valued for its ability to make us feel that we are on scene, with a deeper and 'more visceral understanding of a story' (Wakefield 2015). In this case, the same technology is used to emphasize the significance of engaging with the space around us to try to imagine the invisibilities contained therein—invisibilities that might be visible with the use of technology.[2] This opens up a particular kind of perspective and renders all public spaces potential memorial spaces. It also counters the critiques often posed of digital memory that it can generate information overload (Garde-Hansen, Hoskins, and Reading 2009, p.5). Lastly, it fits strongly with the notion of the counter-monument, which places the onus of maintaining memory on the viewer. While there is a larger politics of visibility at play here, properly accounting for migrant deaths requires a mental labour that is commensurate with Young's idea of the counter-monument.

It also fits the ethical commitments of the project to rethink the relationship between bodies and spaces. In this sense, Freeman characterizes his art as global but not international:

> International art can be exhibited at biennials and in museums worldwide and its meaning remains more or less the same, no matter where it is located. My work relies on site specificity for context and its meaning is derived from its location. I have developed the technology and a methodology that allows me to make work anywhere on earth.[3]

This also responds to some scholarly concerns about visual media and memorialization. Andrew Hoskins (2003, p.9), for example, expresses concern about excessive use of new media technologies in the context of the Holocaust, which may end up 'popularizing' and rendering it banal. In other words, mass representation may reduce the singular quality of the traumatic event, that is, the fact that migrant deaths cannot be fully

---

[2] Freeman's augments can be viewed in a multimedia article, where images are embedded with augments if viewed with the correct smartphone app (see Freeman and Auchter 2015). The purpose of this dissemination is for scholars and artists to view the project and understand its functioning, and it is not designed to serve the memorial function that the project itself is, as discussed in the main text here.

[3] See https://johncraigfreeman.wordpress.com/john-craig-freeman-dossier-2012/external-evaluators/scholarship-and-creativeprofessional-work/

captured by statistics or even by personal stories. To reconnect this with the augmented reality project under discussion, one of its significant contributions seems to be a commitment to unrepresentability. This is one reason why Freeman chose the *calaca* as the augment: it functions as a lasting indicator that references cultural priors: As he tells me in a personal interview (28 July 2013),

> in the tradition of the Mexican Día de los Muertos, or Day of the Dead festivals, this project is designed to honour, celebrate and remember those who have died and to elevate this issue in public consciousness and political debate. The project is intended to provide a kind of lasting conceptual presence in an otherwise ephemeral physical environment and cultural discourse. Calacas are used in commemoration of lost loved ones during Día de los Muertos festivals. Tracing their origins from Aztec imagery and reintroduced in the modern era at the turn of the twentieth century by Mexican artist José Guadalupe Posada, calacas are generally depicted as joyous rather than mournful. According to Aztec beliefs, death should always be celebrated.

The *calaca* acts as a celebratory memorial to the person who lived, yet is also part of a larger political project that rethinks and reimagines landscapes. The reality of the landscape is that it contains within it the deaths of thousands of migrants, and one must engage with the landscape to be able to fully grasp this. In other words, the aim of the project is not simply to make border deaths visible, but rather to account for the way in which border deaths are a function of territoriality, and how discourses of territoriality and the way landscapes are typically envisioned do not leave room for a comprehensive understanding of migrant deaths. These deaths are not solely about the individual victim, but about commemoration and an understanding of the larger politics of space and violence that led to these outcomes.

By augmenting the reality of the landscape depicted in the project, we are forced to reckon with the idea that the landscapes we view with our own eyes may be incomplete, and to consider what may be absent, and what political processes and exercises of power may render these absent. By positing a complex spatiality, its focus is not about seeing the body of the migrant, but about playing with the question of what is real. The user sees through their mobile device both the physical space as it is, and the physical space as it is not: both are realities. As Freeman notes, his work is premised on the changing nature of public space.

For the past eight years, I have worked on the corner of Tremont and Boylston Streets overlooking the historic Boston Common, the first public park in the United States. I walk across the park every morning. As I do, I often contemplate the role that the town square plays in [the] shaping of political discourse and national identity formation. Whereas the public square was once the quintessential place to air grievances, display solidarity, express difference, celebrate similarity, remember, mourn, and reinforce shared values of right and wrong, it is no longer the only anchor for interactions in the public realm. Public discourse has been relocated to a novel space; a virtual space that encourages exploration of mobile location based art in public. Moreover, public space is now truly open, as artworks can be placed anywhere in the world, without prior permission from government or private authorities with profound implications for art in the public sphere and the discourse that surrounds it. In the early 1990s, we witnessed the migration of the public sphere from the physical realm, the town square and its print augmentation, to the virtual realm, the Internet. In effect, the location of public discourse and the site of national identity formation have been extended into the virtual world and the global network. With the emergence of these technologies on widely used mobile devices, the distributed placelessness of [the] Internet, public discourse and identity formation comes crashing back down to place. Imagine now, the entire mobile Internet, and its physical manifestations of place, as a world-wide public square. (Personal interview, 28 July 2013)

In this vein, while Freeman's project is about migrants, it is most substantively about rethinking the way we memorialize, and what this tells us about how certain bodies and spaces come to light as public or are consigned to the private realm. It posits an alternative form of memorialization in public space by presencing deaths that are often consigned to the private realm, yet it does so precisely through forcing us to encounter the absence of migrants, both from the spaces we encounter and from public discourse.

I noted earlier that one of the dilemmas of migrant memorials more broadly is that simply drawing attention to migrant deaths has not led to wider policy change in the US and Europe. I want to emphasize here that Freeman's project, while it is about resistance to territoriality, is not premised on humanizing the migrant *per se*. The *calaca* represents the remains found at that site, rather than personal data or an image of the persons themselves. What Freeman adeptly represents in this project, then, is that empathy and solidarity need not be built on the individual; rather, questioning the very way in which certain deaths become public is significant as a practice of memory and memorialization.

Drift Alignment

Andrew O'Brien's art installation, *Drift Alignment* (2018–2019) (Fig. 10.2), focuses on how our relationship with the sky shapes our understanding of territory. His installation, at museums or community spaces, and in the case described here at a gallery in Tennessee, displays several types of work that shift our looking both up and down. First, O'Brien examined data about found migrant remains in the Arizona desert. He took the terrestrial coordinates of those discoveries and translated them into celestial coordinates, using midnight on the day the remains were recorded into public record. What the viewer ends up seeing, then, is the image of what the night sky would have looked like in the place where and when those remains were found. He then uses astronomical databases to manufacture a corresponding image of the respective night sky. Each square pictured, then, in Fig. 10.2, refers to one individual set of human remains.

Second, O'Brien taught himself to photograph the night sky using a telescope, and he photographed constellations with particular meanings. Some of the images are taken from the same latitude as the border between the US and Mexico, meaning that at a certain time of year, this is what

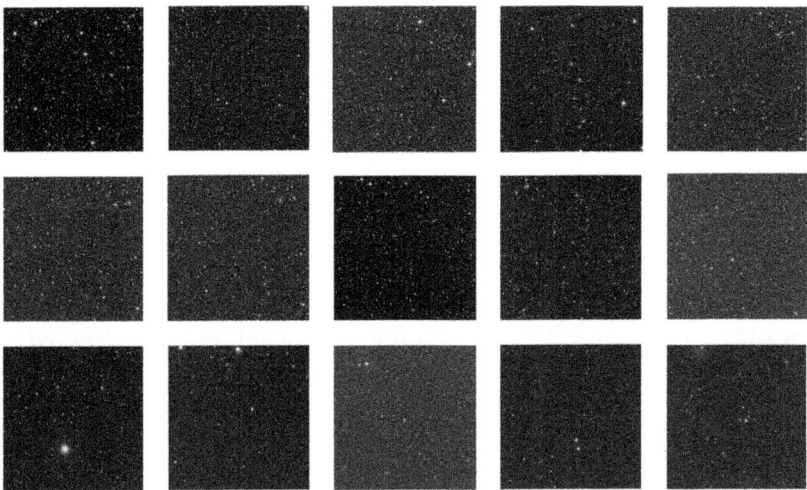

Fig. 10.2 *Drift Alignment*, January 2017 grid, 2019, 15 digital pigment prints, 20″ x 20″ each. Image courtesy of Andrew O'Brien

viewers would see above them while standing on the border itself. The artist calls on a long history of astronomy in the border region to force us to question how we relate to bodies: celestial bodies that occupy spaces above us and the remains of human bodies discovered in the desert.

The third component of O'Brien's installation consists of photographs taken along the US-Mexico border. One photo, in Florence, Arizona, shows a white house containing a migrant rights project, and other buildings that are immigrant detention centres. Behind the photographer is a monument to the founder of the state of Arizona, which cannot be seen in the photograph. O'Brien's photographs depict places that are charged and invisible at the same time. Those who run immigrant detention centres want them to be invisible, and the photograph does not show us signs or markings. Rather, it sits as a counter-monument, forcing the viewer to reflect on the absences inherent in the spaces we interact with: the absent narrative of statehood and its colonial implications; the absent migrants who sustain the functioning of some of the mechanisms of the state; the absent mechanisms of state power itself on bodies and the landscape.

What is most notably absent in O'Brien's project is depictions of migrants. There are no lists of names of the dead or images of migrants or their remains. Rather, our interaction with migrant deaths is mediated through the stars and through the depictions of landscape and space. I asked O'Brien about the framing of such artwork, which is exhibited often without accompanying narrative.[4] He noted that the act of looking at the work matters, and it forces the viewer to consider how images and things relate to each other. While simply looking at the project does not immediately invoke migrant deaths, the gallery brochure does contextualize these images in the larger context of migration, and a proposed book with images and commentary reinforces this explanation for the viewer.

In other words, for O'Brien, simply making migrant deaths visible is insufficient. His project is not about humanizing individual migrant deaths, but rather about contextualizing them in larger narratives about space and place. In one photo, he shows us an artificial horizon, a device that reflects the sun and allows one to find latitude and longitude on land. This banal, scientific tool replicates the historical method by which borders were first drawn, and gestures to the colonization of border regions through scientific tools. As McNevin (2016) has noted, 'The liberal

---

[4] All comments by O'Brien are from this personal interview 14 March 2019, in Chattanooga, Tennessee, USA, at the site of the *Drift Alignment* exhibit.

democratic promise of liberty and prosperity remains open to some, via formal refugee resettlement schemes, precisely and explicitly through violence enacted on others (asylum seekers at the border)'. O'Brien's work, then, does not only mourn migrants, as this same liberal democratic regime does, but rather forces an encounter with the structural violence inherent in such deaths.

Through a practice of critical mimesis, O'Brien's depiction of the tool raises questions about the artificial nature of border formation, and with the other components of the exhibit, grounds such questioning in immediate engagement with the landscape. In this sense, like *Border Memorial: Frontera de los Muertos,* it forces us to rethink what counts as public space and narratives worthy of occupying such space. It generates a monument to movement itself, to the migrant experience. This monument, however, is a virtual one, and it draws on the tradition of the counter-monument to require engagement by the viewer. The burden is on us to understand the origin and meaning of the images of the stars, just as the burden is on us not to oversimplify the larger politics of migrant deaths with reference to concepts like grief and dignity (Squire 2017; Alonso and Nienass 2016), something which fits with Young's notion of the counter-monument.

Conclusions

I have argued that both of the projects discussed above can be broadly understood within the framing of the counter-monument. By drawing on innovative technologies of the virtual and augmented, they disrupt traditional memorial forms in the same way as the counter-monument. They remind us that the permanence of the monument can be illusory, and that memory can be ambiguous. They draw out the significance of monumental forms that change, adapt with the landscape or are adapted to the landscape, or are ephemeral. For example, Freeman's *Border Memorial: Frontera de Los Muertos* shows us something different depending on how we interact with particular landscapes. It reminds us that public space may not in fact be place-bound, and (re)introduces deaths that are normally elided from the public eye. O'Brien's project focuses on the blurring of time by drawing on historical references in how we presently interact with border landscapes. Rather than using the traditional gravesite to commemorate migrant deaths, O'Brien instead encourages us to look both up and down, to consider celestial bodies as monuments themselves, though they are ephemeral. By capturing one moment, he leads us to reflect on the intersections between bodies and spaces and on the potentially ephemeral nature of monuments and memories.

What these projects share is twofold: first, the pursuit of new media forms to reflect on migration and migrant deaths, and second, the absence of actual migrants. Instead, migrants and migration are accounted for through the alternative forms of virtual and augmented reality that seek to give the viewer/user access to a set of shared understandings, meanings and experiences. In addition, they fit the remit of the counter-monument as a project that seeks to 'confront the nation-state with its own crimes and exclusions', in the words of Elizabeth Strakosch (2010, p.268), by moving our focus to the deaths that are a direct result of border security policies which force migrants to use more dangerous routes (Romero 2018).

This chapter has suggested that examining virtual and augmented reality installations can compel us to rethink the very idea of migrants and monuments. While traditional monuments can often account for historical cases, ongoing mobility and movement as in the cases I have discussed requires alternative notions of monumentalization. Similarly, building monuments requires political capital and investment in a community and its identity, something which is not present for undocumented migrants along the US-Mexico border. What remains, then, is the counter-monument, a memorial form which questions memorialization itself by blurring the boundaries between bodies and spaces and encouraging us to look at space in new ways, putting the onus of bearing memory on all of us. John Craig Freeman's work, for example, pushes us to rethink public space as virtual, and to encounter augmented reality and the way it is shaped by the invisible power structures around us governing migration. Andrew O'Brien's work subverts traditional encounters with territoriality by encouraging us to look up at the stars as a way of understanding the landscape around us and the migrants who have died in the Arizona desert. By playing with absence and presence and by providing a disjuncture between the real and the virtual, they allow us to access stories that often remain untold. They encourage the viewer to remember and become active in the story itself, similar to the mechanisms of the counter-monuments discussed in the German context.

It bears mentioning here some of the limits of the counter-monument genre, based on the examples discussed above. One dilemma both of these projects raise is that of voice and representation. A critic might suggest that these projects are examples of American artists speaking on behalf of migrants, whose own voices remain silent. While we should always be cautious about such considerations, it should be emphasized that migrants in this context occupy a vulnerable space of voicelessness due to their precarious legal status. This is further the case in discussing the migrants who die crossing the US-Mexico border. Many remain nameless, without families to speak their lives into existence in the story of what happened to them as a result. Families back home may commemorate them in individual ways, but their deaths are co-opted into larger political projects associated with migration that turn these deaths into statistics to be managed by a security apparatus.

Presencing the individual in an unconventional form can offer a resistance to these totalizing narratives of migration in the same forums in which they occur and in the same country: the US. Memorialization dignifies these lives and deaths. It is also worth noting that these projects do not tell the story of migrants on their behalf as some narrative projects do, but rather disrupt the very idea that we can adequately represent migrant deaths in narrative form. As a result, John Craig Freeman turns to the cultural icon of the *calaca*, and Andrew O'Brien to the sky: interaction with the landscape becomes the story that can memorialize the individual in ways more traditional forms of monumentalization cannot adequately perform.

I should also note that both of these memorial projects, while they rethink the idea of public space, do not in fact occur within public space in the same way as a public memorial; we do not intentionally need to seek it out in order to view it. Freeman's project requires the downloading of an app and a visit to the areas in question. O'Brien's project is interacted with in a gallery space. Engagement with these projects is purposeful, then, not accidental. While this is a limitation in usefulness compared to other memorial forms, and even compared to other uses of new media technologies, it does fit with the framing of the counter-monument, which places the burden of memory on the viewer/visitor.

Additionally, counter-monuments in Young's sense as traced earlier can be stumbled across in the urban fabric and then demand engagement from the visitor. The two projects I have described here are different in that they do require the visitor to prepare themselves for the engagement. Still, the border does not lend itself to a traditional memorial or to a memorial that people can easily come across. If modern forms of violence at the border occur through the very imposition of space, then perhaps the transformative effect occurs first and foremost by shifting memorialization to the level of the virtual. By transgressing the state's desire to impose territory on space and by forcing us to do the labour of engaging our own complicity in these territorial forms of statecraft. This transgressive project, whether it engages few or many, and though it may not enlarge the community of mourners, rethinks public space in new ways and offers a politics beyond empathy that can be transformative.

A counter-monument can offer new ways of thinking about representation in the era of digital media. Both of these artists view their projects as political; they seek to make visible experiences and lives and deaths that tend to be outside the purview of contemporary political debates about migration, particularly in the US. When the burden of memory is placed on all of us, there is increased potential for the formation of empathetic communities that can dignify these deaths. Yet, this requires community members to step up to accept that burden for this to translate into a larger mechanism of social remembrance. The forms of commemoration I have described here may be less successful at circulating memory than large-scale public memorial projects, but this evokes a larger question about the purpose of memorialization. Should monuments focus on ubiquitous access, on representation, on narrative or on something else altogether? It also bears mentioning that conventional monuments, just like counter-monuments, do not always evoke the same response from viewers: indeed, social surroundings tend to alter and shift the meaning of monuments over time and from one individual to another (Osborne 2017), but in the right circumstances, counter-monuments can engage more 'democratic public processes of commemoration' (Moshenska 2010, p.7). Indeed, though 'commemoration that must be actively sought out is unsatisfactory, holding out the possibility of cultural amnesia' (ibid., p.24), those who traverse a highway in Arizona or look up at the sky are inadvertently engaged in a larger story of commemoration that is only waiting to be uncovered.

References

Alonso, A. D., & Nienass, B. (2016). Deaths, Visibility, and Responsibility: The Politics of Mourning at the US-Mexico Border. *Social Research, 83*(2), 421–451.

Andrieu, K. (2009). 'Sorry for the Genocide': How Public Apologies Can Help Promote National Reconciliation. *Millennium, 38*(1), 3–23.

Auchter, J. (2013). Border Monuments: Memory, Counter-Memory, and (B)Ordering Practices Along the US-Mexico Border. *Review of International Studies, 39*, 291–311.

Auchter, J. (2014). *The Politics of Haunting and Memory in International Relations*. New York: Routledge.
Caruth, C. (Ed.). (1995). *Trauma: Explorations in Memory*. Baltimore: Johns Hopkins University Press.
Caruth, C. (1996). *Unclaimed Experience: Trauma, Narrative, and History*. Baltimore: Johns Hopkins University Press.
Cocciolo, A. (2014). Digitally Augmented Remembrance: Public Memory, Mobile Technology and the 9/11 Memorial. Draft paper Available at http://www.thinkingprojects.org/Digitally_Augmented_remembrance_for_web.pdf
DeTurk, S. (2017). Memory of Absence: Contemporary Counter-Monuments. *Art and the Public Sphere*, 6(1 and 2), 81–94.
Doty, R. (1996). The Double-Writing of Statecraft: Exploring State Responses to Illegal Immigration. *Alternatives*, 21(2), 171–189.
Freeman, J. C., & Auchter, J. (2015). Border Memorial: Frontera de los Muertos. *Hyperrhiz: New Media Cultures* 12, unpaginated.
Garde-Hansen, J., Hoskins, A., & Reading, A. (Eds.). (2009). *Save as…Digital Memories*. Basingstoke: Palgrave.
Hess, A. (2007). In Digital Remembrance: Vernacular Memory and the Rhetorical Construction of Web Memorials. *Media, Culture, and Society*, 29(5), 812–830.
Hite, K., & Collins, C. (2009). Memorial Fragments, Monumental Silences and Reawakenings in 21st-Century Chile. *Millennium*, 38(2), 379–400.
Hoskins, A. (2003). Signs of the Holocaust: Exhibiting Memory in a Mediated Age. *Media, Culture, and Society*, 25(1), 7–22.
Hoskins, A. (Ed.). (2017). *Digital Memory Studies: Media Pasts in Transition*. London: Routledge.
Hutchison, E., & Bleiker, R. (2008). Emotional Reconciliation: Reconstituting Identity and Community After Trauma. *European Journal of Social Theory*, 11(3), 385–403.
Lupu, N. (2003). Memory Vanished, Absent, and Confined: The Countermemorial Project in 1980s and 1990s Germany. *History and Memory*, 15(2), 130–164.
Mayo, J. (1988). *War Memorials as Political Landscape: The American Experience and Beyond*. Santa Barbara: Praeger.
McGeough, R.E. (2011). The American Counter-Monumental Tradition: Renegotiating Memory and the Evolution of American Sacred Space. Doctoral Dissertation. Louisiana State University.
McNevin, A. (2016). Borders and the Politics of Mourning. Available at http://www.publicseminar.org/2016/12/borders-and-the-politics-of-mourning-3/
Moshenska, G. (2010). Charred Churches or Iron Harvests? *Journal of Social Archaeology*, 10(1), 5–27.
Osborne, J. (2017). Counter-Monumentality and the Vulnerability of Memory. *Journal of Social Archaeology*, 17(2), 163–187.

Pardes, A. (2018). For Museums, Augmented Reality Is the Next Frontier. *Wired*, September 21.

Pogacar, M. (2018). Culture of the Past. In A. Hoskins (Ed.), *Digital Memory Studies: Media Pasts in Transition* (pp. 27–47). London: Routledge.

Rajaram, P. K. (2004). Disruptive Writings and a Critique of Territoriality. *Review of International Studies, 30*, 201–228.

Resende, E., & Budryte, D. (Eds.). (2014). *Memory and Trauma in International Relations: Theories, Cases, and Debates*. London: Routledge.

Romero, S. (2018). They Have a Mission in the Desert: Finding the Bodies of Border Crossers. *The New York Times*, 13 July.

Rygiel, K. (2016). Dying to Live: Migrant Deaths and Citizenship Politics Along European Borders: Transgressions, Disruptions, and Mobilizations. *Citizenship Studies, 20*(5), 545–560.

Salter, S. (2006). The Global Visa Regime and the Political Technologies of the International Self: Borders, Bodies, Biopolitics. *Alternatives, 31*, 167–189.

Sherman, D. (1996). Art, Commerce, and the Production of Memory in France after World War I. In J. Gillis (Ed.), *Commemorations: The Politics of National Identity* (pp. 186–214). Princeton: Princeton University Press.

Stevens, Q., Franck, K. A., & Fazakerley, R. (2012). Countermonuments: The Anti-Monumental and the Dialogic. *The Journal of Architecture, 17*(6), 951–972.

Squire, V. (2017). Governing Migration through Death in Europe and the US: Identification, Burial, and the Crisis of Modern Humanism. *European Journal of International Relations, 23*(3), 513–532.

Strakosch, E. (2010). Counter-Monuments and Nation-Building in Australia. *Peace Review, 22*(3), 268–275.

Sturken, M. (1997). *Tangled Memories: The Vietnam War, the AIDS Epidemic, and the Politics of Remembering*. Oakland: University of California Press.

Tallon, L. (2012). Museums and Mobile Survey 2012. Available at http://www.museums-mobile.org/survey/

Urry, J. (1995). How Societies Remember the Past. *The Sociological Review, 43*(1), 45–65.

Von Bieberstein, A., & Evren, E. (2016). From Aggressive Humanism to Improper Mourning: Burying the Victims of Europe's Border Regime in Berlin. *Social Research, 83*(2), 453–479.

Wakefield, J. (2015). Virtual Reality Looks for a Role in Journalism. *BBC*, 1 April.

Young, J. (1994). *Texture of Memory*. New Haven: Yale University Press.

CHAPTER 11

Synthesis and Conclusions

Sabine Marschall

Migration and diaspora, whether originating in voluntary mobility or forced displacement, carry personal and collective memories into new social and geo-political environments. Commemorative markers, from large-scale permanent monuments to ephemeral impromptu grassroots memorials and even virtual memorials in cyberspace, mediate such memories, produce novel modes of remembrance and new collective memories that fuse transnational and transcultural elements. Traumatic memories and constructions of victimhood loom large in the arena of migration and displacement, even where ancestors may have migrated in search of better opportunities. Collective memories of suffering, loss, death and trauma—attached to migrant communities and ethnic minorities; marginalized indigenous groups or underpinning national identity of host societies—hence often dominate the public discourse and representation of memory in the context of migration.

While the authors of this volume draw on a range of conceptual approaches, Michael Rothberg's influential theory of multidirectional memory, espoused in his 2009 book and other publications, has inspired

S. Marschall (✉)
School of Social Sciences, University of KwaZulu-Natal,
Durban, KwaZulu-Natal, South Africa
e-mail: marschalls@ukzn.ac.za

© The Author(s) 2020
S. Marschall (ed.), *Public Memory in the Context of Transnational Migration and Displacement*, Palgrave Macmillan Memory Studies,
https://doi.org/10.1007/978-3-030-41329-3_11

many, as it provides what Assmann (2014, p.551) calls 'a remedy against the traps of competitive victimhood'. By examining the memory of the Holocaust and colonialism, both closely allied with dynamics of migration, displacement, flight and refuge, Rothberg (2009) shows the productive connections and intersections between what is often positioned as paradigmatically autonomous memory traditions. Derived from these case studies, he intended the concept of multidirectional memory 'to capture the dialogic emergence of hybrid memories in transnational and multicultural contexts' (Rothberg 2014a, p.125). Although technology plays an important role, the physical mobility of groups and individuals, their concrete behaviour and interactions within a host society environment represent a crucial catalyst for dialogue, contestation, negotiation and the emergence of hybrid identity models and transcultural memory dynamics (Rothberg 2009).

Scholars in the field of memory studies should not simply celebrate the transcultural and transnational dimensions of memory facilitated by high mobility, advanced communication technology and globalized cultural consumption practices, but rather 'foreground located articulations of remembrance embedded in uneven relations of power', suggests Rothberg (2014a, p.129). If one of the key challenges of investigating memory lies in the fluidity of its constellations and the complexity and multiplicity of its modes of mediation, the current volume's concentration on monuments and memorials, physical artefacts permanently or temporarily installed in specific locations, circumscribes a precise focal point and public arena for the manifestation of collective and often transcultural memory. Yet, what is significant is not the monument *per se*, but how social actors engage—discursively and bodily—with such artefacts and how remembering occurs in the process of such engagement. Collectively, the chapters of this volume examine interaction with commemorative markers at the very local and often personal level, yet always connected to larger scales and frames of reference—the city, the host nation, the homeland or transnational political agendas and discourses of identification.

Transcultural, transnational and multidirectional memory are hence important concepts for grounding the migration aspect of this book, the memory carried by migrants and transformed or newly produced in dialogical interaction with the host society. To anchor the monument aspect of this volume, I remain inspired by an older conceptual model espoused by Wulf Kansteiner (2002) in his methodological critique of collective memory studies. Kansteiner (2002, p.180) asserts that

> ... we should conceptualize collective memory as the result of the interaction among three types of historical factors: the intellectual and cultural traditions that frame all our representations of the past, the memory makers who selectively adopt and manipulate these traditions, and the memory consumers who use, ignore, or transform such artifacts according to their own interests.

Kansteiner's (2002:197) suggestion that collective memory studies must be furthered by focussing on the memory makers, memory users and the media of memory will provide some scaffolding for structuring this Conclusion chapter, although the limitations of this hermeneutical triangle and its neat categorization will also become evident.

All contributing authors have drawn their own conclusions at the end of the respective chapters, summing up key points and expounding insights derived from their empirical case studies about the triangular relationship between memory, monuments and migration. Individual readers of this book may find additional, perhaps unexpected, dimensions of meaning and significance in details and elements resonating with their own areas of interest and expertise. The subjectivity of the observations presented below is hence fully acknowledged, as I present some of my own thoughts on what I see each chapter contributing to the objectives of this collection.

MONUMENT AS MEDIUM OF MEMORY

The media of memory or the 'visual and discursive objects and traditions of representations' (Kansteiner 2002, p.197) here refer broadly to the memory culture developed by migrants, diasporas, host societies and homeland societies, of which monuments constitute the central point of interest. The contributions of this volume illustrate how established cultural traditions of memory are rendered transcultural or multidirectional through migration and forced displacement. Commemorative monuments and memorials in the conventional sense, disregarding for now their dissolution in the realm of new media technology, are first and foremost physical objects, tangible artefacts in public space. They primarily rely on images and texts, which can be—and often are—studied and analysed through discursive approaches, but the full complexity of the monument as a semiotic signifier and affective public symbol includes many other visual, spatial, material and discursive elements.

Transcultural Memory

Wolf's art historical examination reveals the complexity of the monument as a visual symbolic artefact and placing this chapter at the beginning of the collection alerts the reader to potential dimensions of analysis that remain marginalized in subsequent chapters. In the Monument of the Syrian Residents to the Argentine Nation, for instance, small visual details and their calculated combination—the fez as a symbol of modernity within the Ottoman homeland context and its combination with a Western suit—(re)construct memory for the immigrant community's identity projects and socio-political agendas vis-à-vis the host society. Carefully crafted and deliberately placed elements address stereotypes (e.g. the Syrian as street peddler) and prevailing anti-immigrant discourses in a settler nation increasingly imagined as racially and religiously homogenous.

The Monument of the Syrian Residents to the Argentine Nation hence visually represents, as Wolf puts it, 'a re-imagined, curated memory of migration', which depends equally on remembering and forgetting. The prominent visual presence of the monument and the seductive, distractive power of its imagery, visual details and textual signifiers, deflect from absence, memories not shared—for instance about the hardships of migration and the hurdles of integration. The visual statement of the Syrian monument is not an appeal for empathy by the marginalized, the subaltern, the victimized, but an assertive declaration of positive self-identification, aspiration and proud belonging to the host nation, emanating from an imagined position of equality with other immigrant groups during the momentous occasion of the Centennial.

Wolf shows how the aesthetic articulation of the Syrian monument in Buenos Aires is in many ways formulaic and non-distinct in its adherence to European academic traditions of style and iconography, local taste and the precedents it emulates, but in details, it is unique and distinct by drawing on Ottoman commemorative traditions and visual elements. Such embedded transcultural visual and textual references represent another dimension of transcultural and transnational memory, forged by migrants themselves in the process of negotiating their identity and—on account of the monument's anticipated permanency—enshrining a particular memory of migration and origin for future generations of the Syrian diaspora.

Rothberg (2014b, p.654) suggests that 'all acts of memory that enter public space necessarily enter simultaneously into dialogue with practices and traditions of memory that seem at first distant from them'. How transcultural and transnational memory is embedded in, and indeed produced by, the visual dimension and aesthetic aspects of commemorative markers is implied in various chapters, but could productively be explored much further within the arena of monuments and migration. What does it mean, for example, when the statue in memory of the comfort women in Glendale, California, is not a locally designed original, but a replica of the sculpture in Seoul, opposite the Japanese embassy? How is public memory produced and legitimated when Ukrainian immigrants in Canada pour their 'mnemonic material' into respected commemorative forms, using visual formulae and Graeco-Roman aesthetics inspired by Canadian and Commonwealth practices of commemorating war veterans? It is through location, scale, material, visual elements and inscriptions, but also calculated references to local landmarks and transnational symbols that migrant monuments seek to establish strategic connections and cross-border associations. The diasporic negotiation of memory and crafting of such artefacts is the result of dialogue, interaction, sometimes tension and even violence, but—as Rothberg asserts (ibid.)—it is above all productive.

Absence and Presence

Beyond discursive engagements with monuments as 'texts' that focus on mnemonic content and intended symbolic meaning, a more comprehensive, affective, multisensory and materialist perspective recognizes that the scale and (semi)permanent physical presence of commemorative markers in public space produces meaning in its own right and creates its own realities. This is well illustrated in Ruberto and Sciorra's comparison between the fate of the enormous Columbus monument in New York City, a prominent landmark embedded in the local urban fabric, and the much smaller statue of Columbus at the city hall in San Jose, California, which was vandalized and ultimately removed. Monuments represent only a small aspect of the comprehensive memory culture nurtured by the Ukrainian diaspora in Canada, but it was the permanent physical presence of these commemorative markers, the undeniable material existence of these symbol of a disputed past that prompted the Russian tweet about the 'monuments for Nazi criminals', resulting in an international diplomatic crisis. (In the digital age, a verbal attack via social media represents a globalized act of iconoclasm that can be more effective than localized physical defacement.) Townsville in Queensland, Australia, has long since carried the name of Robert Towns, but it was the 2005 unveiling of his statue that brought simmering tensions to the fore and prompted protests from the South Sea Islander community and indigenous groups. The material presence of the statue in a prominent city space was perceived as deepening the estrangement of these marginalized groups and glaringly highlighting their exclusion from the local landscape of memory.

Had the Towns' statue been erected half a century earlier, the public reception might have been different. At the time when Syrians erected their monument in Buenos Aires; when Italian Americans sponsored Columbus statues across the United States and when the post-war Ukrainian immigrants first began to establish memorials to their revered veterans, public monuments were regarded (by those empowered to make their voices heard) as largely innocent and unproblematic artefacts. City authorities in the 'New World', in particular, keen to emulate the civilized and 'cultured look' of European metropoles through commemorative public art, were readily prepared to approve and sometimes grateful to accept such monuments, especially when donated.

In more recent decades, reflecting the legacy of post-modern and post-structuralist sensibilities, material presence inevitably draws attention to absence, exclusiveness and the non-represented—a recurrent theme among the contributions of this volume. Monuments virtually cry out 'to be toppled, besmirched, desecrated', observes Taussig (1999, p.20–21), because they rely on selective remembering, and the repressed history is always already pre-installed—like a hidden flaw, awaiting to be revealed. In western societies, emancipatory socio-political developments and migration-related demographic changes have rendered cultural representations in the public domain more sensitive and effected a 'democratization of history' that brings minority memories to the fore (Nora 2002). Previously marginalized and effectively silenced voices, including indigenous groups, migrant communities and ethnic minorities, may now be found to participate and even initiate critical discourses around cultural symbols in public spaces, politicizing monuments and opening them up to intense public scrutiny, but also strategically using monuments to 'write back', present counter-narratives and realize their own identity projects.

The Producers of Public Memory

Monuments are the means of representation that facilitate the process of articulating, structuring and using memory in a social setting; without such social settings, Kansteiner (2002, p.190) notes, building on

Halbwachs' seminal recognition of the social frames of memory, no memories, even those of eyewitnesses, can assume collective relevance. Monuments are not intrinsically able to preserve memory or socially transmit their intended meaning, but require complex processes of interpretation and enculturation; discursive and performative action; and the maintenance of a commemorative tradition to bring the memory of the past into the present. In short, memory work does not end with the establishment of a monument. The degree to which later generations of Ukrainian immigrants in Canada, for instance, comprehend the meaning of images, symbols and acronyms in the memorials created by their parents and grandparents indicates the extent of their induction into and absorption of the memory culture created and nurtured by that generation.

Several chapters of this volume explore the memory makers, those who seek to actively construct, frame and disseminate memory in specific ways. It is those who drive memory discourses and initiate, design and defend monuments; those who seek to rehabilitate suppressed memories and bring them into the public eye in ways that may be referred to as memory activism (Gutman 2017); even those who promote memories for purposes of economic gain and material benefits. As mentioned in the Introduction chapter and much emphasized in memory studies more generally, the establishment of public monuments and indeed the production of memory in multicultural contexts, resulting from dialogue and tension, are always influenced by prevailing relations of power, but not necessarily in simplistically hierarchical and predictable ways. The chapters in this book illustrate that ethnic minorities, migrants and even refugees, marginalized and often discriminated against socially, economically and perhaps politically, can still be effective producers of memory in their host societies, who manage to rearticulate hegemonic narratives and turn repressive power relations in favour of their own agenda.

Vision and Determination

The diaspora environment provides unique conditions for remembrance, both enabling and constraining. Favourable circumstances and specific types of resources are helpful for those who seek to bring memory-based identity projects to fruition, but ultimately these individuals need skill, creativity, persistence and some degree of savviness. Effective producers of memory are able to recognize and successfully harness economic, sociopolitical and intellectual resources provided by the host society; utilize legal frameworks and policy instruments for their own purposes; and strategically exploit gaps and weaknesses of host society systems.

As monuments purport to symbolize the collective memory of specific groups, their initiators present themselves as speaking on behalf of their community or the general public. Yet through careful historical research, the origins of commemorative markers and traditions can often be traced to small groups, grassroots actors and identified individuals with very specific agendas. It was a small elite of Italian immigrants, driven by a minute assembly of prominent persons, that created the symbolic connection between Italian Americans and Columbus as a symbol of Italian civilization and then managed to stabilize and fortify it through the establishment of monuments and commemorative holiday celebrations. It was an intensely organized and politicized group of Ukrainian immigrants that created a specific mnemonic tradition in the Canadian diaspora. It was a small number of local activists who pushed for the erection of statues in memory of Korean comfort women in the United States by prominently mobilizing the victimization discourse and seeking support from strategic coalition partners backed by nationally and internationally recognized policy instruments.

Memory makers are visionaries and passionate advocates of a cause, even if they prefer to retain a low profile and work 'behind the scenes'; they have motivation, purpose and the persistence to drive their interpretation of the past into the public eye and defend it against competing narratives. Despite being part of marginalized populations, they may have useful connections, local and transnational networks and some level of societal or political influence, but their most powerful resource is arguably the passivity of others—the silence, indifference or lack of contestation from those they claim to represent and the public at large.

Naïveté, lack of historical knowledge and tepid interest in the past, among the immigrant community, the host society and even within the Canadian government, provided fertile ground for the Ukrainian immigrants to pursue their memory politics geared at fostering long-distance nationalism. What is more, the absence of overt criticism from victim groups, notably Holocaust survivors, permitted them to not only detract from their own association with Nazi perpetrators, but to cast the Ukrainian people themselves as victims by gaining the Canadian government's support for the official recognition of the *Holodomor*.

Victimhood

Many chapters illustrate the central role of victimhood in migration and diaspora, interweaving and contrasting different scales of victimization and revealing layers of subalternity. The discourse of perpetrator and victim underpins the Korean Americans' efforts at publicly remembering the comfort women and erecting statues to them. The Korean diaspora has been active in creating awareness internationally, but their efforts were particularly successful in the United States, where—as for the Ukrainians in Canada—fertile ground for ethnic minority memorialization is provided through the democratic system and constitutionally enshrined freedom of expression, which includes tolerance towards different understandings of the past. The Korean Americans are not least encouraged and inspired by the Ukrainian community's success in establishing their *Holodomor* memorial right in the midst of the US capital, moreover financed by the US government (along with the Ukrainian government). But the comfort women statues are not only about remembering these women's tragic fate; they serve as epitome and synecdoche of the wider historical victimization of the Korean people through Japanese colonialism. In the context of migration, victim narratives relating to the country of origin or the post-migration settling in the host country may be nurtured over generations, creating a post-memory (Hirsch 2001) of discrimination and trauma that still deeply affects the present generation.

Commemorative symbols are surrounded by, and sometimes the result of, competing narratives of victimization, because discourses of victimhood are employed—and mobilized as strategic resource—by those creating, defending and attacking monuments. Japanese Americans and Japanese nationals perceive the comfort women statue initiatives as an attack on their own national and group identity. Similarly, many Ukrainians in Canada feel offended by the Russian criticism of their diasporic memorials, pushing the public memory of their victimization by the Soviet Union. Migrant identity constructions based on victimhood may be promoted to deflect from one's own role as perpetrator or justify rejecting wider responsibilities in the fight against historical injustice. Italian Americans outraged over demands for the removal of Columbus statues feel victimized, defamed, discriminated against, paralleling their forefathers' experience as first-generation migrants. Yet, the more the Italian Americans are defending Columbus statues as counter-hegemonic sites of memory, symbols of the subaltern histories of Italian immigrants, the more critics are provoked to mobilize the memory of the real subaltern, the indigenous American Indians subjugated by Columbus and his legacy.

Monument ventures are ostensibly about preserving collective memories and celebrating ethnic community identity, but their makers may pursue them to achieve rather different, if disguised, social and political objectives, often motivated by a group consciousness of real or perceived victimhood. A rise in xenophobic nationalist ideology and discriminatory discourses can fuel immigrants' eagerness to initiate monuments to proactively stake a public claim of belonging and pre-empt the threat of exclusion from the national imaginary. The development of a hero cult around Christopher Columbus did not rise to prominence in Italy, but was crafted by Italian immigrants in an American socio-political environment marked by racial prejudice and anti-Italian bigotry.

The Italian immigrants' quest for recognition and addressing stereotypes through commemorative initiatives parallels the Syrians' effort in Argentina in many ways, but also pursues a different strategy. While a carefully designed monument articulating collective memory and community aspiration can itself deepen the community's 'otherness', the Italian Americans appropriate Columbus, a widely recognized transcultural symbol of identification for European American settlers, as an Italian hero and symbol of a civilized, white Italian culture. Eclipsing indigenous perspectives on the explorer, the Italian immigrants' mythologizing through public statues and monuments, mostly donated by the community itself, is once again underscored by the issue of race as a central, if veiled, mainstay of immigrant identity and host society inclusion.

Resources

Resources for the diasporic production of public memory come most obviously in the form of political and economic power, sometimes social or cultural capital. Ukrainian immigrants were able to take full advantage of the Canadian policy of multiculturalism to attract official support and even public funding for their memory project, framed as expressions of ethnic identity and celebration of community history. Even once public attention and international controversy had erupted, the Ukrainians benefitted from—and were emboldened in their demands—by the Canadian government's awareness of the ethnic group's political power as a crucial electorate bloc. This situation of mutual benefit allowed them to preserve their monuments and even influence the Canadian government's foreign policy—with Ukraine, its allies and enemies.

Resources may present themselves in less obvious guises, including conducive geo-social spaces. For a memory culture existing at the fringe of society, the cemetery—initially seen as an apolitical sacred space, but increasingly ideologically charged—presents itself as an advantageous spatial arena for the Ukrainian memorials. Imbued with an aura of solemnity and respect, where one does not speak ill of the dead, the cemetery is simultaneously a valued public space and a sheltered, protected terrain. Here a close-knit community was able to perform nationalist commemorative rituals and performances in folk costumes and military uniforms during anniversary days largely out of the public eye and induct the Canadian-born generation into the nationalist historical culture.

If official host society backing, public acquiesce and the absence of detractors understandably constitute conducive conditions for the diasporic production of memory, McCarthy's chapter illustrates—in support of Rothberg's theory of multidirectional memory—that contestation, active opposition and even virulent protest can become resources in their own right. As memory politics and diaspora politics interact, fierce opposition from Japan and Japanese Americans initially had a curtailing effect on the Korean American memory agenda, moreover because the general American public was also divided on the comfort women issue. However, the push back from the Japanese government hardened the resolve of local activists and raised the public profile of their campaign; using the contestation as a tool to further their cause, they kept pushing for more statues and memorials.

A classic case of the production of memory emerging in a multicultural diasporic context of dialogue, tension and negotiation, McCarthy shows how the favour swayed back and forth, as both groups with their competing narratives learned from the experience of public response and became more strategic and savvy in pursuing their politics of memory. Similar to Rudling's case, stratagems included the use of personal connections, working behind the scenes and serving the interests of the political leadership. The increasing political influence of the Korean Americans as electoral bloc has been noted in the ethnic minority's realization of their commemorative initiatives, but other strategies and resources were more crucial in this case.

Survivors and Coalition-Building

Perhaps the most important resource for the Korean American memory makers was the moral authority and presence of survivors. Just as the 'memory boom' (Winter 2001) of the 1980s may be linked to the imminent disappearance of the communicative memory of the Holocaust, the passing of the Korean eye-witness generation fuels and legitimates measures to preserve and institutionalize this memory of trauma, deeply connected with Korean national identity and cultural memory at home and in the diaspora. At the micro level, survivor women are mobilized to publicly share painful memories next to mute statues. Commemorative markers accrete meaning through such performativity, because for those who witness the testimony, in person or mediated through TV or social media, the memory of the eye-witness account may forever remain attached to the statue. Similarly, participants of refugee-guided tours in Berlin are likely to remember particularly emotional episodes of the refugee's shared memory more vividly than the historical narrative officially associated with the monument.

At the macro level, ethnically, temporally and geographically specific memories of trauma are hence multidirectionally mapped onto widely recognized memory traditions, familiar templates and commemorative paradigms, such as Holocaust remembrance, the memory of slavery and colonialism, and the tragedies of war. Through such contextualization and connection with larger international memory and human rights discourses—reflected in organizational alliances and strategic coalitions between grassroots actors and NGOs with national and international scope—'different layers of memory are "inter-activated"' (Rothberg 2014a, p.136). Universal messaging about human rights, women's rights and historical justice was employed to garner support for the contested memory campaign, justify its wider societal relevance and deflect from perceptions of this being an internal matter between Japan and Korea. In a globalized world, local memory dynamics are hence supported and made visible through contextualization within global debates and international discourses, but the latter also, in turn, gain traction by drawing from multiple strands of local cases (Assmann and Conrad 2010).

Building coalitions and linking the public memory initiative around narratives of victimization to more general rights issues and larger goals not directly or exclusively associated with the immigrant group, similarly played a role in Sullivan and Sullivan's chapter. The provocation caused by the Robert Towns' statue, the credence and official status it lent to the memory of the disputed historical figure, acted as a catalyst for bringing counter-memories to the fore. South Sea Islanders' construction of a traumatic memory of slavery centred on Towns, paralleling Native American activists' depiction of Christopher Columbus, remains historically controversial, yet served an important role in consolidating community identity. But it was the coalition with indigenous Australians, irrespective of historical tensions between the two groups, that bolstered the community's collective spirit and strengthened its lobbying power with government authorities.

Quite contrary to the erstwhile aims and objectives of the Towns' statue initiative, the conflictual interaction between settlers and diasporic groups allied to indigenous people engendered not only the production of an alternative historical memory, but its prominent public institutionalization through the erection of a new monument. Rather than preventing the public memorialization of a disputed hero, the diasporic subaltern memory activist can obtain historical justice by pinning counter-memory to the hegemonic marker and—exploiting its public visibility—open up subversive discursive spaces of memory that may result in meaningful changes in the material landscape of memory.

The monument controversy in Townsville not only mobilized the South Sea Islander community and fostered new relationships with other marginalized groups locally, but allowed the diasporic South Sea Islanders to restore their homeland links with Melanesia, where the transnational memory narrative produced in the diaspora found a place in nationalist mythologies. Importantly, the flow of memories and cultural practices is not simply one-directional, from homeland to diaspora, but occurs in both directions (Landsberg 2004). Vanuatu became independent in 1980, Ukraine in 1991; both sovereign nations embarked on developing their own national identity, fostering foundation myths and historical narratives linked to emotional memories, often involving trauma and historical injustice. In this context, migrants and diasporas constitute useful resources, not only economically, in terms of financial remittances, and politically, in terms of international alliances, but also socio-culturally through 'new imports of mnemonic material' (Rothberg 2014a, p.130).

Rudling's chapter illustrates particularly well how the hostland context becomes a sheltered space for the exilic production, nurturing and 'freezing' of a diasporic memory culture that is later reintroduced into the homeland, where it is embraced as a cornerstone of nationalism. In

McCarthy's chapter, Korea benefits from its diaspora as ambassadors for the home country's national identity politics, who use the conducive conditions provided by the host country environment to fight the home country's memory battles and advance homeland political positions in relation to Japan and relevant international actors. In the present age of globalization, including the globalization of memory, where mobility and technology enable a high level of interconnectedness and exchange, much scholarly research remains one-directionally focused on how migrants and diasporas preserve memories of homeland culture, rather than how collective memory produced in the diaspora may influence and be creatively adopted by the origin country.

Consumers of Memory

Inspired by Kansteiner's (2002) hermeneutic triangle, the consumers or users of memory—one might note here the varying degrees of passivity or agency implied by the two terms—essentially refer to the audience in the context of this book, the public for whom memory markers are ostensibly installed. Users of memory are those with whom memories are shared through personal narration, media and performative traditions, here more specifically the monument and the activities surrounding it. They are those who venerate, visit or simply view the commemorative marker, but also those who casually pass by, surreptitiously ignore or consciously snub the monument and the memory it purports to preserve. It also includes those who more actively reject its intended meaning, perhaps organize protests against it; those who read the monument 'against the grain' and those who subversively transform its meaning to bolster alternative discourses and identity projects. Where the critical engagement with the monument and the development of alternative discourses and counter-memory takes on public dimensions, as illustrated in the case of Townsville, the distinction between memory consumers and memory makers begins to blur.

The vast majority of memory consumers never take on the role of memory makers outside the private realm of their family or profession, maintains Kansteiner (2002, p.193), yet it is equally important for scholars to acknowledge and study passive reception and silent voices. Agency and the exceptional occurrence inevitably draw more attention than passivity, silence and the ordinary. The media, both conventional and new social media, are likely to amplify the significance of singularity, that which is considered newsworthy—incidents of statue vandalism; a protest staged over a monument and a controversial demand for a new commemorative marker. Scholarly research interest similarly (and more easily) focuses on controversy than acquiescence and the uneventful. A comprehensive understanding of memory in society—and more specifically the role of public commemorative monuments—requires researchers to engage with reception processes in ways that do not lose sight of the mundane and the not-newsworthy. This includes the passive consumers of memory, such as the silent majority of passers-by who ignore statues and accept monuments as part of the urban environment, much like street furniture; people who have no opinion and communities that ostensibly do not care about remembering the past.

How viewers and the general public receive and interpret monuments and historical representations more generally is very difficult to establish, and even in-depth interviews and ethnographic participant observation, as conducted by Gensburger and Truc in Paris, can only provide a cursory glimpse. Beyond the immediate, short-term impact, longitudinal studies would be required to gauge the transformative effect (if any) of exposure to public memory markers and other representations of the past. While none of the contributors to this volume specifically explores the passive dimensions of monument reception, many mention the silent voices and the disinterested. McCarthy notes how the comfort women memorial in Palisades Park used to blend into the environment without drawing any attention, until the Japanese consulate contacted the city about removing it. The Columbus statue at the San Jose City Hall remained mostly unnoticed until a violent act of vandalism by a Native American activist drew public attention to it. Rudling mentions how the younger generation of Ukrainians in Canada is not particularly interested in the memory culture developed by their parents and grandparents. Having grown up in an era of open archives and greater awareness about the Holocaust, for these young Ukrainians, silence, distancing and ostensible disinterest may be easier options than taking an active stance against a controversial collective memory fostered in the name of national pride.

People with similar backgrounds are frequently thought to form homogenous interpretive communities, who share substantially related attitudes towards historical symbols, yet this can never be assumed (Kansteiner 2002, p.193). While some Italian-Americans fiercely defend Columbus statues and the contested legacy of the man, other members of the community are indifferent or support the removal of the disputed public monuments. For the early Italian immigrants, identification with

Columbus was a strategy of integration into the American mainstream. For their descendants, in a contemporary society with much popular support for a critical reassessment of Columbus, iconoclast attitudes towards his statues may once again affirm mainstream belonging and a rejection of ethnic particularism. In migratory settings, diasporic monuments are touchstones of divided identification, where friction occurs due to overlapping layers and scales of memory at stake in transcultural and transnational dynamics (Rothberg 2014a, p.139).

In unexpected and certainly under-researched ways, refugees in Paris share the host society's collective grief at the local level and participate in their memorialization processes by visiting the 'informal shrines' erected for the victims of terrorist attacks and taking part in commemorative gatherings and public events staged on anniversary dates. By expressing a direct identification with victims at the local level, they assert belonging at the level of the city, identifying themselves as residents of Paris, who grieve like fellow Parisians. Beyond the demonstrative unity and cross-culturally shared solidarity created through the ritualized processes of mourning and solemn occasions of remembering with public addresses by political officials, close observation reveals simmering tensions. Sometimes disputes manifest themselves between different groups of migrants and individuals who connect larger, cultural frames of reference and transnational memories to the local micro level.

This becomes particularly evident where migrants take part in performative action, such as the commemorative banner with inscribed handprints. The act of participation gives rise to communication, not always amicable, and overt conflict is shown to erupt over contested claims to home and belonging. The boundaries between memory makers and memory users become particularly blurred in the participatory, informal field of grassroots memorials, a non-official, populist-democratic genre of memorialization entirely relying on citizen contribution and spontaneous action. Gensburger and Truc show that refugees also place objects at the memorials and add their own messages and images; some take active part in and even initiate ritualized behaviour with French citizens. Connecting different scales and layers, refugees from Syria use the grassroots memorials to express nationalist sentiments and raise solidarity with their cause, as the trauma of the terror attacks resonates with the memory of their own trauma.

A century after the unveiling of the Syrian monument in Buenos Aires, Syrians are once again fleeing war and political turmoil in their homeland or migrating in search of economic opportunities. They now settle predominantly in Germany and other European countries, where despite many differences in historical and geo-political trajectories, they encounter similar stereotypes and discrimination. Huss references Germany's ambivalent *Willkommenskultur* and the widespread popular distinction between 'deserving refugees' and 'undeserving migrants', involving a hierarchy of victimhood. Once again—in different ways—commemorative markers feature as public objects upon which memories are pinned and through which belonging can be expressed.

As in Paris, Syrian and other refugees in Berlin use monuments to build their own identification with the city and a sense of belonging to the host nation, whilst simultaneously constructing a memory-based transnational bridge with their respective homelands and a transcultural one with members of the host nation. For the refugee tour guides in Berlin, consuming the host society's memory culture and appropriating well-known German monuments for their own purposes constitute an aspect of aspiring citizenship. As Huss mentions, some refugees are proud to be able to tell the Germans about their own monuments. The role of tour guide allows them to assert agency and places them in a position of narrative power, temporarily controlling a discourse of which they are more often passive subjects, whilst the tour participants, including German citizens, become consumers of memory. Vis-à-vis foreign tourists, the refugee guide, in adopting the cultural memories identified by the host nation as integral to national identity, assumes the role of semi-citizen, someone who almost belongs to the nation. By adding new, transnational dimensions, treating 'one memory as a prism for another' (Assmann 2014, p.549), sites of national memory in the capital Berlin are transfigured in multidirectional ways, suggesting the possibility of a redefined national identity in the context of migration.

It remains important to recall Connerton's (1989) caution against a reified thinking about memory, a focus on memory as property or product; his own preference for the term remembering emphasizes that personal and social memory does not exist outside the active process of recall. What counts about monuments then is how precisely they induce remembrance, how they are used by individuals and groups to induce, foster and transmit memory. An exploration of memory as embodied action in relation to the materiality of the commemorative artefact requires an investigative focus on agency, temporality and performativity.

In developing their tours, the refugees in Berlin walk around the city and interpret what they see—a subjective process based on prior knowledge, memory and experience. As some aspects of the city, the narratives attached to some monuments, begin to resonate with their own story, the refugees' selection of sites and crafting of narratives is also a material reflection of their process of remembering and the transnational/transcultural connections they draw. In the guided walking tours, memory work occurs through collective witnessing and testimonial exchange, but also many other dimensions of behaviour and bodily practices—gestures, ritualized action, photographing, observing—most importantly perhaps, walking, an activity that encourages internal processing, reflection and non-scripted types of sharing and caring with the refugee guide and fellow participants.

Collectively reflecting while walking, the haptic experience of placing feet on a treacherous path, is also central to remembering in the annual re-enactment of Walter Benjamin's crossing of the Pyrenees in Gómez' chapter. Both chapters, in different ways, moreover involve 'memory-mixing', connecting the contemporary violence exerted by the external borders of 'Fortress Europe', the traumatic memories of refugees from across the Mediterranean, to the institutionalized memory of the Holocaust and Fascism's tragedy of forced exile epitomized by the fate of Walter Benjamin. The refugee tour guides in Berlin employ the ritual of testifying and witnessing, a powerful vehicle for protesting human rights violations in the post-Holocaust era, to map refugee survivor memories onto the canonical memory narratives of the German state, thereby undermining the state's exclusive national identity construct. The Benjamin memorial in Portbou allows a country like Spain that has not yet come to terms with its own authoritarian past to participate in the construction of a shared, denationalized European memory, whilst closing ranks against migrants who do not accept the centrality and uniqueness of the Holocaust.

European efforts at institutionalizing a mnemonic culture around the Holocaust, a past that is completed, isolate the Holocaust from contemporary developments and create a European memory community from which others are excluded—geopolitically supported by the dissolving of internal, but fortifying and securitizing of external borders. However, contrary to the intentions of the German and Spanish authorities who sponsored the Benjamin memorial and signposted various sites of 'democratic memory' around Portbou, the consumers of memory produce their own narratives. During the re-enactment walks, once the participant's body is attuned to the group's pace, conversation begins to flow, private and family memories are shared and connections are drawn between the victims of the Holocaust, the Republican exiles and the predicament of contemporary refugees attempting to enter Europe.

So far, the inclusion of current refuges in the pantheon of 'the nameless' is only a recent development, notes Gómez, and mostly treated as an appendix. However, Rothberg (2014b, p.654) suggests that in certain contexts, the dialogic production of multidirectional memory can become entrenched and in fact take on normative dimensions, that is, lead to new visions of solidarity and coexistence. This is clearly the goal of memory activists like the refugee tour guides in Berlin, but to some extent, these guides preach to the converted. Those who sign up for such tours are likely to be receptive consumers of alternative memories, who already have some level of awareness, empathy and tolerance. Like the Syrian monument in Buenos Aires, the tours can even perpetuate divisions between locals and migrants and affirm stereotypes. Similarly in Portbou, explains Gómez, not every visitor perceives the ethical demands posed by the memory of Benjamin; there is clearly a difference between individual empathy and collective solidarity.

Such ethical demands, the moral obligation to remember and the individual willingness to accept 'the burden of memory' are invoked through reference to James Young's (1992, 1994) theorization of the counter-monument, which—although developed in a very specific historical and socio-political context of Holocaust remembrance in Germany—remains inspirational for memory scholars working in different empirical settings. Huss contextualizes the refugee tours in Berlin as 'embodied counter-monument', as they attempt to replace the indexing impulse of conventional commemorative markers 'with ever-changing, ever-vanishing, and interactive gestures that question the very premise of a memorial'. Likewise, Auchter's chapter on virtual and augmented reality memorials for migrant victims at the US-Mexican border focuses on absence, disappearance and the requirement of active viewer engagement in performing the work of memory.

Much like the haunting desolation of Portbou, the vast, forbidding space of the Mexican desert landscape along the US border works as an ecology of memory. In the emotional setting of this uninhabited geographical terrain, remembering the dead can occur through affective engagement with the landscape and reflection on silence, absence and the violent nature of borders. Using innovative technology of the virtual and augmented, the two American artists' installations discussed by Auchter intend to draw attention to the experiences, the lives and deaths of migrants attempting to cross the border, but do not aim to tell the migrants' story on their behalf. Rather they 'disrupt the very idea that we can adequately represent migrant deaths in narrative form' and challenge the notion of an unambiguous, stable collective memory represented through monuments and memorials. The installations resemble the counter-monument by refusing all elements of monumentality and permanence, in fact dissolving the very material reality of the monument. They disavow the consumption of a single/simple commemorative metanarrative, as meaning remains obscure and reliant on active physical organization, performativity and mental engagement that includes accepting the onus of bearing memory.

In the current age of advanced digital information and communication technology, much scholarly attention has been drawn to 'global memory' shared via mass media and the internet (Assmann and Conrad 2010); transnationally and transculturally accessible online memorialization processes (Foot et al. 2005); and a networked and connective digital memory that begins to problematize and dissolve collective memory as we know it (Hoskins 2009, 2018). The projects discussed by Auchter, on the contrary, although accessible in some form on the internet, remain tied to specific physical localities and experiencing them requires mobility; neither are they interactive, participatory and accreting—digital versions of informal grassroots memorials. Rather, by technologically engaging with absence, space and time, they aim to illuminate the existence of a reality beyond what is normally seen; in the process, as in Portbou, they invoke the memory of the invisible and the nameless.

Unlike conventional commemorative markers designed to be seen by a large urban public and online memorials that aim to reach a multitude in cyberspace, the artists' installations are not primarily geared at extending the community of mourners or functioning as a larger mechanism of social remembrance. Yet they offer, as Auchter puts it, 'a politics beyond empathy that can be transformative'. To a greater extent than casual tour participants in Berlin, these artistic projects appeal to an educated, elitist or privileged audience; experiencing them requires preparation, purposive action and an implied *a priori* commitment and empathy. Among those opting to consume these media of memory, the experience can deepen compassion, transform passive empathy into active commitment and turn some users into makers of memory in a different context.

CONCLUSION

Future generations might accept monuments, memorials and commemorative rituals as the genuine expression of a past society's historical consciousness, even if such symbols may now be seen as irrelevant or subject to criticism. The chapters in this book illustrate that the collective memory visualized in public monuments does not flow organically from a society's sense of identity and purpose. Rather, monuments are the result of very deliberate campaigns, driven by committed individuals and small groups, who manage to fight their memory battles and negotiate their agendas in a socio-political environment of uneven power relations at the macro and micro levels. In the context of migration, where migrants, refugees, diasporic communities and ethnic minorities feature as both producers and consumers of memory, such relations of power are less predictable than might be expected. Defying neat categorizations of victims and perpetrators, mainstream and marginalized, sometimes revealing shifting layers of the subaltern, the diaspora environment produces memory through the complex interweaving of transnational and transcultural influences in a process of dialogue and contestation.

Given collective memory's reliance on mediation, it is not only the discursive interaction between groups of human actors that engenders potentially novel narratives and memory dynamics, but their strategic use of specific memory practices and media, in this case the monument. Monuments, memorials and statues draw their supposed persuasive power from adherence to respected traditions and time-honoured visual formulae, while simultaneously exploring the possibilities afforded by innovative technological developments and changing aesthetic trends, including, especially in the context of migration, transnational and transcultural influences and sources of inspiration. Straddling these somewhat paradoxical dynamics, the visual articulation of memory through monuments is the result of complex intra- and intergroup negotiations, which touch on the very core of migrant and host society identities.

If the diasporic environment is hence a dynamic space, where transcultural perspectives are added to cultural memory and mono-cultural discourses in host societies, future research can explore under what circumstances a new transcultural memory may gain prominence and even become normative, potentially effecting transformative processes in socio-cultural and geo-political terms. Conversely, more research is needed on how the state and the societal mainstream in host countries defend themselves against migrant-initiated challenges of hegemonic narratives; how borders are affirmed rather than dissolved and what strategies are pursued in a quest to uphold accustomed and state-endorsed memories of home and homeland (Rothberg 2014a; Assmann 2014). While fully acknowledging its limitations—from the restricted range of disciplinary perspectives, to the relatively small scope of the case studies, to confined geographical and socio-cultural diversity—the research featured in this book opens up a previously neglected space of investigation and contributes to our understanding of collective memory in the context of transnational and transcultural dynamics.

References

Assmann, A. (2014). Transnational Memories. *European Review, 22*(4), 546–556.
Assmann, A., & Conrad, S. (Eds.). (2010). *Memory in a Global Age. Discourses, Practices and Trajectories.* New York, et al.: Palgrave Macmillan.
Connerton, P. (1989). *How Societies Remember.* Cambridge, et al.: Cambridge University Press.
Foot, K., Warnick, B., & Schneider, S. M. (2005). Web-Based Memorializing after September 11: Toward a Conceptual Framework. *Journal of Computer-Mediated Communication, 11*(1), 72–96.
Gutman, Y. (2017). *Memory Activism: Reimagining the Past for the Future in Israel-Palestine.* Nashville: Vanderbilt University Press.
Hirsch, M. (2001). Surviving Images: Holocaust Photographs and the Work of Postmemory. *The Yale Journal of Criticism, 14*(1), 5–37.
Hoskins, A. (2009). Digital Network Memory. In A. Erll & A. Rigney (Eds.), *Mediation, Remediation and the Dynamics of Cultural Memory* (pp. 91–108). Berlin: de Gruyter.
Hoskins, A. (Ed.). (2018). *Digital Memory Studies: Media Pasts in Transition.* London/New York: Routledge.
Kansteiner, W. (2002). Finding Meaning in Memory: A Methodological Critique of Collective Memory Studies. *History and Theory, 41*(2), 179–197.
Landsberg, A. (2004). *Prosthetic Memory. The Transformation of American Remembrance in the Age of Mass Culture.* New York: Columbia University Press.
Nora, P. (2002). The Reasons for the Current Upsurge in Memory. *Transit – Europäische Revue, 22*(Spring), 1–8. Available at http://www.eurozine.com/pdf/2002-04-19-nora-en.pdf.
Rothberg, M. (2009). *Multidirectional Memory: Remembering the Holocaust in the Age of Decolonization.* Stanford: Stanford University Press.

Rothberg, M. (2014a). Multidirectional Memory in Migratory Settings: The Case of Post-Holocaust Germany. In C. De Cesari & A. Rigney (Eds.), *Transnational Memory. Circulation, Articulation, Scales* (pp. 123–145). Berlin/Boston: De Gruyter.

Rothberg, M. (2014b). Locating Transnational Memory. *European Review, 22*(4), 652–656.

Taussig, M. (1999). *Defacement, Public Secrecy and the Labor of the Negative*. Stanford: Stanford University Press.

Winter, J. (2001). The Memory Boom in Contemporary Historical Studies. *Raritan, 21*(1), 52.

Young, J. E. (1992). The Counter-Monument: Memory Against Itself in Germany Today. *Critical Inquiry, 18*(2), 267–296.

Young, J. E. (1994). *The Texture of Memory: Holocaust Memorials and Meaning*. New Haven: Yale University Press.

Index[1]

A

Absence, 23, 259, 270–275, 277, 280, 283, 285, 287, 296–298, 300, 303, 311, 312

Activist, 11, 22, 73, 74, 84, 85, 87, 97, 100, 103, 104, 117, 132, 141, 142, 144, 173, 178, 194, 300, 303, 305, 307, 311

Aesthetic, 4, 22, 46, 47, 51, 54, 99, 210, 249, 256, 275, 296, 297, 313

Agent, 1, 18, 160, 168, 208, 209, 256

Alienation, 16, 166

Amnesia, 11, 77, 289

Ancestors, 2, 9, 67, 69, 79, 159, 173, 293

Ancestry, 16, 99, 120, 133, 163, 166, 172, 173, 176, 178, 180

Anniversary, 8–10, 31, 34, 36, 75, 97, 114, 167, 171, 180, 222, 233, 234, 251, 252, 303, 308

Archive, 4, 11, 102, 120, 140, 193, 194, 222–224, 229, 230, 232, 274, 277, 307

Artefact, 4, 5, 62, 232, 294–298, 309

Asylum, 2, 8, 190n1, 286

Attack, 15, 19, 20, 74, 76, 80n21, 128, 131, 220–224, 226, 228–234, 228n7, 230n9, 232n10, 233n11, 236, 236n15, 238, 297, 301, 308

Audience, 1, 6, 15–17, 129, 173, 175, 190, 199, 233, 234, 250, 278, 306, 312

Augmented reality, 23, 267–289, 311

Aura, 249, 303

B

Belonging, 2, 3, 8, 10–12, 20, 40, 128, 135, 138, 152, 204, 210, 228, 231, 237, 296, 302, 308, 309

---

[1] Note: Page numbers followed by 'n' refer to notes.

Bigotry, 69, 116, 302
Border, 3, 7, 21–23, 40, 105, 158,
  181, 190n1, 193, 195, 196,
  199n5, 206, 207, 243–261,
  267–289, 310–312, 314
Bronze, 9, 19, 33, 46–48, 51, 68, 83,
  84, 87, 88, 98–99, 103, 145,
  175, 179–181, 202
Bust, 4, 55, 76, 83n23, 102

C

Celebration, 36, 42, 56, 62, 63, 70,
  72, 74, 75, 77, 80, 106, 114,
  147, 168, 171, 173–175, 179,
  230, 300, 302
Cemetery, 21, 36, 103–108, 115, 119,
  170, 249, 252, 303
Centenary, 9, 10, 15, 169, 173–175
Ceremony, 148, 170, 178, 179, 232,
  234, 247, 253, 254
Citizen, 12, 22, 46, 49, 79, 84n24,
  120, 133–135, 151, 169, 204,
  208, 226, 259, 260, 278, 308
Citizenship, 2, 12, 17, 20, 69, 70,
  100n3, 133, 166, 179, 248, 259,
  278, 309
Classification, 2
Commemoration, 6, 8, 11, 12, 14, 17,
  19, 22, 23, 36, 51, 53, 54, 56,
  63, 64, 67, 71, 74, 76, 79, 106,
  114, 129n2, 144, 167, 169,
  172–174, 180, 193, 194, 205,
  207, 221, 222, 231–239, 245,
  260, 269, 272, 282, 289
Commemorative
  ceremony, 234
  marker, 1, 5, 12, 17–19, 23, 24,
    293, 294, 297, 300, 304, 306,
    307, 309, 311, 312
  monument, 3, 4, 7, 17, 34, 44, 192,
    221, 238, 295, 307

ritual, 303, 313
site, 6, 87
Consensus, 11, 14, 132n8, 222, 233
Contestation, 3, 8, 15, 127–152, 158,
  178, 294, 300, 303, 313
Cosmopolitan, 44, 46, 51, 71, 221,
  224, 228, 231, 260
Counter-monument, 22, 192,
  199–202, 249, 250, 268,
  270–276, 281, 285–289,
  311, 312
Culture, 3–7, 11, 13, 14, 20, 22, 45,
  53, 64, 67, 71, 80, 83, 84, 97,
  99, 103, 108, 109, 115, 119,
  128, 132, 138, 150, 151, 165,
  191, 195, 199–202, 204, 210,
  226, 251, 260, 295, 297, 299,
  302, 303, 305–307, 309, 310

D

Dead, 12, 22, 23, 45, 117, 175, 219,
  228n7, 230, 233, 234, 248, 269,
  278, 282, 285, 303, 311
Death, 13, 19, 21, 23, 35, 106, 110,
  113, 167, 244, 246, 251,
  253, 260, 267–289, 293,
  311, 312
Design, 4, 22, 39, 63, 84, 98, 99,
  145, 147, 191, 209, 256, 299
Diaspora, 1–3, 7–9, 13, 14, 22, 23,
  35–37, 50, 52, 56, 71, 97,
  100n3, 106, 109–112, 118, 127,
  129–132, 135–136, 144, 152,
  179, 181, 192, 257, 293,
  295–297, 299–301,
  303–306, 313
Digital, 23, 180, 276, 277, 281, 284,
  289, 297, 312
Discrimination, 39, 50, 67, 69, 132,
  133, 168, 234, 238, 301, 309
Displaced, 1, 2, 8, 190n1

Displacement, 1, 3, 7, 16, 18, 19, 24, 96, 167, 168, 192, 193, 195, 255, 261, 293–295
Dispute, 10, 11, 81, 148–151, 235, 236, 308

E
Elite, 2, 15, 37, 44, 47, 50, 69, 71, 101, 120, 157, 158, 272, 300
Émigré, 41, 96–97n1, 97, 101, 106, 115, 251
Emotion, 67, 73, 81, 203
Empathy, 14, 20, 206, 207, 258–260, 278, 279, 283, 289, 296, 311, 312
Ephemeral, 4, 272, 273, 275, 276, 282, 286, 287, 293
Ethic, 220n1, 243–261
Ethnic, 2, 3, 5, 8, 10, 15, 16, 42, 51, 61–64, 69, 71–73, 73n11, 83, 86, 99–101, 103, 109–110, 117, 131, 134–136, 139, 152, 190, 196n4, 234, 293, 298, 299, 301–303, 308, 313
Exclusive/exclusion, 6, 10, 12, 172, 178, 193, 204, 208, 221, 222, 224, 232–239, 250, 271, 287, 298, 302, 310
Exile, 105, 244, 245, 247, 249, 251, 254, 257, 260, 310, 311
Expatriate, 2

F
Fascism, 21, 77, 83, 112–114, 244, 254, 259, 260, 270–273, 280, 310
Fatality, 21, 22, 269
Foreigner, 40, 57, 72, 74, 208, 223, 225, 228, 229n8
Forgetting, 7, 204, 205, 276, 296

G
Gender, 3, 50, 208
Generation, 2, 8–10, 12, 16, 18, 39, 68, 97, 101, 107, 116, 127, 128, 134, 157, 159, 169, 180, 296, 299, 301, 303, 304, 307, 313
Genocide, 14, 17, 42, 67, 73, 87, 99, 100n3, 110, 116, 129, 137, 147, 148, 200, 200n6, 249
Globalization, 5, 6, 18, 144, 306
Government, 11, 13, 14, 39, 42, 43, 50, 51, 55, 69, 72, 75, 78n18, 81, 86, 95, 100, 101, 109–112, 114, 116, 118–120, 129, 130, 132–135, 137, 138, 144, 147, 149, 150, 157, 158, 163, 167, 180, 203, 206, 233, 234, 251, 253, 256, 283, 300–303, 305
Grassroots, 11, 147, 197, 219–239, 293, 300, 304, 308, 312
Grassroots memorial, 19, 20, 219–239, 293, 308, 312
Grief, 19, 20, 221, 235, 238, 286, 308

H
Hegemony, 150
Heritage, 3, 4, 15, 17, 18, 35, 35n3, 62, 64, 71, 79, 88, 100, 101, 190, 192, 197–200, 207, 208, 232, 243
Historical consciousness, 9, 250, 313
History, 2, 4, 8, 13, 43, 44, 53, 54, 62, 63n2, 64–68, 73, 74, 96, 99, 110–112, 115, 127, 129, 134–136, 138, 150, 158, 163–168, 189, 194, 198, 199, 220, 226, 235, 243–245, 248, 298, 302
Holocaust, 14, 20, 21, 95, 96, 99, 102, 103, 107, 110, 111, 116,

118, 119, 140, 199, 204, 205, 245, 253, 260, 274–276, 281, 294, 300, 304, 307, 310, 311
Holodomor, 14, 99, 100, 100n3, 110, 129, 300, 301
Homeland, 9, 13, 16, 17, 34, 41, 48, 52, 57, 99, 120, 131, 132, 135, 136, 138, 152, 159, 165, 167, 168, 180, 181, 193, 246, 294–296, 305, 306, 308, 309, 314
Host
 country, 1–3, 8, 10, 12, 13, 54, 128, 136, 301, 306
 society, 2, 3, 7–12, 14, 15, 19–23, 53, 128, 129, 131, 131n7, 135–138, 135n10, 142–144, 150–152, 193, 294, 296, 299, 300, 302, 303, 308, 309, 313
Human rights, 21, 116, 130, 137, 139, 142, 144, 147, 150, 205, 253, 260, 304, 310

I

Icon, 5, 7, 17, 47, 68, 75, 165, 288
Iconoclasm, 297
Iconography, 39, 46, 47, 50, 53, 296
Identity
 cultural identity, 2, 3, 9, 10, 193, 253
 discourse, 3
 ethnic identity, 79, 98, 302
 identity practice, 3
 identity project, 3, 8, 12, 296, 298, 299, 306
 identity statement, 3
 national identity, 9–13, 15, 17, 46, 70, 71, 128, 283, 293, 304–306, 309, 310
Ideology, 10, 13, 43, 62, 68, 97n1, 302
Image/imagery, 4, 45–50, 53, 54, 69, 74, 83, 87, 104, 115, 119, 161, 165, 166, 174, 181, 207–209, 280, 282–284, 296, 308
Imaginary, 12, 68, 244, 302
Imagined community, 20, 220
Immigrant, 1, 2, 5, 8–10, 12–14, 17, 18, 31–57, 65–73, 69n5, 69n7, 70n8, 75, 77, 78, 79n19, 83, 88, 103, 107, 108, 115, 127, 128, 131, 132, 134–136, 152, 161, 163, 166, 168, 180, 200, 202, 209, 268, 285, 296–302, 304, 307
Inauguration, 8, 33–39, 44, 53, 54, 56, 245, 254
Inclusive/inclusion, 20, 50, 71, 178, 193, 221, 222, 224, 225, 228, 238, 257, 302, 311
Indigenous, 12, 15, 16, 43, 62, 68, 73–75, 74n13, 79, 158, 158n1, 160, 161, 163–165, 168, 169, 171–175, 178–181, 200n6, 293, 298, 302, 305
Informal shrine, 308
Information technology, 5, 312
Injustice, 110, 130, 141, 162, 166, 179, 205, 210, 271, 301, 305
Inscription, 4, 9, 33, 48, 84, 106, 143, 170, 172, 177, 180, 236, 244, 247, 255, 259, 271, 297
Installation, 11, 19, 82, 87, 174, 181, 284, 285, 287, 311, 312
Intangible, 3, 4
Intergroup, 128, 135, 135n10, 313
Internet, 270, 283, 312
Intragroup, 2, 4, 128, 131, 132n8, 135

J

Justice, 14, 130n6, 131, 132n8, 133, 137, 144, 146, 147, 181, 259, 272, 304, 305

L

Landscape, 1, 4, 12, 15, 18, 19, 23, 55, 81, 87, 112, 158, 159, 165, 169, 170, 177–179, 191, 193, 194, 197, 199, 203–205, 209, 221, 244, 245, 247, 250, 253, 256, 257, 259, 260, 267, 268, 271, 275, 278–282, 285–288, 298, 305, 311

Legacy, 10, 62, 74, 80, 87, 112–114, 116, 117, 119, 120, 167, 175, 247, 257, 298, 302, 307

Location, 4, 12, 16, 22, 33n1, 34, 48, 55, 86, 87, 142, 147, 152, 172, 178, 180, 189, 198, 206, 231, 238, 243, 256, 268, 269, 279–281, 283, 294, 297

M

Marginalization, 12, 80, 128

Material, 4, 17, 24, 46, 51, 54, 57, 64, 67, 75, 84, 86, 88, 98, 191, 192, 198, 204, 222–224, 229, 234, 245, 254–257, 260, 270, 276, 297–299, 305, 310, 312

Materiality, 209, 246, 272, 309

Media, 3, 5, 8, 15, 18, 19, 22, 23, 33, 51, 54, 70n8, 112, 114, 115, 117–120, 144, 166, 201, 230, 268, 270, 276, 278, 281, 287–289, 295, 297, 304, 306, 312, 313

Memorial, 1, 4, 19, 20, 31–57, 64, 69, 72, 87–88, 95, 98, 103–104, 127–152, 158, 159, 165, 169, 170, 179–180, 189–191, 219–239, 244, 245, 247, 267–289, 293–295, 298, 299, 301

Memory/memories
agents of memory, 1
autobiographical memory, 18
bodily memory, 194, 198
burden of memory, 23, 271, 274, 276, 280, 288, 289, 311
carriers of memory, 18
circulation of memory, 5, 238
collective memory, 6, 7, 11, 14, 18, 39, 52–54, 56, 57, 66, 97, 128, 128n1, 129, 135–136, 138, 158, 165, 166, 172, 179, 181, 191–195, 204, 205, 222, 293–295, 300, 302, 306, 312–314
community memory, 9
consumers of memory, 8, 306–313
counter memory, 15, 73, 157, 158, 172, 174, 180, 181, 270–275, 305, 306
cultural memory, 3, 5, 7, 11, 19, 53, 244, 253, 254, 260, 304, 309, 313
digital memory, 270, 276, 281, 312
dynamics of memory, 3
ecology of memory, 245, 255, 311
episodic memory, 18
ethno-nationalist memory, 6
European memory, 244, 253, 258, 259, 310
exclusive memory, 6, 221
family memory, 2, 3, 129, 257, 310
globalization of memory, 6, 18, 306
global memory, 7, 312
group memory, 128, 130, 139
guardians of memory, 230
life memory, 193

Memory/memories (*cont.*)
  media of memory, 295, 312
  memory activism, 19, 191, 192, 205, 210, 299
  memory agent, 18, 168, 208, 209
  memory boom, 254, 304
  memory community, 6, 158, 269, 310
  memory consumer, 295
  memory culture, 13, 14, 20, 22, 99, 108, 109, 115, 119, 191, 295, 297, 299, 303, 305, 307, 309
  memory discourse, 8, 173, 199, 204, 299
  memory entrepreneur, 239
  memory formation, 7
  memory group, 193
  memory landscape, 1, 12, 18, 221
  memory lens, 24
  memory maker, 295, 299, 300, 304, 306, 308
  memory marker, 1, 3, 8, 9, 18, 19, 170, 234, 274, 306, 307
  memory media, 295, 312
  memory mixing, 191, 202, 204, 205, 310
  memory pilgrim, 253
  memory policy, 109
  memory politics, 136, 300, 303
  memory practice, 6, 313
  memory project, 13, 302
  memory scape, 6
  memory scholar, 23, 257, 311
  memory site, 20, 172
  memory studies, 3, 5, 8, 23, 131, 158, 193, 228, 238, 294, 295, 299
  memory template, 14
  memory tradition, 181, 294, 304
  memory user, 295, 308
  memory work, 66, 81, 131, 206, 299, 310
  multidirectional memory, 5, 158, 165, 180, 181, 205, 293, 294, 303, 311
  national memory, 6, 11, 191, 193, 309
  negotiation of memory, 9, 297
  networked memory, 312
  objects of memory, 3
  official memory, 157, 159, 165, 168–174, 178, 181, 202, 209
  oral memory, 164, 180
  personal memory, 255
  popular memory, 16
  postmemory, 204, 301
  production of memory, 205–208, 299, 303
  public memory, 1, 3, 4, 8, 9, 11–16, 19, 23, 31–57, 76, 128–130, 132, 145, 157–159, 178, 180, 181, 198, 208, 210, 222, 288, 297–307
  realms of memory, 64
  site-bound memory, 5
  sites of memory, 11, 19, 64–67, 159, 192, 270, 301
  transcultural memory, 5, 7, 10, 11, 13–17, 20, 53, 189–210, 294, 296–297, 313
  transnational memory, 6, 7, 12, 165, 191, 231, 238, 254, 296, 297, 305, 308
  traumatic memory, 14, 18, 192, 204, 205, 209, 293, 305, 310
  travelling memory, 159, 228, 238
  urban memory, 15, 179
  vehicles of memory, 4
Message, 4, 11, 20, 50, 75, 95, 119, 129, 197, 201, 210, 223–231, 234, 236, 308

Migrant
  economic migrant, 2
  elite migrant, 2
  illegal migrant, 221
  irregular migrant, 19, 21, 22
  migrant community, 1, 9, 137, 293, 298
  migrant group, 3, 12, 15, 131
  non-migrant, 3
  undocumented migrant, 2, 8, 20, 220, 269, 274, 279–280, 287
Migration
  forced migration, 137
  labour migration, 161
  migration heritage, 3
  mixed migration, 2
  pre-migration, 3, 18
  voluntary migration, 190n1
Minority, 1–3, 8, 11, 12, 15, 16, 42, 56, 67, 72, 128, 131, 157, 158, 161, 165, 171, 172, 180, 181, 200, 226, 261, 293, 298, 299, 301, 303, 313
Mnemonic, 5, 11, 15, 158, 181, 191, 194, 198, 207, 210, 256, 259, 260, 297, 300, 305, 310
Mnemoscape, 16
Mobile, 2, 22, 152, 158, 174, 194, 268, 275, 282, 283
Mobility, 2, 3, 5, 41, 53, 56, 152, 158, 194, 195, 198, 207, 209, 260, 287, 293, 294, 306, 312
Monument, 1–24, 31–57, 61–88, 95–120, 128, 140, 146, 147, 165, 168–171, 189–210, 221, 230, 232–239, 249–252, 268, 270, 289, 293–298
Mourning, 22, 23, 221, 234, 249, 308
Movement, 3, 6, 7, 20, 21, 35, 45, 54, 66, 70, 72–74, 100, 105, 130, 130n6, 131, 133, 137, 140–142, 145, 147, 151, 152, 180, 189, 192, 194, 195, 208, 209, 268, 286, 287
Multiculturalism, 12, 13, 96, 99–102, 109, 110, 119, 120, 165, 200n7, 302
Multidirectionality, 165, 178, 179, 260
Museum, 4, 11, 16, 19, 44, 51, 79, 79n20, 86, 110, 111, 150, 198, 200, 201, 204, 207, 221, 222, 233, 238, 244, 275, 276, 281, 284
Myth, 4, 12, 63, 68, 74, 75, 78, 158, 166, 248, 305
Mythology, 167–169, 305

N
Narrative, 4, 5, 9–16, 18, 20, 43, 53, 63–65, 67, 68, 71, 73, 74, 77, 127–129, 131, 135, 136, 141, 142, 145, 147, 150, 152, 157, 160, 165–169, 172, 173, 191, 194, 204, 205, 208, 225, 228, 244, 247, 248, 255, 257, 268, 272, 278, 285, 286, 288, 289, 299–301, 303–305, 309, 310, 312–314
Nation, 1, 3, 5–8, 10–13, 17, 31, 33, 36, 37, 39, 42–44, 46, 52–57, 63n2, 68, 71, 98, 104, 127–129, 134, 173, 192, 195, 205, 224, 294, 296, 305, 309
Nationalism, 13, 14, 37, 43, 44, 71, 76, 95–120, 300, 305
Neoliberalism, 5, 174
Network, 5, 12, 34, 41, 42, 56, 97, 136, 197, 254, 283, 300
Nostalgia/nostalgic, 3, 255

O

Online, 4, 23, 75, 85, 113, 223, 276, 312
Origin, 2, 6–8, 16, 18, 35n3, 40, 66, 77, 78, 96, 135, 152, 164, 166, 170, 172, 174, 223, 225, 237, 238, 246–249, 278, 282, 286, 296, 300, 301, 306
Other, 1–6, 11, 12, 15–19, 21, 34–36, 38, 45, 48, 51, 55, 62, 63, 68–70, 73, 96, 105, 105n8, 129, 132, 134, 135n10, 137, 138, 140, 141, 144, 157, 164, 166–168, 172, 175, 178, 191–194, 197–201, 204, 219, 220, 222, 223, 227, 228, 230, 243–245, 248, 251, 252, 254, 255, 268, 270, 272, 275, 278–280, 293, 295, 296, 300, 303, 305, 307, 309, 310

P

Patron/patronage, 8, 31–57
Performance, 3, 4, 97, 102, 168, 194, 204, 205, 208, 210, 257, 303
Performativity, 4, 9, 17, 53, 54, 56, 194, 200, 209, 210, 272, 299, 304, 306, 308, 309, 312
Perpetrator, 103, 110, 118, 128, 129, 221, 226, 273, 300, 301, 313
Place of origin, 3, 18
Plaque, 4, 36, 51, 52, 103, 143, 145, 149, 171, 222, 233–235, 249, 254, 270, 271
Political, 5, 7, 8, 11–14, 16–18, 22, 31, 33, 35, 37, 39, 41, 42, 45, 47, 54, 56, 63, 69, 71–73, 77, 78, 81, 83, 87, 95–97, 97n1, 99, 100, 103, 104, 106, 110–115, 119, 120, 127–152, 178, 190n1, 197, 202, 204, 205, 208–210, 228n7, 232, 233, 245, 248, 250, 251, 268, 269, 271–274, 277, 278, 282, 283, 287–289, 294, 300, 302, 303, 306, 308
Postcolonial, 165, 200
Power, 1, 3, 11, 13, 14, 16, 39, 44, 45, 72, 73, 81, 109, 128–131, 129n3, 135, 136, 159, 161, 163, 165, 167, 168, 179, 206, 207, 259, 268, 282, 285, 287, 294, 296, 299, 302, 305, 309, 313
Protest, 4, 16, 62, 73, 74, 78, 81, 85, 111, 145, 148, 175, 192, 194, 205, 208, 210, 236n15, 298, 303, 306

R

Race, 12, 38, 43, 44, 57, 69n5, 98, 160, 161, 168, 169, 208, 302
Racism, 45, 67, 73n11, 75, 87, 116, 163, 174, 238
Recall, 9, 53, 255, 270, 276, 309
Reception, 3, 4, 16, 17, 33, 52, 54, 158, 250, 298, 306, 307
Recollection, 3, 7, 67, 128, 166, 210, 259, 276
Re-enactment, 21, 97, 167, 171, 256–260, 310
Refugee, 1–3, 6–8, 11, 12, 15, 16, 18–23, 96, 97, 189–210, 226, 243–261, 268, 286, 299, 304, 308–311, 313
Religion/religious, 4, 47, 48, 68, 189
Remembrance, 3, 7, 9, 11, 13, 23, 181, 191, 193, 204, 234, 238, 249, 255, 268, 289, 293, 294, 299, 304, 309, 311, 312
Rememoration, 64–68, 74, 78, 86, 88
Removal, 62, 63, 80, 81, 116, 301, 307
Replica, 70, 83, 145, 147, 297

Residence, 2, 19, 209
Resident, 8, 16, 20, 22, 33–35, 39, 46, 52, 75, 147, 149, 158, 159, 169, 171, 173, 175, 177, 179, 196, 220, 244, 254, 260, 273, 308
Ritual, 4, 9, 11, 17, 21, 53, 97, 98, 106, 108, 194, 205, 233, 303, 310, 313
Rootedness, 17, 83
Roots, 2, 38, 42, 132, 141, 159

S

Scale, 4, 7, 33, 51, 55, 68, 111, 181, 194, 195, 198, 234, 238, 294, 297, 301, 308
Sculpture, 4, 8, 9, 31, 33, 34, 36, 39, 44, 46, 48, 50, 51, 57, 86n25, 171, 179, 180, 297
Securitization, 277
Self-identification, 2, 296
Settler, 8, 12, 13, 68, 73n11, 128, 158, 166, 171, 174, 180, 181, 296, 302, 305
Shape, 4, 81, 83, 108, 171, 225, 230, 268, 284
Signifier, 4, 12, 48, 250, 295, 296
Size, 38, 84, 189
Slavery, 131, 141, 147, 162, 164–167, 172–174, 178, 304, 305
Social media, 5, 19, 118, 119, 230, 297, 304, 306
Solidarity, 13, 20, 74, 195, 210, 223–225, 227, 231, 250, 258, 259, 283, 308, 311
Spontaneous shrine, 19–21, 220
Stakeholder, 4, 15
Statue, 4, 10, 15, 16, 19, 31, 35–37, 39, 46, 51, 53, 55, 55n22, 61–64, 66–68, 70, 72–74, 72n9, 73n12, 76, 77, 77n16, 79–87, 86n25, 139, 145, 147, 157–181, 230, 235, 236, 297, 298, 300–305, 307, 308, 313
Stele, 4
Stereotype, 9, 10, 52, 98, 175, 201, 296, 302, 309, 311
Stranger, 267, 268
Struggle, 52, 74, 103–106, 127, 193, 201, 207, 209, 210, 247, 258
Subaltern, 16, 66, 201, 296, 301, 302, 305, 313
Subjectivity, 7, 208, 210, 295
Symbol, 4, 5, 10, 17, 19, 43, 46, 47, 66, 68, 71, 73, 76, 77, 80, 83, 86, 98, 106, 115, 116, 159, 174, 181, 225, 295–302, 307, 313

T

Tangible, 1, 3, 22, 54, 274, 295
Temporality, 245, 309
Terror, 221, 231, 232n10
Testimony, 158, 192, 203–205, 207, 220, 304
Tour, 17–19, 189–210, 304, 309–312
Tour guide, 189, 191, 191n2, 192, 195, 197–202, 204, 206–210, 309–311
Tourism, 174, 195, 225, 246, 251, 252
Tourist, 16, 20, 190, 207, 208, 223, 225, 231, 243, 249, 309
Tradition, 9, 35, 36, 38, 46, 52, 78, 181, 249, 282, 286, 294–296, 299, 300, 304, 306, 313
Transcultural, 1, 5–7, 9–20, 23, 46, 52, 53, 181, 189–210, 293–297, 302, 308–310, 313, 314
Transfer, 3, 5, 70, 165, 167
Transformation, 3, 6, 7, 171
Transnational, 1–3, 5–7, 9, 11–14, 16, 18–20, 22, 23, 32, 36, 38,

46–54, 56, 57, 152, 181, 191, 194, 204, 228, 231, 238, 239, 254, 293, 294, 296, 297, 300, 305, 308–310, 313, 314
Trauma, 18, 19, 67, 80, 128, 129, 137, 166, 167, 192, 194, 202–206, 244, 269, 272, 293, 301, 304, 305, 308
Tribute, 12, 34, 110, 219, 222, 230, 231, 249
Tweet, 96, 114, 115, 118, 297
Twitter, 76, 95, 114–115

V

Vandalism, 73, 81, 85, 106, 306, 307
Victim, 3, 13, 17, 19, 20, 22, 23, 87, 106, 110, 128, 129, 130n6, 143, 146, 148, 200, 204, 208, 219, 221, 223, 225, 228, 230–233, 238, 244, 245, 251, 257, 273, 282, 300, 301, 308, 311, 313
Victimhood, 14, 164, 166, 181, 196, 244, 251, 293, 294, 301–302, 309
Victimization, 13–15, 62, 128, 300, 301, 304
Virtual, 23, 259, 268, 270, 275–279, 283, 286–288, 293, 311
Virtual realty, 275, 281, 283
Visitor, 19, 101, 200, 244, 249, 250, 252, 253, 255–260, 270, 271, 274, 288, 311

W

War memorial, 17, 272
World War, 17, 18, 20, 41, 72, 78, 78n18, 80, 82, 95, 97, 98, 104, 110, 115, 117, 138, 189, 196n4, 245, 249, 260, 261

X

Xenophobia, 50, 69, 196

Printed by Printforce, the Netherlands